Lecture Notes in Computer Science 4902

Commenced Publication in 1973
Founding and Former Series Editors:
Gerhard Goos, Juris Hartmanis, and Jan van Leeuwen

T0223200

Paul Hudak   David S. Warren (Eds.)

Practical Aspects of Declarative Languages

10th International Symposium, PADL 2008
San Francisco, CA, USA, January 7-8, 2008
Proceedings

 Springer

Volume Editors

Paul Hudak
Yale University, Department of Computer Science
P.O. Box 208285, New Haven, CT 06520-8285, USA
E-mail: hudak@yale.edu

David S. Warren
Stony Brook University, Department of Computer Science
Stony Brook, NY 11794, USA
E-mail: warren@cs.sunysb.edu

Library of Congress Control Number: 2007941814

CR Subject Classification (1998): D.3, D.1, F.3, D.2

LNCS Sublibrary: SL 2 – Programming and Software Engineering

ISSN   0302-9743
ISBN-10   3-540-77441-6 Springer Berlin Heidelberg New York
ISBN-13   978-3-540-77441-9 Springer Berlin Heidelberg New York

Springer is a part of Springer Science+Business Media

springer.com

© Springer-Verlag Berlin Heidelberg 2008
Printed in Germany

Typesetting: Camera-ready by author, data conversion by Scientific Publishing Services, Chennai, India
Printed on acid-free paper   SPIN: 12209545   06/3180   5 4 3 2 1 0

Preface

The International Symposium on Practical Aspects of Declarative Languages (PADL) is a forum for researchers and practioners to present original work emphasizing novel applications and implementation techniques for all forms of declarative concepts, including functions, relations, logic, and constraints. Declarative languages build on sound theoretical foundations to provide attractive frameworks for application development. Existing languages have been successfully applied to a wide array of real-world situations, and new developments in theory and implementation have opened up new application areas. Conversely, applications have driven progress in the theory and implementation of declarative systems, as well as benefited from this progress.

The 10th PADL Symposium was held in San Francisco, California during January 7–8, 2008, and was co-located with the ACM Symposium on Principles of Programming Languages (POPL). From 44 submitted papers, the PADL Program Committee selected 20 for presentation at the symposium, based upon at least three reviews for each paper provided from PC members and additional referees. Two invited talks were also presented at the conference: one by John Launchbury entitled "Industrial Functional Programming" and the other by Walter Wilson entitled "Large-Scale Logic Servers in Business and Government."

Following what has become a tradition at PADL symposia, the PADL Program Committee selected one paper to receive the "Most Practical Paper" award. This year the paper judged best in terms of practicality, originality, and clarity was: "Certified Development Tools Implementation in Objective Caml," by Bruno Pagano, Olivier Andrieu, Benjamin Canou, Emmanuel Chailloux, Jean-Louis Colaco, Thomas Moniot, and Philippe Wang. Congratulations to these authors for this award.

We wish to thank the Program Committee for its expertise and hard work in selecting papers and invited talks, and General Chair Hai-Feng Guo for his excellent organizational and administrative efforts. Special thanks also to Gopal Gupta for his guidance and advice. We also wish to acknowledge the authors of the EasyChair on-line paper management software, which greatly facilitated the PC's efforts.

The 10th PADL Symposium was sponsored in part by COMPULOG Americas, and was organized in coordination with the Association for Computing Machinery. Thanks are also due to the University of Nebraska at Omaha for its support. Finally, we wish to thank the authors who submitted papers to PADL 2008 and all who participated in the conference.

November 2007   Paul Hudak
                                                          David Warren

Conference Organization

General Chair

Hai-Feng Guo (University of Nebraska at Omaha)

Program Chairs

Paul Hudak (Yale University)
David Warren (Stony Brook University)

Program Committee

Chitta Baral (Arizona State University)
Manuel Chakravarty (University of New South Wales)
Charles Consel (University of Bordeaux)
Mireille Ducasse (IRISA/INSA of Rennes, France)
Matthew Flatt (University of Utah)
Gopal Gupta (University of Texas at Dallas)
Bharat Jayaraman (University of Buffalo)
Patricia Johann (Rutgers University)
Nicola Leone (University of Calabria)
Simon Marlow (Microsoft Research Cambridge)
Erik Meijer (Microsoft Research Redmond)
David Page (University of Wisconsin)
Axel Polleres (National University of Ireland)
Colin Runciman (University of York)
Martin Sulzmann (National University of Singapore)
Terrance Swift (CENTRIA, Universidade Nova de Lisboa)
Peter Szeredi (Budapest University of Technology and Economics)
Kimberly Voll (University of British Columbia)

External Reviewers

Ajay Bansal
Dariusz Biernacki
Annamaria Bria
Laurent Burgy
András György Békés
Francesco Calimeri
Peggy Cellier

Biernacki Dariusz
Tristan Denmat
Jeremy Dubreil
Wolfgang Faber
Norbert Fuchs
Lorenzo Gallucci
Dick Grune

Hai-Feng Guo
Remy Haemmerle
Hatem Hamdi
Jerzy Karczmarczuk
Gabriele Keller
Uwe Keller
Joel Kelso
Srividya Kona
Edmund Lam
Roman Leshchinskiy
Gergely Lukácsy
Julien Mercadal
Richard Min
Henrik Nilsson
Vit Novacek

Gergely Patai
Simona Perri
Isabelle Puaut
Francesco Ricca
Pierre Rousseau
Laurent Réveillère
Kostis Sagonas
Ratnesh Sahay
Vitor Santos Costa
Peter Sestoft
Francois-Regis Sinot
Giorgio Terracina
Qian Wang
Marcus dos Santos

Table of Contents

Industrial Functional Programming

John Launchbury

Galois Inc.
12725 SW Millikan Way, Suite 290
Beaverton, OR 97005
john@galois.com

Abstract. Functional languages have been the backbone of Galois' business for the past eight years. They have been very good for us, but not without their own share of challenges. In this talk, we shall stand back and examine the practicalities of using declarative methods over a range of projects and products, to see what works well in practice, and conversely where we have found the tools to fall short.

Certified Development Tools Implementation in Objective Caml

Bruno Pagano[1], Olivier Andrieu[1], Benjamin Canou[2,3], Emmanuel Chailloux[3], Jean-Louis Colaço[4,*], Thomas Moniot[1], and Philippe Wang[3]

[1] Esterel Technologies, 8, rue Blaise Pascal, 78890 Elancourt, France
{Bruno.Pagano,Olivier.Andrieu,Thomas.Moniot}@esterel-technologies.com
[2] ENS Cachan, antenne de Bretagne Campus Ker Lann, F-35170 Bruz, France
Benjamin.Canou@eleves.bretagne.ens-cachan.fr
[3] Laboratoire d'informatique de Paris 6 (LIP6 - UMR 7606),
Université Pierre et Marie Curie, Paris 6,
104, avenue du Président Kennedy, 75016 Paris, France
{Emmanuel.Chailloux,Philippe.Wang}@lip6.fr
[4] Siemens VDO Automotive, 1, avenue Paul Ourliac, BP 1149, 31036 Toulouse, France
Jean-Louis.Colaco@siemens.com

Abstract. This paper presents our feedback from the study on the use of Objective Caml for safety-critical software development tools implementation. As a result, Objective Caml is now used for the new Scade™ certified embedded-code generator. The requirements for tools implementation are less strict than those for the embedded code itself. However, they are still quite demanding and linked to imperative languages properties, which are usually used for this kind of development. The use of Objective Caml is outstanding: firstly for its high level features (functional language of higher order, parametric polymorphism, pattern matching), secondly for its low level mechanisms needed by the runtime system (GC, exceptions). In order to develop the tools to check the safety-critical software development rules, it is necessary to reinterpret them for this language, and then to adapt Objective Caml so that it satisfies them. Thus, we propose a language restriction and a simplified runtime library in order that we can define and measure the coverage of a program written in Objective Caml according to the MC/DC criteria. Then we can look forward to seeing this kind of languages spread out the industrial environment, while raising the abstraction level in the conception and implementation of tools for certified programs production.

Keywords: Code coverage, Tests measurement, Functional programming, Objective Caml, Civil avionics.

1 Introduction

Safety-critical softwares are traditionally associated to embedded control systems but some other areas need them. Standards for software development have been

---

* This work started while the author was at Esterel-Technologies.

P. Hudak and D.S. Warren (Eds.): PADL 2008, LNCS 4902, pp. 2–17, 2008.

defined with levels determined from the safety assessment process and hazard analysis by examining the effects, on the final users, of a failure condition in the system. Among the most common applications, we hold up as examples flight commands, railway traffic lights, the control system of a nuclear power plant, but also medical equipment or a car ABS[1]. They share the particularity that their dysfunctions can cause catastrophes with lethal consequences for those in relation with such a system.

The civil avionics authorities defined a couple of decades ago the certification requirements for aircraft embedded code. The DO-178B standard [17] defines all the constraints ruling the aircraft software development. This procedure is included in the global certification process of an aircraft, and declines now for other industrial sectors concerned by critical software (FDA Class III for medical industry, IEC 61508 for car industry, etc).

The DO-178B standard imposes a very precise development process, which preponderant activity is independent verification of each development step. In this paper, we focus on software development and mistakes hunting procedures, whereas DO-178B's scope goes further. Code development as it is recognised by certification authorities follows the traditional V-Model dear to the software engineering industry. Constraints are reinforced but the principles stay the same: the product specifications are written by successive refinements, from high level requirements to design and then implementation. Each step owns an independent verification activity, which must provide a complete traceability of the requirements appearing in this step.

The followed process to realize embedded code satisfying such a certification requires the definition of a "coding standard". This standard must define a set of strict rules for the specifications' definition, for the implementation and for the traceability between specifications and realizations. In particular, the coding standard must put forward the obligation to cover the entire code. The DO-178B certification imposes this coverage to be done according to the MC/DC [10] measure (Modified Condition/Decision Coverage).

The DO-178B standard applies to embedded code development tools with the same criteria as the code itself. This means that the tool development must follow its own coding standard. The certification standard originally targeted only embedded software, so its application for a development tool must be adapted. For instance, for a code generator it is accepted to use dynamic allocation and have recursive functions. The specificity of the certification process for tools is under discussion to be explicitly addressed by the forthcoming DO-178C standard that will be effective in a few years.

In this context, tools development in a particular language must comply with DO-178B constraints, which means having an MC/DC coverage of the program's source. Likewise, the runtime library, if there is one, must be certified. For the C language, this translates to the control of `libc` calls and compiler mechanisms verification. For more modern languages, such as Java, it would demand the certification of the whole library.

---

[1] Anti-lock Braking System.

Objective Caml (OCaml) is particularly suitable for compiler conception and formal analysis tools. As well as itself [13], it is used in Lucid Synchrone [15], the à la Lustre language for reactive systems implementation, or the Coq [16] proof assistant implementation. Even ten years ago, the use of the OCaml language in software engineering for safe real-time programs development interested some major avionics industries (Dassault). The experience of Surlog with AGFL shows that OCaml can be integrated in a critical software development process and that it brings in its well-founded model. With Astrée [8], OCaml proves its adequacy for critical software tools realization.

The Esterel-Technologies company markets Scade [2,4], a model-based development environment dedicated to safety-critical embedded software. The code generator of this suite that translates models into embedded C code is DO-178B compliant and allows to shorten the certification process of avionics projects which make use of it. The first release of the compiler was implemented in C and was available in 1999 (version 3.1 to 5.1 were based on this technology), but since 2001, Esterel-Technologies has prepared its next generation code generator based on a prototype written in OCaml. This work allowed to test new compiling techniques [7] and language extensions [6]. It has now appeared that OCaml allowed to reduce the distance between the specifications and the implementation of the tool, to have a better traceability between a formal description of the input language and its compiler implementation.

In a more classical industrial environment, where C or Ada languages dominate, and where development processes use intensive tests, the introduction of OCaml changes the formulations of qualification problematics. Many of its language features surprise control theory engineers or imperative languages programmers, first because OCaml is an expression language, but also because it provides higher level features such as parametric polymorphism, pattern matching, exception handling and automatic memory management [11] (*Garbage Collector or GC*).

Conversely, code coverage and conditions/decisions notions are defined and well understood for imperative languages like the C language. So we need to adapt this notion to OCaml Boolean expressions. Functional programming and parametric polymorphism are the main concerns in this evolution of MC/DC code coverage specification. It is also necessary to adapt the runtime library to fit the coding standards, and advisable to bring control points between specifications and runtime library for the control (general apply mechanism, exceptions handling) and for automatic memory management. This makes the use of the Inria original language runtime library difficult and militates for the building of an alternate compatible runtime library.

The rest of this paper is organized as follows. Section 2 exposes the validation process in an industrial context. Section 3 explains the adaptation of code coverage for OCaml programs and describes our implementation called *mlcov*. Section 4 shows how to certify OCaml programs and then details how the runtime library must be modified. Section 5 compares different approaches to use OCaml and presents our future work.

2   Code Verification in a Certified Context

The American federal aviation administration (FAA) requires any computer program embedded in an aircraft to respect the DO-178B standard to allow it to fly. Several levels of criticity are defined (A, B, C, etc.) and applied according to the impact of a software bug on the whole system and passengers. For instance comfort application like entertainment or air-conditioning are less critical than flying command system.

The DO-178B is highly rigorous about the development process but does not give any constraint, neither on the programming language to use nor even about the paradigms it has to implement. However rules exist to precise this standard and drastically restrain the type of accepted programs. At level A, which applies to the most critical programs, an embedded program cannot dynamically allocate memory, use recursive function and generally speaking has to work in bounded time and space with known bounds. For this kind of development, using OCaml or any other high level language is not an option. Usually, only assembly language and limited subsets of C and Ada are used.

Nevertheless, it is allowed, and becoming more and more necessary, to use code generators and/or verifiers to help writing these programs, if these tools are themselves certified at the same level of the standard. For example, the code coverage measurement, about which we will speak later, can be done by human code reviewers or by a software if it is itself certified at the appropriate level. This level is a bit relaxed for verification tools as they cannot directly affect the embedded application.

When it comes to tools development, some of the most constraining rules can consensually be broken, given that the fundamental demands are fulfilled. For example, if recursion or dynamic memory allocation are allowed, it must be restrained to memory configurations where the stack and the heap are large enough not to interfere with the ongoing computation. Even if, unlike an embedded software, a tool can fail, it must provably never give a false result. Therefore, the verification activities take a preponderant amount of time in the development process.

Tests: coverage measurement criteria: During an industrial process, the code verification stage takes place after the development and is meant to show that the product matches its specifications. Testing software requires a stoping criteria to state that the behavior of the program is reasonably explored as it is well known that exhaustivness is unreachable. Coverage measurement is the traditional answer from the software engineering community to define the good compromise between loose verification and theoretical limits. On this particular point, the DO-178B standard has a very precise requirement by demanding a complete exploration of the code structure in the MC/DC sense. The DO-178B defines several verification activities and among these a test suite has to be constituted to cover up the set of specifications of the software to verify and thus its implementation. The standard requires each part of the code to be used in the execution of at least one test and conform to its specifications.

The structural coverage criteria can be separated into the data flow ones and the control flow ones. The data flow analysis measures the relation between the assignments and uses of variables. The DO-178B only defines criteria over the control flow. The control flow is measured on executed instructions, Boolean expressions evaluated and branches of control instruction executed. We will now present the main measurements.

- *Statement Coverage:* It is the simplest criterion, to understand as well as to apply. It consists in verifying that each instruction of the tested program is executed by at least one test. Such a criterion is considered fragile as shown in the next example.
- *Decision Coverage:* A *decision* is the Boolean expression evaluated in a test instruction to determine the branch to be executed. This coverage requires each decision to be evaluated to the two possible values during the tests, ensuring that all code branches are taken.

  The following C code example, defining the absolute function over integers, exposes the difference between these two criteria:

  ```
  int abs(int x) {int y; if (x<0) y = -x; return y;}
  ```

  A unique test with a negative value for x is sufficient to cover all the instructions, however the decision coverage needs a second one with a positive value. This little code is sufficient to prove that decision coverage can detect more incorrect programs, since with a positive value, a random value is returned by the function instead of the identity whereas such a test is not needed by the statement coverage.
- *Condition Coverage:* A *condition* is an atomic subexpression of a decision. For example, the decision x && (y<0) || f(z) contains the three conditions x, y<0 and f(z). A condition is covered if tests exist in which it is evaluated to **true** and **false**.
- *Condition/Decision Coverage:* The C/DC is the combination of the two previous criteria.
- *Modified Condition/Decision Coverage:* The MC/DC extends the C/DC criterion by requiring each condition to independently modify the decision value. In other words, for each condition c, two tests have to exist which must change the decision value while keeping the same valuations for all conditions but c.
- *Multiple Condition Coverage:* For this criterion, the tests must generate every Boolean combinations of the conditions of each decision.

Let us now illustrate these definitions by showing the tests required by each of the criteria for the test instruction if ((a || b) && c) { ... }. Eight tests exist for this instruction which are the different valuations of the Boolean variables a, b and c. We shall name these valuations *test vectors* and use the notations [TTT T], [FTT T], [TFT T], [FFT F], [TTF F], [FTT F], [TFT F] and [FFF F]. They correspond to the truth table of the expression.

The required tests vary according to the coverage criterion:

- Statement Coverage: a unique test giving the value T to the condition is necessary

- Decision Coverage: Two tests are necessary, one of them giving T and the other F, for example [TTT T] et [FTT F].
- Condition Coverage: Each condition has to take the two values, therefore two tests which give different valuations to every condition are sufficient, for example [TTF F] et [FFT F] (note that this example does not satisfy the decision coverage criterion).
- C/DC: As in the previous case, we must provide two tests which give different valuations to every condition but now they must give a different value to the decision too, for example [TTT T] et [FFF F].
- MC/DC: For each condition, we must exhibit two tests in which only this condition and the decision result differ. For example, the two test vectors [TFT T] and [FFT F] show the independence of the condition a. The test vectors may be used to show the independence of more than one condition. Usually, N+1 test vectors are necessary for a decision with N conditions. For this example, the four test vectors [TFT T], [FTT T], [TFF F] and [FFT F] are sufficient.
- Multiple Condition Coverage : By definition, the eight vectors of the truth table detailed before has to be be provided.

The DO-178B level A certification requires the whole program code to have a 100% MC/DC measurement. The MC/DC criterion turned out to be a reasonable compromise between a too weak requirement of two tests and an unreachable one of 2^n tests.

The relevance of the MC/DC criterion has been profusely discussed [9,12]. Our aim is to show the meaning of this measurement in OCaml since it is required by the civil avionics agencies. An important point to understand is that the MC/DC analysis of the code is one element of the validation process of every development step. Therefore, even if it is possible to work around the coverage analyses by coding tricks in theory, these tricks will be rejected by the persons in charge of reviewing the code or validating the MC/DC measurement in practice.

3   Code Coverage of OCaml Programs

According to Chilenski et al. [10], code coverage is not a test technique: it should be considered as a measure describing the degree to which the source code of a program has been exercised. In this section, we give a definition of the MC/DC criteria from the viewpoint of OCaml programs. We restrict to the functional and imperative features of OCaml, which correspond to the subset allowed by the coding rules of the Scade to C compiler. This subset remains quite large (cf. paragraph 3.3), for instance, it is sufficient to compile the standard library of the OCaml distribution.

3.1   Coverage of Expressions

We need to adapt the definition of code coverage to a functional language like OCaml. With respect to imperative languages, the notion of coverage is related to the statements of a program. Since OCaml is an expression language, we will be interested in the coverage of the expressions evaluation.

In the imperative paradigm, coverage shall pinpoint that every execution branch in the program has independently been exercised. The same is encountered in the OCaml language, since some sub-expressions (in the case of the conditional expression, for instance) may remain unevaluated.

`if (x<y) {`
`    min = f(x);`
`} else {`
`    min = f(y);`
`}`
	`let min =`
	`  if x<y`
	`    then f x`
	`    else f y`
		As well as the coverage of the C program shows which branch of the `if` control structure has been executed, coverage of the OCaml program examines which sub-expression of the `if` operator has been evaluated.

Coverage is measured by instrumenting the source code of the program. With respect to OCaml, we state that an expression has been covered as soon as its evaluation has ended. The main idea of the instrumentation algorithm is to replace each expression `expr` with `(let aux = expr in mark(); aux)`, where the variable `aux` is not free in `expr` and `mark()` is a side-effect allowing to record that this point of the program has been reached.

Some constructions of the OCaml language (such as `if then else`) may introduce several execution branches. Coverage of expressions entails to trace the evaluation of each one of the branches independently. In order to avoid over-marking, we split the instrumentation algorithm into two mutually recursive translation functions $\mathcal{F}$ and $\mathcal{G}$. Both $\mathcal{F}$ and $\mathcal{G}$ instrument the execution branches of the program, but only $\mathcal{F}$ marks the end of evaluation of expressions. Here is the definition of the instrumentation functions, together with some explanation of the interesting cases:

$$\mathcal{F}(k) = \texttt{mark}();\ k \quad \text{if } k \text{ is a constant or a constant constructor}$$

Since we (statically) know that the evaluation of a constant value or constructor never fails, we can simplify the translation and write $\mathcal{F}(k) = \texttt{mark}();\ k$.

$$\mathcal{F}(id) = \begin{cases} \texttt{fun } x \rightarrow \texttt{mark}();\ id\ x & \text{if } id \text{ has a functional type} \\ \texttt{mark}();\ id & \text{otherwise} \end{cases}$$

Note that $\mathcal{F}$ η-expands every top-level functional value ($\mathcal{F}(id) = \texttt{fun } x \rightarrow \texttt{mark}();\ id\ x$) so that the algorithm is still type-preserving. Otherwise, it would produce weak type variables.

$$\mathcal{F}(f\ x) = \begin{cases} \texttt{mark}();\ \mathcal{G}(f)\ \mathcal{G}(x) & \text{if } f \text{ does not return} \\ \mathcal{G}(f)\ \mathcal{G}(x);\ \texttt{mark}() & \text{if } f\ x \text{ has type } unit \\ \texttt{let } aux = \mathcal{G}(f)\ \mathcal{G}(x) \texttt{ in mark}();\ aux & \text{otherwise} \end{cases}$$

A heuristics is implemented in order not to trace the end of evaluation of a family of functions that do not return, such as `failwith` and `exit`: we look for functions with type $\forall \alpha.\tau \rightarrow \alpha$, where the polymorphic type variable α

does not appear in τ. Indeed, the application of any of those functions does not terminate, which implies that structural coverage would never be reached if they were instrumented in the usual way. Instead of the normal case, we write $\mathcal{F}(f\ x) = \mathtt{mark}();\ \mathcal{G}(f)\ \mathcal{G}(x)$. Unfortunately, this heuristics suffers from both false positives and false negatives, since it may be fooled by type annotations.

As a shortcut, we define $\mathcal{F}(f\ x) = \mathcal{G}(f)\ \mathcal{G}(x);\ \mathtt{mark}()$ when the type of $f\ x$ is $unit$, since the type of $\mathtt{mark}()$ is $unit$ too.

$$\mathcal{F}(\mathtt{fun}\ x\ \rightarrow\ e) = \mathtt{fun}\ x\ \rightarrow\ \mathcal{F}(e)$$
$$\mathcal{F}(e_1;\ e_2) = \mathcal{G}(e_1);\ \mathcal{F}(e_2)$$
$$\mathcal{F}(\mathtt{if}\ e_1\ \mathtt{then}\ e_2\ [\mathtt{else}\ e_3]) = \mathtt{if}\ \mathcal{G}(e_1)\ \mathtt{then}\ \mathcal{F}(e_2)\ [\mathtt{else}\ \mathcal{F}(e_3)]$$
$$\mathcal{F}(\mathtt{while}\ e_1\ \mathtt{do}\ e_2\ \mathtt{done}) = \mathtt{while}\ \mathcal{G}(e_1)\ \mathtt{do}\ \mathcal{F}(e_2)\ \mathtt{done};\ \mathtt{mark}()$$
$$\mathcal{F}(\mathtt{let}\ x\ =\ e_1\ \mathtt{in}\ e_2) = \mathtt{let}\ x\ =\ \mathcal{G}(e_1)\ \mathtt{in}\ \mathcal{F}(e_2)$$
$$\mathcal{F}(\mathtt{match}\ e_1\ \mathtt{with}\ p_i\ [\mathtt{when}\ e_2]\ \rightarrow\ e_i) = \mathtt{match}\mathcal{G}(e_1)\mathtt{with}\ p_i$$
$$[\mathtt{when}\mathcal{G}(e_2) \rightarrow \mathcal{F}(e_i)]$$
$$\mathcal{F}(\mathtt{try}\ e\ \mathtt{with}\ p_i\ \rightarrow\ e_i) = \mathtt{try}\ \mathcal{F}(e)\ \mathtt{with}\ p_i\ \rightarrow\ \mathcal{F}(e_i)$$
$$\mathcal{F}((e_1,\ e_2)) = \mathtt{mark}();\ (\mathcal{G}(e_1),\ \mathcal{G}(e_2))$$
$$\mathcal{F}(C(e)) = \mathtt{mark}();\ C(\mathcal{G}(e))$$

$$\mathcal{G}(x) = x\ \text{if}\ x\ \text{is a constant value or an identifier}$$
$$\mathcal{G}(f\ x) = \mathcal{G}(f)\ \mathcal{G}(x)$$
$$\mathcal{G}(\mathtt{fun}\ x\ \rightarrow\ e) = \mathtt{fun}\ x\ \rightarrow\ \mathcal{F}(e)$$
$$\mathcal{G}(e_1;\ e_2) = \mathcal{G}(e_1);\ \mathcal{G}(e_2)$$
$$\mathcal{G}(\mathtt{if}\ e_1\ \mathtt{then}\ e_2\ [\mathtt{else}\ e_3]) = \mathtt{if}\ \mathcal{G}(e_1)\ \mathtt{then}\ \mathcal{F}(e_2)\ [\mathtt{else}\ \mathcal{F}(e_3)]$$
$$\mathcal{G}(\mathtt{while}\ e_1\ \mathtt{do}\ e_2\ \mathtt{done}) = \mathtt{while}\ \mathcal{G}(e_1)\ \mathtt{do}\ \mathcal{F}(e_2)\ \mathtt{done}$$
$$\mathcal{G}(\mathtt{let}\ x\ =\ e_1\ \mathtt{in}\ e_2) = \mathtt{let}\ x\ =\ \mathcal{G}(e_1)\ \mathtt{in}\ \mathcal{G}(e_2)$$
$$\mathcal{G}(\mathtt{match}\ e_1\ \mathtt{with}\ p_i\ [\mathtt{when}\ e_2]\ \rightarrow\ e_i) = \mathtt{match}\ \mathcal{G}(e_1)\ \mathtt{with}\ e_1$$
$$[\mathtt{when}\mathcal{G}(e_2)] \rightarrow \mathcal{F}(e_i)$$
$$\mathcal{G}(\mathtt{try}\ e\ \mathtt{with}\ p_i\ \rightarrow\ e_i) = \mathtt{try}\ \mathcal{G}(e)\ \mathtt{with}\ p_i\ \rightarrow\ \mathcal{F}(e_i)$$
$$\mathcal{G}((e_1,\ e_2)) = (\mathcal{G}(e_1),\ \mathcal{G}(e_2))$$
$$\mathcal{G}(C(e)) = C(\mathcal{G}(e))$$

Correction of the instrumentation. Since $\mathtt{mark}()$ has type $unit$ (computes by side-effect), the translations defined by functions $\mathcal{F}$ and $\mathcal{G}$ do not alter the types of the expressions being instrumented. Furthermore, they do not alter the value computed by this expression.

A program is structurally covered when every call to $\mathtt{mark}()$ in the instrumented source code has been reached.

Tail recursion: Tail recursion is not a feature of OCaml or of functional languages. It is a property of a function, in which the last operation is a recursive call. Such recursions can be easily transformed into iterations: this is known as the tail call optimization. Replacing recursion with iteration can drastically decrease the amount of stack space used and improve efficiency.

Our instrumentation algorithm, consisting in adding a side-effect after each expression, systematically breaks tail calls, thus forbidding the optimization mentioned above. In pratice (with the Scade compiler typically), we were not confronted with cases in which the instrumentation of the program led to a stack overflow.

3.2 MC/DC Coverage

According to the DO-178B standard, MC/DC is fulfilled when every point of entry and exit in the program has been invoked at least once, every condition in a decision has taken on all possible outcomes at least once, and each condition has been shown to affect that decision's outcome independently.

With respect to the OCaml language, we chose to define an MC/DC decision for each expression of type *bool* (except the Boolean constants `true` and `false`). Then, MC/DC conditions are determined by syntactically looking for the Boolean operators `not`, `&&` and `||`. We propose to transform every Boolean expression into a bunch of nested `if then else`. Here is the translation scheme:

$$\mathcal{F}_b(\texttt{not } e,\ l,\ r) = \mathcal{F}_b(e,\ r,\ l)$$
$$\mathcal{F}_b(e_1 \texttt{ \&\& } e_2,\ l,\ r) = \mathcal{F}_b(e_1,\ \mathcal{F}_b(e_2,\ l,\ r),\ r)$$
$$\mathcal{F}_b(e_1 \texttt{ || } e_2,\ l,\ r) = \mathcal{F}_b(e_1,\ l,\ \mathcal{F}_b(e_2,\ l,\ r))$$
$$\mathcal{F}_b(\texttt{if } e_1 \texttt{ then } e_2 \texttt{ else } e_3,\ l,\ r) = \mathcal{F}_b(e_1,\ \mathcal{F}_b(e_2,\ l,\ r),\ \mathcal{F}_b(e_3,\ l,\ r))$$

$$\mathcal{F}_b(e,\ l,\ r) = \texttt{if set\_condition();}\ e\ \texttt{then}\ l\ \texttt{else}\ r \quad \text{otherwise}$$

Thence, the MC/DC instrumentation $\mathcal{M}$ of a Boolean expression e can be defined straightforwardly:

$$\mathcal{M}(e)\ =\ \mathcal{F}_b(e,\ \texttt{set\_outcome();}\ true,\ \texttt{set\_outcome();}\ false)$$

where `set_condition()` and `set_outcome()` are side-effects (of type *unit*) allowing to update respectively the value of the current condition and the value of the decision's outcome.

Example. The following Boolean expression is composed of four independent conditions. Here they are single variables, but could also be replaced with more complex expressions.

```
let pred a b c d = (a || b) && (c || d)
```

There are 2^4 possible tests. Coverage of expressions requires 2 tests, whereas MC/DC needs 5. The $\mathcal{F}_b$ translation reveals 7 calls to `set_outcome()` ; , thus the 2^4 test cases fall into 7 classes according to the way they affect our counters.

```
let pred a b c d =              (*       a b c d  -> p *)
   if a then
      if c then true            (*  1 :  T _ T _  -> T *)
      else if d then true       (*  2 :  T _ F T  -> T *)
      else false                (*  3 :  T _ F F  -> F *)
   else if b then
      if c then true            (*  4 :  F T T _  -> T *)
      else if d then true       (*  5 :  F T F T  -> T *)
      else false                (*  6 :  F T F F  -> F *)
   else false                   (*  7 :  F F _ _  -> F *)
```

Let us find, for each condition, which test pairs are sufficient to prove that the decision's outcome is independently affected:

   a : (1)+(7)   b : (4)+(7)   c : (1)+(3) or (4)+(6)   d : (2)+(3) or (5)+(6)

which leads us to the following minimal sets:

$$\{(1), (2), (3), (4), (7)\} \quad \text{or} \quad \{(1), (4), (5), (6), (7)\}$$

As a consequence, full MC/DC coverage can be achieved with 5 tests, which confirms the theoretical result. Mind that our translation is only required to measure MC/DC coverage, it isn't a method to derive a minimal set of test cases from the source code: hence the discrepancy between the 5 tests required for full MC/DC coverage and the 7 possible tests. In other words, it is not necessary to cover the translated version of the decision in its entirety to fulfill the MC/DC criterion.

3.3   Implementation

We developed a tool capable of measuring the MC/DC rate of OCaml programs. The tool first allows to create an instrumented version of the source code, together with a trace file. Then, the user has to build the instrumented code with the Inria OCaml compiler. Running the instrumented executable leads to (incrementally) updating the counters and structures of the trace file. Finally, the coverage results are presented through HTML reports, that are generated from the information collected in the trace file.

Our tool is built on top of the front-end of the INRIA OCaml compiler. A first pass is always done, prior to the instrumentation stage, in order to reject OCaml programs that do not comply with the coding rules related to the Scade compiler. For instance, we do not support objects, polymorphic variants, labels and optional arguments, nor the unconventional extensions (multi-threading, support for laziness, recursive values and modules).

Performance Results. Performances are quite good with respect to programs that contain a lot of pattern-matching and a few recursive calls. Thus, the Scade to C compiler has been successfully instrumented and used to compile non trivial

Scade programs. The instrumented version of Scade compiler runs almost as fast as the original one.

	Scade compiler	instrumented Scade compiler
number of lines	30 000	53 500
execution time on a large Scade model (8 120 lines)	27.6 s	28.1 s

On the contrary, performances are very degraded with OCaml programs that use recursion intensively, such as a naive implementation of `fibonacci`. Indeed, in those cases, counters can be hit several millions (even billions) of times, whereas in the case of Scade they are updated a few hundreds or thousands of times only.

The η-expansion of polymorphic variables can introduce a lack of performance with a program that uses intensively the higher-order features of the language. This lack has not been measured, but the cost of abusive closure constructions is well known for any functional language developer.

The lack of performance is not a point to our purpose because the instrumented code is only used to measure the coverage of the code. So it will be used in a large set of tests; but it is used on real application cases. Most of cases, including the Scade compiler, the tests needed by the coverage of the source code are small and the instrumented code performs quite well (less than 5% of overcost). Furthermore, the code coverage analysis is a heavy process: tests building, test validation, coverage results analysis, ... In this context, the slight lack of performance is not relevant.

4   Certification of OCaml Programs

The DO-178B certification of an application applies on the final executable. Thus the analysis must be applied to the source code of the progam itself but also on the library code used by the program. A typical OCaml program such as the Scade compiler uses two kind of library code: the OCaml *standard library* which is itself written in OCaml, and the *runtime library*, written in C and assembler; both libraries are shipped with the OCaml compiler and are automatically linked with the final executable.

The standard library contains the interfaces manipulating the datatypes predefined by the OCaml compiler (integers, strings, etc.), the implementation of some commonly used data structures (hash tables, sets, maps, etc.) and some utilitary modules (command line parsing, `printf`-like formatting, etc.). The runtime library contains:

- the implementation of some library functions that cannot be written in pure OCaml because they need access to the in-memory representation of OCaml values: the polymorphic comparison function, the polymorphic hashing function, the serialization/deserialization functions;

- library functions that need to interact with the host OS, most notably the I/O functions;
- low-level support code that is required for the execution of OCaml programs: memory management functionality, exceptions management, support for some function calls, etc. Use of this code is not always traceable to the original source in OCaml, it is often introduced by the OCaml compiler.

The difficulty of specifying and testing such low-level library code (as required by the DO-178B process) lead us to adapt the runtime library so as to simplify it.

4.1   Modifications to the Runtime Library

The bulk of the modifications was to remove features unessential to our specific application, the Scade compiler. This is a program with a relatively simple control flow and very little interaction with the OS: its inputs consist only of command line arguments and text files, its outputs are also text files.

First, the concurrency support was removed from the runtime. OCaml programs can use POSIX signals and multi-threading but this feature is dispensable when writing a compiler.

Similarly, the support for serialization and deserialization of OCaml values was removed. Furthermore these functions are not type-safe and thus can compromise the safety guarantees of the OCaml type system.

Most of the work consisted in simplifying the automatic memory management subsytem. Indeed the garbage collector (GC) of OCaml is renowned for its good performances; however it is a large and complex piece of code. It is a generational GC with Stop&Copy collection for the young generation and incremental Mark&Sweep collection for the older generation; it supports compaction, weak pointers and finalization functions. We successfully replaced it by a plain Stop&Copy collector, thus eliminating features unnecessary to our compiler such as weak pointers and finalization. The collector is no longer incremental, which implies that the execution of the program may be interrupted for a large amount of time by the collector, however this is of no concern for a non-interactive application such as a compiler.

Simplifying this part of the runtime library was difficult because of its tight coupling with the OCaml compiler. Indeed, both this memory manager code and the compiler must agree on the in-memory representation of OCaml values and on the entry points of the memory manager. Furthermore, the OCaml compiler inlines the allocation function of the memory manager for performance reasons. All in all, we had little leeway in replacing this code: it practically had to be Stop&Copy collector and we had to keep some of the symbol names. However we were able to obtain complete coverage of this simplified GC, despite the fact that it is difficult to test since most of the calls are not explicit in the original OCaml source code.

The OCaml standard library is less problematic concerning certification. Most of it is written in plain OCaml and certification of this library code is no more difficult than that of the application code. Some of the more complex modules such as the printf-like formatters were simply removed.

The only notable modification of the standard library is the support of overflows in integer arithmetics. The built-in integers in OCaml implement a signed 31 bit (or 63-bit, depending on the platform) wrap-around arithmetic. To be able to detect overflows, the basic arithmetic functions were replaced by wrapper function that check the result and raise an exception in case of overflow.

4.2   Performance Results

The modifications of the runtime library that can impact the program's performance are the new GC and the overflow-checking arithmetic operations; other modifications are merely removal of unused code and do not alter performance. Tests were done on the (non-instrumented) Scade compiler running with the same large Scade model as in section 3.3.

To check the impact of overflow checks, we tested our modified runtime library with and without overflow detection. No measurable difference could be seen. This is expected as the Scade compiler does very few arithmetic computations.

To measure the performance of the GC, we measured the total running time of the program and the top memory consumption; individual collection time was not measured (as mentioned earlier, "pauses" in the execution due to the GC are not a concern for a compiler). We found the Scade compiler to be approximately 30% slower than with the regular OCaml GC. The memory footprint reached 256 MB vs. 150 MB with the regular GC. This was expected: Stop&Copy GC are not very memory-efficient: due to their design, no more than half the memory used by the GC is available to store program data.

5   Discussion

5.1   Approaches

Our approach in this article is to focus directly on OCaml programs and on the OCaml compiler from Inria. To ensure compatibility of this approach with the Scade compiler, we have restricted the OCaml language to its functional and imperative core language, including a basic module system. The runtime library pointers, serialization ...) has also been simplified. One pending difficulty is to explain compilation schemes for language features and their composition.

Another approach to certificate OCaml programs would be to use a compiler from ML to C [19,5] and then to certify the generated C code by using tools for C code coverage. Once again the main difficulty is to check the GC implementation of the runtime library; GC with ambiguous roots using [3] or not [5] the C stack may "statistically" fail the certification. The simple GC as Stop&Copy [11] are not appropriate to the C language because they move their allocated values, mainly GC regarding the C stack as roots set.

A third approach, which can be compatible with the first, is to use a byte-code interpretor. Its strengh is to improve control to manage stack and exceptions. Moreover, an interpretor gives the possibility to analyse the program coverage during execution and not only by its instrumentation. A Just in Time translator can be added to improve performances [18]. A JIT transformation is easier to explain and to describe during the certification process than an entire compiler, mainly because its optimisations are less complex.

These three approaches allow the use of high level languages to develop tools for embedded softwares. This will reduce the development life cycle and simplify the certification process.

5.2   Future Work

The pattern matching is one of the most important features of the OCaml language. It can be considered both as a control structure and as the only way to build accessors to complex values. Moreover, the static analysis [14], used by the OCaml compiler, ensure some good properties. In this paper, we consider that a pattern matching instruction is covered by a single test for each pattern of the filter. This is sufficient with respect to the definition of MC/DC requirements which are only applicable on Boolean expressions. An extension of the coverage principles is to consider a pattern matching as multiple conditions and to require to cover the independance between any of the condition. For instance, the pattern x::y::1 -> matches any list of at least two elements; intuitively, it expresses two conditions: the list is not empty and the the the tail of the list is not empty too. A more precise coverage measure can ask to have two different tests for this pattern.

The more modern features of OCaml [1] are not necessarily wished by the certification organizations to design critical softwares. For instance the object programming, *à la C++*, is not yet fully accepted by the DO-178B; and the row polymorphism from the OCaml object extension may not satisfy all their criteria. In the same way, polymorphic variants bring a concept of extensibility that is not compatible with the critical software development, which requires comprehensive specifications for all used data structures.

On the other hand, the genericity of functors (parametric modules) is valuable to build this kind of tools, but when a functor is applied, the same types constraints than parametric polymorphism have to be checked These restrictions are under study. A simple solution to properly cover parametric modules is to consider independently any of its monomorphic instance. But this solution leads to demand more tests than the necessary ones: when a part of a functor does not use some arguments, it can share the same tests to ensure the coverage.

6   Conclusion

For the community of statically typed functional languages, usual arguments on quality, safety and efficiency about code written in OCaml are well known and accepted for a long time. Nevertheless, convincing the authorities of certification requires to respect their measuring criteria of quality. This development has shown that the concepts of MC/DC coverage could be used for a functional/imperative subset of OCaml and its simplified runtime. Although it is not applicable to embbed code written in OCaml, satisfying criteria from DO-178B gives to OCaml the capabilities to specify and to implement tools for design of critical softwares.

The Scade compiler of *Esterel Technologies* is such a tool, it has been certified DO-178B level A by the American and the European civil aviation administrations; it is used for instance by Airbus, Pratt and Whitney and many others. Previously implemented with the C language, the compiler of the version 6 of Scade has been written in OCaml and will be submitted to the qualification procedures. The code coverage analysis will be performed by the *mlcov* tool described in this paper. Notice that *mlcov* needs to be DO-178B level C certified which is a necessary condition to be used in a DO-178B level A cycle development.

References

1. Aponte, M.-V., Chailloux, E., Cousineau, G., Manoury, P.: Advanced Programming Features in Objective Caml. In: 6th Brazilian Symposium on Programming Languages(June 2002)
2. Berry, G.: The Effectiveness of Synchronous Languages for the Development of Safety-Critical Systems. Technical report, Esterel-Technologies (2003)
3. Boehm, H., Weiser, M., Bartlett, J.F.: Garbage collection in an uncooperative environment. Software - Practice and Experience (September 1988)
4. Camus, J.-L., Dion, B.: Efficient Development of Airborne Software with SCADE Suite^{TM}. Technical report, Esterel-Technologies (2003)
5. Chailloux, E.: An Efficient Way of Compiling ML to C. In: Workshop on ML and its Applications. ACM SIGPLAN (June 1992)
6. Colaço, J.-L., Pagano, B., Pouzet, M.: A Conservative Extension of Synchronous Data-flow with State Machines. In: ACM International Conference on Embedded Software (EMSOFT 2005), Jersey city, New Jersey, USA (September 2005)
7. Colaço, J.-L., Pouzet, M.: Clocks as First Class Abstract Types. In: Third International Conference on Embedded Software (EMSOFT 2003), Philadelphia, Pennsylvania, USA (October 2003)
8. Cousot, P., Cousot, R., Feret, J., Mauborgne, L., Miné, A., Monniaux, D., Rival, X.: The astrée analyser. In: European Symposium on Programming. LNCS (April 2005)
9. Dupuy, A., Leveson, N.: An empirical evaluation of the mc/dc coverage criterion on the hete-2 satellite software. In: Digital Aviations Systems Conference (DASC), Philadelphia, Pennsylvania, USA (October 2000)
10. Hayhurst, K.J., Veerhusen, D.S., Chilenski, J.J., Rierson, L.K.:A Practical Tutorial on Modified Condition/Decision Coverage. Technical report, NASA/TM-2001-210876 (May 2001)
11. Jones, R., Lins, R.: Garbage Collection. Wiley, Chichester (1996)
12. Kapoor, K., Bowen, J.P.: Experimental evaluation of the variation in effectiveness for dc, fpc and mc/dc test criteria. In: ISESE, pp. 185–194. IEEE Computer Society, Los Alamitos (2003)
13. Leroy, X.: The Objective Caml system release 3.10 : Documentation and user's manual (2007), http://caml.inria.fr
14. Maranget, L.: Warnings for pattern matching. Journal of Functional Programming (2007)

15. Pouzet, M.: Lucid Synchrone version 3.0 : Tutorial and Reference Manual (2006), www.lri.fr/~pouzet/lucid-synchrone
16. T.C.D.T.L. Project: The Coq Proof Assistant Reference Manual (2006), http://coq.inria.fr/V8.1beta/refman
17. RTCA/DO-178B: Software Considerations in Airborne Systems and Equipment Certification. Radio Technical Commission for Aeronautics RTCA (December 1992)
18. Starynkevitch, B.: OCamljit - a faster Just-In-TIme Ocaml implementation. In: Workshop MetaOcaml (June 2004)
19. Tarditi, D., Lee, P., Acharya, A.: No assembly required: Compiling standard ML to C. ACM Letters on Programming Languages and Systems 1(2), 161–177 (1992)

Automatic Coding Rule Conformance Checking Using Logic Programming*

Guillem Marpons[1], Julio Mariño[1], Manuel Carro[1], Ángel Herranz[1],
Juan José Moreno-Navarro[1,2], and Lars-Åke Fredlund[1]

[1] Universidad Politécnica de Madrid
[2] IMDEA Software
{gmarpons,jmarino,mcarro,aherranz,jjmoreno,lfredlund}@fi.upm.es

Abstract. An extended practice in the realm of Software Engineering and programming in industry is the application of *coding rules*. Coding rules are customarily used to constrain the use (or abuse) of certain programming language constructions. However, these rules are usually written using natural language, which is intrinsically ambiguous and which may complicate their use and hinder their automatic enforcement. This paper presents some early work aiming at defining a framework to formalise and check for coding rule conformance using logic programming. We show how a certain class of rules – *structural* rules – can be reformulated as logic programs, which provides both a framework for formal specification and also for automatic conformance checking using a Prolog engine. Some examples of rules belonging to actual, third-party coding rule sets are discussed, along with the corresponding Prolog code. Experimental data regarding the practicality and impact of their application to real-life software projects is presented and discussed.

Keywords: Coding rule checking, Declarative domain-specific languages and applications, Logic programming, Programming environments.

1 Introduction

Although there is a trend towards increased use of higher-level languages in the software industry, offering convenient programming constructs such as type-safe execution, automatic garbage collection, etc., it is equally clear that more traditional programming languages like C (which is notorious for fostering dubious practices) remain very popular. The reasons for this range from efficiency concerns (especially on embedded platforms), need for compatibility with existing products, or the simple fact that a huge amount of acceptably trained programmers are available.

---

* Work partially supported by PROFIT grants FIT-340005-2007-7 and FIT-350400-2006-44 from the Spanish Ministry of Industry, Trade and Tourism; Comunidad Autónoma de Madrid grant S-0505/TIC/0407 (PROMESAS); Ministry of Education and Science grant TIN2005-09207-C03-01 (MERIT/COMVERS) and EU IST FET grant IST-15905 (MOBIUS).

P. Hudak and D.S. Warren (Eds.): PADL 2008, LNCS 4902, pp. 18–34, 2008.

However, a good usage of a language like C involves using the language in a disciplined manner, such that the hazards brought by its weaknesses and more error-prone features are minimised. To that end, it is common to require that code rely only on a well-defined subset of the language, following a set of coding rules. For C, for example, MISRA-C [1], elaborated by The Motor Industry Software Reliability Association (MISRA), is one of the leading initiatives, mainly fostered by the British automotive industry but later applied to other realms. MISRA-C contains a list of 141 coding rules aimed at writing robust C code for critical systems. Examples of typical coding rules for C are *"all automatic variables shall have been assigned a value before being used"* and *"functions shall not call themselves, either directly or indirectly."* For C++ no equally accepted set of coding rules exists, but a notable initiative is *High-Integrity C++* (HICPP [2]) which provides around a hundred coding rules for C++.

Another use of coding rules is to enforce domain-specific language restrictions. Java Card [3], for example, is a subset of Java for programming Smart Cards. In such an environment memory is scarce, and coding rules typically forbid language constructs that may lead to heavy memory usage. At the other end of the spectrum, each organisation – or even project – can establish its own coding rule sets.

However, no matter who devises and dictates the coding rule set, for it to be of practical use, an automatic method to check code for conformance is needed.[1] Added to the intrinsic difficulty of mechanically checking rules, they are typically described using (necessarily ambiguous) natural language, which shifts the difficulty of interpreting them to whoever implements the checking tool. Still there exists a number of commercial quality assurance tools from vendors such as IAR Systems (http://www.iar.com) and Parasoft (http://www.parasoft.com) that claim to be able to check code for compliance with a subset of MISRA-C. Other tools, for example Klocwork (http://www.klocwork.com), define their own list of informally described checks aimed at avoiding hazards. But, in absence of a formal definition of rules, it is difficult to be certain about what they are actually checking, and two different tools could very well disagree about the validity of some particular piece of code with respect to, e.g., the same MISRA-C rule.

This paper presents a framework to precisely specify rule sets such as MISRA-C and to, later, automatically check (non-trivial) software projects for conformity. In the rule-coder side, a logic-based language will make it possible to easily capture the meaning of coding rules; this language will be compiled into a Prolog program with which code conformity is checked.

This work is developed within the scope of the Global GCC project (GGCC, [4]), a consortium of European industrial corporations and research labs funded under the Eureka/ITEA Programme. GGCC aims at extending the free GNU Compiler Collection (GCC) with project-wide optimisation and compilation capabilities (Global GCC). In the context of GGCC, we seek the inclusion of a facility to define new sets of coding rules, and providing mechanisms to check code compliance using a logic programming engine and making heavy use of the

---

[1] Although some rules may be undecidable, finally needing human intervention.

static analysers and syntax tools already present in GCC. Such a mechanism for extensibility is a requirement for many organisations of the GGCC Consortium having their own coding policies or the necessity to adapt existing ones.

Since GCC is a multi-language compilation framework, it is natural to provide support to express coding rules for different target languages. We have initially focused on C, C++, and Java since they are widely used in industry, in particular by the industrial partners of the GGCC project. Throughout the paper, however, we will only consider C++ (and HICPP).

The rest of the paper is structured as follows: Section 2 contains a classification of coding rules. Our framework for rule validation is presented in Sect. 3. Section 4 explains how structural rules can be specified using logic programs, first introducing some key examples and then focusing on those constructs that occur in rules more often. Experimental results obtained with a small prototype are presented in Sect. 5. Section 6 comments on related work and Sect. 7 concludes.

2   A Classification of Coding Rules

In order to make an initial classification of coding rules, which is needed to have an idea of the difficulty of the task and the type of code schemata we will have to deal with, a survey was conducted within the project partners asking for examples of coding rules internally followed in their organisations. This gave us clues about which types of rules were actually perceived as interesting in order to focus primarily on them. In parallel, We analysed in some detail MISRA-C and HICPP, which resulted in a categorisation, shown below, of coding rules which roughly ranks the difficulty of formalising them and of verifying they are met:

Trivial. The existence in the source code of a simple pattern that can be expressed with a regular expression violates the rule. E.g.: "*Do not call the* `malloc()` *function*" (MISRA-C, rule 20.4).

Syntactic. Slightly modifying the grammar (e.g., by eliminating productions) or the lexical analysis, is enough to catch violations to the rule. E.g.: "*Do not use the 'inline' keyword for member functions*" (HICPP, rule 3.1.7).

Type-enforceable. An extended type system is needed to deal with it. E.g.: "*Expressions that are effectively Boolean should not be used as operands to operators other than* `&&`, `||`, *and* `!`" (MISRA-C, rule 12.6).

Structural. The rule has to do with permanent relations between objects in the code. Information not present in the Abstract Syntax Tree (AST) but completely static, such as the inheritance hierarchy, needs to be analysed. E.g.: "*If a virtual function in a base class is not overridden in any derived class, then make it non virtual*" (HICPP, rule 3.3.6).

Dynamic. The rule refers to sequences of events occurring at runtime. Control flow graph information is typically taken into account, but many other things might be necessary, as a memory model, pointer alias, or data-flow information.

E.g.: *"All automatic variables shall have been assigned a value before being used"* (MISRA-C, rule 9.1). Due to their own nature, automatically checking these rules poses, in general, a series of problems whose solution needs information which can, at best, be approximated using static analysis.

Hard to automate. Either the rule is difficult to formalise or it involves non-computable properties: for instance, whether two procedures compute the same function or not. E.g.: *"Behaviour should be implemented by only one member function in a class"* (HICPP, rule 3.1.9).

As it is clear that very different verification techniques are required to deal with different classes of coding rules, we have decided to focus first on *structural* rules, i.e., those that depend on static relations among objects in the code. On one hand, these were perceived as interesting by industrial project partners and, on the other side, a customary research on the literature threw the result that these aspects of software construction had not been treated with the depth they deserved. More than 20 rules of this kind have been detected in HICPP and MISRA-C.

It is interesting to note that, with the exception of the last category, a significant part of the information needed to deal with these rules are already gathered by modern compilers, in particular by GCC. Needless to say, rules of a certain category may require machinery characteristic of previous categories.

3   Rule Validation Framework

Our selection of basic framework components stems from the observation that, in general, structural coding rules are not very complex (in a linguistic sense). They do not need to deal with time, and they do not need to, e.g., model beliefs or approximate reasoning, either. Therefore, first order logic increased with sorts (as we will see later) seems a well-known and completely adequate formalism.

Detecting whether some software project violates a particular rule can be made as follows:

1. Express the coding rule in a suitable logic, assuming an appropriate representation of the entities the rule needs to know about. This is a one-time step, independent from the particular software project to be checked.
2. Transcribe the necessary program information into the aforementioned representation. This is necessary for every project instance.
3. Prove (automatically) whether there is a counterexample for the rule. In that case the rule is not met; otherwise, the code conforms to the rule.

The framework that we propose for structural coding rule validation of C++ development projects is depicted in Fig. 1. On its left-hand side we see that structural coding rules are formulated in a domain-specific language termed CRISP[2] which is compiled automatically into Prolog predicates for checking. CRISP is

---

[2] CRISP is an acronym for "Coding Rules In Sugared Prolog".

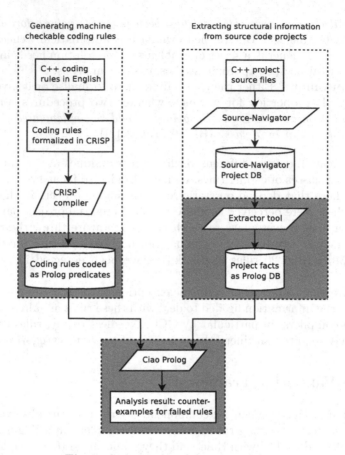

Fig. 1. Coding rule validation workflow

an expressive first-order logic based specification formalism that extends Prolog with *sorts*, full *constructive* negation and *universal quantification*. As some features depend on the programming language being analysed, there is a family of languages ($CRISP_L$) parametrised by the actual programming language (L).

While, as we will see, Prolog can be used to express structural rules, making it the native language for specifying coding rules has several drawbacks: people writing or reading the rules are not likely to be Prolog experts, full Prolog contains too much extra (perhaps non-declarative) stuff that does not fit in our setting and which needs care regarding e.g. evaluation order and instantiation state of variables, etc. Moreover, a proper compilation of rules into Prolog will demand a *careful* use of several extensions to the language. The use of a domain-specific language will therefore maximise declarativeness and will also allow the CRISP compiler to focus on those constructions that appear more often or which are critical in terms of efficiency.

However, as CRISP is still in an early stage of definition – we plan to gather as much information as we can from the experiments and potential users of the language – we will in this paper refrain from discussing it further, and will focus instead on the Prolog implementation of rules.

In our approach we transcribe the *violations* of coding rules as Prolog predicates, their arguments being the entities of interest to the programmer. In this way the verification method can return *references* to the elements in the source code which have to be corrected. Furthermore, coding the negated form of a rule as a logical formula results more natural in many cases.

On the right-hand side of Fig. 1, gathering of structural information from a particular C++ software development project is depicted. To extract this information we are currently taking advantage of the source code analysing tool Source-Navigator [5], that generates a database of architectural and cross-reference information of a software project.[3] A set of Prolog facts representing the same structural information is automatically generated from the Source-Navigator knowledge database.

Validating the C++ software development project against the coding rules is then realised by executing, in the Ciao Prolog System [6], each of the Prolog predicates representing a coding rule violation together with the Prolog facts representing the project structural information. A positive answer to a query will flag a violation of the corresponding rule, and the culprits will be returned in the form of bindings for the predicate arguments. On the other hand, failure to return an answer means that the project conforms to that particular rule.

4 Rule Formalisation

In what follows we will look at how actual HICPP rules can be formalised using logic programming.

Coding the rules requires a set of language-specific predicates representing structural information about, e.g., the inheritance graph of the checked program, its call graph, etc. We use an *order sorted logic* [7] to define these predicates with the purpose of categorising different concepts of the language. Sorts in Prolog are implemented as unary predicates, which is not suitable for constructive negation and the meaning we want to give to quantifiers, as will be seen in Sect. 4.3.

Some representative predicates targeting C++ – in particular those used in the next rule examples –, and a significant fraction of the sorts relevant to them are listed in Table 1. Some predicates appear categorised as *primitive*: they concern base facts that have to be provided by the compiler (i.e. GCC) in the process of compiling a source program. Note that, in general, processing a single compilation unit is not enough: extracting information pertaining a full program or library is required for the analysis we are aiming at. More sophisticated predicates can be constructed in terms of primitive predicates: some examples are given in the table in the *derived* predicates section.

---

[3] We are, however, experimenting with using other source code analysis tools for structural information extraction, including GCC 4.X itself.

Table 1. A subset of sorts and predicates necessary to describe structural relations in C++ code. Sorts of predicate arguments are abbreviated: C for *class* sort, M for *method*, etc. $[S]$ is a list of elements of sort S.

PREDICATE	MEANING
Sorts	
$class(C)$	C is a class.
$method(M)$	M is a member function.
$type(T)$	T is a C++ well-formed type.
$template\_instance(TI)$	TI is an instance of a template
$identifier(I)$	I is a class or method identifier.
Primitive predicates	
$immediate\_base\_of(a : C, b : C)$	Class a appears in the list of explicit base classes of class b.
$public\_base\_of(a : C, b : C)$	Class b immediately inherits from class a with public accessibility. There are analogous predicates for other accessibility choices and also for virtual inheritance.
$declares\_member(a : C, n : N, m : M)$	Class a declares a member m with name n.
$has\_method(c : C, m : M)$	Class c has defined the m method.
$constructor(c : M)$	Method c is a constructor.
$destructor(d : M)$	Method d is a destructor.
$virtual(v : M)$	Method v is dynamically dispatched.
$calls(a : M, b : M)$	Method a has in its text an invocation of method b.
$sig(m : M, i : I, a : [T], r : T)$	Method m has name i, argument type a and result type r.
Derived predicates	
$base\_of(a : C, b : C)$	Transitive closure of $immediate\_base\_of/2$.
$inheritance\_path(a : C, b : C, p : [C])$	Class b can be reached from class a through the inheritance path p.

4.1 Some Examples of HICPP Rule Formalisation

Rule 3.3.15 of HICPP reads "*ensure base classes common to more than one derived class are virtual.*" This can be interpreted as requiring that all classes with more than one immediate descendant class are virtually derived, which seems far too restrictive. In the justification that accompanies the rule, it is made clear that the problem concerns repeated inheritance only (i.e., when a replicated base class is not declared virtual in some of the paths). Whether all paths need to use virtual inheritance, or only one of them, is difficult to infer from the provided explanation and examples. This kind of ambiguity in natural language definitions of coding rules is not uncommon, and is a strong argument in favour of providing, as we do, a formalised rule definition amenable to be used by an automatic checker.

The C++ definition of virtual inheritance makes clear that, in order to avoid any ambiguities in classes that repeatedly inherit from a certain base class, all inheritance paths must include the repeated class as a virtual base. As we want to identify violations of the rule, a reformulation is the following:

> Rule 3.3.15 is violated if there exist classes A, B, C, and D such that: class A is a base class of D through two different paths, and one of the paths has class B as an immediate subclass of A, and the other has class C as an immediate subclass of A, where B and C are different classes. Moreover A is not declared as a virtual base of C.

Fig. 2 shows, among others, the Prolog formalisation of a violation of rule 3.3.15. The success of a query to `violate_hicpp_3_3_15/4` would exemplify an example of violation of HICPP Rule 3.3.15.[4]

Note that the fact that all variables refer to classes is marked at the moment – as Prolog is used – with a predicate `class/1`, whose clauses are provided as part of the project description, and similarly for other sorts in other predicates. A suitable definition of *base_of* is also necessary:

```
base_of(A,A).
base_of(A,B)  :- immediate_base_of(A,C), base_of(C,B).
```

In the case of 3.3.15, the four involved classes are not necessarily distinct, but it is required that B and C do not refer to the same class, and that both are immediate descendants of A. The terms `base_of(B,D)` and `base_of(C,D)` point out that class D must be a descendant of both B and C, through an arbitrary number (maybe zero) of subclassing steps. Finally, for the rule to be violated we require that class A is not virtually inherited by class C. The use of negation in rules is further developed in Sect. 4.3.

Fig. 3 depicts a set of classes and their inheritance relations which make the literal `violate_hicpp_3_3_15('::Animal','::Mammal','::WingedAnimal','::Bat')` deducible, thus constituting a counterexample. If the inheritance from `'::Animal'` to `'::WingedAnimal'` were also *virtual*, the goal would fail (no counterexample could have been found). Note that the rule is more general than it may seem: for example, it does not require that classes B and D are different. Thus, if (nonsensically) `'::Mammal'` and `'::Bat'` in Fig. 3 were the same, a property violation would still be detected.

Another rule that can be easily implemented in this framework but requires disjunction is rule HICPP 3.3.13 specified as "*do not invoke virtual methods of the declared class in a constructor or destructor.*" This rule needs, additionally, information about the call graph of the project.

Rule HICPP 3.3.2 states "*write a 'virtual' destructor for base classes.*" The rationale behind this requirement is that if an object will ever be destroyed through a pointer to its base class, the correct version of the destructor code should be dynamically dispatched. This rule illustrates the necessity of existential quantification; also, the construction "does not exist" appears repeatedly in rule formalisation. Some hints about quantification are also provided in Sect. 4.3.

---

[4] We will use a similar naming convention hereinafter: `violate_hicpp_X_Y_Z/N` is the rule which models the violation of the HICPP rule X.Y.Z.

```
violate_hicpp_3_3_15(A,B,C,D) :-
    class(A), class(B), class(C), class(D),
    B \= C,
    immediate_base_of(A,B), immediate_base_of(A,C),
    base_of(B,D), base_of(C,D),
    \+ virtual_base_of(A,C).
```

```
violate_hicpp_3_3_13(Caller,Called) :-
    method(Caller), method(Called),
    has_method(SomeClass,Caller),
    (
        constructor(Caller)
    ;
        destructor(Caller)
    ),
    has_method(SomeClass,Called),
    virtual(Called),
    calls(Caller,Called).
```

```
violates_hicpp_3_3_2(BaseClass) :-
    class(BaseClass),
    exists_some_derived_class_of(BaseClass),
    does_not_exist_virtual_destructor_in(BaseClass).

exists_some_derived_class_of(BaseClass) :-
    immediate_base_of(BaseClass,_).

does_not_exist_virtual_destructor_in(Class) :-
    \+ (
        has_method(Class,Destructor),
        destructor(Destructor),
        virtual(Destructor)
    ).
```

```
violate_hicpp_16_2(Class) :-
    template_instance(Class),
    has_method(Class,Method1),
    has_method(Class,Method2),
    Method1 \== Method2,
    sig(Method1,Name,ArgsT,ResT),
    sig(Method2,Name,ArgsT,ResT).
```

```
violate_hicpp_3_3_1(Base,Derived) :-
    class(Base), class(Derived),
    (
        private_base_of(Base,Derived)
    ;
        protected_base_of(Base,Derived)
    ).
```

```
violate_hicpp_3_3_11(BaseClass,Super,Class) :-
    class(Class), class(Super),
    base_of(Super,Class), Class \= Super,
    declares_member(Class,ClassMethod),
    declares_member(Super,SuperMethod),
    sig(ClassMethod,Name,Args,Ret),
    sig(SuperMethod,Name,Args,Ret),
    \+ virtual(SuperMethod),
    \+ virtual(ClassMethod).
```

Fig. 2. Formalisation of some HICPP rules

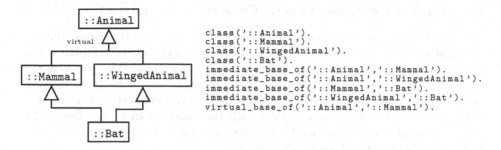

```
class('::Animal').
class('::Mammal').
class('::WingedAnimal').
class('::Bat').
immediate_base_of('::Animal','::Mammal').
immediate_base_of('::Animal','::WingedAnimal').
immediate_base_of('::Mammal','::Bat').
immediate_base_of('::WingedAnimal','::Bat').
virtual_base_of('::Animal','::Mammal').
```

Fig. 3. Violation of rule HICPP 3.3.15 and automatically generated Prolog facts

```cpp
template< typename T > class A {
  public:
  void foo( T );
  void foo( int );
};

template class A< int >;      // void foo(int) declared twice!
```

Fig. 4. Violation of rule HICPP 16.2

Rule HICPP 16.2 reads *"do not define a class template with potentially conflicting methods."* The code snippet in Fig. 4, taken from [2], illustrates how not following the rule can hamper software maintenance and reusability: the template instantiation generates two methods with identical signature.

A formalisation of the rule negation (and, in fact, a program capable of catching non-compliant code) can be easily written using unification and logic variables to represent template parameters (see Sect. 4.2 for more details), as shown in predicate `violate_hicpp_16_2/1` (Fig. 2).

Syntactic rules are also trivially expressible in this framework provided that enough information about the abstract syntax tree is reified into the knowledge base about the program, even if more efficient ways of dealing with these rules exist. Predicate `violate_hicpp_3_3_1/2` (Fig. 2) shows a Prolog representation of rule HICPP 3.3.1, that reads *"use public derivation only."*

HICPP rule 3.3.11, as captured by predicate `violate_hicpp_3_3_11/3` (Fig. 2) forbids overloading or hiding non-virtual functions.

HICPP has a conservative spirit which we want to retain in our rules: any potentially dangerous situation is altogether forbidden, regardless of whether it can actually happen in a given environment (i.e., in a *complete* program). This is very sensible: on one hand, from the point of view of program maintenance, initial conditions may evolve in unforeseeable directions, and protecting the project is very reasonable; on the other hand, when libraries are being developed, these will be used in an *a priori* unknown environment.

The following paragraphs discuss the Prolog translation of rules.

4.2   Types, Classes, and Generic Constructs (Templates)

Parametric polymorphism is realised in C++ by means of *templates*. We are
not dealing, at the moment, with a complete representation of templates, but
only with those whose parameters are classes and basic types. The names of the
parametrised classes are introduced in the knowledge base as function symbols
belonging to the *class* sort. Template parameters are modelled with logic variables, which makes it possible to deal with template instantiation directly by
means of variable instantiation. To illustrate our approach the following Prolog
code would be generated from code in Fig. 4:

```
%% Knowledge base about typing in C++
type(void_type).
type(boolean_type).
...
type(pointer_type(T)) :- type(T).

%% Project-specific data
template_instance(':: A'(T)) :- type(T).
...
```

This code states that, for a particular project, terms of the form ':: A'(*t*) are of
sort *template_instance* if *t* is any *type*. This paves the way for a richer language in
which types are first-order citizens and can be subject to arbitrary constraints (in
particular equality and disequality, but also notions of subsumption, if needed).
This makes up what is necessary to check for violations of rule HICPP 16.2
(recall Fig. 4).

On the other hand, having such power leads to issues as the infinite set of answers for the goal ?- `template_instance(C)`. due to the definition of the scheme
for pointer types being used to construct all possible instances of template 'A'.
Some of these cases can be worked around by using well-known evaluation techniques such as tabled resolution (see, e.g., [8] for a basic reference), delay of
selected goals, and use of a suitable constraint system. A correct treatment
of disequality constraints needs dealing explicitly with negation of non-ground
goals.

4.3   Negation and Quantifiers

Negation appears in coding rules in various forms. On one hand, there is the issue,
already mentioned, that predicates specifying the violation of rules (i.e. their
negation) tend to be easier to translate into Prolog. But this is not necessarily the
case for every structural rule, so some method for automatically generating one
version from the other would be very useful. Also, we have seen that disequalities
and predicates representing the complement of basic relations occur frequently
in the rules.

The main problem with the built-in negation operators in Prolog – see the "\+"
in the last line of `violate_hicpp_3_3_15` – is that correctness is only guaranteed
under certain run-time conditions, i.e. the negated literal must have no free
variables at call time. While experienced Prolog programmers usually develop

a *sixth sense* that allows them to place negated literals only in safe places,[5] a general solution must be provided that allows a CRISP compiler to generate correct Prolog code in all cases. Notice how this problem is shared with the disequality operators – see the "\=" in the third line of `violate_hicpp_3_3_15`.

Extensions to Prolog allowing free variables in negated literals do exist under the name *constructive negation*. Among these, *intensional* approaches apply a source transformation in order to obtain, for a given predicate *p* in the original program, a negative version *neg_p*. Our choice has been to use our own implementation, named *constructive intensional negation* [10], as it deals properly with the kind of knowledge bases that we are generating from the project code – positive and potentially infinite, as explained in Sect. 4.2. Negative constructive answers are possible thanks to a disequality constraint library replacing standard Prolog disequality. This, of course, also solves the problem with disequality operators.

The case of universal quantification is similar to negation. It appears both explicitly in the specification of the rules and also implicitly – generated during the transformation implementing intensional negation of clauses with free variables. Fortunately, our intensional negation library comes equipped with a universal quantification mechanism which is semantically sound and complete for bases satisfying certain conditions.

Finally, for this application, both negation and universal quantification must be implemented in a *sort aware* way, i.e. negated predicates must represent the complement of relations w.r.t. their sorts and the universal quantification of a predicate must hold if, and only if, it holds for every element of its sort, etc. This precludes a naive treatment of sorts as regular Prolog predicates. For example, looking at typical rules like HICPP 3.3.15 or HICPP 16.2, whose violation is formalised in Prolog in Fig. 2, we see that both clauses start with some sort requirements (`class(A)`, `class(B)` ...). A straightforward application of the intensional negation transformation of such clauses would not produce the right code. From a clause of the form

$$r(\overline{X}) \leftarrow sorts(\overline{X}) \wedge p(\overline{X})$$

we would obtain

$$neg\_r(\overline{X}) \leftarrow neg\_sorts(\overline{X})$$
$$neg\_r(\overline{X}) \leftarrow neg\_p(\overline{X})$$

rather than the desired

$$neg\_r(\overline{X}) \leftarrow sorts(\overline{X}) \wedge neg\_p(\overline{X})$$

where *p* is the part of the clause not containing any sort requirements and *neg_p* and *neg_sorts* have been obtained using an standard transformation. Notice how *sorts* must remain positive in the negated version.

---

[5] Static analysis techniques have been developed to actually prove these *tricks* correct, see for instance [9].

Table 2. A brief description of the open-source C++ projects that have been analysed for rule violations. KLOC measured by `sloccount`.

PROJECT	VERSION	DESCRIPTION	KLOC
Bacula	2.2.0	A network based backup program.	20
CLAM	1.1.0	C++ Library for Audio and Music.	46
Firebird	2.1.0.15999-Beta1	Relational database with concurrency and stored procedures.	439
IT++	3.10.12	Library for signal and speech processing.	39
OGRE	1.4.3 (Linux/OSX)	Object-Oriented 3D Graphics Rendering Engine, scene-oriented.	209
Orca	2.5.0	Framework for developing component-based robotic systems.	89
Qt	4.3.1 (X11 opensource)	Application development framework and GUI widgets library.	595

5   Experimental Results

We have developed a prototype that allows for implementing some syntactic and structural coding rules and running them over a C++ source code tree, reporting rule violations.[6] Some of the rules described in Sect. 4.1 have been applied to the C++ open-source software projects appearing in Table 2.

A measure of the size of each project is provided in the table in the form of physical lines of code (KLOC column). All analysed projects can be considered mature but they diverge in their size and application area, covering as a whole a wide range of C++ design techniques. Some of them are final applications, and others are libraries of reusable components. Testing code and examples included in many projects have been excluded from the analysis wherever possible.

Our checking tool has been constructed on top of the Prolog engine Ciao [6]. Until full integration into the GCC pipeline is done, we use, as mentioned before, the open source tool Source-Navigator to extract the needed data about C++ programs. Source-Navigator covers almost the whole C/C++ language and it is able to quickly analyse projects with thousands of source code files. Internally, Source-Navigator stores project facts in Berkeley DB (BDB) tables. The conversion of static information into the Prolog facts shown in Table 1 was realised by a simple Tcl program that traversed the Source-Navigator database using a Tcl Application Programming Interface.

Validating the C++ software development project against its coding rules is then realised by executing, in the Ciao Prolog System, each of the Prolog predicates representing a coding rule violation together with the Prolog facts representing the structural information about the project.

Table 3 shows, for each software project, the number of violations automatically detected for each implemented rule, together with the execution time consumed by

---

[6] The source code of this and subsequent prototypes will be available at `https://babel.ls.fi.upm.es/trac/ggcc/`.

Table 3. Experimental results on a sample of HICPP coding rules and open-source projects. SN TIME is the time spent by Source-Navigator on partially parsing the source code and storing the needed facts into a database. LD TIME is the time taken by loading the facts into the Prolog engine and pre-calculating the closure *base_of*. Cells for rule columns show *no. of violations found (execution time)*. All times are user time expressed in seconds.

PROJECT	SN TIME	LD TIME	RULE 3.3.1	RULE 3.3.2	RULE 3.3.11	RULE 3.3.15
Bacula	1.53	0.24	0 (0.00)	3 (0.03)	0 (0.00)	0 (0.00)
CLAM	1.82	1.62	1 (0.00)	15 (0.47)	115 (0.12)	0 (0.24)
Firebird	6.48	2.61	16 (0.00)	60 (1.02)	115 (0.21)	0 (0.27)
IT++	1.18	0.42	0 (0.00)	6 (0.03)	12 (0.01)	0 (0.00)
OGRE	4.73	3.05	0 (0.00)	15 (0.94)	79 (0.21)	0 (0.31)
Orca	2.51	1.17	1 (0.00)	12 (0.38)	0 (0.09)	0 (0.16)
Qt	12.29	10.42	15 (0.01)	75 (10.53)	1155 (1.32)	4 (1.21)

all the necessary steps of the checking procedure. It can be seen that every project violates some rule and that non-conformant code has been found for every rule.

The fact that rule HICPP 3.3.15 is violated by only one project (Qt) is a direct consequence of the close to zero use of repeated ("diamond-like") inheritance in actual C++ projects. The same infrastructure devoted to check coding rules compliance has been used to detect multiple inheritance and repeated inheritance instances. The conclusion is that multiple inheritance – an important object-oriented design and implementation mechanism – is used very rarely, and the only analysed projects that have taken advantage of repeated inheritance are IT++ and Qt, and even there is applied very few times. Despite the efforts done to include those features into the language [11], its hazards and subtleties seem to have convinced many developers that they have to be completely avoided. Rule HICPP 3.3.15 (in combination with other HICPP rules) is oriented towards permitting a reliable use of multiple and repeated inheritance. A wider adoption of coding standards like HICPP could have the paradoxical effect of popularising some denigrated – but useful – C++ features.

Another interesting aspect of these initial experiments is that they have confirmed that relying solely on manual checking is not a feasible approach to enforce coding rules. Manually approve or reject those violations reported by the checking tool has turn out to be a too tedious and error-prone task. Note that for some rules (e.g. HICPP 3.3.11) the amount of violations is rather big. Moreover, even for simple rules as HICPP 3.3.2 (easy to state and to formalise in Prolog), rule requirements can be fulfilled in many ways, some of them not easy to grasp from the source code. In this particular case a virtual destructor has to be looked for in all the superclasses of a given class.

Execution times have been included in Table 3 to show that a non-negligible amount of time is used to run non-trivial rule violation detectors over the biggest projects, but they are still bearable – as far as rule enforcing machinery is not expected to run in every compilation or, alternatively, that *incremental* rule checking is implemented. SN TIME and LD TIME are executed once per project. The experiments have been run in a 32 bits Intel Dual Xeon 2.0 GHz and code is completely sequential in all measured steps. In a similar way as *base_of*, other intermediate relations could be pre-computed on initialisation for improving performance, or even more general tabling techniques might be used.

6   Related Work

To our knowledge, our proposal is the first attempt at using declarative technology for formally specifying and automatically checking coding rules. A related area where some academic proposals exist that apply first-order logic and logic programming is formalisation and automatic verification of design patterns [12,13,14]. In [14], facts about a Smalltalk program are reified into a logic programming framework. In [13] a very similar setting is developed targeting the Java language. Both formalisms can deal with the structural relations necessary to define the static aspects of design patterns. But none of them use true sorts for quantification nor can cope with infinite domains or recursively defined objects in the target language. This fact makes both approaches unable to represent C++ template parameters as logic variables and reason about hypothetical instantiations of templates as we do in rule HICPP 16.2.

A different area where some interesting ideas can be borrowed from is automatic bug finding techniques. The "bug pattern" term in [15] is very close to our concept of what a rule violation is. It uses structural information, but no mechanism is provided for the user to define its own bug patterns. On the other hand, [16,17] define a domain-specific language to create custom checks for C code, and [18] uses a declarative language for checks on Java. All three are based on automata and syntactic patterns, and are specially oriented to the kind of program properties related with dynamic rules (see Sect.2). The language in [17] is the least expressive of the three but, interestingly, the checking facility has been integrated into a GCC branch.

7   Conclusion

This paper presents a logic programming-based framework to specify industrial coding rules and use them to check code for conformance. These coding rules express what are perceived as good programming practises in imperative/object-oriented programming languages. Our framework is in principle language-agnostic, and the particular characteristics of a given language (kinds of inheritance, etc.) can be modelled seamlessly and with little effort.

The properties we tackle range from syntactic to semantic ones, although in this paper we have focused on the so-called "structural properties", which address programming projects as a whole and have as basic components entities such as classes, methods, functions, and their relations.

In contrast with our approach, current commercial tools like those mentioned in Sect. 1 do not provide the user with any simple – and at the same time powerful enough – mechanism to define new coding rules. If extensibility is possible at all, new checks must be programmed directly in C or C++ and access the internal representation of the analysed code managed by the tool. Moreover, these tools cannot be considered semantically reliable due to the absence of a formal specification of their intended behaviour.

The inference engine we are currently using to perform rule violation detection is plain Prolog, which can be queried to discover witnesses of evil patterns. Speed is, so far, very satisfactory, and we have been able to run non-trivial rules in projects with half a million LOC in around ten seconds using a standard PC. We have specified a good number of coding rules, of which we have selected what we think is a relevant and interesting subset. As expected, the main problem is not in the coding itself, but in understanding clearly what is the exact meaning of the rule. This is, of course, part of the *raison d'être* of the coding rule formalism. Tests have shown rule violations in very well-known and well-regarded projects.

This work is part of a bigger project which is just giving its first results and whose final aim is to be delivered as part of the GCC suite. Defining a stable subset of CRISP is a priority among the directions for future research. The use of a highly enriched logic-based domain-specific language must bridge the gap between the expressive but ambiguous natural language and the rigorous, but somewhat more constraining language of formal logic. In order to keep CRISP declarative while maintaining the efficiency of the Prolog code obtained by hand, a translation scheme must be defined that carefully handles the critical aspects in the Prolog implementation identified so far: negation and disequalities in the presence of free variables, universal quantification, sort constraints, etc.

Mid-term tasks include connecting the framework with other parts of the GGCC project (e.g. static analysis) in order to cover more complex rules and, of course, in order to gain more practical experience both in terms of expressiveness and performance when analysing very large projects. Regarding the latter, there seems to be some room for improvement by discovering recurring patterns – e.g. the fact that transitive closures appear very often in coding rules suggests a potential for tabling, etc.

In the long term, ways of obtaining the needed information about programs directly from the natural language description of the coding rules, can be considered, e.g. by reformulating them into the so called *controlled natural languages* [19] like ACE, CLCE, etc., subsets, for instance, of English, that can be understood unambiguously and automatically. However, the source of ambiguity is not (only) the language itself, but also the assumption of some implicit information (e.g. pertaining to a certain domain or organisation) that may be not be obvious for an external user. The formalisation process, when the target language is declarative and simple enough like CRISP, enforces explicitly including these assumptions and, hence, solve the ambiguities.

References

1. MIRA Ltd.: MISRA-C:2004. Guidelines for the Use of the C Language in Critical Systems (October 2004)
2. The Programming Research Group: High-Integrity C++ Coding Standard Manual (May 2004)
3. Sun Microsystems, http://java.sun.com/products/javacard/
4. Global GCC project website, http://www.ggcc.info/
5. Source-Navigator, http://sourcenav.sourceforge.net/
6. Hermenegildo, M., Bueno, F., Cabeza, D., Carro, M., de la Banda, M.G., López-García, P., Puebla, G.: The CIAO Multi-Dialect Compiler and System: An Experimentation Workbench for Future (C)LP Systems. In: Parallelism and Implementation of Logic and Constraint Logic Programming, Nova Science, Commack, NY, USA, pp. 65–85 (April 1999)
7. Kaneiwa, K.: Order-Sorted Logic Programming with Predicate Hierarchy. Artificial Intelligence 158(2), 155–188 (2004)
8. Ramakrishnan, I.V., Rao, P., Sagonas, K.F., Swift, T., Warren, D.S.: Efficient tabling mechanisms for logic programs. In: ICLP, pp. 697–711 (1995)
9. Muñoz-Hernández, S., Moreno-Navarro, J., Hermenegildo, M.: Efficient negation using abstract interpretation. In: Nieuwenhuis, R., Voronkov, A. (eds.) Logic for Programming, Artificial Intelligence and Reasoning, La Habana (Cuba) (2001)
10. Muñoz, S., Mariño, J., Moreno-Navarro, J.J.: Constructive intensional negation. In: Kameyama, Y., Stuckey, P.J. (eds.) FLOPS 2004. LNCS, vol. 2998, pp. 39–54. Springer, Heidelberg (2004)
11. Ellis, M.A., Stroustrup, B.: The Annotated C++ Reference Manual. Addison-Wesley, Reading (1990)
12. Taibi, T.: An Integrated Approach to Design Patterns Formalization. In: Design Pattern Formalization Techniques. IGI Publishing (March 2007)
13. Blewitt, A., Bundy, A., Stark, I.: Automatic verification of design patterns in java. In: Redmiles, D.F., Ellman, T., Zisman, A. (eds.) ASE 2005. 20th IEEE/ACM International Conference on Automated Software Engineering, Long Beach, CA, USA, November 7-11, 2005, pp. 224–232. ACM Press, New York (2005)
14. Mens, K., Michiels, I., Wuyts, R.: Supporting software development through declaratively codified programming. In: SEKE, pp. 236–243 (2001)
15. Hovemeyer, D., Pugh, W.: Finding bugs is easy. ACM SIGPLAN Notices 39(10), 132–136 (2004)
16. Hallem, S., Chelf, B., Xie, Y., Engler, D.: A system and language for building system-specific, static analyses. ACM SIGPLAN Notices 37(5), 69–82 (2002)
17. Volanschi, E.N.: A portable compiler-integrated approach to permanent checking. In: ASE, pp. 103–112. IEEE Computer Society Press, Los Alamitos (2006)
18. Martin, M., Livshits, B., Lam, M.S.: Finding application errors and security flaws using PQL: A program query language. In: OOPSLA 2005. Proceedings of Object-Oriented Programming, Systems, Languages, and Applications, New York, NY, USA, pp. 363–385. ACM Press, New York (2005)
19. Schwitter, R.: Controlled natural languages, http://www.ics.mq.edu.au/~rolfs/controlled-natural-languages

Comprehension and Dependency Analysis of Aspect-Oriented Programs through Declarative Reasoning

Laleh Mousavi Eshkevari, Venera Arnaoudova,
and Constantinos Constantinides

Department of Computer Science and Software Engineering,
Concordia University,
Montreal, Quebec, H3G 1M8, Canada
Tel.: +1 514 848 2424 Ext. 5374
{l_mousa, v_arnaou, cc}@cse.concordia.ca
http://hypatia.cs.concordia.ca

Abstract. In this paper we discuss an approach to support declarative reasoning over aspect-oriented (AO) programs, adopting AspectJ as a representative technology. The approach is based on the transformation of source code into a set of facts and rules, stored into a Prolog database. Declarative analysis allows us to extract complex information through its rich and expressive syntax. Our approach has two contributions. First, it aims to improve the comprehension of AspectJ programs. The type of knowledge provided is categorized in three main groups: i) general knowledge, ii) bad smells, and iii) quality metrics. The second contribution is the provision of dependency analysis of AspectJ programs. To that end, we identify dependencies in aspect-oriented programs, and translate them into Prolog rules. Expected beneficiaries of our approach include system maintainers who can obtain comprehension and perform dependency analysis through querying the Prolog database during the change planning stage of system evolution.

Keywords: Program comprehension, static analysis, dependency analysis, declarative reasoning, aspect-oriented programming, AspectJ programming language.

1 Introduction

Software maintenance is defined as "the modification of a software product after delivery to correct faults, improve performance (or other attributes) or to adapt the product to a modified environment" (ANSI/IEEE standard 1219-1998). The objective of maintenance is to enhance and optimize an existing system while preserving its integrity [7]. The initial step of software maintenance is program comprehension, and it demands effort and time, initially to understand the software system and then to identify possible problems to be fixed while providing a remedy for them without affecting the overall behavior of the system. Statistics

P. Hudak and D.S. Warren (Eds.): PADL 2008, LNCS 4902, pp. 35–52, 2008.
© Springer-Verlag Berlin Heidelberg 2008

indicate that the amount of time required for software comprehension constitutes a significant proportion of the maintenance process. This is particularly important while comprehension is deployed as the first step during change planning. In this phase, modifications of specific parts of the system would normally affect other parts of the target system due to dependency relationships between entities. Experience shows that making software changes without understanding their effects can lead to underestimated efforts, delays in release schedules, degraded software design and unreliable software products. Estimating and analyzing the potential consequences of carrying out a change provides effective information for the maintainers. To this end, dependency analysis provides feedback about the possible impact of modification of the software system.

The rest of the paper is organized as follows: In Section 2 we provide the necessary theoretical background to aspect-oriented programing and the AspectJ language which we use as a notable representative technology. In Section 3 we discuss the problem and motivation behind this research. In Section 4 we present our proposal. We discuss our methodology in Sections 5, 6 and 7. We illustrate how our approach can be deployed for a typical exploration task with a case study in Section 8. We discuss related work in Section 9 and we provide an evaluation of our approach in Section 10. We conclude our discussion in Section 11.

2   Theoretical Background: Aspect-Oriented Programming (AOP) and AspectJ

The principle of separation of concerns [17] refers to the realization of system concepts into separate software units and it is a fundamental principle of software development. The associated benefits include better analysis and understanding of systems, improved readability of code, increased level of reusability, easy adaptability and good maintainability. Despite the success of object-orientation in the effort to achieve separation of concerns, certain properties in object-oriented systems cannot be directly mapped in a one-to-one fashion from the problem domain to the solution space, and thus cannot be localized in single modular units. Their implementation ends up cutting across the inheritance hierarchy of the system. Crosscutting concerns (or "aspects") include persistence, authentication, synchronization and contract checking. Aspect-oriented programming [13] explicitly addresses those concerns by introducing the notion of aspect, which is a modular unit of decomposition. Currently there exist many approaches and technologies to support AOP. One such notable technology is AspectJ [12], a general-purpose aspect-oriented language, which has influenced the design dimensions of several other general-purpose aspect-oriented languages, and has provided the community with a common vocabulary based on its own linguistic constructs. In the AspectJ model, an aspect definition is a new unit of modularity providing behavior to be inserted over functional components. This behavior is defined in method-like blocks called *advice*. However, unlike a method, an advice block is never explicitly called. Instead, it is only implicitly invoked by an associated construct called a *pointcut* expression. A pointcut expression is a predicate over well-defined points in the execution of the program which are referred to as *join points*. When the program execution reaches a join point captured by a pointcut expression, the associated advice block is executed. Even though the specification and level of granularity of the join point model differ from one language to another, common join points in current language specifications include calls to - and execution of methods and constructors. Most aspect-oriented languages provide a level of granularity which specifies exactly when an advice block should be executed, such as executing before, after, or instead of the code defined at the associated join point. Furthermore, several advice blocks may apply to the same join point. In this case the order of execution is specified by rules of advice precedence specified by the underlying language [14].

3   Problem and Motivation

With an increasing number of tools and support of a community of developers and researchers, the AspectJ programming language is perhaps the most notable aspect-oriented technology. Aspect-oriented programing improves the modularity of systems by allowing programmers to reason about individual concerns in relative isolation. However, the improvement of modularity comes with the cost of overall program comprehension. To achieve comprehension of the entire aspect-oriented program, one must take into consideration not just inter-component dependencies but also all aspect-to-component dependencies. However, the implicit interdependency between aspects and classes demands more careful investigation. The obliviousness property in general-purpose aspect-oriented languages [10] such as AspectJ implies that for a given piece of component functionality f, we need to iterate over all aspect definitions to see which pointcut predicates refer to f and which advice may be combined with f. Manual analysis can be tedious and error prone, particularly for medium- to large-scale systems. To this end, some tool support is currently available. The Eclipse AspectJ plug-in provides some level of visualization (see related work). However, there is certain type of knowledge over an AspectJ program which is neither straightforward to obtain nor can be provided through this plug-in. For example the following information can only be manually extracted:

1. "Fragile aspects" [21]: those which contain pointcuts written in a way which makes them highly vulnerable to any changes in the component code.
2. Aspects that have precedence over a given aspect.
3. Aspects that are advising protected methods only.

Dependency analysis requires program comprehension and it is based on the definition of dependencies that exist among software entities. In the literature many techniques are introduced for dependency analysis, while most of them are adopted for procedural or object-oriented systems. The majority of these techniques are deployed over a system dependency graph (SDG) and slicing methods. However, graph-based analysis lacks scalability which makes the investigation difficult even for a medium-scale system. Moreover, it is very difficult to manually traverse an SDG even for a small-scale system.

The motivation behind this research is to provide a fine-grained model for the representation of program elements and their inter-dependencies in aspect-oriented programs through the deployment of declarative reasoning in order to obtain comprehension and to perform dependency analysis.

4   Proposal: Declarative Reasoning of Aspect-Oriented Programs

We propose the adoption of declarative reasoning to achieve comprehension and dependency analysis of AspectJ systems. To achieve this goal, we need to perform a transformation from source code to a declarative representation. To gain comprehension, we plan to adopt strategies from the literature (see Section 6). These strategies will be translated as rules in a Prolog database. In order to perform dependency analysis, we plan to identify dependencies in an aspect-oriented program and to codify them as Prolog rules. Some of these dependencies will be adopted from the literature [26], while some others will be introduced (see Section 7). Comprehension can then be obtained by executing queries on the Prolog database (see Figure 1).

The expected contribution of this proposal is to provide a proof of concept for an automated environment under which one can obtain knowledge over an

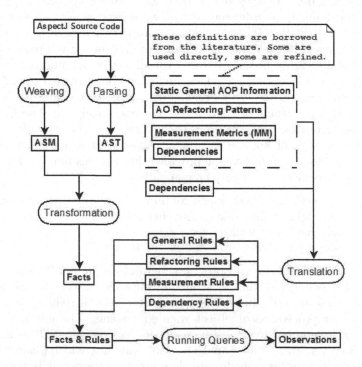

Fig. 1. UML activity diagram illustrating our proposal

AspectJ-like program where this knowledge would otherwise have been difficult or impossible to obtain through existing techniques. Potential beneficiaries of this approach include system maintainers who can perform dependency analysis by querying the database on what elements of the system would be affected should a specific change occur.

The Prolog language has its foundation in logic which allows programmers to define solutions to problems in a logical manner. Its built-in pattern-matching mechanism (unification) makes it possible to bound variables to complex structures which can themselves contain other variables. Moreover, unification provides a mechanism to find multiple solutions for a given problem. In addition to above, Prolog can be deployed as a query language for a database of simple facts for matching complicated patterns. We feel that Prolog is more suitable than other query languages (e.g the Standard Query Language - SQL) for our approach since our database would contain simple facts, but a lot of complex search rules. For example, the derivation rules of Prolog enable us to define relations between facts. However, with SQL we would need to store facts for each relation (views in relational database) and we cannot build view recursively [15]. Deploying SQL would be more beneficial with a great amount of very complex data and with simple search rules. Prolog makes it relatively straightforward to specify, execute and refine complex queries over facts.

5   Model Transformation

In order to transform an AspectJ program into a set of Prolog facts, we have defined a set of transformation rules given in Tables 1 and 2. The transformation process from source code to facts is broken into two steps. First, the abstract syntax tree (AST) corresponding to each compilation unit of the program (.java and .aj files) is retrieved and traversed. Second, the AspectJ structure model (ASM) is retrieved and traversed to provide additional information regarding the relationship among pointcuts, methods and advice blocks. The extracted information from the steps above is then translated to facts according to the transformation rules. These facts are then added to the fact-base and used during the inference process.

6   Model Comprehension

We have added a set of rules to the database in order to capture relationships between entities in the system. These rules are context-free, i.e. they are independent from the particular applications in which they are being deployed. The rules are categorized into three types, based on the motivation by which they were created:

General Rules. We have built certain general rules in order to extract knowledge about the static structure of the program, like inheritance relationships,

Table 1. Transformation rules - Part I

Transformation rules	Definition
`<visibility>:= <public>	<private>	<protected>	<package>`	visibility of a feature is `<public>` or `<private>` or `<protected>`
`[class](<className>, <visibility>)`	class_name is a class with `<visibility>`
`[finalClass](<className>)`	className is a final class
`[abstractClass](<className>)`	className is an abstract class
`[interface](<interfaceName>, <visibility>)`	interfaceName is an interface with `<visibility>`
`[extends](<subClassName> (| <subInterfaceName> | <SubAspectName>),<superClassName> (| <superInterfaceName> | <SuperAspectName>))`	Class subClassName (or subInterfaceName or SubAspectName) extends superClassName (or superInterfaceName or SuperAspectName)
`[implements](<className>, <interfaceName>)`	Class class_name implements interface interface_name
`[aspect](<aspectName>, <visibility>)`	aspectName is an aspect with `<visibility>`
`[privilegedAspect](<aspectName>)`	aspectName is a privileged aspect
`[new](<className1>, <methodName1>, <ClassName2>)`	An instance of `<ClassName2>` is instantiated in method `<methodName1>` in `<className1>`
`<attributeType>:= 0	1	2	3`	`<attributeType>` can be final (1), or static (2), or final-static (3), and if it is not any of the previous types it is marked 0
`[attribute](<className> |<aspectName> | <interfaceName>, <attName>, <Type>, <visibility>, <attributeType>)`	`<attName>` of type `<Type>` is an attribute declared in class className or aspect aspectName or interfaceName with `<visibility>`
`<methodType>:= 0	1	2	3`	`<methodType>` can be abstract(1), or static (3), or final (2) and if it is not any of the previous types it is marked 0
`[method](<className> | <aspectName> | <interfaceName>, <methodName>, <visibility>, <Type>, <ListOfParameters>, <methodType> )`	`<methodName>` , with `<ListOfParameters>` parameters and access modifier public or private or protected and return type `<Type>` is declared in `<className>` or `<aspectName>` or `<interfaceName>`
`[sendMessage](<className1>, <methodName1>, <ListOfParameters1>, <className2>, <methodName2>, <ListOfParameters2>)`	A message methodName2 is sent to `<className2>` from methodName1 in `<className1>`
`[used](<aspectName>, <adviceId>, <ListOfParameters1>, <className>, <methodName>, <ListOfParameters>)`	`<methodName>` in class `<className>` is invoked by `<adviceId>` in `<aspectName>`
`[accessFeature](<className1>, <methodName1>, <className2>, <InstanceVariableName2>)`	`<className1>` accesses `<InstanceVariableName2>` of `<className2>` from `<methodName1>`
`[constructor](<className>, <visibility>, <ListOfParam> )`	`<className>` has a constructor with `<ListOfParam>` parameters

dependencies between aspects and classes, etc. These constitute the core rules defined in our system, and the two subsequent categories of rules are built based on this group. One such example is *Declared Method in Inheritance Hierarchy*, (Figure 2).

We also have defined rules to obtain the following: Aspect monitoring features of a class (methods, attributes) with specific modifiers, Aspects with precedence over a specific aspect, Methods advised by a pointcut, Messages to which a class responds, etc.(see Section 7).

Table 2. Transformation rules - Part II

Transformation rules	Definition
[declareParent](<aspectName>,<Type1>, <Type2>)	<Type2>is declared to be the supertype of <Type1> in <aspectName>
[introducedMethod](<aspectName>,<TypeName>, <methodName>,<visibility>, <ReturnType>, <ListOfParameters>,<methodType>)	<aspectName> declares a method <methodName> with <visibility>, <ReturnType>,and <ListOfParameters> for class <TypeName>
[introducedAtt](<aspectName>,<TypeName>, <AttName>,<Type>,<visibility>, <attributeType>)	<aspectName> declares an attribute <AttName> with, <Type> for a type <TypeName>
[pointcutdesig](<pointcutDesignatorId>,<aspectName>, <pointcutName>,<joinpoint>,<ListOfParam>)	<joinpoint> with a unique id <pointcutDesignatorId> defined in aspectName
<pointcutType>:= 0 |1 |2	<pointcutType> can be abstract (1), static (2), and if it is not any of the previous types it is marked 0
[pointcut](<aspectName>,<pointcutName>,<ListOfParam>, <visibility>,<pointcutType>)	<pointcutName> defined in <aspectName>
<joinpoint>:= call| execution| target| args| this	<joinpoint> can be call, execution, target, args, or this
<adviceType>:= before, after, around	<adviceType> is before , after or around
[triggerAdvice](<aspectName>, <adviceType>, <adviceId>,<ListOfParam>, <returnType>)	Advice <adviceType> belongs to <aspectName> aspect
[advicePointcutMap](<aspectName>, <adviceType>, <adviceId>, <pointcutName>)	Advice <adviceType> defined in <aspectName> aspect is related to the pointcut <pointcutName>
[precedence](<aspectName>, <listOfAspect>)	<precedence> rule is defined in aspect <aspectName>, and <listOfAspect> contains list of aspects according to their precedence

Rules to Identify Bad Smells. Rules to identify potential bad smells (identifying anomalies where refactoring may be required) are influenced by aspect-oriented refactoring strategies such as those discussed in [16] where the authors describe typical situations in aspect-oriented programs which can be problematic along with recommended refactoring strategies. In this work we are only interested in the identification of these conditions as they can provide indications to maintainers where refactoring could perhaps be valuable. One such aspect-oriented refactoring strategy is *Inline Class within Aspect*:

Problem: *A small standalone class is used only by code within an aspect.* This implies that we need to identify a class that is not subclassified, and it is not used as an attribute for other classes, and it does not receive messages from other classes, but it is referenced in an advice body of only one aspect (Figure 3).

Along the same lines and following the strategies in [16], we have defined rules for the following: *Replace Implements with Declare Parents, Introduce Aspect Protection, Replace Inter-type Method with Aspect Method, Extract Superaspect, Pull Up Advice, Pull Up Declare Parents, Pull Up Inter-type Declaration, Pull Up Pointcut* and *Push Down Pointcut*.

%% *Obtain all methods introduced by an aspect for a supertype of a given type*
findDeclaredMethod(AspectName,TypeName,SuperTypeName,MethodName):−
    is_aspect(AspectName), superType(SuperTypeName,TypeName),
    introducedMethod(AspectName,SuperTypeName,MethodName,_,_,_,_).

Fig. 2. Listing for rule `findDeclaredMethod`

%% *Find candidate classes to be moved to an aspect*
is_CandidateForInline(Type):−
    is_class(Type), (get_descendants(Type,L),size(L,0)),
    not(attribute(_,Type,_,_,_)), **not**(sendMessage(_,_,_,Type,_,_)),
    (**findall**(Aspect,(is_aspect(Aspect),used(Aspect,_,_,Type,_,_)),List),
    (size(List,1))).

Fig. 3. Listing for rule `is_CandidateForInline`

Rules to Deploy Measurements. We have defined measurement rules in order to extract information on the quality and the complexity of the program. The complexity of a system depends on a number of measurable attributes such as inheritance, coupling, cohesion, polymorphism, and application size. Some of these attributes like coupling and cohesion are also applicable in an aspect-oriented context. In [26] the authors define coupling as the degree of interdependency among aspects and/or classes. One such metric based on coupling is *Attribute-Class Dependency*: "There is an attribute-class dependence between aspect a and class c, if c is a type of an attribute of a. The number of attribute class dependences from aspect a to the class c can formally be represented as $AtC(a,c) = |\{x|x \in A^a(a) \wedge T(x) = c\}|$." This factor can be calculated through the rule in Figure 4.

attributeClassDependence(AspectName,ClassName):−
    is_aspect(AspectName),
    is_class(ClassName), attribute(AspectName,_,ClassName,_,_).
attributeClassDependenceCount(AspectName,ClassName,Count):−
    count(attributeClassDependence(AspectName,ClassName),Count).

Fig. 4. Listing for rule `attributeClassDependence`

Along the same lines, and following the metrics in [26], we have defined rules to support *Advice-Class Dependency*, *Intertype-Class Dependency*, and *Aspect-Inheritance Dependency* measures.

7 Defining Dependency Relationships between Program Elements

We have classified dependencies in aspect code into three groups: 1) Dependencies between aspects (AO specific dependencies), 2) Dependencies between base classes (OO specific dependencies), and 3) Dependencies between aspects and classes (OO-AO dependencies).

Types of AO Specific Dependencies

Inheritance Dependency. This defines the dependency between a superaspect and its subaspects. In AspectJ, an aspect cannot be extended unless it is defined to be abstract. An abstract aspect needs to have abstract pointcuts which will then be implemented by the concrete subaspects. Normally the advice blocks related to the abstract pointcuts are defined in the superaspect. Detecting the impact of superaspect deletion would not be particularly interesting because this is immediately caught by compiler. However, it is possible that one would delete the content of the superaspect. In the example in Figure 6, there is a direct dependency between **before** advice of the **Superaspect** and the abstract pointcut **p** defined in the **Superaspect** (and also to the concrete pointcut **p** defined in **Subaspect**) as the advice knows which pointcut it is related (bound) to. Therefore, deleting the abstract pointcut would lead to a compiler error. On the other hand, a pointcut does not know about the advice blocks which depend on it. This implies that deleting the advice blocks (related to the abstract pointcut) in the superaspect would result in the program loosing the expected functionality (which was supposed to be supported by **before**, **after**, or **around** of the join point match). Therefore the intended behavior of the program will be changed if this dependency is not realized before the deletion of advice blocks. This dependency can be detected through the rule in Figure 5:

%% Obtain AdviceId in SuperAspect corresponding to given PointcutName in SubAspect
advicePointcutInheritenceDep(SuperAspect,SubAspect,AdviceId,PointcutName):−
      is_aspect(SuperAspect), is_aspect(SubAspect),
      pointcut(SuperAspect,PointcutName,_,_,1),
      pointcut(SubAspect,PointcutName,_,_,0),
      triggerAdvice(SuperAspect,AdviceId,adviceType,_,_),
      advicePointcutMap(SuperAspect,AdviceType,AdviceId,PointcutName).

Fig. 5. Listing for rule `advicePointcutInheritenceDep`

Precedence Dependency. Multiple advice blocks may apply to the same pointcut, and the resolution order of the advice is based on rules on advice precedence [22] under two cases:

1. Precedence rules among advice blocks from different aspects.
2. Precedence rules among advice blocks within the same aspect.

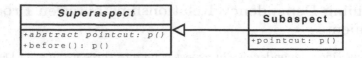

Fig. 6. Inheritance Dependency

The precedence rules create an indirect dependency between advice blocks related to the same pointcut as the execution of advice blocks depends to the precedence rules defined for the aspect(s) to which this advice blocks belong to. The example in Figure 7 corresponds to the first case.

The three advice blocks defined in aspects `AJ1` and `AJ2` are applied to the same join point `call(public void C.m(..)`. According to the precedence rules the `before` advice defined in aspect `AJ1` has precedence over the two advice blocks defined in aspect `AJ2`, and the `before` advice of `AJ2` has precedence over its `after` advice. Figure 7 shows the order of the execution of method `C.m(int)` and the advice blocks. Neither of the advice blocks are aware of the precedence defined in aspect `AJ2`. This implies that there would be no indication about this dependency if one wants to change the `before` advice to `after` or `around` advice. Another type of change can be adding a new advice block for the same join point in aspect `AJ1` or deleting either of the advice blocks.

```
public aspect AJ1 {
      pointcut AJ1_P1(): call(public void C.m(..));
      before(): AJ1_P1() { // Display "Before from AJ1"}}

public aspect AJ2 {
      declare precedence: AJ1, AJ2;
      pointcut AJ2_P1(): call(public void C.m(..));
      before(): AJ2_P1() { // Display "Before from AJ2"
      }
      after(): AJ2_P1() { // Display "After from AJ2"
      }}

public class C {
      public void m(int i){
            ... }}
```

Output:
Before from AJ1
Before from AJ2
...
After from AJ2

Fig. 7. Listing for Precedence Dependency

For certain applications, the correct order of advice and method execution is vital to preserve the semantics of the system. One such example is a concurrent system where a precondition to a service would dictate that authentication would have to be evaluated before synchronization which in turn would have to be evaluated before scheduling. Precedence rules guarantee the correct order, but any changes to the precedence or to the advice should be performed with attention to the dependency that the **declare precedence** creates. On the Eclipse IDE [1] it is possible to obtain the order of advice execution over a method, but it is tedious to detect this dependency. We can detect the precedence dependency through the following strategy:

Precedence dependency between advice blocks of the same aspect. For each pointcut defined in an aspect we need to identify a list of its related advice blocks. If the list contains more than one advice, then according to the precedence rules there would be an order of execution for these advice blocks which implies a dependency (Figure 8).

%% Obtain ListofAdvice bound to PointcutName in AspectName
advicePrecedenceDepPerAspect(AspectName,PointcutName,ListofAdvice)−:
        findall(AdviceId,advicePointcutMap(AspectName,_,AdviceId,PointcutName),
           ListofAdvice),
     size(ListofAdvice,N), N>0.

Fig. 8. Listing for rule `advicePrecedenceDepPerAspect`

We also have defined rules to identify precedence dependencies among advice blocks from different aspects. For the OO-AO dependencies, we have adopted the dependencies defined in the literature. Due to space limitation, only a list of such dependencies are provided: *Pointcut-Class Dependency, Pointcut-Method Dependency, Advice-Class Dependency, Intertype-Class Dependency,* and *Method-Class Dependency.*

8   Case Study

As a proof of concept, we deployed our method over a medium-scale service-oriented system which we developed. The system allows possibly multiple consumers and retailers to have access to a communications hub which controls and coordinates their interactions in order to implement reverse auctions. In this protocol one consumer may place a request to purchase a product. After a collection of sellers is iterated over to find the best price, a message is sent back to the client informing them about the winner and asking for confirmation to place an order. The core functionality is provided by the definitions of classes **Infomediator** and **ReverseAuction** (defining the hub and protocol respectively - not shown). For

```
public abstract aspect ObserverProtocol {
        protected interface Subject {
                public void addObserver(Observer o);
                public void removeObserver(Observer o);
                private List observers = new LinkedList();}
        private synchronized void Subject.notifyObserver(PotentialOrder po){...}
        public interface Observer {
                public void notifyOfchange(Subject s, PotentialOrder po);}
        protected abstract pointcut subjectChange(Subject s, PotentialOrder po);
        after(Subject s, PotentialOrder po): subjectChange(s, po){...}
        protected abstract pointcut findObservers(Infomediator info,
                                Subject s, String service, String rule);
        after(Infomediator info, Subject s, String service,String rule):
                        findObservers(info, s, service, rule){..}}


privileged public aspect CoordinateObserver extends ObserverProtocol {
        declare parents : Retailer implements Observer;
        declare parents : Customer implements Subject;
        private int Retailer.NumberSold = 0;
        public void Retailer.notifyOfchange(Subject s, PotentialOrder po)
                        {NumberSold++;...}
        protected pointcut subjectChange(Subject s, PotentialOrder po):
                execution(* Customer.buy(PotentialOrder))
                && target(s) && args(po);
        protected pointcut findObservers(Infomediator info, Subject customer,
                                String service, String rule):
                execution (* Infomediator.initiateReverseAuction(Customer,
                                                String,
                                                String))
                && target(info) && args(customer, service, rule);}
```

Fig. 9. Listing for aspects `ObserverProtocol` and `CoordinateObserver`

each reverse auction request, a potential order is created and associated with the consumer and the winner of the reverse auction. The system routes the auction result back to the consumer and informs the winner using the callback pattern, implemented in Java RMI. Supported semantics and other technical services (such as the subject-observer protocol, contract checking, authentication, synchronization, transaction logging, throughput and persistence) are provided by a number of aspect definitions. One notable example is the aspectual behavior of the aspect `ObserverProtocol`: This is implemented as an abstract aspect which defines the Observer design pattern, where retailers are viewed as observers and customers are viewed as subjects. The definition of `CoordinateObserver` extends `ObserverProtocol` and provides concrete pointcuts. A list of all retailers that participate in the auction and provide the services that a customer wants is created when a reverse auction is initiated. If the customer eventually purchases

aspect(coordinateObserver,public).
extends(coordinateObserver,observerProtocol).
privilegedAspect(coordinateObserver).
declareParent(coordinateObserver,retailer,observer).
declareParent(coordinateObserver,customer,subject).
introducedAtt(coordinateObserver,retailer,numberSold,int,private,0).
introducedMethod(coordinateObserver,retailer,notifyOfchange,public,
                    [subject,potentialOrder],0).
pointcut(coordinateObserver,subjectChange,[subject,potentialOrder],protected,0).
pointcutdesig(1,coordinateObserver,subjectChange,execution,
                [public,_,customer,buy,[potentialOrder]]).
pointcutdesig(2,coordinateObserver,subjectChange,target,[subject]).
pointcutdesig(3,coordinateObserver,subjectChange,args,[potentialOrder]).
pointcut(coordinateObserver,findObservers,
                [infomediator,subject,string, string],protected,0).
...

Fig. 10. Listing for aspect `coordinateObserver` transformed to Prolog facts

findDeclaredMethod(Aspect,customer,SuperType,Method).

Result:
Aspect = ObserverProtocol, SuperType = Subject, Method = addObserver;
Aspect = ObserverProtocol, SuperType = Subject, Method = removeObserver;
Aspect = ObserverProtocol, SuperType = Subject, Method = notifyObserver;

Fig. 11. Listing for the result of rule `findDeclaredMethod`

the service from the winner retailer of the auction, the corresponding retailer will be notified with the information about the number of items sold. A partial view of the transformation of aspect `coordinateObserver` to Prolog facts is provided in Figure 10. Here we want to calculate *Declared Method in Inheritance Hierarchy* for class `Customer`. Manually, this task would be tedious because one needs to check the body of all aspect definitions in the system in order to obtain this information. According to Section 6 we need to run the following query (the result of which is shown in Figure 11): `findDeclaredMethod(Aspect,customer, SuperType, Method)`.

Automation and tool support: We have developed a tool (called AJsurf) as an Eclipse plug-in that reads the source code and creates a database composed of a collection of Prolog facts. The transformation process from source code to facts is transparent to the end-users. The tool allows end-users to execute statements in form of queries. Moreover, the tool supports the execution of predefined, parameterized or direct queries (in the form of Prolog goals).

9   Related Work

There is currently tool support to ease the comprehension process of both procedural [24], and object-oriented programs. For the latter, tools can be categorized according to the type of transformation and the artifacts they provide:

- Reverse engineering of source code to the design model (such as Poseidon-UML [4], and Eclipse-Omondo [3]).
- Reverse engineering of source code to graphs (data dependency graph, control dependency graph, formal concept analysis lattice).
- Knowledge extraction (facts and rules) from the source code to produce structural relations of elements which serve as a knowledge base over which queries can be executed.

For aspect-oriented systems, tool support can be categorized in three groups [18]: 1) Text-based tools: They provide different views such as editors, outline, and package explorer. 2) Visualization-based tools: They create aspectual relationship views (e.g calls, advice, advised-by) between aspects and classes. 3) Query-based tools: They can be considered as a subset of text-based or visualization-based tools as they provide the result of a query either in text or in a visualization view.

In [8] the authors present a reverse engineering tool called Ciao. Ciao is a graphical navigator tool which allows users to formulate queries, generate a graph, interact with graph nodes, and to perform various graph analysis tasks in order to extract information from a software repository. The software repository is a collection of source code artifacts with all related documents, configuration management files, modification requests and manuals together with an associated database that describes the components and relationship among them. CQL is used as the query language associated with the repository. Ciao supports repositories which have AERO style architecture (Attributes, Entity, Relationship, and Operator), and it has been designed for C and C++ program database and program difference database. Each node in the navigation graph corresponds to a query that generates a specific view on the system. The edges of the navigation graph represent historic dependencies between query views. However, the nodes in the navigation graph only indicate the type of query executed and for each query executed the corresponding graph is shown. To reconstruct the structural relationships that connect different queries on a path, one must compare their corresponding views.

In [20] the authors, model static and dynamic information of an object-oriented system in term of Prolog facts. Declarative queries are defined to allow filtering of the collected data and defining new queries. By running these queries, maintainers can have a view of the system at a higher level of abstractions for a better understanding.

SOUL is a logic meta-language based on Prolog which is implemented in Visual Work Smalltalk [25]. It provides a declarative framework that allows reasoning about the structure of Smalltalk programs based on the parse tree representation. This makes facts and rules to be independent from a particular base language. Moreover, facts and rules are collected based on basic relationships in the object-oriented system. High level relationships like design patterns can be expressed and then implemented in code. The declarative framework of SOUL consists of two layers of rules: basic layer and advanced layer. The basic layer includes representational and structural rules. The representational rules define object-oriented elements (classes, methods, and statements) in the logical meta-language using Smalltalk terms. These rules are the only parts of SOUL which are language base dependent, and the rest are language independent. Using Smalltalk terms facilitates the translation of object-oriented classes to logical facts, and only the relationships between the classes are formulated in rules on the meta-language. The structural rules are defined over the representational rules and formulate some other relationship in Smalltalk systems. Using these rules one can run basic queries on the system.

Lost [19] is an Eclipse plug-in query tool developed for code navigation and browsing for AspectJ programs, deploying a variant of the Object Query Language (OQL), developed by the authors. For its query language, end-users need to write the queries in the query editor area and an instance error feedback feature of the tool allows users to correct the errors while writing queries. Users of Lost need to know the query language as there is no predefined queries available. This tool can be also used for navigation of Java programs. Like other Eclipse plug-ins, this tool deploys Eclipse IDE features like syntax highlighting, and auto-compilation.

In [23] the author implements a Java browser called JQuery as an Eclipse plug-in. The tool creates a database from the source code and provides an interface for the end-users to run queries. The query language used for this tool is a logic programming language called TyRuBa. Using this tool, users can run default (predefined) queries to extract information about their Java programs. Moreover, the tool allows users to write their own queries in order to obtain more information about the given Java code. One of the strengths of this tool is the ability to explore complex combinations of relationships through the declarative configuration interface. Users who only need the basic features do not need to know TyRuBa. However, users would have to know TyRuBa should they want to have more complex queries, as they would need to edit the existed queries or write new ones.

JTransformer [2] is a Prolog-based query and transformation engine for storing, analyzing and transforming fact-bases of Java source code. JTransformer creates an AST representation of a Java project, including the complete AST of method bodies as a Prolog database. Using JTransformer, developers can run powerful queries and transformations on the logic fact-base.

CodeQuest [11] is a source code querying tool which uses *safe Datalog* as its query language, mapping Datalog queries to a relational database system.

In [9] the authors present a prototype tool for analysis and performance optimization of Java programs called DeepWeaver-1. This tool is an extension of the abc AspectJ compiler [5] which has a declarative style query language,

(Prolog/Datalog-like query language) to analyze and transform code within and across methods.

In [6] the authors, describe the representation of aspects in terms of a logic programming language, albeit for a different purpose.

Eclipse IDE [1] provides different editors and views. Views are visual components allowing navigation through a hierarchy of information. Editors are components that allow editing or browsing a file. Views and editors provide different types of representation of the resources for the developers. AspectJ Development Tools (AJDT) provides support for aspect-oriented software development using AspectJ within the Eclipse IDE.

10   Evaluation

From the query language perspective, there have been two common approaches: The first (implemented by Lost) adopts predefined predicates and combines them using relational calculus. In this approach the predicates are stored in named sets and the relational calculus query is translated to common relational algebra operations. The advantage of this approach is the speed and efficiency of the algorithm and the ease of transporting to a persistent storage mechanism. The disadvantage is the limitation of its expressive power. The second approach (implemented by JQuery) adopts a resolution inference mechanism to find the values of variables as they are resolved during unification, while having more expressiveness and power. By defining a query with some additional rules, the end-user can gain the power of a full programming language. There are also disadvantages to this approach including 1) the possibility of running into infinite loops in case of badly written queries and 2) taking a lot of time and memory because of the nature of the reasoning algorithm. For the purpose of our investigation there are a number of tasks, which require logical inference. Furthermore, there are a number of recursive rules like the ones about inheritance hierarchies and call graph traversal. The recursive queries on tree structures are not part of standard have relational query languages like SQL and OQL, even though there exist some vendor specific extensions to support these queries. We utilized the logic based querying approach. However, for highly complex queries, one would have to be familiar with the query language (Prolog). In addition, there are strategies (for example, finding all the methods defined for a type through inter type declaration) or measurements, that can be tedious to compute manually or with other approaches, and our approach supports an environment to do that automatically.

11   Conclusion and Recommendations

In this paper we discussed an approach to support declarative (static) analysis of aspect-oriented programs, adopting AspectJ as a representative technology aiming at improving comprehension. Our approach is based on the transformation of source code into a set of facts and data, provided as a Prolog database over which queries can be executed. Declarative analysis allows us to extract complex information through its rich and expressive syntax. The type of knowledge provided through these queries is categorized in three main groups, such as those which address bad smells (identifying problematic situations where refactoring may be needed), those which address measurements (providing the degree of complexity of the system through metrics) and general (providing static information about the system). We have automated our approach and integrated all activities in a tool provided as an Eclipse plug-in. End-users can execute predefined, parameterized or direct queries in the form of Prolog goals. In the future we plan to extend our approach to support change impact analysis.

References

1. Eclipse website (last accessed: November 15, 2007), http://www.eclipse.org/
2. JTransformer Framework website (last accessed: November 15, 2007), http://roots.iai.uni-bonn.de/research/jtransformer/
3. Omondo website (last accessed: November 15, 2007), http://www.eclipsedownload.com/
4. Poseidon UML website (last accessed: November 15, 2007), http://jspwiki.org/wiki/PoseidonUML
5. Avgustinov, P., Christensen, A.S., Hendren, L., Kuzins, S., Lhoták, J., Lhoták, O., de Moor, O., Sereni, D., Sittampalam, G., Tibble, J.: abc: An extensible AspectJ compiler. In: Proceedings of the 4th International Conference on Aspect-Oriented Software Development (AOSD) (2005)
6. Avgustinov, P., Hajiyev, E., Ongkingco, N., de Moor, O., Sereni, D., Tibble, J., Verbaere, M.: Semantics of static pointcuts in AspectJ. In: Proceedings of the 34th Annual ACM SIGPLAN-SIGACT Symposium on Principles of Programming Languages (POPL) (2007)
7. Bennett, K.H., Rajlich, V.T.: Software maintenance and evolution: a roadmap. In: Proceedings of the International Conference on Software Engineering (ICSE) track on The Future of Software Engineering (2000)
8. Chen, Y.-F.R., Fowler, G.S., Koutsofios, E., Wallach, R.S.: Ciao: a graphical navigator for software and document repositories. In: Proceedings of the 11th International Conference on Software Maintenance (ICSM) (1995)
9. Falconer, H., Kelly, P.H.J., Ingram, D.M., Mellor, M.R., Field, T., Beckmann, O.: A declarative framework for analysis and optimization. In: Krishnamurthi, S., Odersky, M. (eds.) CC 2007. LNCS, vol. 4420, Springer, Heidelberg (2007)
10. Filman, R.E., Friedman, D.P.: Aspect-oriented programming is quantification and obliviousness. In: Proceedings of the OOPSLA Workshop on Advanced Separation of Concerns in Object-Oriented Systems (2000)
11. Hajiyev, E., Verbaere, M., de Moor, O.: CodeQuest: Scalable source code queries with Datalog. In: Thomas, D. (ed.) ECOOP 2006. LNCS, vol. 4067, Springer, Heidelberg (2006)
12. Kiczales, G., Hilsdale, E., Hugunin, J., Kersten, M., Palm, J., Griswold, W.G.: An overview of AspectJ. In: Knudsen, J.L. (ed.) ECOOP 2001. LNCS, vol. 2072, Springer, Heidelberg (2001)
13. Kiczales, G., Lamping, J., Menhdhekar, A., Maeda, C., Lopes, C., Loingtier, J.-M., Irwin, J.: Aspect-oriented programming. In: Aksit, M., Matsuoka, S. (eds.) ECOOP 1997. LNCS, vol. 1241, Springer, Heidelberg (1997)

14. Kienzle, J., Yu, Y., Xiong, J.: On composition and reuse of aspects. In: Proceedings of the AOSD Workshop on Foundations of Aspect-Oriented Languages (FOAL) (2003)
15. Kniesel, G., Hannemann, J., Rho, T.: A comparison of logic-based infrastructures for concern detection and extraction. In: Proceedings of the 3rd AOSD Workshop on Linking Aspect Technology and Evolution (LATE) (2007)
16. Monteiro, M.P., Fernandes, J.M.: Towards a catalog of aspect-oriented refactorings. In: Proceedings of the 4th International Conference on Aspect-Oriented Software Development (AOSD) (2005)
17. Parnas, D.L.: On the criteria to be used in decomposing systems into modules. Communications of the ACM 15(12), 1053–1058 (1972)
18. Pfeiffer, J.-H., Gurd, J.R.: Visualisation-based tool support for the development of aspect-oriented programs. In: Proceedings of the 5th International Conference on Aspect-Oriented Software Development (AOSD) (2006)
19. Pfeiffer, J.-H., Sardos, A., Gurd, J.R.: Complex code querying and navigation for AspectJ. In: Proceedings of the OOPSLA Workshop on Eclipse Technology eXchange (ETX) (2005)
20. Richner, T., Ducasse, S., Wuyts, R.: Understanding object-oriented programs with declarative event analysis. In: Proceedings of the ECOOP Workshop on Experiences in Object-Oriented Re-Engineering (1998)
21. Störzer, M., Koppen, C.: CDiff: Attacking the fragile pointcut problem. In: Proceedings of the Interactive Workshop on Aspects in Software (EIWAS) (2004)
22. The AspectJ Team: The AspectJ programming guide (last accessed: November 15, 2007), http://www.eclipse.org/aspectj/doc/released/progguide/index.html
23. De Volder, K.: JQuery: A generic code browser with a declarative configuration language. In: Van Hentenryck, P. (ed.) PADL 2006. LNCS, vol. 3819, Springer, Heidelberg (2005)
24. Scitools website (last accessed: November 15, 2007), http://www.scitools.com/products/understand/cpp/product.php
25. Wuyts, R.: Declarative reasoning about the structure of object-oriented systems. In: Proceedings of the 26th International Conference on Technologies of Object-Oriented Languages and Systems (TOOLS USA) (1998)
26. Zhao, J.: Measuring coupling in aspect-oriented systems. In: Proceedings of the 10th International Software Metrics Symposium (Metrics) session on Late Breaking Papers (2004)

Efficient Reasoning for Nogoods in Constraint Solvers with BDDs

Sathiamoorthy Subbarayan

Computational Logic and Algorithms Group
IT University of Copenhagen, Denmark
sathi@itu.dk

Abstract. When BDDs are used for propagation in a constraint solver with nogood recording, it is necessary to find a small subset of a given set of variable assignments that is enough for a BDD to imply a new variable assignment. We show that the task of finding such a minimum subset is NP-complete by reduction from the hitting set problem. We present a new algorithm for finding such a minimal subset, which runs in time linear in the size of the BDD representation. In our experiments, the new method is up to ten times faster than the previous method, thereby reducing the solution time by even more than 80%. Due to linear time complexity the new method is able to scale well.

1 Introduction

Many useful functions have compact *Binary decision diagram* (BDD) [1] representations. Hence, the BDDs has attracted attention as a constraint representation [2,3,4,5,6,7,8]. The BDDs have been used in many applications, including: verification, configuration and fault-tree analysis.

The *nogood recording* [9,10] is a technique in constraint solvers to find a subset of the variable assignments made upto a dead-end in a search tree, such that the found subset could independently lead to dead-ends. By recording such subsets called *nogoods* and by preventing similar assignment patterns, the search effort can be drastically reduced.

For a given set of variable assignments X, if the propagation of X in a constraint c implies a variable assignment $(v := a)$, denoted $X \wedge c \Rightarrow (v := a)$, then a *reason* R is a subset of X, such that $R \wedge c \Rightarrow (v := a)$. Finding small reasons is essential for nogood recording. The nogood recording plays a major part in the successful SAT solvers. The adoption of the nogood recording in general constraint solvers requires efficient methods for finding small reasons in every important constraint representation, including BDDs.

This paper focuses on finding small reasons in BDDs. We show that the task of finding a minimum-sized reason in BDDs is NP-complete by reduction from the hitting set problem. We also present a new algorithm for finding minimal-sized reasons, which runs in time linear in the size of the BDD representation. We then empirically demonstrate the usefulness of the new algorithm over a previous method. In our experiments, the new method scales better, and is upto 10 times faster than the previous one.

P. Hudak and D.S. Warren (Eds.): PADL 2008, LNCS 4902, pp. 53–67, 2008.

2   Definitions

2.1   The Constraint Satisfaction Problem

A *constraint satisfaction problem* (CSP) instance is a triple (V, D, C), where V is a set of variables, D is a set of finite domains, one domain $d_i \in D$ for each variable $v_i \in V$, and C is a set of constraints. Each constraint $c_i \in C$ is a pair of the form (s_i, r_i), where $s_i \subseteq V$ and r_i is a *relation* over the variables in s_i.

An *assignment* X is a set like $\{v_{x_1} := a_{x_1}, v_{x_2} := a_{x_2}, \ldots, v_{x_{|X|}} := a_{x_{|X|}}\}$. The variable assignment $(v_{x_i} := a_{x_i})$ fixes the value of v_{x_i} to a_{x_i}, where $a_{x_i} \in d_{x_i}$. An assignment X is *full* if $|X| = |V|$, *partial* otherwise. A *solution* to a CSP is a full assignment S, such that for any constraint $(s_i, r_i) \in C$, the assignment S restricted to s_i belongs to the relation r_i, i.e., $S_{|s_i} \in r_i$. For a given assignment X, a constraint c_i *implies* a variable assignment $(v := a)$, denoted $X \wedge c_i \Rightarrow (v := a)$, if every tuple in the relation r_i containing $X_{|s_i}$ also contains $(v := a)$.

2.2   The Binary Decision Diagrams

A *reduced ordered binary decision diagram* (BDD) [1] is a *directed acyclic graph* with two terminal nodes, one marked with 1 (true) and the other with 0 (false). The Figure 2 (a) and Figure 3 (a) show two example BDDs.

Each non-terminal node n is associated with a Boolean variable $var(n)$. Each node n has two outgoing edges, one *dashed* and another *solid*. The occurrence of variables in any path has to obey a *linear order*. Also, isomorphic subgraphs will be merged together, and a node n with both its outgoing edges reaching the same node n_c will be removed with all the incoming edges of n made to reach n_c directly. A BDD will be represented by its root node. The size of a BDD b, $|b|$, is the number of non-terminal nodes. For a given BDD, the term $solid(n_1)$ evaluates to n_2 iff (n_1, n_2) is a solid edge in the BDD. Similarly, $dashed(n_1)$ evaluates to n_2 iff (n_1, n_2) is a dashed edge.

The variable assignment *corresponding to an edge* (n_1, n_2) is $(var(n_1) := a)$, where $a = true$ iff $n_2 = solid(n_1)$. Consider a path $p =< n_1, n_2, \ldots, n_l >$ in a BDD with $n_l = 1$, from a node n_1 to the 1-terminal. The assignment X_p *corresponding to the path* p is $X_p = \{(var(n_i) := a) \mid 1 \leq i \leq (l-1), (n_{i+1} = solid(n_i)) \Leftrightarrow (a = true)\}$. The X_p is the set of the variable assignments corresponding to each edge in the path. The path p is a *solution path* if $n_1 = b$ and $n_l = 1$, i.,e, starts from the root node.

A BDD b represents a Boolean function f iff for any solution S to f, there exists a solution path p in b, such that $X_p \subseteq S$. We may denote the function represented by a BDD b by b itself. If S is a solution of f, we may specify $S \in f$. The set of solutions S_p corresponding to a solution path p is $S_p = \{S \mid X_p \subseteq S, S \in b\}$. We denote $(v := a) \in p$ to specify that there exists a $S \in S_p$ such that $(v := a) \in S$. Similarly, we denote $X \in p$ if there exists a $S \in S_p$ such that $X \subseteq S$. Note, $(v := a) \in p$ mentions that either there occurs an edge (n_i, n_{i+1}) in p whose corresponding assignment is $(v := a)$, or there is no node n_i in the path p such that $var(n_i) = v$.

Although a BDD representing a Boolean function could be exponential in the number of variables in the function, for several practically useful functions the equivalent BDDs are of small size. Hence, the BDDs have found widespread usage in several applications.

2.3 Representing Constraints Using BDDs

To simplify the presentation, we assume that all the variables in a given CSP have Boolean domain. Given a general CSP, we can encode it using Boolean variables. For example, using the *log-encoding* method, a non-Boolean variable $v \in V$ with domain d can be substituted by $\lceil log\,|d| \rceil$ Boolean variables, matching each value in d to a unique assignment of the introduced $\lceil log\,|d| \rceil$ Boolean variables.

Each constraint $c_i \in C$ is hence a Boolean function defined over s_i, with the function mapping an assignment for s_i to true iff the assignment belongs to r_i.

For $X = \{v_{x_1} := a_{x_1}, v_{x_2} := a_{x_2}, \ldots, v_{x_{|X|}} := a_{x_{|X|}}\}$, the Boolean function obtained by the conjunction of the variable assignments in X is also denoted by X, i.e., $X = \bigwedge_{1 \le i \le |X|}(v_{x_i} = a_{x_i})$, which will be clear from the context.

Given a CSP with several constraints, some of the constraints' function might be represented by compact BDDs. The BDDs of some of the constraints might result in obtaining helpful inferences to speed-up the constraint solver. Hence, the BDDs has attracted attention as a constraint representation [2,3,4,5,6,7,8].

2.4 The Nogoods

A *nogood* [9,10] of a CSP is a partial assignment N, such that for any solution S of the CSP, $N \not\subseteq S$. Hence, a nogood N cannot be part of any solution to the CSP. In a typical constraint solver, an initial empty assignment $X = \{\}$ will be extended by both the *branching decisions* and the variable assignments *implied* by the decisions, and the partial assignment X will be reduced by the *backtracking steps*. The extensions and reductions will go on until either X becomes a solution or all possible assignments are exhausted.

A backtracking step occurs when the assignment X cannot be extended to a solution. The *nogood recording*, if implemented in a constraint solver, will be invoked just before each backtracking step. The nogood recording involves finding and storing a subset N of the partial assignment X, such that N is a nogood. Such nogoods can be used to prevent some bad branching choices in the future and hence speed-up the solution process. This paper focuses on a building block of nogood recording and can be understood independently. We refer the interested reader to [9,10,11,12,7] for details on the whole nogood recording process.

2.5 The Reasons for Variable Assignment

A building block of nogood recording is to find a small subset R of an assignment X that is a *reason* for the implication of a variable. If $X \wedge c \Rightarrow (v := a)$, then the reason R is a subset of X, $R \subseteq X$, such that $R \wedge c \Rightarrow (v := a)$. Heuristically, smaller sized reasons are preferred, since that would lead to smaller nogoods resulting in better pruning. We show that when a BDD represents a constraint, the task of finding a *minimum* sized reason is NP-complete. We also show that a *minimal* sized reason can be found in time linear in the size of the BDD.

Given a BDD b, an assignment X and $(v := a)$ such that $X \wedge b \Rightarrow (v := a)$, let $R_{all} = \{ R \mid R \subseteq X, R \wedge b \Rightarrow (v := a) \}$. The set R_{all} contains all the reasons.

Now, we formally define the problems for finding minimum and minimal reasons in BDDs. We specify the decision version for the minimum problem.

MINIMUM BDD-REASON :

Input: A BDD b, an assignment X, and $(v := a)$, such that $X \wedge b \Rightarrow (v := a)$ and a positive integer K.
Output: Yes, if there is a R, such that $R \in R_{all}$, and $|R| \leq K$. No, otherwise.

MINIMAL BDD-REASON :

Input: A BDD b, an assignment X, and $(v := a)$, such that $X \wedge b \Rightarrow (v := a)$.
Output: R, such that $R \in R_{all}$, and $\forall R' \in R_{all}$. if $R' \subseteq R$ then $R = R'$.

3   The MINIMUM BDD-REASON Is Intractable

We prove that MINIMUM BDD-REASON is NP-complete by using reduction from the HITTING SET problem.

HITTING SET [13]:

Input: A collection Q of subsets of a finite set P, and a positive integer $K \leq |P|$.
Output: Yes, if there is a set P' with $|P'| \leq K$ such that P' contains at least one element from each subset in Q. No, otherwise.

Lemma 1. *A relation r with q tuples, defined over k Boolean variables, can be represented by a BDD of size at most qk nodes.*

Proof. If the BDD b represents the relation r, then there will be exactly q solutions in b, one for each tuple in r. Since representing each solution by b requires at most k nodes, there will be at most qk non-terminal nodes in b.   □

Lemma 2. *Given a BDD m of a function over the variables in $\{b_1, b_2, \ldots, b_k\}$, using the order $b_1 < b_2 < \ldots < b_k$, if $m \Rightarrow (b_k := \text{false})$ then the size of the BDD m' representing $m \vee (b_k = \text{true})$ is $|m|$.*

Proof. Since the variable b_k is at the end of the variable order, given m we can obtain m' by just the following two steps.

1. Add a new node n' with $var(n') = b_k$. The *dashed* edge of n' will reach the 0-terminal and the *solid* edge will reach the 1-terminal. The n' represents the function $(b_k = true)$. Now, for each *dashed* (resp. *solid*) edge of the form $(n, 0)$ for any node n, where $n \neq n'$, replace the *dashed* (resp. *solid*) edge $(n, 0)$ with a new *dashed* (resp. *solid*) edge (n, n').

2. There will be only one n'' such that $var(n'') = b_k$ and $n'' \neq n'$, representing the function $(b_k = false)$, otherwise $m \Rightarrow (b_k := false)$ is not possible. Remove n'' and make the incoming edges of n'' to reach the 1-terminal.

Exactly one node n' is added and one node n'' is removed. Hence, $|m'| = |m|$. □

Theorem 1. *The MINIMUM BDD-REASON is NP-complete.*

Proof. The problem is in NP, as we can quickly check the correctness of any R. Now, we reduce the HITTING SET problem into MINIMUM BDD-REASON.

Let the set $P = \{p_1, p_2, \ldots, p_{|P|}\}$, $Q = \{q_1, q_2, \ldots, q_{|Q|}\}$ with $q_i \subseteq P$ and an integer K define an instance of the HITTING SET problem.

Let r be a relation defined over the $|P| + 1$ Boolean variables in the set $\{b_1, b_2, \ldots, b_{|P|+1}\}$. The Figure 1 shows the structure of the relation r. There will be $|Q|$ rows in r. The row i of r will correspond to the $q_i \in Q$. Let the Boolean term a_{ij} be *false* iff $p_j \in q_i$.

b_1	b_2	.	.	.	$b_{|P|}$	$b_{|P|+1}$
a_{11}	a_{12}	.	.	.	$a_{1|P|}$	*false*
a_{21}	a_{22}	.	.	.	$a_{2|P|}$	*false*
.	.				.	.
.	.				.	.
.	.				.	.
$a_{|Q|1}$	$a_{|Q|2}$	.		.	$a_{|Q||P|}$	*false*

Fig. 1. The relation r

The row i of the relation r will contain the tuple $(a_{i1}, a_{i2}, \ldots, a_{i|P|}, false)$. Let the BDD b_r represents the function of r, using the order $b_1 < b_2 < \ldots < b_{|P|+1}$.

Let the BDD b' represents the function $(b_{|P|+1} = true)$. The b' is trivial with just one non-terminal node. Let the BDD b represents $b_r \vee b'$, i.e., $b = b_r \vee b'$. Let $X = \{b_1 := true, b_2 := true, \ldots, b_{|P|} := true\}$.

By the definition of r, in each solution S of b_r the $b_{|P|+1}$ takes *false* value. Also, if S is a solution of b', then $b_{|P|+1}$ takes *true* value in S. Due to the different values for $b_{|P|+1}$, the solutions of b_r and b' are disjoint. So for any $S \in b$, either $S \in b_r$ or $S \in b'$, but not both.

For any $q_i \in Q$, $|q_i| \geq 1$, therefore, for each row i of r there exists a $p_j \in q_i$ such that $a_{ij} = false$. So, for any $S \in b$, $S \in b_r$ implies that there exists an i, $1 \leq i \leq |P|$, such that $a_{ij} = false$, and hence b_i takes *false* value in S. As, for $1 \leq i \leq |P|$, b_i takes *true* in X, $X \wedge b_r$ is *false*. So, $X \wedge b = X \wedge b'$ and since $b' = (b_{|P|+1} = true)$, $X \wedge b \Rightarrow (b_{|P|+1} := true)$.

So, the assignment X, the BDD b, the variable assignment $(b_{|P|+1} := true)$ and the integer K define an instance of the MINIMUM BDD-REASON problem.

So given a HITTING SET instance (P, Q, K), we can obtain a corresponding instance of MINIMUM BDD-REASON defined by $(X, b, (b_{|P|+1} := true), K)$.

We now have to show that given (P, Q, K), we can obtain $(X, b, (b_{|P|+1} := true), K)$ in polytime and also that the output to $(X, b, (b_{|P|+1} := true), K)$ is *Yes* iff the output for (P, Q, K) is *Yes*.

To show that we can obtain $(X, b, (b_{|P|+1} := true), K)$ in polytime, we just have to show that we can obtain b in polytime. By Lemma 1, $|b_r|$ is bounded by $|Q|(|P| + 1)$. Also, by Lemma 2, $|b|$ which is equivalent to $b_r \vee (b_{|P|+1} = true)$ is at most $|b_r|$. Hence, we can obtain $(X, b, (b_{|P|+1} := true), K)$ in polytime.

Now, we just have to show that the instance (P, Q, K) has the *Yes* output iff the instance $(X, b, (b_{|P|+1} := true), K)$ has the *Yes* output.

($\Rightarrow$): Let $P' = \{p_{t_1}, p_{t_2}, \ldots, p_{t_{|P'|}}\}$, where $1 \leq t_i \leq |P|$, be an answer for the *Yes* output of (P, Q, K). Then consider R to be $\{b_{t_1} := true, b_{t_2} := true, \ldots, b_{t_{|P'|}} := true\}$. We show that $R \wedge b \Rightarrow (b_{|P|+1} := true)$, which proves the ($\Rightarrow$) case.

Since P' is a *Yes* answer, by definition, for each row i of r, there will be a j, such that $p_j \in P'$ and $(a_{ij} = false)$. So for each row i, there will be a j, such that $(a_{ij} = false)$ and b_j takes *true* value in R. Hence, the solution $S \in b_r$ corresponding to any row i cannot be a solution of $R \wedge b_r$. So, $R \wedge b_r = false$, which implies $R \wedge b = R \wedge (b_r \vee b') = ((R \wedge b_r) \vee (R \wedge b')) = ((false) \vee (R \wedge b')) = R \wedge b'$. Since, $(R \wedge b') \Rightarrow (b_{|P|+1} := true)$, $R \wedge b \Rightarrow (b_{|P|+1} := true)$. Hence the ($\Rightarrow$) case.

($\Leftarrow$): Let $R = \{b_{r_1} := true, b_{r_2} := true, \ldots, b_{r_{|R|}} := true\}$ be a solution for the *Yes* answer of $(X, b, (b_{|P|+1} := true), K)$. Let $P' = \{p_{r_1}, p_{r_2}, \ldots, p_{r_{|R|}}\}$. We have to show that P' has at least one element $p_j \in q_i$ for each $q_i \in Q$.

Since $R \wedge b \Rightarrow (b_{|P|+1} := true)$, $b' \Rightarrow (b_{|P|+1} := true)$ and $b_r \Rightarrow (b_{|P|+1} := false)$, $R \wedge b_r = false$. So, there is no solution S such that $S \in (R \wedge b_r)$.

For each row i of the relation r there exists a j such that $(a_{ij} = false)$ and $(b_j := true) \in R$. Otherwise, i.e., if there does not exist such a j for a row i then, the solution S corresponding to the row i belongs to $(R \wedge b_r)$, which is a contradiction to $R \wedge b_r = false$.

So, for each row i, there exists a j such that $(a_{ij} = false)$ and $(b_j := true) \in R$, hence, $p_j \in q_i$ and $p_j \in P'$, which proves the ($\Leftarrow$) case.   □

4   A Linear-Time Algorithm for MINIMAL BDD-REASON

A dashed edge (n_1, n_2) in a BDD b is a *conflicting edge* with respect to an assignment X if $(var(n_1) := true) \in X$. Similarly, a solid edge (n_1, n_2) in b is a *conflicting edge* with respect to X if $(var(n_1) := false) \in X$.

Suppose $X \wedge b \Rightarrow (v := a)$, then the removal of all the conflicting edges w.r.t X in b will result in removing each solution path p with $(v := \neg a) \in p$. Otherwise, there will be a p such that $X \in p$ and $(v := \neg a) \in p$, which is a contradiction to $X \wedge b \Rightarrow (v := a)$.

Example 1. Consider the BDD b in the Figure 2 (a) and the assignment $X = \{v := true, x := true, z := false\}$, then $X \wedge b \Rightarrow (y := true)$. Hence, the removal of the conflicting edges, as shown in the Figure 2 (b), removes every solution path p with $(y := false) \in p$.

Example 2. Consider the BDD b in the Figure 3 (a) and the assignment $X = \{v := false, w := true, y := false\}$, then $X \wedge b \Rightarrow (x := false)$. Hence, the removal of the conflicting edges, as shown in the Figure 3 (b), removes every solution path p with $(x := true) \in p$.

Suppose $X \wedge b \Rightarrow (v := a)$, a conflicting edge (n_1, n_2) is a *frontier edge* if there exists a solution path p using (n_1, n_2), such that $(v := \neg a) \in p$, and the subpath of p from n_2 to the 1-terminal does not use any conflicting edge.

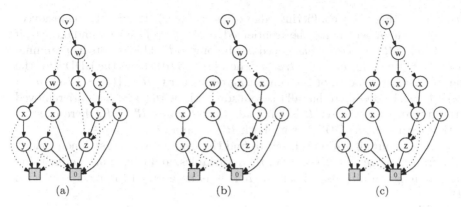

Fig. 2. *Example 1, $X \wedge b \Rightarrow (y := true)$.* (a) The BDD b, (b) The BDD b without the conflicting edges w.r.t X, (c) The BDD b without the frontier edges.

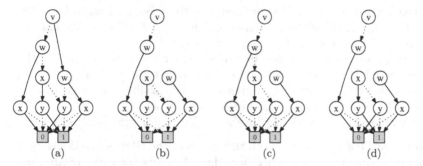

Fig. 3. *Example 2, $X \wedge b \Rightarrow (x := false)$.* (a) The BDD b, (b) The BDD b without the conflicting edges w.r.t X, (c) The BDD b without the frontier edges, (d) The BDD b without the conflicting edges w.r.t $R = \{(v := false), (w := true)\}$.

In any solution path p with $(v := \neg a) \in p$, the frontier edge is the conflicting edge nearest to the 1-terminal. Hence, removal of all the frontier edges will result in removing every solution path with $(v := \neg a)$. Otherwise, there will exist a solution path p without using any frontier edge, such that $(v := \neg a) \in p$, which is a contradiction to $X \wedge b \Rightarrow (v := a)$. The Figure 2 (c) and Figure 3 (c) show the BDDs of the two examples without just the frontier edges. In both the cases, the removal of the frontier edges removes every solution path p with the corresponding variable assignment.

The idea of our minimal reason algorithm is to first find the frontier edges. Then, to find a subset of the frontier edges such that the inclusion of the variable assignments conflicting the subset in R will ensure that $R \wedge b \Rightarrow (v := a)$ and R is minimal.

In the Example 1, as in the Figure 2 (c), all the frontier edges conflict with just $(x := true)$. Hence, the set $R = \{(x := true)\}$ is such that $R \wedge b \Rightarrow (y := true)$.

In the Example 2, as in the Figure 3 (c), each assignment in X has a frontier edge. There is only one solution path with a frontier edge of $(y := false)$. Also, in that path there is a conflicting edge of ($w := true$). Hence, the inclusion of ($w := true$) in R will make the frontier edge of ($y := false$) redundant. So, if ($w := true$) $\in R$ then ($y := false$) need not belong to R. This results in a minimal reason $R = \{(v =: false), (w := true)\}$. The Figure 3 (d) shows the BDD b for the Example 2 after removal of the conflicting edges w.r.t. $R = \{(v := false),(w := true)\}$. It can be observed that all the solution paths with ($x := true$) are removed in the figure. Also, the set R is minimal, since for any $R' \subsetneq R$, there exists a solution path p in the BDD b, with both $R' \in p$ and ($x := true$) $\in p$.

The idea of our algorithm is hence to find the frontier edges first. Then to look at the frontier edges, in the order of their variables, and decide on the inclusion of a matching variable assignment in R if it is necessary to remove a solution path.

The Figure 4 presents the *MinimalReason* procedure. The *MinimalReason* uses the *FindFrontier* procedure in Figure 5 to mark the nodes with an outgoing frontier edge. The assumptions made in presenting the procedures are:

1. The BDD b represents a function defined over the k Boolean variables in the set $\{b_1, b_2, \ldots, b_k\}$, using the variable order $b_1 < b_2 < \ldots < b_k$. We assume $X \wedge b \Rightarrow (v := a)$ where $v = b_i$ for an i, $1 \leq i \leq k$.
2. The *visited*, *reach1*, and *frontier* are three Boolean arrays, indexed by the nodes in the BDD b. The entries in the three arrays are initially *false*.
3. The *reachedSet* is an array of sets indexed by the variables in the BDD. The entries in the *reachedSet* array are initially empty sets.
4. The set V_X denotes the variables in X, i.e., $V_X := \{b_i \mid (b_i := a') \in X\}$.

The procedure *FindFrontier* visits all the nodes in the BDD b in a depth first manner and if an edge (n_1, n_2) is a frontier edge, then sets the entry *frontier*$[n_1]$ to *true*. The procedure uses the *visited* array to make sure it visits a node only once. At the end of the procedure, the entry *reach1*$[n]$ is *true* iff there exists a path from n to the 1-terminal without using a conflicting edge or an edge corresponding to ($v := a$).

The lines 1-2 of the *MinimalReason* procedure appropriately initializes the *reach1* and *visited* entries for the two terminal nodes and makes a call to *Find-Frontier*. The lines 1-3 of the *FindFrontier* procedure ensure that a node is visited only once and the child nodes are processed first. In the case ($var(n) = v$) at line-4, based on the value of 'a' the procedure appropriately sets *reach1*$[n]$, ignoring the edge corresponding to ($v := a$). Since we are just interested in removing solution paths with ($v := \neg a$), we can ignore the edge corresponding to ($v := a$). In the case ($var(n) \notin V_X$) at line-9, the procedure sets the *reach1*$[n]$ to *true* if any of the child nodes of n has *true* entry in *reach1*. The lines 12-13 correspond to the case where $var(n) \in V_X$, in which an outgoing edge of the node n could be a frontier edge. Based on the value $var(n)$ takes in X and the *reach1* entries of the child nodes, the procedure decides whether *frontier*$[n]$ is *true* or not. Note, the value *frontier*$[n]$ becomes *true* if an outgoing edge of the node n is a frontier edge.

At the end of the first recursive call made to *FindFrontier* at the line-2 of *MinimalReason*, all the nodes with an outgoing frontier edge are identified by the entries in the *frontier* array. At the line-3 of the *MinimalReason* procedure,

MinimalReason $(X, b, (v := a))$

1 : $reach1[0] := false$; $reach1[1] := true$; $visited[0] := true$; $visited[1] := true$
2 : *FindFrontier*(b)
3 : $reachedSet[var(b)] := \{b\}$; $R = \{ \ \}$; $T := \{0, 1\}$ // T - *terminal nodes*
4 : **for** $i := 1$ **to** k // *i.e., for each variable* b_i
5 : $foundFrontier := false$
6 :   **for each** $n \in reachedSet[b_i]$
7 :   **if** $(frontier[n])$ $foundFrontier := true$
8 :   **if** $(foundFrontier)$
9 :   **if** $((b_i := true) \in X)$
10:                $R.Add((b_i := true))$
11:                **for each** $n \in reachedSet[b_i]$
12:                     **if** $(solid(n) \notin T)$ $reachedSet[var(solid(n))].Add(solid(n))$
13:           **else** // *i.e.,* $((b_i := false) \in X)$
14:                $R.Add((b_i := false))$
15:                **for each** $n \in reachedSet[b_i]$
16:                     **if** $(dashed(n) \notin T)$ $reachedSet[var(dashed(n))].Add(dashed(n))$
17:      **else** // *i.e.,* $(foundFrontier = false)$
18:           **for each** $n \in reachedSet[b_i]$
19:                **if** $(solid(n) \notin T)$ $reachedSet[var(solid(n))].Add(solid(n))$
20:                **if** $(dashed(n) \notin T)$ $reachedSet[var(dashed(n))].Add(dashed(n))$
21: **return** R

Fig. 4. The MinimalReason Procedure

FindFrontier (n)

1 : $visited[n] := true$
2 : **if** $(\neg visited[solid(n)])$ *FindFrontier*$(solid(n))$
3 : **if** $(\neg visited[dashed(n)])$ *FindFrontier*$(dashed(n))$
4 : **if** $(var(n) = v)$
5 :   **if** (a)
6 :   **if** $(reach1[dashed(n)])$ $reach1[n] := true$
7 :   **else** // *i.e.,* $(a = false)$
8 :   **if** $(reach1[solid(n)])$ $reach1[n] := true$
9 : **else if** $(var(n) \notin V_X)$
10:      **if** $(reach1[dashed(n)] \vee reach1[solid(n)])$ $reach1[n] := true$
11: **else** // *i.e.,* $var(n) \in V_X$
12:      **if**$((var(n) := true) \in X)$
13:           **if** $(reach1[dashed(n)])$ $frontier[n] := true$
14:           **if** $(reach1[solid(n)])$ $reach1[n] := true$
15:      **else**
16:           **if** $(reach1[solid(n)])$ $frontier[n] := true$
17:           **if** $(reach1[dashed(n)])$ $reach1[n] := true$

Fig. 5. The FindFrontier Procedure

the set $reachedSet[var(b)]$ is assigned a set with just the root node. At the end of *MinimalReason*, if a node n belongs to the set $reachedSet[var[n]]$, then it means the node n could be reached from the root node b without using any conflicting edge w.r.t R, where R is the output minimal reason. At the line-3 of the procedure, the set R is initialized to be empty and T is initialized to a set with both the terminal nodes. At the line-4, the procedure starts to loop over each variable in the BDD, in the variable order. During each loop, if any node n belongs to the $reachedSet[var(n)]$ with $(frontier[n] = true)$, then the procedure adds the assignment of $var(n)$ in X to R and ignores the child node of n which can be reached by the frontier edge of n by not adding it to the $reachedSet$. In the case there was no frontier node in $reachedSet[b_i]$, then the lines 18-20 adds both the child nodes of each $n \in reachedSet[b_i]$ to the $reachedSet$ if they are not terminal nodes. At the line-21, the procedure returns the obtained minimal reason R, such that $R \wedge b \Rightarrow (v := a)$.

Lemma 3. *If (n_f, n_{f+1}) is a frontier edge, then the FindFrontier results in $frontier[n_f] = true$.*

Proof. Let a solution path p for which (n_f, n_{f+1}) is a frontier edge be $p =< n_1, n_2, \ldots, n_f, n_{f+1}, \ldots, n_l >$, where $n_1 = b$ and $n_l = 1$. We know $(v := \neg a) \in p$.

It can be observed that the *FindFrontier* procedure ensures that, for $f < j \leq l$, $reach1[n_j] = true$. Since $n_l = 1$, this trivially holds for n_l, as initialized at the line-1 of the *MinimalReason* procedure. For $f < j < l$, the edge (n_j, n_{j+1}) is not a conflicting edge by frontier edge definition, also (n_j, n_{j+1}) does not correspond to the assignment $(v := a)$ as $(v := \neg a) \in p$. Hence, for $f < j < l$, the *FindFrontier* procedure ensures that $reach1[n_{j+1}] \Rightarrow reach1[n_j]$. Therefore, for $f < j \leq l$, $reach1[n_j] = true$, which implies $reach1[n_{f+1}] = true$.

Since $reach1[n_{f+1}] = true$ during the call *FindFrontier*(n_f), the lines 12-17 of the procedure will ensure that $frontier[n_f] = true$.   □

Theorem 2. *If MinimalReason $(X, b, (v := a))$ returns R then $R \wedge b \Rightarrow (v := a)$.*

Proof. We show that in any solution path p in the BDD b with $(v := \neg a) \in p$, there exists a conflicting edge w.r.t. R. Hence, for any solution $S \in b$, if $(v := \neg a) \in S$, then $S \notin (R \wedge b)$, which proves the theorem.

The proof is by contradiction. Suppose there exists a solution path p in the BDD b with $(v := \neg a) \in p$. Let $p =< n_1, n_2, \ldots, n_f, n_{f+1}, \ldots, n_l >$, where $n_1 = b$, $n_l = 1$ and (n_f, n_{f+1}) is the frontier edge. Lets assume the path does not use any conflicting edge w.r.t R. Then, we show that $n_f \in reachedSet[var(n_f)]$ and hence the assignment of $var(n_f)$ in X, which conflicts (n_f, n_{f+1}), belongs to R, which is a contradiction.

Since by assumption the path p does not contain any conflicting edge w.r.t R, for any edge (n_i, n_{i+1}) in p, if the assignment corresponding to the edge is $(var(n_i) := a')$, then $(var(n_i) := \neg a') \notin R$.

Then for $1 \leq i \leq f$, $n_i \in reachedSet[var(n_i)]$. This holds trivially for $i = 1$ as initialized at the line-3. For $1 \leq i < f$, since by assumption the edge $(n_i, n_i + 1)$ is not a conflicting edge w.r.t R, the procedure would have added n_{i+1} to $reachedSet[var(n_{i+1})]$, irrespective of the value of the *foundFrontier* flag during the loop at the line-4 for $var(n_i)$. Hence, $n_f \in reachedSet[var(n_f)]$.

During the loop corresponding to $var(n_f)$, at the line-4 of the *MinimalReason* procedure, since $n_f \in reachedSet[var(n_f)]$ and by Lemma 3, $frontier[n_f] = true$, the *foundFrontier* flag will be *true*. Hence, the assignment to $var(n_f)$ in X will be in R, with (n_f, n_{f+1}) being a conflicting edge w.r.t. R, which is a contradiction.

□

Theorem 3. *If MinimalReason* $(X, b, (v := a))$ *returns R then R is a minimal reason.*

Proof. Let $(v' := a') \in R$. The *MinimalReason* includes $(v' := a')$ in R only if there exists a node n with $frontier[n] = true$, $var(n) = v'$ and $n \in reachedSet[v']$. Hence, by the frontier edge definition, an edge of the form (n, n') is the only conflicting edge w.r.t R in a solution path p with $(v := \neg a) \in p$. Hence, the removal of $(v' := a')$ from R would imply $R \wedge b \Rightarrow (v := a)$ is not true. Therefore, R is minimal.   □

Theorem 4. *The MinimalReason procedure takes time at most linear in $|b|$.*

Proof. The total amount of space used by all the used data-structures is at most linear in b. We can ignore the number of variables k when compared with $|b|$, as $|b|$ could be exponential in k.

After excluding time taken by the descendant calls, each call to the *Find-Frontier* procedure takes constant time. Hence, the call *FindFrontier(b)* in total takes time at most linear in $|b|$.

The running time of *MinimalReason* procedure, excluding the call to *Find-Frontier*, is dominated by the loop at line-4. The loop iterates k times. Since a node n in the BDD b is added to $reachedSet[var(n)]$ at most once during all the k iterations, the total time required for all the k loops is linear in b.

Hence, the *MinimalReason* procedure takes time at most linear in $|b|$ to find a minimal reason.   □

5   Related Work

A method for finding minimal reasons in BDDs was presented in [7], which we call as the PADL06 method. The authors did not specify the worst case running time of the PADL06 method. But, the PADL06 method uses existential quantification operations on BDDs and hence quite costly when compared to our new linear-time method. If the BDD b is defined over the variables in V_b, the PADL06 method existentially quantifies the variables in $(V_b \setminus V_X)$ from the BDD b for finding a minimal reason. Note, the time and space complexity of each existential quantification operation in the worst case could even be *quadratic* [1] in $|b|$. Precisely, some of the advantages of our new method over the PADL06 [7] method are:

1. Worst case linear running time.
2. No costly BDD operations like existential quantifications.

3. No creation of new BDD nodes, the BDDs remain *static* during our solution process. Our new minimal reason method just uses the underlying directed acyclic graph of the BDDs, and hence does not require a full BDD package, while the PADL06 method requires a full BDD package.

In [14], the authors did not give details of their method for generating minimal reasons in BDDs, even the complexity of their method was not mentioned.

6   Experiments

We have implemented our new minimal reason algorithm as part of a constraint solver with nogood learning. Our solver uses the BuDDy[1] BDD package. Our solver just uses the lexicographic variable order.

Given a CSP instance in the CLab [15] input format, we use the CLab tool to compile BDDs, one BDD for each constraint in the CSP. This will convert the input CSP instance into a list of Boolean variables and a set of BDDs defined over those variables. Our tool takes the set of BDDs as input and uses our constraint solver to find a solution. Our tool is designed after the BDD-based hybrid SAT solver in [14], which requires a method for MINIMAL BDD-REASON .

We use the 34 CSPs modelling *power supply restoration* problem in our experiments. The instances are available online[2], in the CLab format. All the instances are satisfiable.

We have also implemented the PADL06 [7] method in our tool for comparison. To study the scalability of the PADL06 method and our new method, for each input CSP, we create three types of instances in BDD format with increasing BDD sizes. The first type called *Group*-1 instance, as mentioned above, is obtained by building one BDD for each constraint in the CSP. The second type called *Group*-5 instance is obtained by first partitioning the constraints into $\lceil |C|/5 \rceil$ disjoint groups of constraints in the CSP. Each group will have at most five consecutive constraints, in lexicographic order. Then one BDD will be built to represent the conjunction of the constraints in each group. The third type called *Group*-10 instance is created similar to Group-5, but by using groups of size ten. Since the size of a BDD representing conjunction of five constraints will be usually larger than the sum of the sizes of five BDDs representing each one of the five constraints, the sizes of the BDDs in a Group-5 instance will usually be larger than those in the matching Group-1 instance. Hence, by using Group-1, Group-5 and Group-10 instances of an input CSP, we can study the scalability of the new method and the PADL06 method over increasing BDD sizes.

All our experiments are done in a Cygwin environment with Intel Centrino 1.6 GHz processor and 1 GB RAM.

The conversion of the 34 CSPs into Group-k types, for $k \in \{1, 5, 10\}$, resulted in 102 instances in BDD representation. To compare our new method with the PADL06 method, we used our solver to find a solution for each one of the 104

---

[1] http://buddy.sourceforge.net/
[2] http://www.itu.dk/research/cla/externals/clib

Table 1. Instance Characteristics. $|V|$: the number of variables in the input CSP. $|V'|$: the number of Boolean variables required to encode the original variables. $|C|$: the number of constraints. **Max**: the size of the largest BDD in the corresponding Group-k instance. **Total**: the sum of the sizes of all the BDDs in the corresponding Group-k instance.

Instance				BDD Size					
				Group-1		Group-5		Group-10	
Name	$|V|$	$|V'|$	$|C|$	Max	Total	Max	Total	Max	Total
and-break-complex	414	998	852	755	38808	3540	110340	62735	459564
complex-P1	299	731	592	755	24055	13523	77414	139048	356546
complex.10	414	998	849	631	33923	4271	89448	38901	262059
complex.11	414	998	849	608	32937	4371	89168	40235	276547
complex.12	414	998	849	724	37902	5443	108263	55494	349829
complex	414	998	849	755	38804	5823	112873	60903	381951

Table 2. Solution Time (**ST**) and Minimal Reason Time (**MRT**)

Name	Group-1		Group-5		Group-10	
	PADL06	NEW	PADL06	NEW	PADL06	NEW
	ST, MRT	ST, MRT	ST, MRT	ST, MRT	ST, MRT	ST, MRT
and-break-complex	3.20, 1.03	2.94, 0.00	13.12, 7.49	7.40, 1.21	50.54, 41.02	14.62, 4.40
complex-P1	1.24, 0.76	1.14, 0.03	3.88, 2.27	2.98, 0.16	37.13, 21.52	18.17, 2.32
complex.10	5.04, 1.48	4.44, 0.01	9.19, 5.27	5.55, 0.90	58.01, 45.10	15.96, 4.89
complex.11	5.81, 1.54	5.14, 0.01	6.47, 3.86	3.95, 0.60	17.26, 12.81	6.73, 1.31
complex.12	2.65, 1.21	2.14, 0.04	3.15, 2.43	2.07, 0.27	22.40, 18.10	6.96, 1.75
complex	3.19, 1.08	2.94, 0.01	19.91, 9.94	12.29, 1.88	227.75, 189.04	41.77, 15.20

instances, first using our new method and then using the PADL06 method. We repeated each experiment thrice and obtained the average values. For each instance, we noted the total time taken to find a solution, and the total time taken for the calls made to the corresponding minimal reason method. We used the *gprof* tool to measure the time taken by the minimal reason procedure calls.

Since we do not have space to list the details for all the 34 instances, we picked five relatively large instances and present their characteristics in Table 1. The Table 2 presents the time taken for finding a solution and the total time taken for finding minimal reasons in both the type of experiments on the five instances.

The Figure 6 and Figure 7 plots the solution time and minimal reason time for the both the minimal reason methods, for all the instances.

The tables and figures show that the new method is at least as fast as the PADL06 method in all the used instances. The new method is even 10 times faster than the PADL06 method. Also, the new method scales better than the PADL06 method as the run-time difference between the new method and the PADL06 method widens from a Group-1 instance to the matching Group-10 instance.

In the case of the *complex* Group-10 instance, the PADL06 method dominates the solution time taking 83% of the solution time, while the usage of the new method reduces the solution time to less than a fifth.

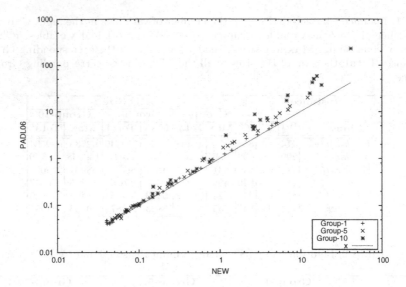

Fig. 6. Solution Time

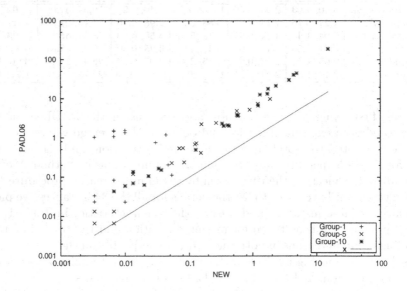

Fig. 7. Minimal Reason Time

7   Conclusion

We have shown that the problem of finding a minimum reason for an implication by a BDD is NP-complete. We have also presented a linear-time algorithm for finding minimal reasons, which can be used to improve the nogood reasoning process in hybrid constraint solvers using BDDs. Our experiments shows that the new method for finding minimal reasons is better than the previous method for several instances and also scales well due to linear time complexity.

Acknowledgement

Thanks to Lucas Bordeaux and Youssef Hamadi for discussions related to this work.

References

1. Bryant, R.E.: Graph-based algorithms for boolean function manipulation. Transactions on Computers 8, 677–691 (1986)
2. Bouquet, F., Jégou, P.: Using OBDDs to handle dynamic constraints. Information Processing Letters 62, 111–120 (1997)
3. Hadzic, T., Subbarayan, S., Jensen, R.M., Andersen, H.R., Møller, J., Hulgaard, H.: Fast backtrack-free product configuration using a precompiled solution space representation. In: PETO, pp. 131–138 (2004)
4. van der Meer, E.R., Andersen, H.R.: BDD-based recursive and conditional modular interactive product configuration. In: CP 2004 CSPIA Workshop, pp. 112–126 (2004)
5. Subbarayan, S., Jensen, R.M., Hadzic, T., Andersen, H.R., Hulgaard, H., Møller, J.: Comparing two implementations of a complete and backtrack-free interactive configurator. In: CP 2004 CSPIA Workshop, pp. 97–111 (2004)
6. Lagoon, V., Stuckey, P.: Set domain propagation using ROBDDs. In: Wallace, M. (ed.) CP 2004. LNCS, vol. 3258, pp. 347–361. Springer, Heidelberg (2004)
7. Hawkins, P., Stuckey, P.J.: A hybrid BDD and SAT finite domain constraint solver. In: Van Hentenryck, P. (ed.) PADL 2006. LNCS, vol. 3819, pp. 103–117. Springer, Heidelberg (2005)
8. Cheng, K.C.K., Yap, R.H.C.: Maintaining generalized arc consistency on ad-hoc n-ary Boolean constraints. In: ECAI, pp. 78–82 (2006)
9. Dechter, R.: Enhancement schemes for constraint processing: Backjumping, learning and cutset decomposition. Artificial Intelligence 41, 273–312 (1990)
10. Schiex, T., Verfaillie, G.: Nogood recording for static and dynamic constraint satisfaction problems. International Journal of Artificial Intelligence Tools 3, 187–207 (1994)
11. Katsirelos, G., Bacchus, F.: Unrestricted nogood recording in CSP search. In: Rossi, F. (ed.) CP 2003. LNCS, vol. 2833, pp. 873–877. Springer, Heidelberg (2003)
12. Zhang, L., Madigan, C.F., Moskewicz, M.W., Malik, S.: Efficient conflict driven learning in boolean satisfiability solver. In: ICCAD, pp. 279–285 (2001)
13. Garey, M.R., Johnson, D.S.: Computers and Intractability-A Guide to the Theory of NP-Completeness. W.H. Freeman and Co (1979)
14. Damiano, R.F., Kukula, J.H.: Checking satisfiability of a conjunction of BDDs. In: DAC, pp. 818–823 (2003)
15. Jensen, R.M.: CLab: A C++ library for fast backtrack-free interactive product configuration. In: Wallace, M. (ed.) CP 2004. LNCS, vol. 3258, p. 816. Springer, Heidelberg (2004), http://www.itu.dk/people/rmj/clab/

Flexible, Rule-Based Constraint Model Linearisation

Sebastian Brand, Gregory J. Duck, Jakob Puchinger, and Peter J. Stuckey

NICTA, Victoria Research Lab, University of Melbourne, Australia

Abstract. Nonlinear constraint satisfaction or optimisation models need to be reduced to equivalent linear forms before they can be solved by (Integer) Linear Programming solvers. A choice of linearisation methods exist. There are generic linearisations and constraint-specific, user-defined linearisations. Hence a model reformulation system needs to be flexible and open to allow complex and novel linearisations to be specified. In this paper we show how the declarative model reformulation system CADMIUM can be used to effectively transform constraint problems to different linearisations, allowing easy exploration of linearisation possibilities.

1 Introduction

The last decade has seen a trend towards high-level modelling languages in constraint programming. Languages such as ESRA [1], Essence [2], and ZINC [3] allow the modeller to state problems in a declarative, human-comprehensible way, without having to make subordinate modelling decisions or even to commit to a particular solving approach. Examples of decisions that may depend on the target solver are: the representation of variables of a complex type such as sets or graphs, and the translation of constraints into those provided by the solver to be used. Such decisions need to be taken if a concrete solver such as Gecode, ILOG Solver, CPLEX or Eclipse is to be used directly.

The problem solving process is thus broken into two parts. First, a high-level, solver-independent, conceptual model is developed. Second, the conceptual model is mapped to an executable version, the design model. Typically, an iterative process of solver selection, model formulation or augmentation, and model transformation, followed by experimental evaluation, is employed.

An imbalance exists in how the steps of this process are supported in practice. For the task of model formulation, there are well-designed, open, high-level modelling languages. In contrast, the task of model transformation is typically done by fixed procedures inaccessible to the modeller. It is hard to see that there is a single best set of transformations that can be wrapped and packed away. We therefore conclude that a strong requirement on a model transformation process and platform is *flexibility*.

In this paper we describe how we transform high-level models written in the modelling language MINIZINC [4] (a subset of ZINC) into Integer Linear Programming (ILP) models. The transformations are written in our term-rewriting

P. Hudak and D.S. Warren (Eds.): PADL 2008, LNCS 4902, pp. 68–83, 2008.

based model transformation language CADMIUM [5]. The rules and transformations are directly accessible to the modeller and can be freely examined, modified, and replaced. A major strength of CADMIUM is its tight integration with the ZINC modelling language. The rules operate directly on ZINC expressions; as a result, transformations are often very compact and comprehensible. Another strength of the approach is easy reusability. For example, in the linearisation of MINIZINC models we reused transformations originally designed for transforming MINIZINC models to FLATZINC (a low-level CP solver input language).

Our computational experiments, where MINIZINC models are transformed into CPLEX LP format, demonstrate the advantages of our system. It allows the user to experiment with different ways of linearising logical constraints as well as high-level constraints such as all_different [6,7].

2 Languages and Systems

2.1 The ZINC Family of Modelling Languages

ZINC [3] is a novel, declarative, typed constraint modelling language. It provides mathematical notation-like syntax (arithmetic and logical operators, iteration), high-level data structures (sets, arrays, tuples, Booleans), and extensibility by user-defined functions and predicates. Model and instance data can be separate. MINIZINC [4] is a subset of ZINC closer to existing CP languages that is still suitable as a medium-level constraint modelling language. FLATZINC, also described in [4], is a low-level subset of ZINC designed as a CP solver input language. It takes a role for CP systems comparable to that taken by the DIMACS and LP/MPS formats for propositional-satisfiability solvers and linear solvers, resp.

A ZINC model consists of an unordered set of *items* such as variable and parameter definitions, constraints, type definitions, and the solving objective. As an example, consider the following MINIZINC model of the Golomb Ruler problem. The problem consists in finding a set of small integers of given cardinality such that the distance between any pair of them differs from the distance between any other pair.

```
int: m = 4;
int: n = m*m;
array[1..m] of var 0..n: mark;
array[1..(m*(m-1)) div 2] of var 0..n: differences =
    [ mark[j] - mark[i] | i in 1..m, j in i+1..m ];
constraint mark[1] = 0;
constraint % The marks are ordered, and differences distinct
    forall ( i in 1..m-2 ) ( mark[i] < mark[i+1] )
    ∧ all_different(differences);
constraint mark[2] - mark[1] < mark[m] - mark[m-1];   % Symmetry
solve minimize mark[m];
```

Let us consider the items in textual order.

- The first and second lines declare the parameters m and n, both of type int.
- The following two lines declare the decision variables in arrays mark and differences. The variables of either array take integer values in the range 0..n. The index set of mark are the integers in the range 1..m. The array differences is defined by an array comprehension.
- Next is a *constraint* item fixing the first element of mark to be zero. The remaining constraints order the marks, make the differences distinct, and finally break a symmetry.
- The final item is a *solve* item, which states that the optimal solution with respect to minimising the final mark at position m should be found.

More detail about the ZINC language family is available in [3,8,4].

2.2   The CADMIUM Model Transformation System

CADMIUM [5] is a declarative, rule-based programming language based on associative, commutative, distributive term rewriting. CADMIUM is primarily targetted at ZINC model transformation, where one ZINC model is transformed into another by a CADMIUM program (mapping). A rule-based system for constraint model transformation is a natural choice as such transformations are often described as rules in the first place.

CADMIUM is well-suited for ZINC model transformation because of the tight representational integration between the two languages. A CADMIUM program is a sequence of rules of the form

$$CCHead \setminus Head \Leftrightarrow Guard \mid Body$$

where *Head* and *Body* are arbitrary terms that in particular can involve ZINC expressions. Any expression from the current model matching *Head* is rewritten to the expression *Body* if the rule application requirements given by *CCHead* and *Guard* are satisfied (either of which can be absent). The rules in the program are repeatedly applied until no more applications are possible. The obtained model is the result of the transformation.

CADMIUM has its roots in CHR [9] but substantially extends it by several features, briefly described in the following. See [5] for a thorough exposition.

Associative Commutative Matching. An operator $\circ$ is *Associative Commutative* (AC) if it satisfies $x \circ (y \circ z) = (x \circ y) \circ z$ and $x \circ y = y \circ x$. AC operators are common, e.g. $+$, $*$, $\wedge$, $\vee$, $\cup$, $\cap$. CADMIUM supports *AC matching*, which means the order and nested structure of expressions constructed form AC operators does not matter; e.g. 0 + a can match X + 0 with X = a. This reduces the number of rules required to express a transformation. AC matching is a standard feature of other term rewriting languages, e.g. Maude [10].

Conjunctive Context Matching. CADMIUM supports *matching* based on the pseudo-distributive property $X \wedge f(Y_1, ..., Y_n) = X \wedge f(Y_1, ..., X \wedge Y_i, ..., Y_n)$ of conjunction for all functions f. This is in contrast to *performing* classical distribution where the X disappears from the top-level and is distributed to all arguments at once. Using this approach, conjunct X is *visible* in any sub-expression S of f: we say that X is in the conjunctive context (CC) of S.

A CADMIUM rule in which a *CCHead* prefix is present uses CC matching. In order for the rule to fire, *CCHead* must match (part of) the conjunctive context of the expression that matches *Head*. CC matching can for example be used to implement parameter substitution in constraint models by the rule

X = C \ X ⇔ C.

If an equation X = C appears in the conjunctive context of an X, then this rule rewrites X to C. Consider the expression f(a,a+b,g(a)) ∧ a = 3. Equation a = 3 is in the CC of all occurrences of a in the rest of the expression. After exhaustively applying the rule, the result is f(3,3+b,g(3)) ∧ a = 3.

CC matching is very powerful because it allows the user to match against non-local information. As far as we are aware, CC matching is unique to CADMIUM.

User-Definable Guards. CADMIUM supports rule with guards. A rule in which a guard is present can only be applied if the guard holds, that is, if the *Guard* expression can be rewritten to **true**. CADMIUM provides a number of simple guards, such as is_int(X) to test whether X is an integer constant. Importantly, guards can also be defined by the user via rules.

Staged Transformations. Beyond atomic transformations that consist of a single rule set, CADMIUM also supports composite, staged transformations: sequences of atomic transformations. Each atomic transformation is applied to the model in sequence, with a commitment to the intermediate results.

2.3   Representation of ZINC Models in CADMIUM

Conceptually, CADMIUM operates directly on ZINC expressions and items (we emphasise this by printing ZINC keywords in bold). The following details of the ZINC representation in CADMIUM term form are worth pointing out:

- All ZINC items in the model are joined by conjunction. Thus the ZINC model

    constraint X = 3;
    solve satisfy;

  is treated as

    constraint X = 3 ∧ **solve satisfy**.

  The advantage is that ZINC items are in each other's conjunctive context.
- The conjunction of ZINC items is wrapped by a top-level **model** functor. This representation allows top-down model transformation in the way non-term-rewriting-based approaches work, rewriting the entire model at once:

    model Model ⇔ ...

  However, in our experience, top-down model transformations are almost never needed.

3 Transforming Nonlinear MiniZinc into linear Integer Programming format

There are several ways of linearising constraints. A generic method is the *Big-M* approach, used to convert a logical combinations of linear constraints into a conjunction of linear constraints. A finite domain constraint can always be written as a logical combination of linear constraints, by reverting to some logical definition of it.

For some high-level constraints, alternative definitions can be given that tightly reflect their structure onto auxiliary variables, for example, $0/1$ integer variables encoding assignments of original variables.

3.1 The Generic *Big-M* Transformation

At the core of this linearisation approach is the fact that a disjunction $(x \leqslant 0) \vee b$, where b is a propositional variable, is equivalently written as the inequation $x \leqslant ubound(x) \cdot b$, where $ubound$ is an upper bound on the value of the variable x. Our transformation first normalises a MiniZinc model and then transforms it into negation normal form. The next steps are based on the work by McKinnon and Williams [6] and Li et al. [11]. We simplified their transformation and made some steps, such as Boolean normalisation, more explicit.

Li et al. [11] define the modelling language $\mathcal{L}^+$, which consists of linear arithmetic constraints, Boolean operators, and some additional constraints such as at_most and at_least. Steps of the transformation described in [11] are:

- Transformation of $\mathcal{L}^+$ into negation normal form.
- Transformation of simplified $\mathcal{L}^+$-formulas into Γ-formulas. A Γ-formula is of the form $\Gamma_m\{P_1, \ldots, P_n\}$ and is true if at least m of $\{P_1, \ldots, P_n\}$ are true. Each P_i is a Γ-formula, a linear constraint, or a propositional literal.
- Flattening of nested Γ-formulas.
- Transformation of Γ-formulas into linear constraints.

Our transformation is based on this procedure. After several normalisation and decomposition steps, we generate Γ-formulas which are then further transformed into a linear form of MiniZinc. In the decomposition steps we provide several alternative transformations, and we allow the user to experiment with possible combinations of those alternatives. As a final step, we currently write out the obtained linear model in CPLEX LP format, for directly feeding it into most of the currently available ILP solvers.

We outline the major transformation steps in the following, giving actual CADMIUM example rules for illustration.

Model Normalisation. MiniZinc allows substantial freedom in the way models are written and so adapts to the preferred visual style of the model writer. The first step in our conversion is to rewrite simple, equivalent notations into a normal form. Examples are the joining of constraint items and the replacement of synonyms:

    (constraint C) ∧ (constraint D) ⇔ constraint C ∧ D;
    X == Y ⇔ X = Y;

Predicate Inlining. We currently use a top-down transformation, traversing the entire model term, to replace a call to a predicate (or function) by the respective instantiated predicate body.

This is our only case of a model-wide top-down transformation. We are currently moving towards a modified ZINC term representation in which predicate applications are wrapped in a reserved functor. Matching can then take place against this functor, and the need for a top-down transformation will be removed.

Parameter Substitution and Comprehension Unfolding. The next steps, while defined separately and listed in sequence, depend on and enable one another. In a non-term-rewriting approach, an explicit iteration loop would be needed to compute the mutual fixpoint. In CADMIUM, each individual atomic transformation corresponds to a set of rules, and the composite transformation is the union of these rule sets. Once the composite transformation has reached stabilisation, the mutual fixpoint of the separate rule sets is obtained.

1. Parameter substitution.
   We use the conjunctive context of a parameter to retrieve its value:
   ```
   X = C \ X ⇔ is_int(C) | C;
   ```
2. Evaluation.
   Parameter substitution may allow us to simplify the model. We here apply rules that do so by taking into account the semantics of ZINC constructs:
   ```
   X ∨ true ⇔ true;
   X + Y ⇔ is_int(X) ∧ is_int(Y) | X !+ Y;
   X ≤ C ⇔ is_int(C) ∧ ubound(X) !≤ C | true;
   ```
   The first rule simplifies a Boolean expression, the second evaluates addition of integer constants using the CADMIUM built-in !+, while the third removes constraints $X \leq C$ that are redundant w.r.t. to the declared domain of X.
3. Compound built-in unfolding.
   This step inlines predicates/functions such as **forall**, **sum** that are compound built-ins in MINIZINC:
   ```
   sum([]) ⇔ 0;
   sum([E ! Es]) ⇔ E + sum(Es);
   ```
   Note the CADMIUM syntax for array literal decomposition shown here.
4. Comprehension unfolding.
   An example for a simple case are these rules:
   ```
   [E | X in L..U] ⇔ L > U | [];
   [E | X in L..U] ⇔ [subst(X=L, E) ! [E | X in L+1..U]];
   ```
   The subst term denotes a substitution and is reduced accordingly.

These transformations are not specific to the MINIZINC linearisation task. Indeed, they are also used in the MINIZINC to FLATZINC transformation.

Decomposition of High-Level Constraints. In addition to the previously defined normalisations and decompositions, we decompose different generic constraints such as the **domain** constraint, here in ZINC notation:

```
X in A..B ⇔ is_int(A) ∧ is_int(B) | A ≤ X ∧ X ≤ B;
X in S    ⇔ is_set(S) | exists([ X = D | D in S ]);
```

We discern two cases of the respective set. If it is in range form, the constraint can be mapped onto two inequalities. Otherwise, it is mapped to a disjunction over the set values, which can be written using ZINC comprehension notation.

An array lookup with a variable index, corresponding to an `element` constraint, is transformed into a disjunction over all possible index values:

```
Y = A[X] ⇔ is_variable(X) |
    exists([ X = D ∧ A[D] = Y | D in dom(X) ]);
```

The expression **dom**(X) using the ZINC built-in **dom** is rewritten into the declared domain of the variable X, by rules we omit here. ZINC has a variety of such built-ins; **index_set** to retrieve an array index set is another useful one.

An `all_different` constraint is simply decomposed into a conjunction of inequations of the variable pairs:

```
all_different(X) ⇔
    forall([ X[I] ≠ X[J] | I,J in index_set(X) where I < J ]);
```

Minimum and maximum constraints are similarly decomposed. Furthermore, strict inequalities and disequalities are rewritten into expressions using only inequalities.

Since the decomposition of high-level constraints may introduce comprehensions and since further expression simplification can often be done, the rules for comprehension unfolding and expression evaluation are again imported into this stage.

Negation Normal Form. We transform formulas into negation normal form in the usual way. For example

$$(x - y < 5 \land y - x < 5) \rightarrow (z \geqslant 1)$$

is rewritten into

$$((x - y \geqslant 5) \lor (y - x \geqslant 5)) \lor (z \geqslant 1).$$

N-Ary Conjunction and Disjunction. We conjoin these binary connectives into an n-ary form, (using functors `conj,disj`), which is then transformed into Γ-formula form:

```
disj(Cs) ⇔ gamma(Cs, 1);
conj(Cs) ⇔ gamma(Cs, length(Cs));
```

The second argument to `gamma` is the minimum number of subformulas that need to hold. The formula from the example above becomes:

```
gamma([gamma([x - y ≥ 5, y - x ≥ 5], 1), z ≥ 1], 1).
```

Big-M Linearisation. This is the central step. It relies on the fact that all constraints were previously normalised. We proceed top-down, starting at the top-most `gamma` formula.

```
constraint gamma(Cs, M) ⇔
    constraint implied_gamma(true, Cs, M, []);
implied_gamma(B, [], M, Bs) ⇔ B → sum(Bs) ≥ M;
implied_gamma(B, [C ! Cs], M, Bs) ⇔
    let { var bool: Bi } in
    ((Bi → C) ∧ implied_gamma(B, Cs, M, [bool2int(Bi) ! Bs]));
B → E ≥ F ⇔ E-F ≥ lbound(E-F) * (1-bool2int(B));
```

The second and third rule transform a formula $B \to \Gamma_m(C)$ into a conjunction of implications $B_i \to C_i$. The B_i are accumulated in a list, which is used for the constraint $B \to \sum_i B_i \geq m$. An implication whose consequence is a **gamma** formula is turned into **implied_gamma** form again (not shown here for brevity). The last rule finally rewrites a simple implied linear inequation into pure linear form. The **lbound** term is rewritten into a safe lower bound of its argument expression which may include decision variables.

We optimise the linearisation by distinguishing special cases such as in

```
implied_gamma(B, [Bi ! Cs], M, Bs) ⇔ is_variable(Bi) |
    implied_gamma(B, Cs, M, [bool2int(Bi) ! Bs]);
```

which leads to fewer auxiliary Boolean variables being created.

Let us revisit part of our example. Assume x and y are in 0..10.

```
gamma([x - y ≥ 5, y - x ≥ 5], 1)
```

is stepwise transformed as follows (where we omit **bool2int** for brevity):

```
B → gamma([x - y ≥ 5, y - x ≥ 5], 1)
implied_gamma(B, [x - y ≥ 5, y - x ≥ 5], 1)
(B1 → x - y ≥ 5) ∧ (B2 → y - x ≥ 5) ∧ (B → B1+B2 ≥ 1)
(x - y - 5 ≥ -15*(1 - B1)) ∧ (y - x - 5 ≥ -15*(1 - B2)) ∧
    (B1 + B2 - 1 ≥ -1*(1 - B))
```

Boolean Variables to 0/1 Variables. In this step, we recast Boolean variables as 0/1 integer variables, by simply substituting the type:

```
bool ⇔ 0..1;
bool2int(B) ⇔ B;
```

Output to LP Format. The concluding stage prints out the linear model in CPLEX LP format using CADMIUM's I/O facilities. The result of applying the transformations to the Golomb Ruler problem of Section 2.1 is given in the Appendix.

3.2   Equality Encoding for High-Level Constraints

For a constraint such as **all_different**, the *Big-M*-linearisation applied to its naive decomposition does not result in a so-called *sharp* formulation: one that represents the convex hull of the constraint. Sharp formulations for a number of common constraints are given in Refalo [7]. At the core of many sharp formulations is the explicit encoding of variable assignments. Given a variable x with domain $D(x)$, for each $a \in D(x)$ a propositional variable for the assignment $x = a$ is introduced. We write such a variable as $[\![x = a]\!]$.

In this way, a sharp linear formulation of the domain constraint $x \in S$ is

$$\sum_{a \in D} [\![x = a]\!] = 1 \quad \wedge \quad x = \sum_{a \in D} a[\![x = a]\!].$$

For the all_different constraint over variables x_i with respective domain $D(x_i)$, one can use the linear constraints

$$\sum_{i=1}^{n} [\![x_i = a]\!] \leqslant 1 \quad \text{for each} \quad a \in \bigcup_{i=1}^{n} D(x_i).$$

They represent the fact that each value in any variable domain can be used by at most one variable. The CADMIUM rule setting up this encoding is as compact:

```
all_different_equality_encoding(Xs, Xi_eq_a) ⇔
    forall([ sum([ Xi_eq_a[I,A] | I in index_set(Xs) ]) ≤ 1
        | A in array_union([ dom(Xs[I]) | I in index_set(Xs) ]) ]);
```

The array Xi_eq_a collects the $[\![x = a]\!]$ variables. In order to share these encoding variables between different high-level constraints, the link between an original variables x and its associated encoding variables is maintained by encoding tokens (terms). These tokens are installed at the model top-level during the encoding stage and are thus in the conjunctive context of any constraint whose translation needs them.

To contrast the available approaches for all_different, consider the MINI-ZINC fragment:

```
array[1..n] of var -n..n: x;
constraint all_different(x);
```

The *Big-M* translation of all_different gives:

```
array[1..n, 1..n] of 0..1: B1;
array[1..n, 1..n] of 0..1: B2;
constraint
    forall(i in 1..n, j in i+1..n) (
        x[i] - x[j] + 1 ≤ (2 * n + 1) * (1 - B1[i, j]) ∧
        x[j] - x[i] + 1 ≤ (2 * n + 1) * (1 - B2[i, j]) ∧
        B1[i, j] + B2[i, j] ⩾ 1 );
```

while the transformation using the equality encoding results in:

```
array[1..n, -n..n] of 0..1: xv;
constraint
    forall(i in 1..n) (
        sum([ a * xv[i, a] | a in -n..n ]) = x[i] ∧
        sum([     xv[i, a] | a in -n..n ]) = 1 );
constraint
    forall(a in -n..n) ( sum([ xv[i, a] | i in 1..n ]) ≤ 1 );
```

The **element** constraint $z = a[x]$ for a variable x and an array a of integer constants can be represented as

$$z = \sum_{i \in D(x)} a[i] \cdot [\![x = i]\!],$$

which is embodied in the rule

```
element_equality_encoding(A, X, Y, X_eq_d) ⟺
    Y = sum([ A[D] * X_eq_d[D] | D in dom(X) ]);
```

This encoding is not applicable in the case when the array has variable elements. Our transformation verifies this and falls back to the naive *Big-M* decomposition approach if needed.

The basis for these linearisations of high-level constraints comes from the linear representation of disjunctive programs [12]. A further generalisation would be to directly apply this linearisation to the constraint in negation normal form.

3.3   Context-Dependent Constraint Generation

If we take into account the context of a constraint we may be able to simplify its translation. The Tseitin transformation [13] for converting Boolean formulas into clausal form takes this into account, usually reducing the number of clauses by half. For (Integer) Linear Programming there are common modelling "tricks" that make use of context. For example, the **max(y,z)** expression in both of the following cases

```
constraint 8 ⩾ max(y,z);
solve minimize max(y,z);
```

can be replaced by a new x constrained by $x \geqslant y \wedge x \geqslant z$. In the first case, we only need to require the existence of any value between 8 and y,z, and in the second case, minimisation will force x to equal either y or z.

In general if a variable is only bounded from above in all constraints, we can translate an equation defining the variable as an inequality that bounds it from below. For example x = **max(y,z)** is replaced by $x \geqslant y \wedge x \geqslant z$ as above if x is only bounded from above, and replaced by $x \leqslant t \wedge (t \leqslant y \vee t \leqslant z)$, where t is a new variable, if x is only bounded from below.

This reasoning can be concisely implemented in rule form:

```
max(X, Y) ⟺ pol(ID, pos, max_context(X,Y, ID));

E + pol(ID, P, F) ⟺ pol(ID, P, E + F);
E - pol(ID, P, F) ⟺ pol(ID, invert(P), E - F);

pol(ID, P, E) ⩽ F ⟺ pol(ID, P, E ⩽ F);
pol(ID, P, E) ⩾ F ⟺ pol(ID, invert(P), E ⩾ F);
pol(ID, _, E) = F ⟺ pol(ID, all, E = F);

constraint pol(ID, P, E) ⟺ pol(ID, P) ∧ constraint E;
solve minimize pol(ID, P, E) ⟺ pol(ID, P) ∧ solve minimize E;

pol(ID, all) \ max_context(X,Y, ID) ⟺ max_complete(X,Y);
pol(ID, pos) \ max_context(X,Y, ID) ⟺ max_bounded_above(X,Y);
```

We add a polarity marker to each occurrence of a nonlinear expression in question. Polarity markers then travel upwards in the expression tree until the top-level, recording possible polarity changes. (The rules for invert, not shown here, map pos to neg and vice versa, and all to itself). Once at the top-level, the polarity of the expression occurrence is known, and it can be replaced accordingly.

3.4 Constraint Relaxations

Given we have completely captured the meaning of a high-level constraint such as element or all_different by some linearisation, we are free to add other linear relaxations of the constraints to the model in order to improve the solving behaviour. Hooker [14] describes a number of simple and complex linear relaxations for various high-level constraints.

As an example, consider the element constraint $Y = A[X]$ where A is a fixed array. We can add bounds to Y as follows:

```
Y = A[X] ⇔ is_variable(X) ∧ fixed_array(A) |
    exists([X = D ∧ A[D] = Y | D in dom(X)]) ∧
    Y ⩾ min([A[D] | D in dom(X)]) ∧
    Y ⩽ max([A[D] | D in dom(X)]);
```

4 Case Studies

In this section we report on evaluations of various choices in transforming MINI-ZINC into LP format. We show that the best choice is problem-dependent and, therefore, that an open transformation system facilitating experimentation is important. For reference, we also give results on transforming MINIZINC to the low-level CP solver input language FLATZINC.

The experiments were performed on a 3.4 Ghz Intel Pentium D with 4 Gb RAM computer running Linux. The FLATZINC models were solved by the G12 finite domain solver using its default (first-fail) search. The LP models were solved using CPLEX 10.0 with default parameter settings. The solvers were aborted if they did not return a result within a reasonable amount of time; this is indicated in the tables.

4.1 *Big-M* Decomposition and Equality Encoding

For this comparison we use the following examples:

- eq20: twenty linear constraints;
- jobshop: square job scheduling (2×2, 4×4, 6×6, 8×8);
- mdknapsk: multidimensional knapsack problem ($\langle n, m \rangle \in \{\langle 5, 3 \rangle, \langle 100, 5 \rangle\}$);
- packing: packing squares into a rectangle (size 4);
- queens: the N-queens problem (sizes 8, 10, 20);
- alpha: a crypt-arithmetic puzzle;
- golomb: the Golomb ruler problem ($m \in \{4, 6, 8\}$);

Table 1. Results of the described transformations on several different models

name	MINIZINC lines	FLATZINC lines	transl.	solve	LP Big-M decomp. lines	transl.	solve	LP equality enc. lines	transl.	solve
eq20	63	82	0.31s	0.18s	43	0.44s	0.00s	"		
jobshop2x2	20	18	0.28s	0.10s	37	0.40s	0.00s	"		
jobshop4x4	22	141	0.31s	0.18s	227	0.48s	0.02s	"		
jobshop6x6	24	492	0.49s	8.65s	749	0.67s	1.72s	"		
jobshop8x8	26	1191	0.73s	>300s	1771	1.11s	>300s	"		
mdknapsk5_3	21	16	0.29s	0.07s	25	0.42s	0.00s	"		
mdknapsk100_5	75	176	0.60s	>300s	217	1.36s	0.61s	"		
packing	32	237	0.33s	0.16s	378	0.53s	0.00s	"		
queens_8	9	86	0.31s	0.17s	613	0.56s	0.06s	"		
queens_10	9	137	0.32s	0.15s	974	0.72s	0.36s	"		
queens_20	9	572	0.49s	0.21s	4039	2.42s	>300s	"		
alpha	52	53	0.29s	0.16s	2356	1.64s	0.13s	1511	1.32s	0.51s
golomb4	11	14	0.30s	0.07s	144	0.46s	0.00s	272	0.47s	0.01s
golomb6	11	25	0.31s	0.18s	807	0.69s	0.10s	1249	1.02s	0.53s
golomb8	11	40	0.32s	1.49s	2763	1.70s	19.36s	3878	3.28s	>300s
perfsq10	16	89	0.28s	0.17s	949	0.91s	0.12s	493	0.60s	0.10s
perfsq20	16	161	0.30s	1.55s	3069	3.36s	1.92s	1353	1.14s	0.42s
perfsq30	16	233	0.29s	111.29s	6389	9.10s	21.00s	2613	2.34s	0.66s
warehouses	45	476	0.45s	2.29s	1480	1.14s	1.34s	1322	0.96s	0.08s

- perfsq: find a set of integers whose sum of squares is itself a square (maximum integer 10, 20, or 30);
- warehouses: a warehouse location problem.

The results are shown in Table 1. The problems are grouped according to the translation features they can make use of. The eq20 and mdknapsk problems are linear and used to gauge the performance of the parts of the transformation not concerned with linearisation as such. The job-shop, packing and queens problems are nonlinear models without the use of high-level constraints, so the equality encoding variant does not differ from the Big-M variant for them. The alpha and golomb problems use all_different constraints, whereas element constraints occur in perfsq and warehouses.

First, from these experiments we can see that while the FLATZINC translations are often smaller, and faster to achieve than the LP format, the speed of the ILP solver means that the LP translations are often better overall.

That the translation to LP is typically slower than to FLATZINC is not unexpected as linearisation creates more constraints. A second, central factor is that, while FLATZINC is output by a non-CADMIUM ZINC pretty printer, the LP format generator uses a preliminary, primitive CADMIUM I/O module to write the files. We plan to address this issue by passing the linear model to the ILP solver directly rather than via files; and we will also optimise CADMIUM I/O.

Some of the slightly bigger examples (golomb8, jobshop8x8, mdknapsk100_5, perfsq30, and queens_20) show that translations times do scale, but the solve times can increase dramatically. For some examples (queens, golomb, jobshop) we can see a clear advantage of the FD solver, whereas for other examples (mdknapsk, perfsq) the ILP solver performs better.

For the linearisation choice, we find that for our example problems the sharp equality encodings works well for `element`, whereas surprisingly `all_different` does not benefit from it.

4.2 Context-Dependent `max` Constraints

For this set of benchmarks we use a model of a cancer radiation therapy problem [15]. The model is linear with the exception of multiple occurrences of `max` constraints. We compare the generic, complete linearisation and the context-dependent one (Section 3.3). Table 2 shows the results.

One observation is that the LP translation time grows quickly with the instance size. In good part this is due to CADMIUM's current suboptimal I/O module: for example, approximately one third of the time for size 8 instances is spent in the final step of printing the LP format text file.

The major observation in these benchmarks results, however, is the very surprising fact that the complete linearisation is *better* in the majority of cases than the context-dependent translation, which is less than half the size. This appears to be a consequence of an ill-guided ILP search in CPLEX in the context-dependent case. While correct bounds on the solutions are often found quickly, the search struggles to find integer solutions. We have been able to drastically

Table 2. Radiation problems: generic and context-dependent translations

Instance	MINIZINC lines	FLATZINC lines	transl.	LP complete lines	transl.	solve	LP context-dependent lines	transl.	solve
8_0	12	2387	3.20s	7458	16.30s	5.86s	2530	3.92s	287.27s
8_1	12	2387	2.74s	7458	16.23s	3.53s	2530	3.58s	1.71s
8_2	12	2387	2.76s	7458	16.16s	1.11s	2530	3.61s	1.11s
8_3	12	2387	2.70s	7458	16.10s	3.42s	2530	3.66s	22.32s
8_4	12	2387	2.73s	7458	16.22s	1.22s	2530	3.64s	1.38s
8_5	12	2387	2.70s	7458	16.07s	1.74s	2530	3.63s	>20min
9_0	13	3008	3.92s	9547	25.63s	2.87s	3211	5.46s	5.28s
9_1	13	3008	3.90s	9547	25.62s	2.35s	3211	5.45s	2.55s
9_2	13	3008	3.94s	9547	25.61s	6.42s	3211	5.47s	2.29s
9_3	13	3008	3.88s	9547	25.69s	14.01s	3211	5.35s	170.71s
9_4	13	3008	3.90s	9547	25.40s	1.63s	3211	5.42s	588.70s
9_5	13	3008	3.93s	9547	25.76s	20.88s	3211	5.49s	21.04s
10_0	14	3701	5.72s	11894	39.28s	16.21s	3974	8.02s	1.83s
10_1	14	3701	5.73s	11894	38.74s	14.25s	3974	8.02s	660.17s
10_2	14	3701	5.67s	11894	39.43s	7.88s	3974	8.00s	8.90s
10_3	14	3701	5.68s	11894	39.07s	1.45s	3974	7.96s	5.50s
10_4	14	3701	5.67s	11894	39.44s	11.82s	3974	7.95s	7.52s
10_5	14	3701	5.65s	11894	39.31s	1.76s	3974	8.01s	>20min

improve the behaviour for some instances by an informed modification of CPLEX parameters.[1]

A study of this unexpected observation is not the task of this paper. This puzzling result does, however, support our claim that the flexibility to experiment with different model translations is important.

5 Concluding Remarks

CADMIUM is one of only a few purpose-built systems targetting constraint model transformation, and among these, has particular strengths. Constraint Handling Rules (CHR) is less powerful in the sense that CHR rules can only rewrite items at the top-level conjunction. CHR implementations are also not deeply integrated with high-level modelling languages in the way CADMIUM and ZINC are.

The Conjure system [16] for automatic type refinement accepts models in the high-level constraint specification language ESSENCE and transforms them into models in a sublanguage, ESSENCE', roughly corresponding to a ZINC-to-MINI-ZINC translation. Conjure's focus is on automatic modelling: the generation of a family of correct but less abstract models that a given input model gives rise to. Our current goal with CADMIUM somewhat differently is to have a convenient, all-purpose, highly flexible 'plug-and-play' model rewriting platform.

We have only really begun to explore the possibilities of linearisation of MINI-ZINC models using CADMIUM. There are other decompositions based on Boolean variables $[\![x \leqslant d]\!]$ which could be explored; see e.g. [17,18]. There are many relaxations and combinations to explore. We can investigate how many IP modelling "tricks" can be implemented using concise CADMIUM analysis and rewriting.

On the technical side, we believe data-independent model transformation is a promising direction to take. It would for example mean to postpone unfolding comprehensions, and to transform according to the *derived* rather than present kind of an expression (i.e. constant vs. variable at solve time). We would expect transformation efficiency to greatly improve in this way.

Acknowledgements. This work has taken place with the support of the members of the G12 project.

References

1. Flener, P., Pearson, J., Ågren, M.: Introducing ESRA, a relational language for modelling combinatorial problems. In: LOPSTR 2003, pp. 214–232 (2003)
2. Frisch, A.M., Grum, M., Jefferson, C., Hernandez, B.M., Miguel, I.: The design of ESSENCE: A constraint language for specifying combinatorial problems. In: IJCAI 2007 (2007)
3. Garcia de la Banda, M.J., Marriott, K., Rafeh, R., Wallace, M.: The modelling language Zinc. [19], 700–705

---

[1] Interestingly an FD approach outperforms ILP when a specialised search approach is used [15], but this is not currently expressible in MINIZINC.

4. Nethercote, N., Stuckey, P.J., Becket, R., Brand, S., Duck, G.J., Tack, G.: Mini-Zinc: Towards a standard CP modelling language. [20], 529–543
5. Duck, G.J., Stuckey, P.J., Brand, S.: ACD term rewriting. In: Etalle, S., Truszczyński, M. (eds.) ICLP 2006. LNCS, vol. 4079, pp. 117–131. Springer, Heidelberg (2006)
6. McKinnon, K., Williams, H.: Constructing integer programming models by the predicate calculus. Annals of Operations Research 21, 227–246 (1989)
7. Refalo, P.: Linear formulation of constraint programming models and hybrid solvers. In: Dechter, R. (ed.) CP 2000. LNCS, vol. 1894, pp. 369–383. Springer, Heidelberg (2000)
8. Rafeh, R., Garcia de la Banda, M.J., Marriott, K., Wallace, M.: From Zinc to design model. In: Hanus, M. (ed.) PADL 2007. LNCS, vol. 4354, pp. 215–229. Springer, Heidelberg (2006)
9. Frühwirth, T.: Theory and practice of Constraint Handling Rules. Journal of Logic Programming 37(1-3), 95–138 (1998)
10. Clavel, M., Durán, F., Eker, S., Lincoln, P., Martí-Oliet, N., Meseguer, J., Talcott, C.: The Maude 2.0 system. In: Nieuwenhuis, R. (ed.) RTA 2003. LNCS, vol. 2706, pp. 76–87. Springer, Heidelberg (2003)
11. Li, Q., Guo, Y., Ida, T.: Modelling integer programming with logic: Language and implementation. IEICE Transactions of Fundamentals of Electronics, Communications and Computer Sciences E83-A(8), 1673–1680 (2000)
12. Balas, E.: Disjunctive programming: Properties of the convex hull of feasible points. Discrete Applied Mathematics 89(1-3), 3–44 (1998)
13. Tseitin, G.: On the complexity of derivation in propositional calculus. In: Studies in Constructive Mathematics and Mathematical Logic, pp. 115–125 (1968); Reprinted in Siekmann, J., Wrightson, G.(eds.) Automation of Reasoning, vol. 2, pp. 466–483, Springer, Heidelberg (1983)
14. Hooker, J.: Integrated Methods for Optimization. Springer, Heidelberg (2007)
15. Baatar, D., Boland, N., Brand, S., Stuckey, P.J.: Minimum cardinality matrix decomposition into consecutive-ones matrices: CP and IP approaches. LNCS, vol. 4510, pp. 1–15. Springer, Heidelberg (2007)
16. Frisch, A.M., Jefferson, C., Hernández, B.M., Miguel, I.: The rules of constraint modelling. In: Kaelbling, L.P., Saffiotti, A. (eds.) 19th International Joint Conference on Artificial Intelligence (IJCAI 2005), pp. 109–116 (2005)
17. Tamura, N., Taga, A., Kitagawa, S., Banbara, M.: Compiling finite linear CSP into SAT. [19], 590–603
18. Ohrimenko, O., Stuckey, P., Codish, M.: Propagation = lazy clause generation. [20], 544–558
19. Benhamou, F.: 12th International Conference on Principles and Practice of Constraint Programming. In: Benhamou, F. (ed.) CP 2006. LNCS, vol. 4204, Springer, Heidelberg (2006)
20. Bessière, C.: 13th International Conference on Principles and Practice of Constraint Programming. In: CP 2007. LNCS, vol. 4741. Springer, Heidelberg (2007)

A   Resulting LP Format

The following is the result of applying the MINIZINC-to-LP format transformation (using the *Big-M* linearisation of all_different) to the Golomb Ruler problem of Section 2.1:

```
Minimize mark{3}
Subject To
   mark{0} = 0
   mark{1} >= 1
   mark{2} - 1 differences{3} - 1 mark{1} = 0
   mark{3} - 1 differences{4} - 1 mark{1} = 0
   mark{3} - 1 differences{5} - 1 mark{2} = 0
   differences{0} - mark{1} = 0
   differences{1} - mark{2} = 0
   differences{2} - mark{3} = 0
   mark{1} + mark{2} - 1 mark{3} <= -1
   mark{1} - 1 mark{2} <= -1
   differences{5} + 17 V_107 - 1 differences{4} <= 16
   -1 V_108 - 1 V_107 <= -1
   differences{4} + 17 V_108 - 1 differences{5} <= 16
   differences{5} + 17 V_105 - 1 differences{3} <= 16
   -1 V_106 - 1 V_105 <= -1
   differences{3} + 17 V_106 - 1 differences{5} <= 16
   differences{4} + 17 V_103 - 1 differences{3} <= 16
   -1 V_104 - 1 V_103 <= -1
   differences{3} + 17 V_104 - 1 differences{4} <= 16
   differences{5} + 17 V_101 - 1 differences{2} <= 16
   -1 V_102 - 1 V_101 <= -1
   differences{2} + 17 V_102 - 1 differences{5} <= 16
   differences{4} + 17 V_99 - 1 differences{2} <= 16
   -1 V_100 - 1 V_99 <= -1
   differences{2} + 17 V_100 - 1 differences{4} <= 16
   differences{3} + 17 V_97 - 1 differences{2} <= 16
   -1 V_98 - 1 V_97 <= -1
   differences{2} + 17 V_98 - 1 differences{3} <= 16
   differences{5} + 17 V_95 - 1 differences{1} <= 16
   -1 V_96 - 1 V_95 <= -1
   differences{1} + 17 V_96 - 1 differences{5} <= 16
   differences{4} + 17 V_93 - 1 differences{1} <= 16
   -1 V_94 - 1 V_93 <= -1
   differences{1} + 17 V_94 - 1 differences{4} <= 16
   differences{3} + 17 V_91 - 1 differences{1} <= 16
   -1 V_92 - 1 V_91 <= -1
   differences{1} + 17 V_92 - 1 differences{3} <= 16
   differences{2} + 17 V_89 - 1 differences{1} <= 16
   -1 V_90 - 1 V_89 <= -1
   differences{1} + 17 V_90 - 1 differences{2} <= 16
   differences{5} + 17 V_87 - 1 differences{0} <= 16
   -1 V_88 - 1 V_87 <= -1
   differences{0} + 17 V_88 - 1 differences{5} <= 16
   differences{4} + 17 V_85 - 1 differences{0} <= 16
   -1 V_86 - 1 V_85 <= -1
   differences{0} + 17 V_86 - 1 differences{4} <= 16
   differences{3} + 17 V_83 - 1 differences{0} <= 16
   -1 V_84 - 1 V_83 <= -1
   differences{0} + 17 V_84 - 1 differences{3} <= 16
   differences{2} + 17 V_81 - 1 differences{0} <= 16
   -1 V_82 - 1 V_81 <= -1
   differences{0} + 17 V_82 - 1 differences{2} <= 16
   differences{1} + 17 V_79 - 1 differences{0} <= 16
   -1 V_80 - 1 V_79 <= -1
   differences{0} + 17 V_80 - 1 differences{1} <= 16
Bounds
   0 <= mark{0} <= 16
   0 <= mark{1} <= 16
   0 <= mark{2} <= 16
   0 <= mark{3} <= 16
   0 <= differences{0} <= 16
   0 <= differences{1} <= 16
   0 <= differences{2} <= 16
   0 <= differences{3} <= 16
   0 <= differences{4} <= 16
   0 <= differences{5} <= 16
   0 <= V_99 <= 1
   0 <= V_97 <= 1
   0 <= V_98 <= 1
   0 <= V_95 <= 1
   0 <= V_96 <= 1
   0 <= V_93 <= 1
   0 <= V_94 <= 1
   0 <= V_91 <= 1
   0 <= V_92 <= 1
   0 <= V_89 <= 1
   0 <= V_90 <= 1
   0 <= V_87 <= 1
   0 <= V_88 <= 1
   0 <= V_85 <= 1
   0 <= V_86 <= 1
   0 <= V_83 <= 1
   0 <= V_84 <= 1
   0 <= V_81 <= 1
   0 <= V_82 <= 1
   0 <= V_79 <= 1
   0 <= V_80 <= 1
   0 <= V_107 <= 1
   0 <= V_108 <= 1
   0 <= V_105 <= 1
   0 <= V_106 <= 1
   0 <= V_103 <= 1
   0 <= V_104 <= 1
   0 <= V_101 <= 1
   0 <= V_102 <= 1
   0 <= V_100 <= 1
General
   mark{0}
   mark{1}
   mark{2}
   mark{3}
   differences{0}
   differences{1}
   differences{2}
   differences{3}
   differences{4}
   differences{5}
   V_80
   V_79
   V_82
   V_81
   V_84
   V_83
   V_86
   V_85
   V_88
   V_87
   V_90
   V_89
   V_92
   V_91
   V_94
   V_93
   V_96
   V_95
   V_98
   V_97
   V_99
   V_100
   V_102
   V_101
   V_104
   V_103
   V_106
   V_105
   V_108
   V_107
End
```

The Role of Abduction in Declarative Authorization Policies

Moritz Y. Becker[1] and Sebastian Nanz[2]

[1] Microsoft Research, Cambridge, CB3 0FB, UK
Tel.: +44-1223-479826; Fax: +44-1223-479999
moritzb@microsoft.com
[2] Informatics and Mathematical Modelling
Technical University of Denmark, Denmark
nanz@imm.dtu.dk

Abstract. Declarative authorization languages promise to simplify the administration of access control systems by allowing the authorization policy to be factored out of the implementation of the resource guard. However, writing a correct policy is an error-prone task by itself, and little attention has been given to tools and techniques facilitating the analysis of complex policies, especially in the context of access denials. We propose the use of abduction for policy analysis, for explaining access denials and for automated delegation. We show how a deductive policy evaluation algorithm can be conservatively extended to perform abduction on Datalog-based authorization policies, and present soundness, completeness and termination results.

Keywords: access control, abduction, authorization language, Datalog.

1 Introduction

Authorization is the task of granting or denying access to a system's resources according to a policy. Traditionally, authorization policies have been implemented by access control lists (ACL) or capabilities provided by the operating system, sometimes augmented by groups or roles. However, there are many applications for which these mechanisms are too inflexible, not sufficiently expressive and provide the wrong level of abstraction. For example, access to electronic health records is regulated by a huge number of laws that are both complex and prone to change. Decentralized applications such as grid systems require support for delegation of authority and attribute-based constraints.

Such requirements have led to the development of trust management systems and declarative authorization languages for flexible, expressive application-level access control (e.g. [1,2,3,4,5]). An authorization policy is then written as a set of rules that are both human readable and machine enforceable. This approach aims to increase the usability and scalability of access control systems: policies written in such languages are more concise and have a lower viscosity than ACLs, and provide a much higher level of abstraction, thus facilitating a closer representation of the intended policy.

P. Hudak and D.S. Warren (Eds.): PADL 2008, LNCS 4902, pp. 84–99, 2008.

However, comprehending and predicting the consequences of a policy is difficult, as policies can be complex and contain hundreds of rules, and each access grant is based on the construction of a logical proof of compliance with respect to this policy. Thus, writing a correct policy is still a highly error-prone task. We conjecture that the current lack of tools for analyzing policies remains a major obstacle to a wider adoption of authorization languages.

In this paper, we develop algorithms for analyzing the consequences of declarative authorization policies. Many existing authorization languages are based on negation-free Datalog or are translated into Datalog for evaluating access requests. (A Datalog clause is a first-order definite Horn clause without function symbols.) Datalog is sufficiently expressive for a wide range of policies, including delegation, which requires recursion. Furthermore, Datalog is decidable and can be evaluated efficiently. Hence, to maximize generality, our algorithms work on policies specified in Datalog.

In particular, we focus on the tasks of *explaining* access grants and access denials. In the former case, the question we are trying to answer is *"why is a given request granted?"*. It is easy to see that the proof graph contains exactly the necessary information for constructing the (possibly textual) explanation. The basic evaluation algorithm that is used for deciding access requests can be easily extended to construct a copy of the proof graph during evaluation.

In the case of access denial, the question is *"which authorization facts or credentials were missing that would have led to an access grant?"*. This turns out to be a harder question, as the failed partial proof does not contain enough information to answer it. Moreover, there are in general infinitely many different answers, but often only finitely many "interesting" or "useful" ones. We propose to apply *abductive* techniques for finding the set of meaningful answers. Abduction [6] is a reasoning paradigm that has been used for planning, fault diagnosis and other areas in AI, but has not previously been considered for analyzing authorization policies. Many algorithms have been developed for various variants of abduction (see [7] for an extensive survey); in this paper, we show that a deductive evaluation algorithm that is used for deciding access requests can be conservatively extended to perform abduction of authorization facts and credentials. Thus we show that existing implementations of Datalog-based authorization engines can be leveraged and extended with little effort to facilitate this kind of analysis. Moreover, we show that this algorithm can be used for multiple purposes: (1) as the basis of a tool helping security administrators to write and to debug policies, (2) for providing users with an answer in the case of an access denial that is more helpful than a mere "no", and (3) to compute sets of missing credentials in automated distributed delegation scenarios.

The remainder of the paper is structured as follows: Section 2 first presents a non-deterministic terminating algorithm for evaluating policies. The algorithm is extended to construct proof graphs. A second extension is developed that computes sets of missing facts that, if added, would lead to a positive access decision. Section 3 presents techniques for guaranteeing that the algorithm terminates. Section 4 discusses three application scenarios to illustrate the different ways in which the algorithm could be used. In Section 5 we discuss related work and conclude. A technical report [8] contains full proofs.

2   Adding Abduction to Policy Evaluation

The basic authorization problem consists of deciding whether an access request complies with an authorization policy and a set of credentials. For Datalog-based policies, this amounts to deductive query evaluation. Tabling resolution algorithms are proposed in [9] and [5] for evaluating queries against Datalog-based authorization policies. These algorithms are easy to implement and are guaranteed to terminate due to tabling [10,11].

Here we provide a generalization of these algorithms, presented as state transition systems. The non-deterministic presentation lends itself to parallel implementations; moreover, it also leads to simpler soundness, completeness and termination proofs. Section 2.2 instantiates this generalized tabling scheme to a purely deductive policy evaluation algorithm. The evaluation algorithms in [9] and [5] can be seen as straightforward deterministic implementations of this general scheme. Section 2.3 illustrates a simple extension of the first one, which facilitates the construction of proof graphs, e.g. for explaining positive access decisions. Finally, Section 2.4 extends it further to perform *abduction*, which computes the *dual* of the basic authorization problem, namely the sets of facts or credentials which, according to the policy, would grant an authorization request. As shown in Section 4, this algorithm can be applied to explain access denials, to analyze policies and to provide automated distributed delegation.

2.1   An Extensible Scheme for Policy Evaluation

Preliminaries. We use the terms *groundness, substitution, unifier, most general unifier (mgu)* and *(fresh) variable renaming* in their standard meanings. We assume a denumerable set of variables $\mathcal{X}$ and a first-order signature with a countable (possibly infinite) set of constants $\mathcal{C}$ and a finite set of predicate names (but no function symbols). An *atom* P consists of a predicate name applied to an ordered list of terms, each of which is either a variable or a constant. *Clauses* are of the form $P_0 \leftarrow \vec{P}$. The atom P_0 is referred to as the *head*, and the (possibly empty) finite sequence of atoms $\vec{P}$ as the *body* of the clause. A clause with an empty body is also called a *fact*. A *policy* $\mathcal{P}$ is a finite set of clauses.

The semantics of a policy $\mathcal{P}$ is given by the least fixed point of the *immediate consequence operator* $T_{\mathcal{P}}$ [12]:

$$T_{\mathcal{P}}(I) = \{P_0\theta \ : \ (P_0 \leftarrow P_1,\ldots,P_n) \in \mathcal{P}, \ P_i\theta \in I \text{ for each } i, \ P_0\theta \text{ ground}\}$$

We denote the least fixed point of $T_{\mathcal{P}}$ by $T_{\mathcal{P}}^{\omega}(\emptyset)$. Intuitively, it contains all ground atoms that are deducible from the policy. The most general unifier of atoms P and Q is denoted by $mgu(P,Q)$. We say that P *is subsumed by* Q (also written $P \preceq Q$) iff $P = Q\theta$ for some substitution θ.

In our examples, we write variables in *italics*, constants in `typewriter` font, and predicate names in sans serif.

An authorization policy defines authorization-relevant predicates such as canRead, canWrite etc. Upon an access request, the resource guard issues a query (e.g. "canRead(`Alice`,`Foo`)?") to be evaluated against the policy. Usually, the policy is composed of the locally stored policy plus a set of facts obtained from (user-submitted or fetched) *credentials* that may support the request. We will later show examples of policies and their uses.

Description of the Scheme. The algorithms described in the following subsections are instantiations of a state transition system that processes nodes of the following form:

Definition 2.1 (Nodes). A *node* is either a *root node* $\langle P \rangle$ where P is an atom, or a *tuple* (with at least 3 fields) of the form $\langle P; \vec{Q}; S; ... \rangle$, where the atom P is called the *index*, the (possibly empty) sequence of atoms $\vec{Q}$ the *subgoals*, and the atom S the *partial answer*. If the list of subgoals $\vec{Q}$ is empty, a node is called an *answer node* with *answer* S. Otherwise it is called a *goal node*, and the first atom in $\vec{Q}$ is its *current subgoal*.

Intuitively, the list of subgoals $\vec{Q}$ contains the atoms that still have to be solved for the goal P. The subgoals are solved from left to right, hence the head of the list is the current subgoal. The current subgoal can be resolved against another answer node, which may entail instantiations of variables which will narrow down the partial answer S. The partial answer may eventually become a proper answer if all subgoals have been solved.

Note also that tuples may have more than three fields, which allows us to instantiate the algorithm scheme to perform various computational tasks. In its standard form, it implements ordinary deduction as outlined in Section 2.2. We may add an additional field $\vec{n}$ containing the nodes which justify the derivation of the current node; this will allow us to reconstruct proof graphs in Section 2.3. Lastly, we will introduce a field Δ containing atoms which were just assumed to hold when deriving the current node, and thus yield an abductive algorithm in Section 2.4.

Furthermore, the algorithm makes use of two tables:

Definition 2.2 (Answer and Wait Tables). An *answer table* is a partial function from atoms to sets of answer nodes. A *wait table* is a partial function from atoms to sets of goal nodes.

We denote the answer and wait tables in the algorithm by *Ans* and *Wait*, respectively. The set *Ans*(P) contains all answer nodes pertaining to the goal $\langle P \rangle$ found so far. The set *Wait*(P) contains all those nodes whose current subgoal is waiting for answers from $\langle P \rangle$. Whenever a new answer for $\langle P \rangle$ is produced, the computation of these waiting nodes is resumed.

The algorithm is given in Table 1 as a transition system defined by a relation $\rightarrow$ on states of the following form:

Table 1. Generic tabling algorithm

(root) $(\{\langle P\rangle\} \uplus \mathcal{N}, \mathit{Ans}, \mathit{Wait}) \rightarrow (\mathcal{N} \cup \mathcal{N}', \mathit{Ans}, \mathit{Wait})$
     if $\mathcal{N}' = \mathbf{generate}_{\mathcal{P}}(P)$

(ans) $(\{n\} \uplus \mathcal{N}, \mathit{Ans}, \mathit{Wait}) \rightarrow (\mathcal{N} \cup \mathcal{N}', \mathit{Ans}[P \mapsto \mathit{Ans}(P) \cup \{n\}], \mathit{Wait})$
     if n is an answer node with index P
          $\not\exists n' \in \mathit{Ans}(P) : n \preceq n'$
          $\mathcal{N}' = \bigcup_{n'' \in \mathit{Wait}(P)} \mathbf{resolve}(n'', n)$

(goal$_1$) $(\{n\} \uplus \mathcal{N}, \mathit{Ans}, \mathit{Wait}) \rightarrow (\mathcal{N} \cup \mathcal{N}', \mathit{Ans}, \mathit{Wait}[Q' \mapsto \mathit{Wait}(Q') \cup \{n\}])$
     if n is a goal node with current subgoal Q
          $\exists\, Q' \in \mathit{dom}(\mathit{Ans}) : Q \preceq Q'$
          $\mathcal{N}' = \bigcup_{n' \in \mathit{Ans}(Q')} \mathbf{resolve}(n, n')$

(goal$_2$) $(\{n\} \uplus \mathcal{N}, \mathit{Ans}, \mathit{Wait}) \rightarrow (\mathcal{N} \cup \{\langle Q\rangle\}, \mathit{Ans}[Q \mapsto \emptyset], \mathit{Wait}[Q \mapsto \{n\}])$
     if n is a goal node with current subgoal Q
          $\forall\, Q' \in \mathit{dom}(\mathit{Ans}) : Q \not\preceq Q'$

Definition 2.3 (States). A *state* is a triple $(\mathcal{N}, \mathit{Ans}, \mathit{Wait})$ where $\mathcal{N}$ is a set of nodes, *Ans* is an answer table, and *Wait* is a wait table.

A state of the form $(\{\langle P\rangle\}, \{P \mapsto \emptyset\}, \{P \mapsto \emptyset\})$ is an *initial state*. A state $\mathcal{S}$ is a *final state* iff there is no state $\mathcal{S}'$ and such that $\mathcal{S} \rightarrow \mathcal{S}'$.

We have left the description of the algorithm generic with respect to the following choices:

1. the structure of tuples (beyond the first three fields)
2. the subsumption relation $\preceq$ on answer nodes
3. the procedure **resolve**(n, n')
4. the procedure **generate**$_{\mathcal{P}}(P)$

Intuitively, if $n \preceq n'$ (*n is subsumed by n'*) holds, then the answer node n provides no more information than n'; in the algorithm, we can thus discard n and potentially ensure that the answer set is kept finite. The procedure **resolve**(n, n') is intended to take a goal node n and an answer node n' and combine the current subgoal of n with the answer provided by n' to get a new node with a simpler subgoal. The procedure **generate**$_{\mathcal{P}}(P)$ is intended to generate a set of tuples for a given query $\langle P\rangle$ by resolving P against the rules of program $\mathcal{P}$.

Starting in an initial state, rule (root) generates answer and goal nodes for a query $\langle P\rangle$. Answer nodes are processed by (ans) which inserts them into $\mathit{Ans}(P)$ if they are not subsumed by the answers already present there; likewise they are resolved against all nodes currently waiting for an answer to P. Goal nodes are either handled by (goal$_1$) or (goal$_2$), depending on whether the current subgoal is subsumed by an atom in the domain of the answer table. If it is, the already existing answers to that atom can be reused for the current subgoal, and the goal node is added to the wait table in (goal$_1$). Otherwise, (goal$_2$) spawns a new root node, and initializes the answer and wait tables.

2.2   Deductive Policy Evaluation

In its simplest instantiation, the algorithm performs ordinary deduction, i.e. starting in an initial state with root node $\langle P \rangle$ it will terminate in a state where $Ans(P)$ represents all instantiations of P which are deducible from the policy $\mathcal{P}$. We obtain this instantiation by defining:

1. Tuples are of the form $\langle P; \vec{Q}; S \rangle$.
2. $\langle P; [\,]; S \rangle \preceq_D \langle P; [\,]; S' \rangle$ iff $S \preceq S'$.
3. Let $n = \langle \_; [\,]; Q' \rangle$ be an answer node, and Q'' a fresh renaming of Q'.
$$\mathbf{resolve}^D(\langle P; [Q, \vec{Q}]; S \rangle, n) = \begin{cases} \{\langle P; \vec{Q}\theta; S\theta \rangle\} & \text{if } \theta = mgu(Q, Q'') \text{ exists,} \\ \emptyset & \text{otherwise} \end{cases}$$
4. $\mathbf{generate}_\mathcal{P}^D(P) = \bigcup_{(Q \leftarrow \vec{Q}) \in \mathcal{P}} \mathbf{resolve}^D(\langle P; [Q, \vec{Q}]; Q \rangle, \langle P; [\,]; P' \rangle)$
   where P' is a fresh renaming of P.

The subsumption relation $\preceq_D$ causes all answer nodes to be discarded whose partial solutions are "more instantiated" and therefore less general than already existing answers.

Example 2.4. The following policy allows the file Foo to be read by Bob and every employee who is associated with any work group (in particular, Alice):

    canRead(x, Foo) ← isEmployee(x), inWorkgroup(x, y).
    canRead(Bob, Foo).
    isEmployee(Alice).
    inWorkgroup(Alice, WG23).

Suppose the algorithm is started in an initial state with query $\langle \mathrm{canRead}(z, \mathrm{Foo}) \rangle$. The only possible start transition is (root), thus $\mathbf{generate}_\mathcal{P}^D(\mathrm{canRead}(z, \mathrm{Foo}))$ is called and produces a goal node

$$n_0 \equiv \langle \mathrm{canRead}(z, \mathrm{Foo}); [\mathrm{isEmployee}(x), \mathrm{inWorkgroup}(x, y)]; \mathrm{canRead}(x, \mathrm{Foo}) \rangle$$

and an answer node $\langle \mathrm{canRead}(z, \mathrm{Foo}); [\,]; \mathrm{canRead}(\mathrm{Bob}, \mathrm{Foo}) \rangle$. Eventually, the goal node will be resolved against the last two facts in the policy to yield a second answer $\langle \mathrm{canRead}(z, \mathrm{Foo}); [\,]; \mathrm{canRead}(\mathrm{Alice}, \mathrm{Foo}) \rangle$. The algorithm terminates with no further answers.

2.3   Constructing Proof Graphs

A simple extension of the above instantiation reconstructs the proof graphs for every answer in $Ans(P)$:

1. Tuples are of the form $\langle P; \vec{Q}; S; \vec{n}; Cl \rangle$, where Cl is a clause in $\mathcal{P}$ and $\vec{n}$ is a sequence of answer nodes called *child nodes*.
2. $\langle P; [\,]; S; \_; \_ \rangle \preceq_G \langle P; [\,]; S'; \_; \_ \rangle$ iff $S \preceq S'$.
3. Let $n = \langle \_; [\,]; Q'; \_; \_ \rangle$ be an answer node, and Q'' a fresh renaming of Q'.
$$\mathbf{resolve}^G(\langle P; [Q, \vec{Q}]; S; \vec{n}; Cl \rangle, n) = \begin{cases} \{\langle P; \vec{Q}\theta; S\theta; [\vec{n}, n]; Cl \rangle\} \\ \qquad \text{if } \theta = mgu(Q, Q'') \text{ exists,} \\ \emptyset \qquad \text{otherwise} \end{cases}$$

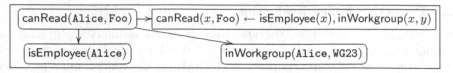

Fig. 1. Proof graph related to Example 2.4

4. Let P' be a fresh renaming of P.

$$\textbf{generate}_{\mathcal{P}}^{\mathsf{G}}(P) = \bigcup_{(Q \leftarrow \vec{Q}) \in \mathcal{P}} \textbf{resolve}^{\mathsf{G}}(\langle P; [Q, \vec{Q}]; Q; []; Cl \rangle, \langle P; []; P'; []; Cl \rangle)$$

When resolving a goal against an answer node, the answer node is inserted as a new child node, as justification for the resolution step. In order to reconstruct the proof graph, an answer node is interpreted to have edges pointing to each of its child nodes and an edge pointing to the rule Rl which has been used to derive that particular answer. Figure 1 shows a proof graph for the derivation of canRead(Alice, Foo) in Example 2.4.

Proof graphs are useful for auditing and explaining positive access decisions. If the predicates are associated with meta-information on how they can be translated into natural language, the proof graph could also be represented as a sentence such as "Alice can read Foo because Alice is an employee and Alice is in workgroup WG23".

2.4 Abductive Policy Evaluation

In our setting, the term abduction relates to the following problem. Given an atom P and a policy $\mathcal{P}$, find all sets A of atoms such that P is deducible from $\mathcal{P}$ augmented by A. The set A is called an *abductive solution* for query P, and we require that the predicate names occurring in A are from a given set of *abducible* predicate names. The choice of the abducibles usually depends on the application domain and the kind of analysis we want to perform. In many cases, we are interested in all possible abductive solutions, so we specify all predicate names in $\mathcal{P}$ to be abducible. We define $\mathcal{A}$ to be the set of all ground instantiations of abducible predicates.

In the context of decentralized authorization, the parameters of the abductive solution may be unknown and may thus have to be left uninstantiated. For example, the solution could specify a delegation chain where the identities of the intermediate delegators cannot be fixed a priori. Therefore, the abductive solutions we are interested in may contain variables that can be arbitrarily instantiated; this is sometimes referred to as *floundering* abduction. This way, each solution can represent an infinite number of ground solutions. We can provide a relatively simple algorithm to solve the floundering abduction problem (compared to e.g. [13,14]) mainly because our policies are monotonic.

The generic tabling scheme is instantiated as follows:

1. Tuples are of the form $\langle P; \vec{Q}; S; \Delta \rangle$, where Δ is a set of atoms called the *residue*.

2. $\langle P;[\,];S;\Delta\rangle \preceq_{\mathtt{A}} \langle P;[\,];S';\Delta'\rangle$ iff $|\Delta| \geq |\Delta'|$ and there exists a substitution θ such that $S = S'\theta$ and $\Delta \supseteq \Delta'\theta$.

3. Let $n = \langle \_;[\,];Q';\Delta'\rangle$ be an answer node, and Q'',Δ'' fresh renamings of Q',Δ'.

$$\mathbf{resolve}^{\mathtt{A}}(\langle P;[Q,\vec{Q}];S;\Delta\rangle, n) = \begin{cases} \{\langle P;\vec{Q}\theta;S\theta;\Delta\theta \cup \Delta''\theta\rangle\} \\ \qquad\qquad \text{if } \theta = mgu(Q,Q'') \text{ exists,} \\ \emptyset \qquad\qquad \text{otherwise} \end{cases}$$

4. $\mathbf{generate}^{\mathtt{A}}_{\mathcal{P},\mathcal{A}}(P) = \bigcup_{(Q \leftarrow \vec{Q}) \in \mathcal{P}} \mathbf{resolve}^{\mathtt{A}}(\langle P;[Q,\vec{Q}];Q;\emptyset\rangle, \langle \_;[\,];P;\emptyset\rangle) \cup$
$\{\langle P;[\,];P;\{P\}\rangle : P \text{ is abducible}\}$

The main idea is thus to extend tuples with a *residue* Δ, containing atoms which are just *assumed* to hold in the process of the algorithm. Such atoms are initially inserted into the residue by $\mathbf{generate}^{\mathtt{A}}_{\mathcal{P},\mathcal{A}}$ whenever an abducible goal $\langle P\rangle$ is encountered. They are then propagated using $\mathbf{resolve}^{\mathtt{A}}$ such that for each hypothetical answer S obtained, Δ expresses which atoms must be added to $\mathcal{P}$ in order to be able to deduce it.

In general, there are infinitely many abductive solutions: by monotonicity, any extension of an abductive solution is trivially also an abductive solution. Clearly, the abductive algorithm should only consider solutions that are not simple supersets of already existing ones. Similarly, we are not interested in a new solution that is an instantiation of (and thus less general than) an already existing one. The subsumption relation $\preceq_{\mathtt{A}}$ makes sure that such "uninteresting" answers are not considered.

The correctness of the algorithm is formalized by the following theorems.

Theorem 2.5 (Soundness). *If $(\mathcal{N}, \mathrm{Ans}, \mathrm{Wait})$ is reachable from an initial state $\mathcal{S}_0$ then for all $P \in dom(\mathrm{Ans})$: $\langle P';[\,];S;\Delta\rangle \in \mathrm{Ans}(P)$ implies that for all substitutions ϑ such that all elements of $\Delta\vartheta$ are ground it holds that $P = P'$, $S\vartheta \preceq P$, and $S\vartheta \in T^{\omega}_{\mathcal{P} \cup \Delta\vartheta}(\emptyset)$.*

Theorem 2.6 (Completeness). *If $\mathcal{S}_f \equiv (\mathcal{N}, \mathrm{Ans}, \mathrm{Wait})$ is a final state reachable from an initial state $\mathcal{S}_0$ then for all $P \in dom(\mathrm{Ans})$: $S \in T^{\omega}_{\mathcal{P} \cup \mathcal{A}}(\emptyset)$ and $S \preceq P$ implies that there exists a substitution ϑ, an atom S', and a residue Δ such that $S'\vartheta = S$, $\Delta\vartheta \subseteq \mathcal{A}$, and $\langle P;[\,];S';\Delta\rangle \in \mathrm{Ans}(P)$.*

Example 2.7. Consider again the program of Example 2.4, but assume that it no longer contains the atom inWorkgroup(Alice, WG23). Furthermore, suppose that both isEmployee and inWorkgroup are abducible predicate names.

For query $\langle \mathsf{canRead}(z, \mathsf{Foo})\rangle$ the procedure $\mathbf{generate}^{\mathtt{A}}_{\mathcal{P},\mathcal{A}}$ executes as the one described in Example 2.4, and produces in particular the goal node n_0. Using (goal_2), a new root $\langle \mathsf{isEmployee}(x)\rangle$ will be inserted. The call to the function $\mathbf{generate}^{\mathtt{A}}_{\mathcal{P},\mathcal{A}}(\mathsf{isEmployee}(x))$ produces answer nodes

$\langle \mathsf{isEmployee}(x)\rangle;[\,];\mathsf{isEmployee}(\mathsf{Alice});\emptyset\rangle$
$\langle \mathsf{isEmployee}(x);[\,];\mathsf{isEmployee}(x);\{\mathsf{isEmployee}(x)\}\rangle$

Upon termination of the algorithm, $Ans(\mathsf{canRead}(z, \mathsf{Foo}))$ contains answer node which exhibit the following answer/residue pairs:

$(\mathsf{canRead}(\mathtt{Bob}, \mathsf{Foo}),\quad \emptyset)$
$(\mathsf{canRead}(\mathtt{Alice}, \mathsf{Foo}), \{\mathsf{inWorkgroup}(\mathtt{Alice}, y)\})$
$(\mathsf{canRead}(x, \mathsf{Foo}),\quad \{\mathsf{isEmployee}(x), \mathsf{inWorkgroup}(x, y)\})$

The first one does not require any assumptions, and the other two give sets of hypothetical assumptions in order for answers of a particular shape to hold. For example, to grant read access for $\mathtt{Alice}$, she would have to show that she is member of some work group y. All other possible abductive solutions are subsumed by these three answers.

3   Termination Conditions

The abduction algorithm from Section 2.4 is guaranteed to terminate if there is a finite set of answers such that every valid answer would be subsumed by some element in the set. However, there are cases in which every complete set of answers is infinite and the algorithm does not terminate.

Example 3.1. Consider the policy

$$\mathsf{canRead}(\mathit{user}, \mathit{file}) \leftarrow \mathsf{deleg}(\mathit{delegator}, \mathit{user}, \mathit{file}), \mathsf{canRead}(\mathit{delegator}, \mathit{file}).$$

In this example, $\mathsf{canRead}(x, y)$ indicates that principal x has read access to resource y, and $\mathsf{deleg}(x, y, z)$ indicates that principal x delegates read access for resource z to principal y. This policy implements a simple variant of discretionary access control: users can delegate read access if they have read access themselves. The abductive query $\mathsf{canRead}(\mathtt{Alice}, \mathsf{Foo})$ has an infinite set of answers with growing residues:

$\{\mathsf{canRead}(\mathtt{Alice}, \mathsf{Foo})\}$
$\{\mathsf{deleg}(x_1, \mathtt{Alice}, \mathsf{Foo}), \mathsf{canRead}(x_1, \mathsf{Foo})\}$
$\{\mathsf{deleg}(x_1, \mathtt{Alice}, \mathsf{Foo}), \mathsf{deleg}(x_2, x_1, \mathsf{Foo}), \mathsf{canRead}(x_2, \mathsf{Foo})\}$
$\{\mathsf{deleg}(x_1, \mathtt{Alice}, \mathsf{Foo}), \mathsf{deleg}(x_2, x_1, \mathsf{Foo}), \mathsf{deleg}(x_3, x_2, \mathsf{Foo}), \mathsf{canRead}(x_3, \mathsf{Foo})\}$
$\dots$

The answers do not subsume each other: being able to provide the missing facts corresponding to one of these answer does not imply being able to provide the facts corresponding to any other answer. Clearly, the algorithm does not terminate.

There are different ways to approach this problem. If the algorithm is used for debugging policies or for explaining access denials to users, non-termination may not be a serious problem, if the answers can be returned one by one. Ideally, the answers would be returned in some meaningful order, e.g. sorted by simplicity. This can be achieved by serializing the non-deterministic algorithm into a deterministic one with a fixed order of transitions.

Sometimes, however, it is important to ensure both termination and completeness. For example, the algorithm could be used to verify that there is *no* abductive answer of a certain form; this would require a complete set of abductive solutions. This section discusses various strategies of ensuring termination.

3.1   Subsumption Weakening

One such strategy is to replace the subsumption relation $\preceq_A$ by a weaker relation. Intuitively, a weaker subsumption relation has the effect of filtering out more answers in the (ans)-transition; in other words, fewer answers are deemed "relevant" or "interesting". As long as this alternative subsumption relation enjoys a sort of compactness property (essentially that it is not possible to indefinitely keep adding new answers that are not subsumed) then the algorithm is guaranteed to terminate.

Theorem 3.2. *Let $\sqsubseteq$ be a partial order on nodes such that in every infinite sequence of nodes $n_1, n_2, \ldots$ containing only a finite number of distinct constants, there are nodes n_i and n_j with $i < j$ and $n_j \sqsubseteq n_i$. If the subsumption relation $\preceq_A$ on nodes in the algorithm is replaced by $\sqsubseteq$ then all transition paths starting from an initial state are of finite length.*

The following definition specifies two examples of subsumption relations that satisfy the condition of the theorem.

Definition 3.3. *Let $n = \langle P; [\,]; S; \Delta \rangle$ and $n' = \langle P; [\,]; S'; \Delta' \rangle$. Then $n \sqsubseteq_0 n'$ iff $S \preceq S'$ and the predicate names occurring in Δ' are a subset of the predicate names occurring in Δ. Let M be a positive integer. Then $n \sqsubseteq_M n'$ iff $|\Delta| > M$ or $n \preceq_A n'$.*

The first relation, $\sqsubseteq_0$, is useful if one is only interested in the predicate names of the missing facts, not their parameters. For example, a security administrator may be interested in the question *"is it possible for Alice to gain read access to Foo if someone, no matter who, is granted write access?"*. Here, the administrator is only interested in whether an abductive answer containing canWrite exists.

The second relation, $\sqsubseteq_M$, is parameterized on a constant M and filters out answers with more than M missing facts. This method could be used in the non-termination example above to ensure termination by cutting off the delegation chain at a certain maximum length.

3.2   Static Termination Analysis

The advantage of weakening the subsumption relation is a strong termination guarantee for all possible policies, queries and sets of abducibles. The downside of this approach is a correspondingly weaker completeness result: completeness only holds with respect to the subsumption relation.

We now develop an alternative approach that guarantees termination under the original subsumption relation, as long as the policy satisfies a certain property. To gain an intuition for this property, consider the necessary conditions for non-termination. The algorithm does not terminate only if there is an infinite sequence of abductive answers, each of which is not subsumed by any previous answer. This is only possible if the residues Δ are growing unboundedly. Since the answers can only contain the (finitely many) predicate names and constants occurring in the policy and the query, it must be the case that there is a predicate name p such that for all integers N there is always a residue in the sequence in which there are more than N occurrences of p. But this is only possible if the policy is recursive.

Verbaeten [15] provides a sufficient termination condition for general abductive logic programs that requires non-recursivity. But recursion plays an important role in authorization policies, for example for specifying delegation. Fortunately, due to the subsumption check, recursion does not always lead to non-termination. In order for the sequence to pass the subsumption condition, the p-atoms in the residues must form increasingly bigger structures that are connected via an unbounded number of shared variables. In Example 3.1, we can see that non-termination stems from the recursive canRead condition, and furthermore the sharing of the variable *delegator* with a second body predicate which is not in the head of the clause: this essentially causes the creation of an increasing linked structure of deleg atoms with newly created, shared variables.

This leads to a necessary condition for non-termination, the negation of which is then a sufficient condition for termination. The following definition is used in the formalization of the condition.

Definition 3.4. A clause $R \leftarrow \vec{R}$ is an *unfolding* of a clause $P \leftarrow P_1, ..., P_i, ..., P_n$ if there exists a clause $Q \leftarrow \vec{Q} \in \mathcal{P}$ such that P_i and Q unify with mgu θ, and $R = P\theta$ and $\vec{R} = (P_1, ..., P_{i-1}, \vec{Q}, P_{i+1}, ..., P_n)\theta$. A clause C can be *unfolded* to yield a clause C' if C' is obtained from C by 0 or more unfolding transformations.

Theorem 3.5. *Let $\mathcal{P}$ be a set of clauses such that no clause can be unfolded to yield a clause with the following property:*

- *The head predicate occurs in a body atom P.*
- *It has a second body atom Q that is abducible and shares a variable with P which does not occur in the head.*

Then all transition paths starting from an initial state are of finite length.

The condition in Theorem 3.5 is decidable; in fact, a static analyzer for checking it can be written in Prolog in less than a hundred lines. The static analyzer could then be run before an abductive query, and if the condition is not satisfied, the user could be warned that evaluation of the query may not terminate. Preliminary experiments have shown that the condition gives a relatively accurate approximation for non-termination. In particular, many recursive policies can be shown to guarantee termination.

4   Application Scenarios

This section illustrates three possible applications of the abduction algorithm in the area of policy-based access control.

4.1 Explaining Access Denials to Users

In current access control systems, the user is often left without guidance if access is denied. Consider the following policy of some company:

canRead(x, /workgroup23/) ← isEmployee(x), inWorkgroup(x, WG23).
canRead(x, /workgroup23/) ← isManager(x).

Suppose employee Alice submits the credential isEmployee(Alice) upon log-on to the authorization system, but forgets to submit the credential that she is member of workgroup WG23. If she then tries to access the folder /workgroup23/, she will just get the answer "access denied". Using the abduction technique, the produced residues {inWorkgroup(Alice, WG23)} and {isManager(Alice)} could be used to construct the more helpful message "access would have been granted if you had shown that you are a member of work group WG23 or that you are a manager".

If parts of the policy itself are considered confidential, the abductive solutions can be filtered by a *disclosure* meta-policy. Disclosure policies have been studied extensively in the area of automated trust negotiation (e.g. [16,17,18]). A simpler (but slightly less fine-grained) approach would be to tag particular atoms in clause bodies that must not be abduced.

4.2 Administration of Authorization Policies

The next example illustrates the use of the abduction algorithm in a policy analysis and debugging tool. Consider the following example rules that are part of a policy of an electronic health record (EHR) service:

$$\text{treatingClinician}(cli, pat) \leftarrow \tag{1}$$
$$\text{roleMember}(pat, \texttt{Patient}), \text{roleMember}(cli, \texttt{Clinician}), \text{consent}(pat, cli).$$

$$\text{canReadEHR}(cli, pat, subj) \leftarrow \tag{2}$$
$$\text{treatingClinician}(cli, pat), \text{nonSensitive}(subj).$$

$$\text{canReadEHR}(cli, pat, \texttt{Psych}) \leftarrow \tag{3}$$
$$\text{treatingClinician}(cli, pat), \text{isCertifiedPsychiatrist}(cli).$$

$$\text{canReadEHR}(pat, pat, subj) \leftarrow \tag{4}$$
$$\text{roleMember}(pat, \texttt{Patient}), \text{nonSensitive}(subj).$$

Rule (1) specifies that a clinician *cli* is a *treating clinician* of patient *pat* if the patient has given consent to treatment. The predicate canReadEHR(x, *pat*, *subj*) is used to check if principal x is permitted to read patient *pat*'s record items on subject matter *subj*, where subject matters range over categories such as psychiatry, cardiology, radiology etc. Some subject matters, such as Psych, are deemed sensitive and have stricter access requirements. The predicate nonSensitive(*subj*) defines the range of subjects that are deemed non-sensitive. Rule (2) allows clinicians to read their patients' record items on non-sensitive subjects. Rule (3) specifies that only psychiatrists are permitted to access their patients' psychiatric data. Finally, Rule (4) permits patients to view their own data, but only the items regarding non-sensitive subject matters.

The rationale behind Rule (4) is that patients should not be allowed to access data that could potentially distress them if read without professional guidance. In particular, they should not be able to autonomously access their psychiatric data. In order to check if the policy really implements the intended behavior, the security administrator can issue the abductive query canReadEHR(pat, pat, Psych) to see if there is a way for patients to access their own psychiatric data.

Assuming that all predicates apart from canReadEHR and treatingClinician are abducible, we obtain an answer with residues

{roleMember(pat, Patient), nonSensitive(Psych)}.

This is easily dismissed as unproblematic if the administrator can verify that there is no way of inserting a fact nonSensitive(Psych). But we also get a second answer with residue

{roleMember(pat, Patient), roleMember(pat, Clinician),

isCertifiedPsychiatrist(pat), consent(pat, pat)}.

This answer is more troublesome: a patient can read what her psychiatrist has written if she happens to be a certified psychiatrist too and has given consent to treat herself. This may or may not be regarded as a bug in the policy; but in any case, as there are no further abductive answers, and by completeness and termination of the algorithm, it is guaranteed that there are no further loopholes in the policy.

4.3   Automated Delegation

The following scenario takes place in a multi-domain grid computing environment. Alice is a user who wishes to submit a job to be computed on a grid compute cluster. She knows that during the execution of her job, a node from the compute cluster will have to access her file `alice.dat` stored on a file server in a different domain. Therefore, at some point, an authorization query of the form canRead(Node, `alice.dat`) will be evaluated on the file server. Suppose the file server's policy contains the rule from Example 3.1 and the fact canRead(Alice, `alice.dat`).

As Alice's job may take many days to complete, she wants to know in advance which delegation credentials she has to submit to the file server, so she sends the abductive query canRead($node$, `alice.dat`) to the server. Her query contains a variable $node$ in place of the node that will eventually access her file, because she cannot know its identity in advance.

The first returned answer is the trivial answer where *node* is instantiated to `Alice` and the residue is empty. The second answer is uninstantiated and has the singleton residue {deleg(`Alice`, *node*, `alice.dat`)}. This would require direct delegation to the node, which is not convenient as its identity is not known to Alice. The third answer has residue

{deleg(`Alice`, x, `alice.dat`), deleg(x, *node*, `alice.dat`)}.

This answer represents a delegation chain of depth 2 and is the most useful in this situation, because Alice knows the identity of the compute cluster's scheduling service. Thus she can submit a delegation credential

deleg(`Alice`, `Scheduler`, `alice.dat`)

to the scheduling service along with her job and a partially instantiated missing-credential "template"

{deleg(`Scheduler`, *node*, `alice.dat`)}.

The service will then execute the job on some node, e.g. `Node42`, passing along Alice's delegation credential as well as a newly created (or cached) credential instantiated from the template, namely deleg(`Scheduler`, `Node42`, `alice.dat`). When the node eventually requests access to Alice's file on the file server, it submits both Alice's and the scheduler's delegation credentials to support the request. Access is then guaranteed to be granted as long as the file server's policy has not been changed in the meantime.

5   Discussion

Related work. There has been very little research on improving the usability of authorization systems in the case of access denial. The *Know* system [19] can provide helpful feedback to the user in the form of a list of conditions under which the policy allows access. A separate disclosure policy restricts the information revealed by the feedback. However, the authors only consider policies of rather limited expressiveness, namely those that can be written as propositional boolean formulas; hence the feedback can be computed using Ordered Binary Decision Diagrams (OBDDs).

Bonatti et al. [20] have developed a framework for explaining both positive and negative access decisions in the context of a Datalog-based authorization language. For explaining access denials, they essentially compute a tabled failed proof graph (called explanation graph) for the query. Users can navigate through the graph, which is represented in controlled natural language, to see where the proof failed. To keep the overhead as low as possible, they do not attempt to search for the missing facts that would complete the failed proof. We have shown in this paper that we can compute the sets of missing facts while maintaining a low implementation overhead.

Koshutanski and Massacci [18] employ abduction for interactive credential retrieval: if the credentials presented by the user are not sufficient to allow access, the service computes a set of missing credentials (filtered by a disclosure policy) and returns it to the user who can either supply the required credentials or decline, in which case the process iterates. This process terminates because it is assumed that the set of constants that could be used as credential parameters is finite and known to the service in advance. The policy can then be reduced to propositional (variable-free) formulas. However, we believe that this is an unreasonable assumption, particularly in decentralized applications where authorization is based on attributes as the identities of principals in delegation chains are not known a priori.

Becker and Nanz [21] have developed an algorithm for analyzing authorization policies in which facts (such as current role activations) can be added and removed dynamically by commands (such as activating or deactivating a role). The paper presupposes a function for computing sufficient preconditions for executing such commands, but does not explain how it can be implemented. The abductive procedure presented in this paper could be used to implement the required function.

Implementation. Prototypes of the abductive algorithm and the static termination analysis have been implemented in OCaml and in XSB Prolog, respectively. The SecPAL system [5] supports proof graph generation based on the algorithm presented here. Current and future work on the SecPAL system will include integration of tools based on our abduction algorithm. As SecPAL is compiled into Datalog with constraints, the implementation will also have to handle constraints. Extending the abduction algorithm with constraints is relatively simple, assuming the existence of satisfiability and subsumption checking operations. In essence, tuples are extended to include a constraint on variables occurring in the predicate and the residue. In the resolution step, the conjunction of the constraints from the two input nodes is computed and checked for satisfiability. Furthermore, the subsumption check is extended to also check if the constraint from one node is subsumed by the constraint from the other node.

Conclusion. Declarative authorization languages can increase the flexibility, scalability, and manageability of access control systems. However, they are not without their own usability problems, as many authorization policies are intrinsically complex. To alleviate this complexity, tools are needed for facilitating access auditing and review, meaningful user feedback, policy diagnosis and debugging, and automated credential retrieval. In this paper, we have shown how a tabled resolution algorithm for policy evaluation can be extended to create proof graphs and to compute sets of missing proof facts using abduction. For the abductive algorithm, we have explored methods for guaranteeing termination and complete answers. The algorithms are general enough to be applicable to a wide range of existing systems. We believe that tools based on these algorithms will help the declarative policy approach gain wider adoption in the industry.

References

1. Li, N., Mitchell, J.C., Winsborough, W.H.: Design of a role-based trust management framework. In: Symposium on Security and Privacy, pp. 114–130 (2002)
2. DeTreville, J.: Binder, a logic-based security language. In: IEEE Symposium on Security and Privacy, pp. 105–113 (2002)
3. Li, N., Mitchell, J.C.: Datalog with constraints: A foundation for trust management languages. Practical Aspects of Declarative Languages, 58–73 (2003)
4. Becker, M.Y., Sewell, P.: Cassandra: Flexible trust management, applied to electronic health records. In: IEEE Computer Security Foundations Workshop (2004)
5. Becker, M.Y., Fournet, C., Gordon, A.D.: Design and semantics of a decentralized authorization language. In: IEEE Computer Security Foundations Symposium (2007)
6. Peirce, C.: Abduction and Induction. In: Philosophical Writings of Peirce (1955)
7. Kakas, A.C., Kowalski, R.A., Toni, F.: The role of abduction in logic programming. In: Gabbay, D.M., Hogger, C.J., Robinson, J.A. (eds.) Handbook of Logic in Artificial Intelligence and Logic Programming, vol. 5, pp. 235–324 (1998)
8. Becker, M.Y., Nanz, S.: The role of abduction in declarative authorization policies. Technical Report MSR-TR-2007-105, Microsoft Research (2007), http://research.microsoft.com/research/pubs/view.aspx?tr_id=1348
9. Becker, M.Y., Sewell, P.: Cassandra: distributed access control policies with tunable expressiveness. In: IEEE International Workshop on Policies for Distributed Systems and Networks, pp. 159–168 (2004)
10. Tamaki, H., Sato, T.: OLD resolution with tabulation. In: Shapiro, E. (ed.) ICLP 1986. LNCS, vol. 225, pp. 84–98. Springer, Heidelberg (1986)
11. Chen, W., Warren, D.S.: Tabled evaluation with delaying for general logic programs. Journal of the ACM 43(1), 20–74 (1996)
12. Abiteboul, S., Hull, R., Vianu, V.: Foundations of Databases. Addison-Wesley, Reading (1995)
13. Alferes, J.J., Pereira, L.M., Swift, T.: Abduction in well-founded semantics and generalized stable models via tabled dual programs. Theory and Practice of Logic Programming 4(4), 383–428 (2004)
14. Denecker, M., Schreye, D.D.: SLDNFA: An abductive procedure for abductive logic programs. Journal of Logic Programming 34(2), 111–167 (1998)
15. Verbaeten, S.: Termination analysis for abductive general logic programs. In: International Conference on Logic Programming, pp. 365–379 (1999)
16. Winsborough, W.H., Seamons, K.E., Jones, V.E.: Automated trust negotiation. In: DARPA Information Survivability Conference and Exposition, vol. 1 (2000)
17. Winsborough, W.H., Li, N.: Towards practical automated trust negotiation. In: IEEE International Workshop on Policies for Distributed Systems and Networks (2002)
18. Koshutanski, H., Massacci, F.: Interactive access control for web services. In: International Information Security Conference, pp. 151–166 (2004)
19. Kapadia, A., Sampemane, G., Campbell, R.H.: Know why your access was denied: regulating feedback for usable security. In: ACM conference on computer and communications security, pp. 52–61 (2004)
20. Bonatti, P.A., Olmedilla, D., Peer, J.: Advanced policy explanations on the web. In: European Conference on Artificial Intelligence, pp. 200–204 (2006)
21. Becker, M.Y., Nanz, S.: A logic for state-modifying authorization policies. In: European Symposium on Research in Computer Security (2007)

Unification of Arrays in Spreadsheets with Logic Programming

Philip T. Cox and Patrick Nicholson

Faculty of Computer Science, Dalhousie University,
6050 University Avenue, Halifax, NS, Canada B3H 1W5
{Philip.cox,Pat}@Dal.ca

Abstract. Unification, one of the key processes underlying logic programming (LP), provides a powerful mechanism for assembling and disassem-
bling structures, lists in particular, by matching patterns. In recent work, we
showed how spreadsheets can be enhanced by adding a visual form of LP in
which lists, the fundamental structures of LP, are replaced by rectangular
arrays, the fundamental structures of spreadsheets. The benefits include enhanced programmability and a way to specify high level templates for spreadsheet structures. Here, we focus on the structure of arrays, and describe the
array unification algorithm underlying our current implementation.

Keywords: Spreadsheet, logic programming, array, unification.

1 Introduction

Spreadsheets first appeared in 1979 with the introduction of VisiCalc on the Apple
II, contributing significantly to the rapid adoption of personal computers [2]. Spreadsheets were perhaps the first applications to allow non-technical users to solve problems
of importance to them in their work and daily lives. Since spreadsheets present a
straightforward visualisation of calculations organised on ledger-like sheets, they were
ideally suited to the graphics-based PCs which arrived in the mid-80s, accelerating the
proliferation of computer use by non-technical people. As a result, spreadsheet languages, of which Microsoft Excel is the prototypical example, are among the most successful
and widely used end-user programming languages.

Unfortunately, the characteristics of spreadsheets that have made them popular,
have also made them dangerous. Companies which would normally invest heavily in
thoroughly engineered, reliable tools for important tasks, began to entrust spreadsheets,
cobbled together by nonprogrammers, with complex and critically important calculations. Spreadsheets, however, were never intended for this purpose. They provide sim-
plistic and cumbersome programming capabilities, and no sound software engineering
tools or methodology. As a result, not only are spreadsheets among the most widely
used programming tools, but spreadsheet programs are among the most likely to contain
errors.

Researchers have recently turned their attention to these problems, at least partly
motivated by widely publicised instances of costly accounting errors due to faulty

P. Hudak and D.S. Warren (Eds.): PADL 2008, LNCS 4902, pp. 100–115, 2008.
© Springer-Verlag Berlin Heidelberg 2008

spreadsheets, and legislation assigning liability for these errors to company managers and directors [12]. This work focusses on testing and debugging methodologies and tools [8,15], higher level design of spreadsheet structures [1,7,11], and improved programmability [3,13,19].

Since the mid-80s, various combinations of logic programming (LP) and spreadsheets have been proposed. Some representative examples are as follows. In NEXCEL, an array can represent a predicate defined by a set of clauses, the bodies of which consist of literals referring to other arrays as predicates [4]. Similarly, an array in LogiCalc can be a table defining a relation, and cells can contain queries, lists or any other terms [10]. In XcelLog, cells contain expressions which are translated into clauses for execution by an underlying LP execution mechanism [14]. In two other early systems, spreadsheets provided an interface for displaying the values of variables instantiated by a logic program separate from the sheet [16,18]. In these systems, the normal data flow computational model of spreadsheets is replaced with some form of LP, resulting in a programming environment significantly different from that provided by Microsoft Excel and similar products. They do not, therefore, help to alleviate the shortcomings of spreadsheets discussed above.

Although rectangular arrays of cells are fundamental components in the structure of all but the most trivial spreadsheets, they are not directly supported by common spreadsheet languages, and must be managed by the user according to some conventions that he or she has established. This is analogous to assembly languages, in which high level structures such as while loops are not provided, and must be constructed from individual instructions according to some pattern. In a spreadsheet, an array is established by filling the cells in a rectangle with contents that are related to each other in some way, and, if they are formulae, possibly refer to the contents of cells in another array. Hence, to a large extent, spreadsheet programming involves specifying the structure of arrays, relationships between arrays and computations that fill arrays with values. Similarly, logic programming involves specifying the structure of terms, relationships between terms, and computations that bind variables occurring in terms. Based on this analogy, L-sheets, a recently proposed extension to spreadsheets, incorporates a form of LP in which unification of terms is replaced by unification of arrays [6]. In contrast to previous spreadsheet/LP combinations, L-sheets delivers the following benefits:

- A visual, high-level specification of spreadsheet structure.
- Enhanced programmability.
- The existing "formula-in-cell" model, familiar to current users, is preserved.
- User-defined abstractions are built in the sheet interface, allowing for a smooth transition from novice to expert user.

The work reported here focusses on issues that have arisen during the implementation of an L-sheets prototype, array unification in particular. Section 2 informally describes L-sheets via a sequence of examples which illustate both typical use in a business setting, and more unusual applications. In Section 3, we describe the unification of arrays by presenting the Prolog implementation of the array matching algorithm which underlies the current prototype. We conclude with a discussion in Section 4 of the current state of this project and issues for future investigation.

2   L-Sheets

In this section, we present several examples to illustrate the main features of L-sheets. The reader is encouraged to consult [6] for a more formal description. An L-sheets application consists of a collection of *worksheets*, like the familiar Microsoft Excel worksheets, and *program sheets*. Program sheets contain definitions as described below. Cells in a worksheet can contain formulae possibly referring to other cells. In addition, definitions from program sheets can be applied to a worksheet, resulting in formulae being added to the content of some cells.

2.1   Templates

This example, from Erwig *et al.* [7], illustrates what we envisage to be one of the most common uses of L-sheets, and involves specifying the structure of a budget worksheet, an example of which is shown in Figure 1. This worksheet is an example of a family of worksheets in which blocks of three columns headed Qnty, Cost and Total, each containing data for one year, are repeated as many times as necessary. Similarly, rows for budget items are repeated as necessary. Clearly, formulae in repeated cells and formulae referring to repeated cells conform to a pattern.

Fig. 1. Budget worksheet displaying formulae (from [7] p.299)

Figure 2 depicts an L-sheets program sheet consisting of two definitions, **budget** and **years**, which together specify the family of budget worksheets exemplified by that in Figure 1. The **budget** definition has a single *case*, the *head* of which is a *template* named **budget**, represented by a pale grey rectangle. The *body* of this case consists of a single template, named **years**. Body templates are dark grey. Templates contain *parameters*, which are arrays, drawn as grids similar to a worksheet grid. In our example, the **budget** template has a single parameter, while the **years** template in the body of the case of the **budget** definition has two.

A definition is analogous to a set of clauses defining a predicate in Prolog. In particular, a case corresponds to a clause, a template to a literal, and the parameters of a template to the list of terms from which a literal is composed.

The structure of an array in a template is indicated by the colour of its grid lines. A vertical grey line indicates that the width of the subarray in which the line lies is variable. For example, consider the array in the **budget** template. Although the subarray with the heavy outline labelled **A** is drawn with two columns, the line separating these columns is grey, so the subarray **A** is variable in width. Similarly, grey horizontal lines indicate variable height. With this is mind, we see that the array in the **budget** template has one column, followed by a variable number of columns, followed by two columns. It also has two rows, followed by a variable number of rows, followed by one row. Values of subarrays are displayed when they are known. For example, the value of the 1x1 subarray at the left end of the second row is the string "Category". The annotation *F1* on the 1x1 subarray at the bottom right corner is not part of the program. It has been added to indicate that the subarray contains an Excel-like formula, as shown in the legend.

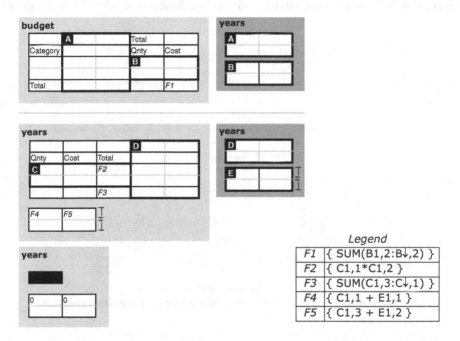

Fig. 2. An L-sheets program defining a family of budget spreadsheets. The annotations *F1, F2,...* are not part of the program, but have been added to indicate cells which contain formulae, shown in the legend. (from [6]).

The definition **budget** specifies that an array is an instance of a budget worksheet if it has the structure described in the previous paragraph and contents as shown, and the subarrays named **A** and **B** have the structure and content specified by the definition **years**.

To apply this definition to a worksheet, the user selects a rectangular array of cells in the sheet to correspond to the parameter (Figure 3a). A (virtual) *goal template* named **budget** is created with the selected array as its parameter. As in Prolog execution, this goal template is unified with the head of the first (and only) case for **budget**. This involves unifying the selected array with the parameter of the head template, using the algorithm described in Section 3, which matches the structure of the two arrays and adds the contents of the subarrays of the parameter array of the head template to the corresponding cells of the goal parameter array (Figure 3b). In particular, the formula $F1$ is rewritten to refer to the appropriate cells in the worksheet, then added to the content of the bottom-right cell of the rectangular array selected in the worksheet. Since the second column of the subarray **B** corresponds to column J in the sheet and stretches from row 5 to row 7, $F1$ is rewritten to SUM(J5:J7). Note that the syntax of formulae in a program sheet differs from that of formulae in a worksheet. In particular, in a program sheet formula a reference consists of a subarray name followed by row and column indices, while a reference in a worksheet is to a named column and numbered row in the whole sheet. Also the ↓ in the formula SUM(B1,2:B↓,2) denotes the last row of the referenced subarray **B**. Note that the content of a cell in a worksheet or a subarray in a program

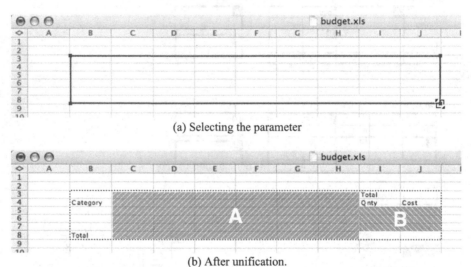

(a) Selecting the parameter

(b) After unification.
The dotted outline and shaded areas have been added for explanatory purposes.

(c) Spreadsheet after execution, displaying formulae.

Fig. 3. Applying **budget** definition to a sheet

sheet is a set of formulae, rather than a single formula. This is because a cell is analogous to a Prolog variable, which may be bound to several terms provided they are unifiable, unlike cells in a normal spreadsheet, which are data flow variables subject to the single-assignment rule [5]. If a cell contains several formulae, then they must all produce the same value, otherwise evaluation fails.

The above execution step replaces the initial goal template with a **years** template, derived from the body of the applied case, and containing the two rectangular arrays from the worksheet, indicated by shading, to which subarrays **A** and **B** were bound by the unification. Execution then proceeds in a fashion analogous to Prolog.

The first case of **years** contains two *rulers*, used here to indicate that the second parameter of the head templates and the array **E** in the body template both have height H. The black rectangle in the head of the second case of the **years** definition represents an array which is 0 in at least one dimension. Also, if a subarray which is variable in one or both dimensions contains a formula, then when the subarray is unified with an array of fixed size, the formula is extended in the same way that a formula in Excel is extended; that is, by appropriately incrementing the indices of references in the formula. Note that, in this example, formulae need not be evaluated during execution. Instead, they are combined appropriately and eventually added to the content of cells in the worksheet. We leave it to the reader to follow the example through to its conclusion, verifying that the final state of the worksheet is as shown in Figure 3c. Note that execution proceeds according to the normal Prolog execution order: that is, cases of a definition are tried in the order in which they are listed, and failure causes backtracking.

2.2 Gaussian Elimination

Although L-sheets' primary goal is to alleviate the reliability and robustness problems of spreadsheets used in strategic applications (Section 1), it can be applied to other kinds of programming tasks as well. This is illustrated by the next two examples, chosen to highlight certain aspects of array unification, the focus of this paper.

Figure 4 depicts a definition **gauss**, and associated definitions **triangularise** and **backsubstitute**, for solving simultaneous linear equations by Gaussian elimination with partial pivoting, with which we assume the reader is familiar. The array labelled **A** in the head of the first case of **gauss** must be bound to an $n \times n+1$ array containing the coefficients and right-hand sides of the equations to be solved. The array **C** must be bound to a $1 \times n$ array for the solution vector.

The templates of the second case of **triangularise** contain several *rulers*, used here to constrain array sizes. For example, the width of the first parameter of the **triangularise** goal template is constrained to be one less than the width of the first parameter of the head by ruler W. To improve efficiency, we could also add rulers to the array **A** in the head of **gauss** to make the above-noted constraint on its dimensions explicit.

The first goal template of this case, with a striped background, no name, and arrays containing only boolean valued expressions, is an example of a *guard*. During execution, the arrays in the guard must be instantiated to arrays of fixed size, and their formulae extended as described above. The guard succeeds if all the formulae in each of its arrays produce **true**. Note that $ in a program sheet formula has the same meaning as in a worksheet formula: that is, it indicates the the following row or column index is not incremented when the formulae is extended. The guard in this case specifies that the leading coefficient of the equation represented by subarray **B** is greater than or equal to the leading coefficient of any other equation, and not zero. If the guard succeeds, then **B** is the pivot row.

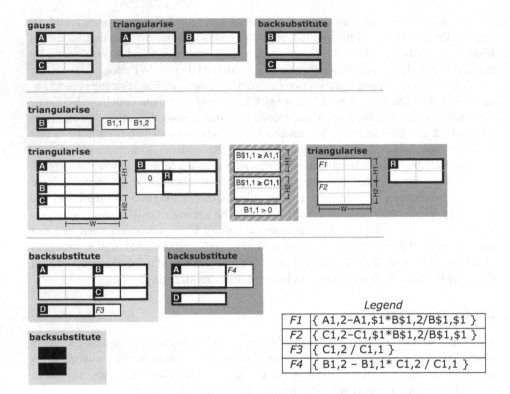

Fig. 4. Gaussian elimination

This example illustrates that array unification, unlike term unification, is not unique. If the array to be unified with the first array in the head of the second case of **triangularise** has *n* rows, then there are *n* ways of unifying the two arrays, so during execution of this case, unification generates successive matches until one is approved by the guard template. Note that execution of the guard template forces some formulae to be evaluated during the execution. Formulae constructed for the result vector are, however, returned to the worksheet unevaluated, then evaluated in the usual way. This implies that if the value of any cell corresponding to a coefficient in the set of equations is changed, **gauss** must be re-executed, possibly depositing different formulae in the cells of the result vector. This is in contrast to the example in Section 2.1, where no formulae are evaluated, and changing a cell need not initiate re-execution.

2.3 Removing Duplicate Values from an Array

In every unification in the preceding examples, one of the arrays involved is of fixed size, starting with the selection of rectangular arrays of cells of known size in the worksheet to correspond to the parameters of the **gauss** or **budget**. This may not always be the case, however, as shown by the example in Figure 5. Two arrays of height 1 satisfy the definition **unique** if every value in the first array occurs in the second exactly once. When **unique** is applied to a worksheet, the user selects some cell in the sheet to correspond to the upper left corner of the second parameter, and annotates this selection as a variable-size array. The size of the rectangle occupied by the result depends on the values in the first array in the sheet, and is determined by execution. When execution begins, the variable-size array from the sheet is unified with the second parameter of **unique**, which is of variable size in the first and second cases.

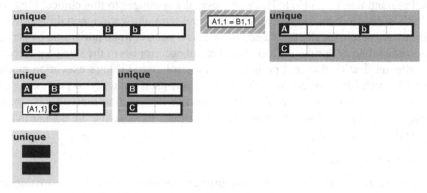

Fig. 5. Removing duplicate values from a vector

3   Array Unification

As demonstrated in the last section, in L-sheets, computations operate on rectangular structures assembled from smaller rectangular structures, which may be of variable height or width. We note that the inclusion of variable-size subarrays in L-sheets is similar to the inclusion of segment variables in LISTLOG lists [9]. As a result, unification is nondeterministic in both systems.

To provide a firm footing for the unification algorithm explained below, we first formalise the intuitive notion of "array" inherent in these examples.

A *cell* consists of *content*, a set of formulae which may be empty, and *width* and *height*, each of which is either an integer, or an integer-valued variable constrained to be at least 0. A *row* is a list of cells, all of the same height. The *height* of a row is the height of its cells. The *width* of a row is the sum of the widths of its cells. An *array* is a list of rows, the widths of which are constrained to be equal. A *null* array is an array, the height or width of which is 0. Note that "cell" is a generalisation of the usual worksheet cell, which is 1 in both dimensions.

If A and B are arrays, each with n rows, such that the heights of corresponding rows of A and B are the same, we denote by A*B the array $(A_1B_1, A_2B_2, \ldots, A_nB_n)$, where juxtaposition denotes list concatenation. Clearly * is associative. If A and B are arrays, then B is a *subarray* of A iff there exist arrays C, D, E and F such that A = C(D*B*E)F.

As illustrated in the previous section, two arrays may have a subarray in common. In Figure 4 for example, in the first case of **backsubstitute**, the array labelled **A** occurs as a subarray of the first parameter of the head, and the first parameter of the body template. This is analogous to two occurrences of the same variable in a Prolog clause, and has analogous results. That is, any changes occurring during unification involving one occurrence affect other occurrences.

Although the definition of array presented here differs slightly from that in [6], it is equivalent to it, and more appropriate for implementation purposes.

3.1   Implementation

Our algorithm for array unification is implemented in SICStus Prolog with Constraint Logic Programming (CLP) [17]. There are several advantages to this choice. First, because of similarities between array unification and term unification, certain features of the former are automatically delivered by the latter. For example, horizontal or vertical division of a subarray during unification affects all occurrences of the subarray. Second, since array unification does not produce a unique solution, Prolog's execution mechanism will search for a correct one. Third, CLP lends itself naturally to processing and finding common instances of arrays, since a unification solution must satisfy dimensionality constraints. Before presenting the algorithm, we describe the data structures used to represent an array.

3.2   Array Structure

The representation of an array consists of three components, *structure*, *constraints* and *content map*. We invite the reader to relate the following description of these to the example in Figure 6.

The *structure* component is a list of rows, each a triple of the form (S, H, C) where S is initially an uninstantiated variable; H is a variable representing the height of the row; and C is a list of cells.

Each cell is a triple of the form (S, W, C), where S is initially uninstantiated,; W is a variable representing the width of the cell; and C is a variable that is associated with the actual content of the cell via the *content map*.

The triples described above are called *structure triples*. The elements of a structure triple are called the *structure variable*, *size* and *content*, respectively. We also use *size* to mean the *height* of a row, or *width* of a cell, and the *content* of a cell triple as the *content variable*.

Note that in both kinds of structure triple, the structure variable S, if it is bound, is bound to a binary tree. In the case of a row, this binary tree records the (vertical) divisions of the row into smaller rows during unification. In the case of a cell, the tree records both horizontal and vertical divisions (Figure 8).

The *constraints* component of an array is a set of integer constraints on the heights of rows and widths of cells. It also includes equalities that ensure that the rows of the array are the same width.

The *contents* component of an array consists of a list of pairs of the form (C, L), where C is the content variable of one of the cells in the array, and L is a possibly empty

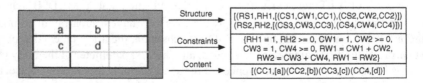

Fig. 6. Data structures for an array

list of the formulae the cell contains. When an instance of an array is created during execution, its *contents* component is appended to a master list called the *content map*. During unification, content variables of cells are bound together, and their entries in the content map are merged. Also, as cells are divided horizontally or vertically during unification, new elements are added to the content map corresponding to the cells produced by these divisions.

If the structure variable of a row or cell is bound only to other structure variables, rather than to a compound term, the row or cell is said to be *simple*.

3.3 Structure Splitting

During unification, a simple row may be split vertically into two rows and a simple cell horizontally into two cells. In this section, we describe the predicate `split`, listed in Figure 7, and how it affects the data structures described above.

```
split(horiz,(S,W,C),(S1,W1,C1),(S2,W2,C2),MapIn,MapOut) :-
    S = h((S1,W1,C1),(S2,W2,C2)),
    { W = W1+W2, W1 >= 0, W2 >= 0 },
    lower(W1,Gap),
    split_cell_content(horiz,C,C1,C2,Gap,MapIn,MapOut).

split(vert,(S,H,C),(S1,H1,C1),(S2,H2,C2),MapIn,MapOut) :-
    S = [(S1,H1),(S2,H2)],
    { H = H1+H2, H1 >=0, H2 >= 0 },
    get_first(vert,[(S,H,C)],[(S1,H1,C1),(S2,H2,C2)],MapIn,MapOut).
```

Fig. 7. The `split` predicate

The first parameter of `split` is a flag indicating the direction; `vert` for row splitting, or `horiz` for horizontal cell splitting. The second parameter is a structure triple, as described in the previous section, corresponding to the row or cell to be divided, while the third and fourth are structure triples, `T1` and `T2`, corresponding to the resulting rows or cells. The last two parameters are input and output content maps.

In horizontal splitting, the unbound structure variable `S` is bound to the term `h(T1,T2)`, and the call to `split_cell_content` determines the contents of the two new cells and updates the content map. In the process of propagating the formulae stored in the undivided cell to the newly created cells, it is necessary to know the distance between them; this is obtained through the call to `lower`. In vertical splitting, `S` is bound to the list `[T1,T2]`, and the call to `get_first` vertically splits cells in the row, by binding cell structure variables to terms of the form `v(V1,V2)` where `V1` and `V2` are the structure triples of cells resulting from the vertical splitting. The call to `get_first` both also updates the content map as it vertically splits the cells in the row. In both kinds of split, the size variables of the three structure triples are appropriately constrained.

Clearly, after repeated splitting of a row, its structure variable is bound to a binary tree. Similarly, the structure variable of a split cell is bound to a binary tree, but a somewhat more detailed one, recording both vertical and horizontal divisions, as illustrated

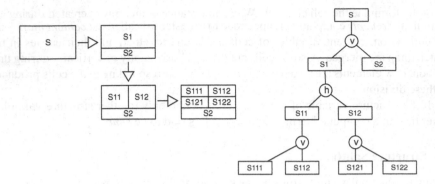

Fig. 8. The binary tree of structure variables created by repeated splitting of a cell

in Figure 8, where the sequence of cell divisions on the left results in the binary tree of structure variables on the right.

3.4 Array Matching

We now turn our attention to the unification algorithm, listed in Figure 9. The predicate `unify` unifies two arrays, receiving as inputs their structure components, `A1` and `A2`, and `MapIn`, which is the input content map obtained by concatenating the content maps of the two arrays. First, `unify` preprocesses `A1` and `A2` by applying `get_first`, producing `A1n` and `A2n`, the first rows of which are simple. The output content map, `MapOut`, records the contents of the cells in the arrays after unification.

The predicate `match` attempts to divide the rows and columns of the two arrays, as conservatively as possible, to make the arrays structurally identical. The processing required is essentially the same for matching the lists of rows that constitute the arrays, and for matching the lists of cells that constitute rows. Hence the same code accomplishes both. The first parameter of `match` is a flag indicating the processing direction; `vert` for array matching, or `horiz` for row matching. The second and third parameters are either array structures or rows, depending on the value of the first parameter.

To simplify the narrative, we describe the operation of `match` on rows; however, the description also applies to the matching of arrays.

The base cases of `match` apply if one of the input rows is empty, and succeed if the other is eliminable, that is, either empty or composed entirely of cells the widths of which can be constrained to equal 0.

In the third clause of `match`, `get_first` is applied to each of the incoming rows, transforming them into rows the first cells of which are simple. For purposes of discussion, we will call these leading simple cells L_1 and L_2. The body of the clause then divides into three subcases, dealing with the three possible ways of matching L_1 and L_2. Figure 10 illustrates the first and third cases.

In the first case, L_1 is split into two cells, L_{1a} and L_{1b}, say, the widths of L_{1a} and L_2 are constrained to be equal, their contents are unified (see below), and the height of L_{1b}

```
unify(A1,A2,MapIn,MapOut) :-
    match(vert,A1,A2,MapTemp2,MapOut).

match(Type,A1,A2,MapIn,MapIn) :-
    empty(A1),!,
    eliminable(A2).

match(Type,A1,A2,MapIn,MapIn) :-
    empty(A2),!,
    eliminable(A1).

match(Type,A1,A2,MapIn,MapOut) :-
    get_first(Type,A1,[(S1,W1,C1)|R1],MapIn,Map1),
    get_first(Type,A2,[(S2,W2,C2)|R2],Map1,Map2),
    !,
    ( split(Type,(S1,W1,C1),(S2,W2,C11),(S12,W12,C12),Map2,Map3),
      { W12 >= 1 },
      unify_content(Type,C11,C2,Map3,Map4),
      A1n = [(S12,W12,C12)|R1],
      A2n = R2
    ;
      split(Type,(S2,W2,C2),(S1,W1,C21),(S22,W22,C22),Map2,Map3),
      { W22 >= 1 },
      unify_content(Type,C21,C1,Map3,Map4),
      A2n = [(S22,W22,C22)|R2],
      A1n = R1
    ;
      { W1 = W2 },
      S1 = S2,
      unify_content(Type,C1,C2,MapIn,Map4),
      A1n = R1,
      A2n = R2
    ),
    match(Type,A1n,A2n,Map4,MapOut).
```

Fig. 9. The unify and match predicates

is constrained to be at least one. In other words, L_1 is forced to be strictly wider than L_2, and L_2 is unified with the "prefix" of it. Matching then continues with the remaining portions of the two rows, the first of which starts with the cell L_{1b}. The second case is analogous to the first, except the roles of the two rows are reversed. In the third case, the widths of L_1 and L_2 are constrained to be equal, and the cell contents are unified. In each case, the structure variables of matched cells are unified, so the cells are not only equal in size, but are identical.

3.5   Unifying Content

As discussed in the previous section, after selecting two rows or cells to unify, match unifies their content. This is achieved via a call to unify_content, in which the first

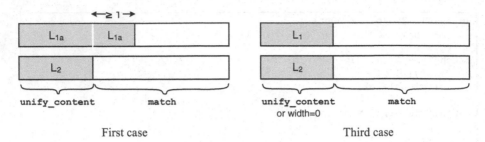

Fig. 10. Matching two non-empty rows

parameter is `vert` or `horiz`, for unifying the content of rows or cells, respectively. To unify the content of rows, `unify_content` applies `match` with first parameter `horiz` to the two rows. To unify cell contents, `unify_content` binds the content variables of the cells together, finds the two entries in the content map corresponding to the content variable, removes them, and adds a single entry containing the concatenation of the content lists from the two removed entries.

4   Discussion and Future Directions

The error-proneness of spreadsheets and its widespread, devastating and expensive effects are well known, and have led in recent years to intense research on techniques and tools for developing reliable spreadsheet programs. Among the approaches taken to this problem are enhancing the programmability of spreadsheets, and providing a means to specify spreadsheet structures.

In recent work, we proposed improving the programmability of spreadsheets, not by replacing the data flow semantics, but by augmenting it with a form of logic programming in which unification of terms is replaced by unification of rectangular arrays [6]. In the resulting language, L-sheets, the user can program worksheets in the usual way, and in addition, apply definitions to them, where definitions are visual, sheet-based logic programs, depicting operations that divide and assemble arrays.

Several advantages of this approach are outlined in [6]. First, while the "formula-in-cell" model familiar to current spreadsheet users is preserved, user-defined abstractions are built within the same sheet interface. Hence the sharp division between the end-user programmer and the expert is removed. Second, although manipulation of array structures is the main focus, logic programs can be created that operate at the level of individual cells, as in other logic programming spreadsheet languages that have been proposed. Third, the array unification on which L-sheets is based provides a natural means for specifying spreadsheet structures, as illustrated by the **budget** example in Section 2.1.

It could be argued that logic programming is a niche computational model, appealing to a relatively small proportion of programmers, and therefore has little chance of being accepted by spreadsheet users. However, there are significant differences between normal logic programming and L-sheets. In particular, unification has a much more concrete (visual) foundation, the assembly and disassembly of arrays, which are fundamental to spreadsheet structure. Nevertheless, the real utility of the approach can be determined only by testing it with users.

In this paper we have focussed on implementation matters, and in particular, we have described the array unification algorithm. The prototype of L-sheets is implemented in two parts. The user interface, written in Java, communicates with the execution mechanism written in SICStus Prolog. At the time of writing, it can deal with any examples with the characteristics of **budget**, **gauss**, and **unique**. It is not possible at present to apply more than one definition to a sheet.

As this project proceeds, various areas will be further explored. Some are as follows.

Unification modes. In the **budget** example, formulae are not evaluated during unification, but in **gauss** and **unique** they are. Further research is necessary to determine the context in which a formula should be evaluated.

Re-execution of the worksheet. More than one definition may be applied to a worksheet, overlapping each other, and interacting with formulae inserted by the user. When a formula is added or deleted, or a definition applied or its application removed, parts of the sheet need to be re-executed. In the simple data flow of standard spreadsheets, determining the parts to execute is straightforward, but not in the case of L-sheets. This problem has received some inconclusive study [6], but further investigation is necessary.

Triggering re-execution. Various actions will clearly trigger re-execution of a definition. For example, changing any value in the coefficient array will cause full re-execution of **gauss**, and resizing the worksheet parameter array will cause re-execution of **budget**. A complete study of triggering is required.

Interface enhancements. Clearly, the worksheet array selected when applying **budget** must have $3n$ columns for some non-zero n, and at least 3 rows. Such constraints should be enforced as the user selects parameters. Formats such as font, cell colours and borders, should be included in program sheets, and transferred to the worksheet during unification. Such formats would become part of a cell's content, so it will be necessary to determine how to resolve conflicts when differing formats are applied to the same cell via unification.

Debugging facilities. Various debugging tools and methodologies have been proposed for standard spreadsheets [15]. Research is required to determine the extent to which they can be incorporated into L-sheets. Since unification failure may occur several levels deep when either the shape-matching of arrays or evaluation of cell contents causes failure, tools for locating and rectifying errors due to such failures will be necessary, requiring some kind of visualisation and traversal of execution.

Acknowledgements

This work was partially supported by the Natural Sciences and Engineering Research Council of Canada via Discovery Grant OGP0000124, and an Undergraduate Student Research Award.

References

1. Abraham, R., Erwig, M.: Inferring templates from spreadsheets. In: 28th ACM International Conference on Software Engineering, Shanghai, China, pp. 182–191 (May 2006)
2. Bricklin, D., Frankston, R.: VisiCalc: Information from its creators (July 2007), http://www.bricklin.com/visicalc.htm
3. Burnett, M., Atwood, J., Djang, R., Gottfried, H., Reichwein, J., Yang, S.: Forms/3: A First-Order Visual Language to Explore the Boundaries of the Spreadsheet Paradigm. Journal of Functional Programming 11(2), 155–206 (2001)
4. Cervesato, I.: A Spreadsheet for Everyday Symbolic Reasoning. In: AAAI Fall Symposium on Integrating Reasoning into Everyday Applications, Arlington VA, pp. 1–8 (October 2006)
5. Chamberlin, D.D.: The "single-assignment" approach to parallel processing. In: Proc. AFIPS Fall Joint Computer Conference, Las Vegas NV, pp. 263–270. AFIPS Press, Montvale, N.J (1971)
6. Cox, P.T.: Enhancing the Programmability of Spreadsheets with Logic Programming. In: Proc. IEEE Symposium on Visual Languages and Human-Centric Computing, Coeur d'Alène ID (to appear, 2007)
7. Erwig, M., Abraham, R., Cooperstein, I., Kollmansberger, S.: Gencel: A Program Generator for Correct Spreadsheets. Journal of Functional Programming 16(3), 293–325 (2006)
8. Erwig, M., Burnett, M.: Adding Apples and Oranges. In: Krishnamurthi, S., Ramakrishnan, C.R. (eds.) PADL 2002. LNCS, vol. 2257, pp. 173–191. Springer, Heidelberg (2002)
9. Farkas, Z.: LISTLOG - A Prolog Extension for List Processing. In: Ehrig, H., Levi, G., Montanari, U. (eds.) TAPSOFT 1987 and CFLP 1987. LNCS, vol. 250, pp. 82–95. Springer, Heidelberg (1987)
10. Gupta, G., Akhter, S.: Knowledgesheet: A graphical spreadsheet interface for interactively developing a class of constraint programs. In: Pontelli, E., Santos Costa, V. (eds.) PADL 2000. LNCS, vol. 1753, pp. 308–323. Springer, Heidelberg (2000)
11. Paine, J.: Excelsior: Bringing the benefits of modularisation to Excel. In: Proc. EuSpRIG 2005, Greenwich UK (July 2005)
12. Panko, R.R.: Spreadsheets and Sarbanes-Oxley: Regulations, Risks, and Control Frameworks. Communications of the Association for Information Systems 17(29), 647–676 (2006)
13. Peyton Jones, S., Blackwell, A., Burnett, M.: A user-centred approach to functions in Excel. In: 8th ACM SIGPLAN International Conference on Functional Programming, Uppsala, Sweden, pp. 165–176 (August 2003)
14. Ramakrishnan, C.R., Ramakrishnan, I.V., Warren, D.S.: Deductive Spreadsheets Using Tabled Logic Programming. In: Etalle, S., Truszczyński, M. (eds.) ICLP 2006. LNCS, vol. 4079, pp. 391–405. Springer, Heidelberg (2006)
15. Ruthruff, J.R., Prabhakararao, S., Reichwein, J., Cook, C., Creswic, E., Burnett, M.: Interactive, visual fault localization support for end-user programmers. Journal of Visual Languages & Computing 16(1-2), 3–40 (2005)

16. Spenke, M., Beilken, C.: A spreadsheet interface for logic programming. In: ACM Conference on Human Factors in Computing Systems, Austin TX, pp. 75–80 (1991)
17. Swedish Institute of Computer Science, SICStus Prolog, http://www.sics.se/sicstus/
18. van Emden, M.H., Ohki, M., Takeuchi, A.: Spreadsheets with Incremental Queries as a User Interface for Logic Programming, ICOT Technical Report, TR-44 (October 1985)
19. Wilson, S.: Building a Visual Programming Language, MacTech 13(4) (July 2007), http://www.mactech.com/articles/mactech/Vol.13/13.04/Spreadsheet2000/

Specialising Simulator Generators
for High-Performance Monte-Carlo Methods[*]

Gabriele Keller[1], Hugh Chaffey-Millar[2], Manuel M.T. Chakravarty[1],
Don Stewart[1], and Christopher Barner-Kowollik[2]

[1] Programming Languages and Systems, School of Computer Science and
Engineering, University of New South Wales
{keller,chak,dons}@cse.unsw.edu.au
[2] Centre for Advanced Macromolecular Design, School of Chemical Sciences and
Engineering, University of New South Wales
h.chaffey-millar@student.unsw.edu.au, c.barner-kowollik@unsw.edu.au

Abstract. We address the tension between software generality and performance in the domain of simulations based on Monte-Carlo methods. We simultaneously achieve generality and high performance by a novel development methodology and software architecture centred around the concept of a *specialising simulator generator*. Our approach combines and extends methods from functional programming, generative programming, partial evaluation, and runtime code generation. We also show how to generate parallelised simulators.

We evaluated our approach by implementing a simulator for advanced forms of polymerisation kinetics. We achieved unprecedented performance, making Monte-Carlo methods practically useful in an area that was previously dominated by deterministic PDE solvers. This is of high practical relevance, as Monte-Carlo simulations can provide detailed microscopic information that cannot be obtained with deterministic solvers.

1 Introduction

The tension between software generality and performance is especially strong in computationally intensive software, such as scientific and financial simulations. Software designers usually aim to produce applications with a wide range of functionality, which in the case of simulations means that they are highly parameterisable and, ideally, target different types of high-performance hardware. Scientific software is often used for new research tasks, and financial software is often employed for new products and new markets. In both cases, there is a high likelihood that the boundary of previous uses will be stretched. However, generality often comes with a performance penalty, as computations become more interpretive, require more runtime checks, and use less efficient data structures.

As an example, consider a computational chemistry simulation, using a Monte-Carlo method, that in its innermost loop repeatedly selects a random chemical

---

[*] This work was funded by the UNSW FRGP *High Performance Parallel Computing for Complex Polymer Architecture Design*.

reaction from a set of possible reactions. The probabilities of the reactions are determined by the reactions' empirical rate coefficients and the reactants' concentrations. If we aim for generality, the code will have the capability to handle a wide range of reactions. These reactions and their probabilities will be stored in a data structure that the code will have to traverse over and over when making a selection and when updating the concentrations of the various reactants. This is an interpretive process whose structure is not unlike that of an interpreter applying the rules of a term rewriting system repeatedly to the redexes of a term. The more general the rules handled by the interpreter, the higher the interpretive overhead, and the fewer rewrites will be executed per second.

To maximise performance, we need to eliminate all interpretive overhead. In the extreme, we have a program that hard-codes a single term rewriting system; i.e., we compile the term rewriting system instead of interpreting it. We can transfer that idea to the chemistry simulation by specialising the simulator so that it only applies a fixed set of reactions. Such specialisation can have a very significant impact on the performance of simulators that execute a relatively small part of the code very often; i.e., even minor inefficiencies of a few additional CPU cycles can add significantly to the overall running time. Giving up on generality is not an option. We also cannot expect the user to manually specialise and optimise the simulation code for the exact reactions and input parameters of a particular simulation; instead, we automate the generation and compilation of specialised code.

In programming languages, the move between interpreter and compiler is well known from the work on partial evaluation [1]. More generally, research on generative programming [2] and self-optimising libraries [3] introduced approaches to code specialisation in a range of application areas, including numerically intensive applications [4,5]. Much of this work is concerned with providing general libraries that are specialised at compile time. In this paper, we transfer these ideas from libraries to applications and combine them with runtime code generation and a development methodology based on prototyping.

More precisely, we introduce a novel software architecture for simulators using Monte-Carlo methods. This architecture uses *generative code specialisation* to reconcile generality and performance in a way that is transparent to the end user. Specifically, instead of an interpretive simulator in a low-level language, we implement a *specialising simulator generator* in a functional language and use it to generate optimised C code specialised for a particular simulator configuration. Moreover, we outline how a specialising simulator generator can be developed by way of prototyping the simulator in a functional language.

We discuss the design of specialising simulator generators and the parallelisation of the generated simulators for Monte-Carlo methods. Moreover, we demonstrate the practical relevance of our approach by a concrete application from computational chemistry, namely a simulator for polymerisation kinetics using a Markov-chain Monte-Carlo method.

We achieved unprecedented performance for the polymerisation simulator. For the first time, it makes Monte-Carlo methods practically useful in an area that is dominated by deterministic PDE solvers. This is of high practical relevance, as Monte-Carlo simulations can provide detailed microscopic information about generated polymeric species. Such microscopic information—which is not available from deterministic simulators, specifically those using the h-p-Galerkin method [6,7]—includes (yet is not limited to) information on polymer species with more than one chain length index (i.e., star polymer systems often applied in polymeric drug, gene, and vaccine delivery systems [8]), cross-linking densities, and branching in complex polymer networks as well as detailed information on copolymer compositions. Finally, we demonstrate good parallel speedups for our Monte-Carlo method, whereas no parallel h-p-Galerkin solvers for polymerisation exist to the best of our knowledge. Parallelisation is a pressing practical problem, as multicore counts have replaced clock rates as the main parameter increased in new processor generations.

In summary, our main contributions are the following:

- A development methodology and software architecture using generative code specialisation for Monte-Carlo simulations (Section 2 & Section 3).
- A parallelisation strategy for Markov-chain Monte-Carlo methods (Section 4).
- A detailed performance evaluation of our Monte-Carlo simulator for polymerisation kinetics, which shows that the application of methods from functional programming can lead to code that is significantly more efficient than what can be achieved with traditional methods (Section 5).

As aforementioned, we build on a host of previous work from generative programming, partial evaluation, and runtime code generation. We discuss this related work as well as other work on polymerisation kinetics in Section 6.

2   A Generative Code Specialisation Architecture

Simulations based on Monte-Carlo methods are popular in the study of complex systems with a large number of coupled degrees of freedom, this includes applications ranging from computational physics (e.g., high energy particle physics) to financial mathematics (e.g., option pricing). The underlying principle is the *law of large numbers;* that is, we can estimate the probability of an event with increasing accuracy as we repeat a stochastic experiment over and over. This principle applies to any system that we can model in terms of *probability density functions (PDFs)*. This includes the numerical approximation of purely mathematical constructs with no apparent stochasticity or randomness, such as approximating the value of π or the numerical integration of complex functions [9].

Monte-Carlo methods use probability density functions to drive sampling during a simulation. This can be the repeated evaluation of a function at random points, e.g. to integrate it numerically, or it can be a sequence of system state changes, each of which occurs with a certain probability—e.g., a solution of chemical reactants changes depending on the likelihood of the reactions.

To exploit the law of large numbers, all Monte-Carlo simulations repeat one or more stochastic experiments a large number of times, while tallying the results, and possibly continuously evolving some system state and computing variance reduction information. With increasing complexity of the system and increasing need for precision, more and more stochastic experiments need to be performed. This highly repetitive nature of Monte-Carlo simulations is one of the two key points underlying the software architecture that we are about to discuss.

The second key point is that, in many application areas, Monte-Carlo simulations should admit a wide variety of different simulations. For example, in reaction kinetics, we would like to handle many different chemical reactions and, in financial modelling, we would like to model many different financial products. We call this the *configuration space*. The more general a simulator, the larger its configuration space. To explore new chemical processes and new financial products, we need to have short turn-arounds in an interactive system to explore a design space by repeatedly altering configurations. In contrast, when the user finds a point in the design space that they want to simulate in more detail, a simulation may run for hours or even days.

In summary, the two crucial properties of Monte-Carlo simulations guiding the following discussion are thus:

- *Property 1:* The simulation repeats one or more stochastic experiments and associated bookkeeping a large number of times, to achieve numeric accuracy.
- *Property 2:* It simulates complex systems with a large number of degrees of freedom and a rich configuration space.

2.1   The Classical Approach: A Simulator in C, C++, or Fortran

Property 1 makes Monte-Carlo simulators very computationally intensive—e.g., sophisticated simulations in the domain of polymerisation kinetics can run for hours or even days. Hence, manually optimised simulator code in low-level languages like C, C++, and Fortran is the state of the art, and the use of functional languages is out of the question, unless the same level of performance can be achieved.

While Property 1 encourages the use of a low-level language, the number of optimisations that can be performed in such a language is limited by Property 2. A simulator in a low-level language must be sufficiently generic to handle a large configuration space in which it has to evaluate functions with a large number of inputs. In other words, the code in the repeatedly executed inner loop will be complex and possibly traverse sophisticated data structures. However, given the number of repetitions, each CPU cycle counts significantly towards the final running time. Additional instructions required to implement a more general solution lead to notable inefficiencies compared to specialised implementations.

To illustrate this situation, consider reaction kinetics again. Each reaction occurs with a probability that depends on the relative concentration of the various reactants. If it occurs, it will consume one or more reactants and release new reactants into the solution. A Monte-Carlo simulator will have to keep track of these concentrations and the associated reaction probabilities. It has to select reactions according to the implied probability density function. The reactions have to be modelled in a data structure and the more variations we allow, the more interpretive the process in the inner loop will be. In other words, the larger the configuration space, the slower the simulator.

2.2   A Generative Approach

This situation calls for a generative approach. The simulator has a large configuration space and its inner loop will be executed many times for a single configuration, making it worthwhile to specialise the inner loop for one configuration, thus, effectively giving us a custom simulator for one problem. This specialisation has to be transparent to the user and has to occur in an interactive environment to admit exploratory uses. Hence, we propose the use of online generative code specialisation: that is, depending on user input, the application specialises its inner core to produce highly optimised code, and then, dynamically loads and links that code into the running application.

2.3   From Haskell to C to a C Generator

We propose the following development methodology:

1. Implement a *prototype simulator* in a functional language like Haskell as an executable specification, to explore alternative designs.
2. Implement a *specialised simulator* in a low-level language like C by specialising the prototype simulator for one or more concrete simulator configurations. Use it to explore possible low-level optimisations including selecting appropriate imperative data structures.
3. Replace the simulator core of the prototype simulator with a *simulator generator* that, when executed on the same configuration, produces the specialised simulator we manually implemented in the previous step.

Both the specialised simulator and the simulator generator are validated against the prototype simulator, which is much more compact and easier to reason about. This development methodology is especially worthwhile when extending the boundaries of existing simulators, as was the case in the project in which we developed it. We had undertaken to implement the first simulator to compute detailed microscopic information for reactions of star polymers and to achieve higher levels of efficiency than existing simulators. Existing systems either oversimplified complex molecular structures [10] or lacked performance and generality [6]. Moreover, no existing system was parallelised, and we aimed for good scalability on high-latency networks, such as Ethernet-based PC clusters.

Consequently, we developed a new simulator from scratch in Haskell and placed particular emphasis on data structures for the system state that are sufficiently small to enable cheap network transmission, while still allowing for a highly efficient innermost loop of the simulator. Subsequently, we parallelised the prototype simulator using a generic master/worker skeleton based on the standard network library distributed with the Glasgow Haskell Compiler (GHC).

Only after we convinced ourselves of the efficiency of the data structures and algorithms implemented in the prototype using GHC's heap profiler and scalability benchmarks on a PC cluster, did we turn to Step 2 of our development methodology and implement a specialised simulator in C. This enabled problem-oriented, explorative development without too much attention to low-level details and avoiding premature optimisations.

The concrete specialisation opportunities in Step 2 are domain-specific and to find them specialisation-time data must be separated from runtime data; i.e., the variables in the inner loop of the simulator that are fixed by the simulator configuration and do not change between loop iterations must be identified. In our case, this was the number and type of reactions and reactants; i.e., we can pre-calculate and hardcode all possible one-step changes of the system state.

In Step 3, we exploit the fact that the performance-critical code is in the inner loop of the simulator. Hence, the simulator generator does not need to generate the C code for an entire simulator. Instead, it inserts into a simulator skeleton only system-state initialisation code, state-changing code of the inner loops, and other configuration-depended code, such as some I/O. For example, in the simulator for polymerisation kinetics, the most important piece of specialised and generated code is the body of one C `switch` statement that, depending on the randomly selected reaction, effects the update of the system state—c.f., Section 3.2.

2.4   Runtime Compilation and Loading

The use of a simulator generator implies runtime code generation and compilation. In our case, the latter consists of invoking a standard C compiler, such as GNU's `gcc` or Intel's `icc` to compile the generated specialised simulator. Given the long running times of typical Monte-Carlo simulations, we can even amortise time-consuming compilation with costly optimisations enabled. In addition to the simplification of data and control structures explicitly performed by the specialising simulator generator, the C compiler can exploit the fact that many of the variables of the generic simulator are now embedded as constants. This leads to additional constant folding, loop unrolling, etc.

After code generation, the simulator executable can be executed in a separate process or, as in our implementation, loaded into the main application using dynamic code loading [11]. The latter is attractive for interactive applications that, for example, animate the simulation graphically.

3   Generative Monte-Carlo Methods

We will now discuss two examples of Monte-Carlo methods. The first is a toy example to illustrate the basic structure of Monte-Carlo methods and the second is a real-world application, namely the aforementioned polymerisation simulator.

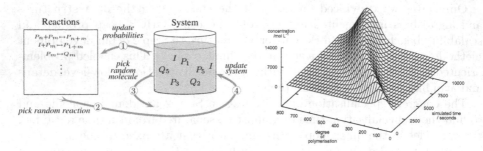

Fig. 1. Structure of polymerisation simulator (left) and computed molecular weight distribution (right)

3.1 Computing π

The probably simplest Monte-Carlo method is the one to compute an approximation of π. We know that the area of a circle is $A = \pi r^2$. Hence, $\pi = A/r^2$; i.e., $\pi/4$ is the *probability* that a point picked at random out of a square of side length $2r$ is within the circle enclosed by that square. As explained in the previous section, the fundamental idea underlying Monte-Carlo methods is to *estimate the probability of an event with increasing accuracy by repeating a stochastic experiment over and over*. Here the stochastic experiment is to pick a point in the square at random, and we use that experiment to approximate the probability that picked points lie inside the circle. By multiplying that approximated probability with 4, we approximate π.

3.2 Modelling Polymerisation Kinetics

Our main example is a simulator for polymerisation kinetics. This is a complete application incorporating a significant amount of domain knowledge; hence, we cannot sensibly display and explain its source code in a paper. However, the code is publicly available[1] for inspection and use—in fact, we have two versions of the application, the prototype simulator (entirely in Haskell) and the specialising simulator generator (with the generator in Haskell and the simulator skeleton in C). In the following, we will discuss the innermost loop of the simulator, containing all the performance-critical code, as well as sketch the work distribution between the simulator generator (in Haskell) and the simulator skeleton (in C). Due to space constraints and to avoid having to explain too much of the chemistry, we will abstract over many of the simulator data structures; more details, from a chemist's perspective, are in a companion paper [8].

Chemical reactions in four steps. The four steps performed by the innermost loop of the simulator are illustrated in Figure 1 (left): ① computation of the reaction probabilities; ② random selection of a reaction; ③ random selection of the

---

[1] http://www.cse.unsw.edu.au/~chak/project/polysim/

```
                                              #define I_Star 2
                                              ...
                                              #define DECOMPOSITION 0
  ...                                 simulator ...
  D:Comment;DECOMPOSITION            generator  #define DO_REACT_BODY \
  Elementalreaction I 0 I* I* 0 kd   in Haskell   {case DECOMPOSITION:\
  ...                                  ⟹            resMolCnt = 2;\
         Model as .rsy file                        resMol1Spec = I_Star;\
                                                   resMol2Spec = I_Star;\
                                                   break;\
                                                   ...

                                              Generated genpolymer.h
```

```
#include "genpolymer.h"
void oneReaction () { // updates global system state
  int reactIndex, mol1Len, mol2Len;        // consumed molecules
  int resMol1Spec, resMol2Spec,            // produced...
      resMol1Len[CHAINS], resMol2Len[CHAINS]; // ...molecules
  int resMolCnt = 1;                       // number of produced; default is one
```

① Compute reaction probabilities as product of the reaction's statically determined relative probability and the current concentration of the reactants involved.

```
updateProbabilities ();
```

② Randomly pick a reaction according to the current reaction probabilities; e.g., from the list in Figure 1 (left), we might pick $P_n + P_m \mapsto P_{n+m}$.

```
reactIndex = pickRndReact ();
```

③ Randomly pick the molecules involved in the reaction. In some systems polymers with different chain lengths react with different probability. For the reaction $P_n + P_m \mapsto P_{n+m}$, we have to pick two random chain lengths n and m.

```
mol1Len = pickRndMol (reactToSpecInd1 (reactIndex));
if (consumesTwoMols (reactIndex))
  mol2Len = pickRndMol (reactToSpecInd2 (reactIndex));
```

④ Compute reaction products, and update the concentration of molecules accordingly; for our example, we add P_{n+m}. The consumed molecules, P_n and P_m, were already removed in Step ③. Also, the system clock is incremented.

```
switch (reactIndex) // compute reaction products
  DO_REACT_BODY      // defined by simulator generator; sets resMol1Spec etc.
incrementMolCnt (resMol1Spec, resMol1Len);
if (resMolCnt == 2)
  incrementMolCnt (resMol2Spec, resMol2Len);
advanceSystemTime (); // compute Δt of this reaction
}
```

Fig. 2. Task of the specialising generator (top) and simulator skeleton (bottom)

consumed molecules; and ④ update of the system with the produced molecules. These steps are further explained in Figure 2 (bottom), where the corresponding C code of the simulator skeleton, in form of the function `oneReaction()`, is also given. In fact, the C code of `oneReaction()` is almost the same for a generic simulator and a specialised simulator. The main difference is the `switch` statement and its body `DO_REACT_BODY`, which is a placeholder for code inserted by the specialising simulator generator—we will come back to this below.

Chemistry basics. Generally, polymerisation kinetics features two kinds of molecules: *simple molecules* that have no chain length (such as the I in the example) and *polymers* that have a chain length specified by a suffix (such as the P_n in the example). Polymers with multiple chains, are called *star polymers*, which are often applied in polymeric drug, gene, and vaccine delivery systems. Our simulator is the first to compute detailed microscopic information for this important class of polymers. In our simulator, a reaction consumes one or two molecules and also produces one or two molecules; this is encoded in the conditionals in Step ③ and ④, respectively. Reactions involving polymers are specific w.r.t. the type of molecules involved, but are parametrised over the chain length; e.g., $P_n + P_m \mapsto P_{n+m}$ consumes two polymers with lengths n and m and produces one with length $n+m$. In Step ③, the probability always depends on the current concentration of the molecules of varying chain lengths, but may be adjusted by a factor that models how the chain length influences the reactivity of a molecule.

Computing molecular weight distributions. Each invocation of `oneReaction()` corresponds to one chemical reaction and to one stochastic experiment of the Monte-Carlo method. These reactions slowly alter the concentration of polymer molecules with particular chain lengths. An indirect measure of chain length is molecular weight, and Chemists like to see the evaluation of polymer concentrations in the form of *molecular weight distributions*, as in Figure 1 (right), which was computed by our simulator.

Specialisation. Figure 2 (top) illustrates the task of the specialising simulator generator: it reads a reaction specification, as an `.rsy` file, and compiles it into a C header file `genpolymer.h`. This header file contains all reaction-specific *data and code,* and is `#included` by the simulator skeleton. To avoid overheads due to sophisticated data structures, the different types of molecules and reactions are simply encoded as integers (e.g., the `#defines` for `I_Star` and `DECOMPOSITION` in the displayed code fragment). This, most importantly, enables the use of a simple `switch` statement to compute the produced molecules in Step ④. The body of that switch statement is one of the most important pieces of generated code and `#defined` by `DO_REACT_BODY` (underlined). The code fragment in Figure 2 (top) gives the switch `case` for a simple decomposition reaction. The cases for polymers are somewhat more involved, as chain lengths have to be computed.

In Section 1, we discussed that the aim of a specialising simulator generator is to eliminate interpretive overhead. In the polymerisation simulator, we achieve this by (a) hardcoding the reactants involved in each reaction and (b) using an array with fixed size and layout that maps molecule types (including chain length for polymers) to the number of that type of molecule in the system. Point (a) is crucial to be able to use a `switch` statement with a few simple operations per `case`/reaction in Step ④. In contrast, a generic simulator needs to consult a dynamic reaction table to achieve the same. For a complex reaction, this specialisation reduces the number of executed assembly instructions in our code from 31 (including 5 branches) to 6 (including one branch and one indirect jump) when compiled with the Intel C compiler.

3.3   A Specialiser in Haskell

In general, the reaction specifications are significantly more involved than the .rsy file fragment in Figure 2 (top). The file format originates from the PREDICI system [12,13] and, by using it, we can create chemical models with PREDICI's graphical frontend. Parsing reaction specifications, extracting the information necessary for the simulator generation, and generating the specialised C data structures and code fragments makes heavy use of algebraic data types, pattern-matching, list manipulation, and higher-order functions; i.e., it is the type of code where functional languages excel.

As an example, take the fragment of the specialisation code in Figure 3, which is a simplified version of the actual code used in the generator. We model chemical reactions with the type `Reaction`, which specifies the involved kinds of molecules and the reaction's rate coefficient (i.e., the probability of that reaction happening in dependence on the concentrations of the involved reactants). Molecules can be of three kinds determined by the data type `Kind` (i.e., simple molecules, linear polymer chains, and star polymers). Moreover, the variant `NoSpec` is used to when any of the two reactant or product slots in a `Reaction` are not used (e.g., reactions where two reactant molecules result in a single product molecule). In addition to `Reaction`s, we have `ReactionSchemas` that determine the length of polymers produced by a reaction using values of type `ResLen`. Figure 3 only shows part of the definition of `ResLen`; in general, it models arithmetic expressions over the two input chain lengths with support for inclusion of random variables. The latter is required to represent the splitting of a polymer chain at a random position. For star polymers, `ResLen` calculations become slightly more complicated, as we need to express a sequence of calculations on a star's chains. As an example, take the reaction discussed previously: $P_n + P_m \mapsto P_{n+m}$. It's representation as a `ReactionSchema` is by the value `RS (Poly, Poly) (Poly, NoSpec) (AddLen FstLen SndLen, NoLen)`.

Figure 3 also gives the code for the function `specialiseReacts`, which uses a list comprehension to combine each reaction with its matching schema, as determined by the auxiliary function `matchesSchema`. The function then derives from each matching reaction-schema pair a specialised reaction `SpecReaction`. These specialised reactions are subsequently fed into the code generator to produce the code for DO_REACT_BODY.

— Concrete reaction:
```
data Reaction =
  Reaction
   Name
   RateCoef   — rate coefficient
   Kind Kind  — reactants
   Kind Kind  — products
```

```
data ResLen   — Reaction product length:
  = FstLen             — length of 1st reactant
  | SndLen             — length of 2st reactant
  | AddLen ResLen ResLen
                       — sum of 1st & 2nd
  | ConstLen Int — constant length
  — some further variants
```

```
type RateCoef = Double
type Arms     = Int
```

— Various kinds of molecules:
```
data Kind
  = Simple     — regular molecule
  | Poly       — linear polymer
  | Star Arms  — star polymer
  | NoSpec     — not present
```

— How to compute polymer lengths:
```
data ReactionSchema
  = RS (Kind, Kind)   — reactants
       (Kind, Kind)   — products
       (ResLen, ResLen)
                      — product lengths
```

— Desc. of a specialised reaction:
```
data SpecReaction =
  SpecReaction
   Name
   Kind Kind      — reactants
   Kind ResLen    — product #1
   KInd ResLen    — product #2
```

```
specialiseReacts :: [Reaction] -> [ReactionSchema] -> [SpecReaction]
specialiseReacts reactions schemata = map specialiseReaction reactSchema
  where
  reactSchema = [(r,s) | r <- reactions, s <- schemata, matchesSchema r s]
    specialiseReaction ((Reaction name _ react1 react2 prod1 prod2),
                        (RS name _ _ (resLen1, resLen2)))
      = SpecReaction react1 react2 prod1 resLen1 prod2 resLen2

matchesSchema :: Reaction -> ReactionSchema -> Bool
matchesSchema r s = ⟨check whether reaction r fits schema s⟩
```

Fig. 3. Fragment of the specialisation code

The specialiser generates all C code that is dependent on the type of molecules and reactions in the system. In the C skeleton, these code fragments are represented by C pre-processor macros, such as DO_REACT_BODY. Similarly, all system parameters (e.g., the maximum number of chains per molecule CHAINS) and tag values to represent molecules and reactions (e.g., I_Star and DECOMPOSITION) are computed by the specialiser and emitted as macro declarations. All parameters of reactions, such as rate coefficients, are hardcoded into the macros that form the system initialisation code. After macro expansion, the C compiler is presented with a program manipulating integers, floats, and arrays that has a simple control structure and is littered with constant values—i.e., it has ample opportunities to apply standard compiler optimisations.

4   Parallelisation

Monte-Carlo methods where the individual stochastic experiments are independent—such as the approximation of π—are almost trivial to parallelise. The large number of independent stochastic experiments can be easily distributed over multiple processors, as long as we ensure that the statistic properties of our source of randomness are robust with respect to parallel execution. The only communication between the parallel threads is at the end of the simulation when the local results need to be combined into a global result. This can be efficiently achieved with standard parallel reduction operations (e.g., parallel folds).

The parallelisation of the polymerisation simulator is more involved. The probability of the various types of reactions changes over time with the changing concentration of the molecules involved in a reaction. In other words, the stochastic experiments are dependent and we have a *Markov-chain* Monte-Carlo method. Previous proposals to parallelise Monte-Carlo polymerisation involve running the same simulation several times and calculating the average [6]. Different instances of the same simulation can run in parallel, and the average over the individual results will be more accurate than any single simulation. However, it is important to keep in mind that running the same simulation ten times will not, in general, lead to a result of the same quality as a single simulation of a system ten times the size, since the concentration of some of the reactants is so low, that, for small systems there would be less than one molecule available and the fact that the simulation is discrete would distort the result. This is not just a theoretical problem, we have observed it in production-sized simulations [8].

We solved this problem by exploiting the following observation: a common simplification in simulations of reaction kinetics is to abstract over the spatial location of the molecules in the system. If two molecules are far apart, they would, in reality, be less likely to react. We can use this for parallelisation by splitting the system into several subsystems, running the simulation of the subsystems independently in parallel, but ensuring that we *mix*—i.e., gather, average, and re-distribute—the states of the subsystems with sufficient frequency to model the Brownian motion of the molecules. Thus, we parallelise the application without compromising the quality of the result. The speed up is slightly less than for a trivially parallel Monte-Carlo simulation, as mixing triggers communication. However, as the following benchmarks show, the parallelisation is still very good.

Although, our approach of regularly averaging over a set of Monte-Carlo simulations running in parallel was motivated by the physical intuition of spatial separation and Brownian motion in a liquid, we conjecture that the same approach to parallelisation is more generally applicable to Markov-chain Monte-Carlo methods. Regular averaging over a set of parallel simulations will improve the accuracy of the intermediate results and so usually accelerate convergence. However, the ideal frequency for mixing will depend on the concrete application.

5   Performance

To quantify the performance benefits of our approach, we will now discuss three aspects of the performance of our system: (a) the performance improvement due to specialisation, (b) the speedup due to parallelisation, and (c) the performance relative to existing systems. We used two types of hardware for benchmarking the Monte-Carlo code: (1) a PC cluster with Intel Pentium 4, 3.2GHz, processors connected by GigaBit Ethernet (called *P4 cluster* in the following) and (2) a shared-memory computer containing 8x dualcore AMD Athlon 64 3200+, 2.2GHz, processors connected by a HyperTransport 1.0 bus (called *Athlon SMP* in the following). Both systems ran GNU/Linux. All C code was compiled with the Intel C compiler `icc`, version 9.1, except where we explicitly noted the use of the GNU C compiler `gcc`, version 4.1. We generated random numbers using Matsumoto & Nishimura's Mersenne Twister MT19937, version 2002/1/26. All

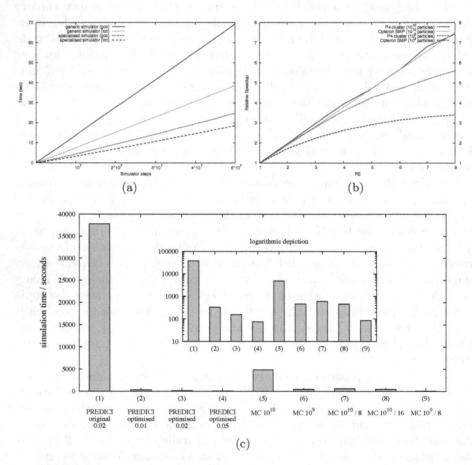

Fig. 4. (a) Generic versus specialised polymerisation simulator; (b) parallel speedup on shared memory and cluster hardware; (c) deterministic versus Monte-Carlo simulator

communication between parallel processes was via MPICH2. We only used one core per processor of the Athlon SMP system to avoid skewing the benchmarks by bus contention on the processor-memory interface.

Generic versus specialised simulator. We start by quantifying the performance benefit gained from specialisation. Figure 4(a) plots the running time of a generic simulator, manually implemented in C, and a simulator produced by our specialising simulator generator. For this particular simulation (a simple model of the polymerisation of bulk styrene [8, Fig. 4]), the specialisation leads to a performance improvement between a factor of 2 and 2.5, depending on whether we compile with gcc or icc. The benchmark was executed on one node of the P4 cluster—icc produces only marginally better code than gcc on AMD processors.

Accurate comparisons with other Monte-Carlo simulators for polymerisation kinetics are difficult, as published data is scarce and no software is available for benchmarking. However, we reproduced the methyl acrylate model of Drache et al. [6] to the best of our knowledge and the performance of the processors in our Athlon SMP system is very similar to the hardware used by Drache et al. The results suggest that the performance of our generic simulator, at least for Drache's methyl acrylate model, is essentially the same as that of Drache's simulator. In summary, our novel specialising simulator generators advance the state-of-the-art in uniprocessor performance of Monte-Carlo simulators for polymerisation kinetics by around a factor of two.

Parallel speedup. Figure 4(b) graphs the speedup of the specialised simulator for the simple styrene model for both the P4 cluster and the Athlon SMP. It does so for a solution containing 10^9 and a solution containing 10^{10} particles. With 10^{10} particles, we get very good scalability (close to 7.5 for 8 PEs) on both architectures. Given the rather simple commodity hardware of the P4 cluster, this is a very positive result. For 10^9 particles, scalability is clearly limited. In essence, the 10^9 particle system is too small to efficiently utilise more than 4 PEs in the cluster and 5 PEs in the SMP system.

Deterministic versus Monte-Carlo simulator. From an end-user perspective, it is irrelevant whether a simulator uses a Monte-Carlo or a deterministic method, such as the popular h-p-Galerkin method to compute a molecular weight distribution by solving partial differential equations. What counts is (a) the amount of detail in the information produced by the simulator and (b) the speed with which the information is computed. Monte-Carlo methods are attractive as they can compute information detail that is not available from deterministic simulators, such as information on polymer species with more than one chain length index, cross-linking densities, and branching in complex polymer networks as well as information on copolymer compositions [6,7]. However, Monte-Carlo methods are rarely used in practice as they have until now required much longer simulation times.

We already showed that our use of specialising simulator generators improves the performance over generic Monte-Carlo simulators, such as Drache's system [6], even for simple polymerisation models. However, the acid test for the practical usefulness of our approach is a comparison with the fastest available deterministic solvers. The undisputed leader in this space is the commercial package PREDICI (of CiT GmbH) [12,13]. We originally benchmarked the distributed version 6.36.1 of PREDICI, but after supplying CiT with a draft of our companion paper [8] and after some discussion about the reasons for the poor performance of PREDICI between CiT and us, CiT supplied us with a custom optimised version of PREDICI, which performs much better on the complex styrene model [8, Fig. 5] used for the benchmarks. All PREDICI benchmarks were on a 3.4GHz Xeon machine running Windows; i.e., slightly faster hardware than the P4 cluster, which we measured our code on.

The results are depicted in Figure 4(c). The bars labelled "MC 10^9" and "MC 10^{10}" are for the uniprocessor performance of our specialised Monte-Carlo simulator for 10^9 and 10^{10} particles, respectively, on the P4 cluster. "MC $10^9/8$" and "MC $10^{10}/8$" are for the same code running in parallel on 8 PEs. "MC $10^{10}/16$" is also *only on 8 PEs*, but using 16 processes to gain some further slight speedup by using the HyperThreading capabilities of the processors of the P4 cluster.

Our uniprocessor performance is several times better than the original performance of PREDICI. However, after the optimisation, PREDICI improved by two orders of magnitude[2] and we need to use 4 PEs to achieve roughly the same performance with Monte-Carlo. (At this stage, it is not entirely clear how general the optimisation of PREDICI is.) The number of particles for Monte-Carlo and the accuracy value of PREDICI that give comparable results depend on the simulated model. In this benchmark, Monte-Carlo with 10^9 particles is comparable to PREDICI with an accuracy of 0.02; so, with 8 PEs, we are nearly twice as fast—note that this is on a cheap Ethernet-based cluster.

In summary, our combined performance improvement by specialisation and parallelisation has made Monte-Carlo methods for polymerisation kinetics a practical alternative to deterministic solvers for complex models; especially so, when microscopic detail is of interest that deterministic solvers cannot produce. Moreover, with the increasing number of cores in commodity processors, the lack of parallelisation will be an ever more serious obstacle for deterministic solvers.

6 Related Work

Generative programming. FFTW [4] was clearly an inspiration for us and shares with our approach the use a functional language to generate optimised low-level code. This is, however, where the similarity ends. FFTW provides a library of composable solvers, whereas we presented an application architecture. FFTW heavily relies on dynamic optimisations, whereas our approach is purely static.

ATLAS [14] applies techniques similar to FFTW to the implementation of optimised BLAS algorithms. In particular, it runs benchmarks kernels at installation time to determine important architecture parameters and compose optimised BLAS routines from a range of kernels using a code generator.

---

[2] PREDICI's dramatic improvement is due to an algorithmic change, after studying the behaviour of our complex styrene model with our Monte-Carlo simulator.

Partial evaluation. Partial evaluators for C, such as C-Mix [15] and Tempo [16], share with our work the objective of high-performing, yet easily maintainable code, and they also rely on the C compiler to apply standard optimisations that have been enabled by specialisation. However, there are also significant differences: We changed the core data structures when moving from generic to specialised simulator. It is unlikely that the same kind of changes could have been achieved automatically, as we relied on domain knowledge. Our specialising simulator generator makes heavy use of higher-order functions, pattern matching and algebraic data types. These language features are not or not particularly well supported in C, and so would not be available when implementing a fully generic simulator in C (for specialisation by a partial evaluator tool); i.e., we would lose the benefit of doing most of the algorithmic work in a declarative language.

C++ templates as a substrate for partial evaluation, as in [17], allow the addition of domain specific information, and it would be interesting to investigate if it is possible to get similar results as we have with our approach. However, it would definitely be necessary to push the limits of C++ template programming, a technique which can be fairly tricky and error prone.

Polymerisation kinetics. We based the development of our Monte-Carlo method on [18,19,20,6]. Although Drache et al. [6] use multiple processors to run independent simulations in parallel, to increase the accuracy of the result, we are the first to implemented a parallel version of a *single* simulation. We discussed this and compared our performance with Drache's in Section 5.

7   Conclusion

The classic approach to high-performance Monte-Carlo simulations is to design, implement, and optimise a generic simulator in an imperative language. Using a functional language, we outperformed the classic approach in generality (we fully simulate star polymers) and execution time (we are more than twice as fast on a uniprocessor and scale well in parallel) by exploring the design space with a functional prototype and generating specialised data structures and performance critical code. For the first time, Monte-Carlo methods are now a viable alternative to deterministic solvers for polymerisation kinetics.

Acknowledgements. We would like to thank Dr. Michael Wulkow from CiT GmbH for the stimulating and interesting discussions that have benefited both the PREDICI and parallel Monte Carlo approach. We also thank the anonymous reviewers for their helpful comments.

References

1. Jones, N.D., Gomard, C.K., Sestoft, P.: Partial Evaluation and Automatic Program Generation. Prentice Hall International, Englewood Cliffs (1993)
2. Czarnecki, K., Eisenecker, U.W.: Generative programming: methods, tools, and applications. ACM Press/Addison-Wesley (2000)

3. Veldhuizen, T.L., Gannon, D.: Active libraries: Rethinking the roles of compilers and libraries. In: Proc. of the SIAM Workshop on Object Oriented Methods for Inter-operable Scientific and Engineering Computing (OO 1998) (1998)
4. Frigo, M., Johnson, S.G.: The design and implementation of FFTW3. Proceedings of the IEEE 93(2), 216–231 (2005)
5. Veldhuizen, T.L., Gannon, D.: Active libraries: Rethinking the roles of compilers and libraries. In: Proc. of the SIAM Workshop on Object Oriented Methods for Inter-operable Scientific and Engineering Computing (OO 1998), SIAM Press (1998)
6. Drache, M., Schmidt-Naake, G., Buback, M., Vana, P.: Modeling RAFT polymerization kinetics via Monte Carlo methods: cumyl dithiobenzoate mediated methyl acrylate polymerization. Polymer (2004)
7. Tobita, H., Yanase, F.: Monte Carlo simulation of controlled/living radical polymerization in emulsified systems. Macromolecular Theory and Simulation (2007)
8. Chaffey-Millar, H., Stewart, D.B., Chakravarty, M., Keller, G., Barner-Kowollik, C.: A parallelised high performance Monte Carlo simulation approach for complex polimerization kinetics. Macromolecular Theory and Simulations 16(6), 575–592 (2007)
9. Robert, C., Casella, G.: Monte Carlo Statistical Methods. Springer, Heidelberg (2004)
10. Chaffey-Millar, H., Busch, M., Davis, T.P., Stenzel, M.H., Barner-Kowollik, C.: Advanced computational strategies for modelling the evolution of full molecular weight distributions formed during multiarmed (star) polymerisations 14 (2005)
11. Pang, A., Stewart, D., Seefried, S., Chakravarty, M.M.T.: Plugging Haskell in. In: Proc. of the ACM SIGPLAN Workshop on Haskell, pp. 10–21. ACM Press, New York (2004)
12. Wulkow, M.: Predici (2007), http://www.cit-wulkow.de/tbapred.htm
13. Wulkow, M.: The simulation of molecular weight distributions in polyreaction kinetics by discrete galerkin methods. Macromolecular Theory Simulation 5 (1996)
14. Whaley, R.C., Petitet, A., Dongarra, J.J.: Automated empirical optimization of software and the ATLAS project. Parallel Computing 27(1–2), 3–35 (2001)
15. Glenstrup, A.J., H.M., Secher, J.P.: C-Mix – specialization of C programs. In: Partial Evaluation: Practice and Theory (1999)
16. Consel, C., Hornof, L., Lawall, J.L., Marlet, R., Muller, G., Noy, J., Thibault, S., Volanschi, E.N.: Tempo: Specializing systems applications and beyond. ACM Computing Surveys 30(3) (September 1998)
17. Veldhuizen, T.L.: C++ templates as partial evaluation. Partial Evaluation and Semantic-Based Program Manipulation, 13–18 (1999)
18. Lu, J., Zhang, H., Yang, Y.: Monte carlo simulation of kinetics and chain-length distribution in radical polymerization. Macromolecular Theory and Simulation 2, 747–760 (1993)
19. He, J., Zhang, H., Yang, Y.: Monte carlo simulation of chain length distribution in radical polymerization with transfer reaction. Macromolecular Theory and Simulation 4, 811–819 (1995)
20. Prescott, S.W.: Chain-length dependence in living/controlled free-radical polymerizations: Physical manifestation and Monte Carlo simulation of reversible transfer agents. Macromolecules 36, 9608–9621 (2003)

A Generic Programming Toolkit for PADS/ML: First-Class Upgrades for Third-Party Developers

Mary Fernández[1], Kathleen Fisher[1], J. Nathan Foster[2], Michael Greenberg[1,2], and Yitzhak Mandelbaum[1]

[1] AT&T Research
[2] University of Pennsylvania

Abstract. Domain-specific languages facilitate solving problems in a targeted domain by providing features particular to the domain. Declarative domain-specific languages have the additional benefit that users specify *what something means* rather than *how to do something*. As a result, the language compiler is free to choose the best implementation strategies and to generate multiple artifacts from a single description. PADS/ML is a declarative data description language designed to facilitate ad hoc data management. From a single description, the compiler generates a myriad of artifacts, including data structures for the in-memory representation of the data and parsers and printers. In this paper, we describe a new generic programming infrastructure for PADS/ML that allows third-party developers to define additional useful artifacts without modifying the compiler. We report on two case studies that use this infrastructure. In the first, we build a version of PADX for PADS/ML, allowing any data source with a PADS/ML description to be queried as if it were XML. In the second, we extend Harmony with the ability to synchronize any data with a PADS/ML description.

1 Introduction

Domain-specific languages provide enormous leverage precisely because they have limited scope, allowing their designers to tailor the abstractions they provide to the targeted domain. Declarative domain-specific languages bring an additional benefit in that they specify *what something means*, rather than *how to do something*. As a result, the compiler is free to decide how to accomplish the task and even what tasks need to be accomplished. This freedom allows the designers of declarative domain-specific languages to generate more than one software artifact from a single specification.

The PADS/ML language is a declarative domain-specific language for specifying the format of ad hoc data [MFW+07]. An *ad hoc* data format is any semi-structured data representation for which parsing, querying, analysis, or transformation tools are not readily available. Despite the existence of standard formats like XML, ad hoc data sources are ubiquitous, arising in industries as diverse as finance, health care, transportation, and telecommunications as well as in scientific domains, such as computational biology and physics. Figure 1 summarizes a variety of such formats, including ASCII and binary encodings, with both fixed and variable-width records arranged in linear sequences and in tree-shaped hierarchies.

P. Hudak and D.S. Warren (Eds.): PADL 2008, LNCS 4902, pp. 133–149, 2008.
© Springer-Verlag Berlin Heidelberg 2008

Name	Use	Representation
Gene Ontology (GO) [Con]	Gene Product Information	Variable-width ASCII records
SDSS/Reglens Data [MHS$^+$05]	Weak gravitational lensing analysis	Floating point numbers, et al
Web server logs (CLF)	Measuring web workloads	Fixed-column ASCII records
AT&T Call detail data	Phone call fraud detection	Fixed-width binary records
Newick	Immune system response simulation	Fixed-width ASCII records in tree-shaped hierarchy
OPRA	Options-market transactions	Mixed binary & ASCII records with data-dependent unions
Palm PDA	Device synchronization	Mixed binary & character with data-dependent constraints

Fig. 1. Selected ad hoc data sources

Common characteristics of ad hoc data make it difficult to perform even basic data-processing tasks. To start, data analysts have little control over the format of the data; it typically arrives "as is," and the analysts can only thank the supplier, not request a more convenient format. The documentation accompanying ad hoc data is often incomplete, inaccurate, or missing entirely, which makes understanding the data format more difficult. Ad hoc data sources frequently contain errors, which poses another challenge. For some applications, like system monitors, erroneous data is more important than error-free data; it may signal, for example, where two systems are failing to communicate. Unfortunately, writing code that reliably handles both error-free and erroneous data is difficult and tedious.

The PADS/ML system, like its close ancestor PADS/C [FG05], solves these problems by providing a declarative data description language. A PADS/ML specification describes the physical layout and semantic properties of an ad hoc data source. The language provides a type-based model: basic types specify atomic data such as integers, strings, dates, *etc.*, while structured types such as tuples, records, and datatypes describe compound data. Leveraging the declarative nature of such descriptions, the PADS/ML compiler generates from each description a suite of useful data structures and tools, including a canonical in-memory representation of the data, a canonical meta-data representation called a *parse descriptor*, a parser, and a printer.

Ideally, a system like PADS/ML would permit third-party developers to build new tools for specifications without modifying the compiler. With that goal in mind, the original PADS/ML compiler generated an OCAML functor for traversing the canonical data structure. Although an improvement over PADS/C, which requires modifying the compiler to generate new tools, the PADS/ML infrastructure was insufficient because it only supported tools that *consume* a PADS data representation in a single depth-first, left-to-right traversal. This limitation precludes many useful tools, *e.g.,* those that require a different traversal strategy or that *produce* a PADS/ML data representation rather than consuming one.

To rectify this deficiency, we redesigned the generic tool infrastructure of PADS/ML, leveraging ideas from type-directed programming [Yan98, Hin04]. Given a PADS/ML description, third-party developers can now build a wide variety of generic tools relating to the description's in-memory representation and parse descriptor. To illustrate the power of this generic infrastructure, we describe two third-party tools that did not require making tool-specific changes to the compiler: an implementation of PADX [FFGM06], a system for querying any PADS data source as though it were XML; and an extension to Harmony [FGK+07, PBF+], a system for synchronizing data.

The contributions of this paper are:

- An extension of PADS/ML with a generic tool infrastructure, which permits third parties to easily build new tools for processing PADS data (Section 3).
- A demonstration of how to implement generic programming constructs in OCAML (Section 3).
- Case studies of two non-trivial ad hoc data tools whose functionality was enhanced by using PADS/ML's generic tool infrastructure (Section 4).

We briefly review the PADS/ML data description language in Section 2. We then describe the generic tool framework in Section 3. In Section 4, we describe how the framework was used to build PADX and Harmony. We survey related work and conclude in Section 5.

2 A Review of PADS/ML

In this section, we briefly describe PADS/ML; a more complete description appears in earlier publications [MFW+07, Man06]. A PADS/ML description specifies the physical layout and semantic properties of an ad hoc data source. These descriptions are formulated using types. Base types describe atomic data, such as ASCII-encoded, 8-bit unsigned integers (puint8), binary 32-bit integers (pbint32), dates (pdate), strings (pstring), and the singleton types corresponding to literal values. Certain base types take additional OCAML values as parameters. For example, pstring(c) describes strings that are immediately followed by the character c. Structured types describe compound data built using standard type constructors such as tuples and records for specifying ordered data, variants for specifying alternatives, and lists for specifying homogeneous sequences of data. Type constraints describe data satisfying arbitrary programmer-specified semantic conditions—*e.g.*, that a string pstring has at least ten characters. The following subsections illustrate PADS/ML types further using Cisco router configuration files as an example.

2.1 Example: Cisco Router Configuration

A configuration file for a Cisco router sets the values of parameters that control the router's behavior. The configuration language contains hundreds of commands, and a typical configuration file has hundreds of commands with thousands of parameters. A configuration file lists commands, one per line, where the first word on the line is the command and the remaining words are parameters. A command may depend on

```
version 12.0
!
hostname anaconda
username viking password 5 AF334003CC2
policy-map mis_policy_90:100_output_12K
  class rt_class
    priority
    police cir percent 90 conf-act tx
end
```

Fig. 2. A tiny excerpt of a Cisco router configuration file

```
ptype command = cmd_name * ' ' * cmd_args
ptype section (min_indent : int) = {
  indent: [i: pstring_ME("/^ */") | length i >= min_indent];
  start_cmd: command; peol;
  sub_cmds: section(length indent + 1) plist(No_sep,Error_term)
}
ptype config_element =
    Section of section (0)
  | Comment of pre "/ *[!].*$/" * peol
ptype source = config_element plist(No_sep,No_term)
```

Fig. 3. Simplified description of Cisco configuration files

other commands, indicated by indentation. Additionally, configurations may include comments, marked by "!". Figure 2 shows an excerpt of such a file.

Figure 3 contains a simplified PADS/ML description of the Cisco configuration file format. The description is a sequence of type definitions. The first definition, command, describes a single command consisting of a command name followed by its arguments. The section type describes a group of related commands. A command is deemed to be a child of an earlier command if its indentation is greater. To express this constraint, section is parameterized by the expected minimum indentation, and its identation is checked against the parameter. The section type is a record with three fields. The first field indent describes the indentation preceding every command. It detects a decrease in indentation level signals, which signals the end of a command group, using a *constraint*. The second field, start_cmd, describes the first command of the section, and the third field, sub_cmds, describes the list of its subcommands.

The plist constructor defining the subcommand list takes three parameters: on the left, the element type; on the right, an optional *separator* that delimits list elements, and an optional *terminator*. In this example, the list has no separators; it terminates when it encounters an element with an error. Next, config_element uses a variant type to indicate that an element of a configuration file can be either a section or a comment line. Lastly, the type source describes a complete Cisco configuration file as a list of elements with no separator and no special terminator. It is terminated with the default terminator of the end-of-file.

```
type source = Config_element.rep plist
type source_pd_body = Config_element.pd_body plist_pd_body Pads.pd
module Source :
  sig
    type rep = source
    type pd_body = source_pd_body
    type pd = pd_body Pads.pd
    val   parse : Pads.handle -> rep * pd
    val   print : rep -> pd -> Pads.handle -> unit
    module MakeTyrep (GenFunTys:GenFunTys.S) : sig
      val tyrep : ...
    end
    ...
  end
```

Fig. 4. Selected software artifacts generated from the `source` type

2.2   Compiling PADS/ML

Given a description, the PADS/ML compiler creates an OCAML library containing types for the in-memory representation and for the parse-descriptor body for each type in the PADS/ML description. It also contains a module with functions for parsing and printing the data, and a functor for creating a runtime representation of the types. Figure 4 shows the signature of the module produced for the type `source` from Figure 3.

For reference, we note that the structure of the parse descriptor reflects that of the representation. Every parse descriptor has a header with meta data describing the entirety of the corresponding representation (error information, *etc.*), and a body, consisting of descriptors for each subcomponent. Therefore, every parse descriptor has the type `pd_header * 'pdb`, for some parse-descriptor body type `'pdb`. We use the abbreviation `'a pd = pd_header * 'a` to express this structure.

3   Generic Programming for Ad Hoc Data

In a data-processing pipeline, several steps typically occur between parsing and printing. Some steps may be application specific, but many others can be expressed generically and applied to data of any type. Examples include compression and decompression, pretty printing, flattening, database formatting, cleaning, querying, conversion to and from generic formats such as XML and S-expressions, summarization, data generators (*e.g.,* for testing), and transformations like those described in the "scrap-your-boilerplate" series [LP03, LP04, LP05]. Given the variety and number of generic operations, we wish to provide third-party developers with a mechanism to express such operations, without having to modify the PADS/ML compiler.

We use the term "generic" to mean *type indexed*. A type-indexed function defines a family of functions, with one member of the family for every type in the index. A type-indexed function can be constrasted with a *polymorphic* function, which is a single function that can be used at many different types. Because PADS/ML descriptions

```
type summary = ... (* uniform data summary type. *)
type seed =  ... (* seed value used in data generation. *)
('r,'b) pretty_print = 'r -> 'b Pads.pd -> string
('r,'b) flatten     = 'r -> 'b Pads.pd -> (string * string) list
('r,'b) decompress  = in_channel -> 'r * ('b Pads.pd)
('r,'b) summarize   = 'r -> 'b Pads.pd -> summary -> summary
('r,'b) clean       = 'r * 'b Pads.pd -> 'r * 'b Pads.pd
('r,'b) generate    = seed  -> 'r * ('b Pads.pd)
```

Fig. 5. Type constructors for selected generic functions

consist of types, it is natural to express algorithms that are generic to any description as functions indexed by the types of the in-memory representation and the parse descriptor.

Previously, we introduced a generic-tool framework for PADS/ML to support third-party tool development [MFW+07]. While this framework was sufficient to code a number of useful functions, it had limitations. Specifically, it only supported functions that could be implemented by consuming the in-memory representation of PADS/ML data in a single depth-first, left-to-right traversal.

In this section, we present a fully redesigned framework that supports a much broader range of generic functions. We begin with an overview of our new framework. Then, we provide two examples of how the system is used, from the perspectives of both the user and the tool developer. Finally, we will describe the implementation of the generic tool framework, including the details of type representations.

3.1 Overview

In our generic-programming architecture, three different "actors" cooperate to build and use each generic function f: the end user, the PADS/ML compiler, and the tool developer. When a user wants to apply a generic function f to data of a particular type τ, she needs to *specialize* f to τ, that is, select the member of f appropriate to τ. We use the notation $f[\tau]$ to denote this member. Note that for every type-indexed function f, there is a type constructor σ that relates the type indices of f to the types of members of f—specifically, $f[\tau] : \sigma(\tau)$. For example, Figure 5 lists type constructors for some useful generic functions.

While, conceptually, specialization involves types τ, in reality, OCAML provides no way to manipulate, or even access, types in code. Therefore, we must encode type indexes as runtime values, which we call *type representations*. A function specialize, defined in the PADS/ML runtime, instantiates generic functions to particular types using the type's runtime representation. All type representations are built from a set of combinators, which we will describe in greater detail at the end of this section. In principle, the user can use the combinators to construct type representations by hand. In practice, though, such constructions are tedious boilerplate and therefore best generated automatically. Therefore, the PADS/ML compiler generates the runtime representations for each PADS/ML type, along with all of the other generated software artifacts.

The tool developer is responsible for writing f as a type-indexed function. In OCAML, a natural way to express such functions is by pattern matching on a representation of

```
<Left>
  <fst>""</fst>
  <snd>
    <fst><fst>version</fst><snd>12.0</snd></fst>
    <snd/>
  </snd>
</Left>
```

Fig. 6. Cisco config command `version 12.0` encoded in XML using a canonical, sums-of-products schema

the type. Therefore, the developer implements f by specifying the generic function's behavior for each PADS/ML type constructor, including base types, records, tuples, variants, and user-defined types. Note that the role of "tool developer" might be played by a range of users, from PADS/ML developers to data analysts. Our goal is that tool developers should not need any expertise in PADS/ML internals to be productive, although we do expect a higher level of programming expertise for tool developers than for average PADS/ML users.

3.2   Example: Conversion to XML

We begin with an example use of a generic function `to_xml` that translates any PADS data to a corresponding canonical XML representation.[1] This canonical representation uses one schema to encode all data as anonymous sums of products. We explain our choice of this simple encoding when we dicuss the implementation of `to_xml`.

In the example, the end-user wants to translate Cisco configuration data into XML, so she needs to specialize the generic function `to_xml` to the `source` type from the Cisco description of Figure 3. The user might perform this conversion as follows:

```
module SourceTyrep = Cisco.Source.MakeTyrep(TXTys)
let source_to_xml = specialize to_xml SourceTyrep.tyrep
let r,pd = ... Cisco.Source.parse ... ;;
let source_xml = source_to_xml r pd "Config"
```

In the first line, she creates a representation of the type `source` by applying the functor `MakeTyRep`, generated by the compiler for this purpose, to the module `TXTys` defined by the `to_xml` tool writer to specify the type structure of that tool. In the second line, she specializes the generic function `to_xml` to the type `source`, creating the function `source_to_xml`. She then parses the configuration file to create a data representation `r` and its corresponding parse descriptor `pd`. Finally, she applies the specialized conversion function to `r`, `pd`, and a tag for the resulting XML element, yielding an XML representation of the data. Figure 6 shows the result of converting the command "`version 12.0`" in Figure 2 into XML using the `to_xml` function.

Next, we turn to the tool developer's task of implementing the generic function `to_xml`. Figure 7 shows an excerpt of the code. The first four lines define the type

---

[1] We presume a type `xml` with two constructors: `PCData`, for atomic values, and `Element`, for structured values; and a pretty-printer for such values.

```
module ToXMLTycon =
struct
  type ('a,'pdb) t = 'a -> 'pdb pd -> string -> xml
end
module TXTys = GenFunTys.MakeGeneric(ToXMLTycon)
let rec to_xml = { TXTys.
  int = (fun i (hdr,()) tag ->
    Element(t,[PCData(string_of_int i)])));
  tuple = (fun a_ty b_ty (a,b) (hdr,(a_pd,b_pd)) tag ->
    let a_xml = specialize to_xml a_ty a a_pd "fst" in
    let b_xml = specialize to_xml b_ty b b_pd "snd" in
      Element(tag,[a_xml;b_xml])
  );
  sum = (fun a_ty b_ty v (hdr,v_pdb) tag ->
    match v,v_pdb with
      Left a, Left a_pd  ->
        Element(tag,[specialize to_xml a_ty a a_pd "Left"])
    | Right b,Right b_pd ->
        Element(tag,[specialize to_xml b_ty b b_pd "Right"])
  );
  defined = (fun a_ty (from_t, to_t) (from_pdb, to_pdb)
                 t (hdr,t_pdb) tag ->
    specialize to_xml a_ty (from_t t) (hdr,(from_pdb t_pdb)) tag
  );
}
```

Fig. 7. Excerpt of a generic converter to XML

constructor TXTys, which describes the types of the specializations of the generic function to_xml. The implementation of the generic function follows. It is actually a record with one field for each type constructor that can appear in a type index. Each field defines a function that specifies how the generic function behaves for the corresponding type constructor.

For the sake of brevity, we have simplified the implementation of to_xml. In the full implementation, there are cases for most of OCAML's base types and a default case. The cases for sums and products have additional parameters to support n-ary sums and products with field and constructor names, and nullary constructors, thereby fully supporting OCAML's named records and variant types. Additionally, parse descriptor headers are included in the XML when they indicate an error in the data.

The case (*i.e.,* field) for integers, int, takes the representation of a parsed integer and its parse descriptor as arguments. It returns a representation of that integer wrapped in the XML constructor PCData. More interesting is the field tuple, which corresponds to the case for binary products. The first two arguments, a_ty and b_ty, represent the types of the tuple components. They are used to specialize to_xml for use with those components. The next two arguments are the tuple to be converted and its parse descriptor. The last argument is the tag to be used when constructing the XML element. The first two lines of the function body translate the components into XML by specializing to_xml to the type of each tuple component and applying the result to the appropriate

```
module FromXMLTycon =
struct
  type ('a,'pdb) t = xml -> ('a * 'pdb pd)
end
module FXTys = GenFunTys.MakeGeneric(FromXMLTycon)
let rec from_xml = { FXTys.
  int = (fun Element(_,[PCData(s)]) ->
    try int_of_string s, (good_hdr,())
    with Failure "int_of_string" -> 0, (error_hdr,()));
  tuple = (fun pos a_name a_ty b_ty Element(_,[a_xml;b_xml]) ->
    let (a,a_pd) = a_ty from_xml a_xml in
    let (b,b_pd) = b_ty from_xml b_xml in
      (a,b),(valid_hdr,(a_pd,b_pd))
  );
  sum = (fun pos a_name a_ty a_empty b_ty b_empty -> function
      Element(_,[Element("Left",_) as a_xml]) ->
        let a,a_pd = a_ty from_xml a_xml in
          Left a, (valid_hdr, Left a_pd)
    | Element(_,[Element("Right",_) as b_xml]) ->
        let b, b_pd = b_ty from_xml b_xml in
          Right b, (valid_hdr, Right b_pd)
  );
  defined = (fun a_ty (from_t, to_t) (from_pdb, to_pdb) a_xml ->
    let a,(h,a_pdb) = a_ty from_xml a_xml in
      (to_t a),(h,to_pdb a_pdb)
  );
}
```

Fig. 8. Generic converter from XML

component. Note that this "appropriateness" is statically checked by the OCAML compiler (that is, unless the components have the same type, inverting the type representations will result in a type error.) Finally, the XML for the components is bundled into a single element with the tag specified by the final argument.

The case for binary sums follows the same pattern as that of binary tuples. For user-defined types, we borrow from Hinze [Hin04], requiring the tool writer to use functions that convert between the user-defined type and a sum-of-products type (similarly for the parse descriptor). These compiler-generated conversions are supplied by the caller of the tool as the second and third arguments of the defined field (the first argument is a representation of the sum-of-products type). In our example, we are mapping from a type to XML, so we use the "from" conversion function.

3.3 Example: Conversion from XML

A significant improvement in the new generic interface for PADS/ML is that it does not limit developers to writing functions that consume data. To illustrate this point, we define in Figure 8 the implementation of a generic function from_xml that *produces* data of a given type from XML input.

The implementation mirrors that of to_xml. The first four lines specify the type constructor for the generic function and create the type of the from_xml generic function. The field definitions for from_xml follow the same pattern as those for to_xml, producing data rather than consuming it. One difference relates to parse descriptors. The type constructor for from_xml requires a parse descriptor along with the reconstructed data. But we discarded such descriptors when converting to XML, so we need to recreate them now. In most cases, we simply provide a place-holder valid_hdr to indicate the data is error free. For the int field, however, we check that the string in the XML is a valid integer and report errors using the parse descriptor.

3.4   Other Generic Functions

All our example tools are self contained in that they make no reference to other generic functions. Our framework, however, permits generic functions that depend on other generic functions, and even mutually recursive generic functions. The only limitation is that such functions must all share the same generic-function type constructor.

3.5   Type Representations

We now discuss the implementation of type representations, reusing the to_xml generic function from above for an example. The tool developer implemented to_xml as a record with one field for each type constructor. The end user specialized this generic function implementation to a particular PADS/ML type τ by applying the specialize function to a representation of the type τ. The expression specialize to_xml has the polymorphic type

```
specialize to_xml : ('r,'p) tyrep -> 'r -> 'p pd -> xml
```

Notice that the type constructor σ of to_xml is expressed implicitly in this type.

While the runtime provides the definition of the specialize function, it is the task of the compiler to produce the representation of the PADS/ML type τ. Following Yang's approach [Yan98], we choose to represent each PADS/ML type τ as a function that takes as an argument a generic function, (*i.e.*, a record of functions, each field specifying the behavior of the generic function for one type constructor) and selects the field of the generic function corresponding to τ. If τ is a simple type, that is all the type representation function need do. If τ is a type constructor, the type representation function then applies the selected function to the representations of the arguments of the type constructor.

For example, the representation of the PADS/ML type (pint*pint) is:

```
fun gf -> gf.tuple (fun gf -> gf.int) (fun gf -> gf.int)
```

This function takes a generic function gf as an argument and selects the tuple field. Because tuples are type constructors with two arguments, the type representation function for the pair then applies this selected function to the type representation of the arguments, pint. This representation type function simply selects the int field from the generic function gf.

```
type to_xml_record = {
   int     : int -> unit pd -> xml
   tuple   : 'a 'b 'p 'q. ('a,'p) type_rep -> ('b,'q) type_rep
             -> ('a * 'b) -> ('p pd * 'q pd) pd -> xml
   sum     : 'a 'b 'p 'q. ('a,'p) type_rep -> ('b,'q) type_rep
             -> ('a,'b) sum -> ('p pd,'q pd) sum pd -> xml
   defined : 'a 'p 'u 'q. ('a,'p) type_rep -> ('a,'u) iso
                   -> ('p,'q) iso -> 'u -> 'q pd -> xml
}
and ('r,'p) type_rep = to_xml_record -> 'r -> 'p pd -> xml
```

Fig. 9. The type of to_xml

With this choice for the representation of types, the definition of the specialize function is trivial— it is just function application: fun gf ty -> ty gf. This one definition handles all generic functions and all type representations. In contrast, the compiler must generate a different type representation for each PADS/ML type in a description.

The type system of OCAML ensures that the application of a generic function to a type representation will never go wrong, but getting our choice for type representations as functions to typecheck in OCAML takes a bit of engineering. To illustrate, we again turn to the to_xml example. Figure 9 defines the type to_xml_record, which is the type of the generic function implementation to_xml. Notice that the record fields contain first-class polymorphic functions. This flexibility is essential because the representation of a PADS/ML type might need to apply the same field to several distinct types, *e.g.*, for a PADS/ML type containing more than one kind of tuple. Figure 9 also defines the type constructor type_rep, which is the type of the representation of all PADS/ML types for the to_xml generic function. As an example, the type of the representation of the the PADS/ML type (pint*pint) is

```
to_xml_record -> int*int -> (int_pd*int_pd) pd -> xml
```

which is just (int*int,int_pd*int_pd) type_rep.

3.6   Tool-Independent Type Representations

The types in Figure 9 describe the to_xml generic function very precisely; too precisely, in fact. Those types and the type representations built from them are specific to to_xml and could not be used for other generic function, for example, from_xml. To support a wide range of different generic functions, we follow Yang's approach and provide tool-*independent* type representations and record types, by abstracting away the pieces that are particular to each generic function. Specifically, we must abstract away the type constructor associated with the generic function.

Here we encounter a problem: abstracting over a type constructor requires support for higher-order polymorphism, a feature not provided in OCAML's core language. Therefore, we turn to OCAML's module system and use a functor to do the abstraction. Figure 10 shows a simplified excerpt of such a functor, MakeGeneric, provided by the PADS/ML runtime. This functor defines the type of the representation of PADS/ML types

```
type 'a pd = pd_hdr * 'a
type ('a,'t) iso = ('t -> 'a) * ('a -> 't)
type ('l,'r) sum = Left of 'l | Right of 'r
module MakeGeneric(GenFunTycon: sig type ('r,'pdb,'s) t end) :
sig
  type ('r,'pdb,'s) gf_tycon = ('r,'pdb,'s) GenFunTycon.t
  type 's gf_record = {
    int    : (int,    unit, 's) gf_tycon;
    tuple : 'a 'b 'a_pdb 'b_pdb.
        ('a,'a_pdb,'s) type_rep ->
        ('b,'b_pdb,'s) type_rep ->
        ('a * 'b, ('a_pdb pd * 'b_pdb pd) pd, 's) gf_tycon;
    sum : 'a 'b 'a_pdb 'b_pdb.
        ('a,'a_pdb,'s) type_rep ->
        ('b,'b_pdb,'s) type_rep ->
        (('a,'b) sum, ('a_pdb pd,'b_pdb pd) sum pd, 's) gf_tycon;
    defined : 'a 'r 'a_pdb 'r_pdb.
        ('a,'a_pdb,'s) type_rep ->
        ('a,'r) iso -> ('a_pdb,'r_pdb) iso ->
        ('r,'r_pdb,'s) gf_tycon;
  }
  and ('r,'pdb,'s) type_rep =
    's gf_record -> ('r,'pdb,'s) gf_tycon
end
```

Fig. 10. A simplified excerpt of the signature of functor MakeGeneric for making generic-function types. This functor is located in the GenFunTys module, which is part of the PADS/ML runtime.

type_rep and the type of the generic-function record for all generic functions associated with the type constructor t, passed as an argument to the functor. Conceptually, the types we described earlier in this section, to_xml_type, *etc.*, result from applying this functor, although in doing the abstraction, we added a parameter to the type constructor t so that a single instance of this functor will be able to express the necessary types for a wider range of generic functions. Note that we have simplified the presentation of this functor in the same way that we simplified to_xml and from_xml – specifically, we have left out a number of cases and the parameters to tuple and sum that provide full support for OCAML's records and variant types.

The issue of higher-order polymorphism arises in the definition of the representation of PADS/ML types as well because the representations reference the labels of the generic-function record. Hence, the definition of the representation of each PADS/ML type is given in a compiler-generated functor MakeTyrep, parameterized by the type of the generic function.

To summarize, the generic function infrastructure provided by PADS/ML has three main components: the function specialize and the functor MakeGeneric, defined once, and the functor MakeTyrep, which is generated for each PADS/ML type in a given description. A tool developer writing a generic function with associated type constructor σ uses the functor MakeGeneric to produce the type of the generic function that she

```
('a, 'pdb, 's) consumer = 'a -> 'pdb Pads.pd -> 's
('a, 'pdb, 's) producer = 's -> 'a * ('pdb Pads.pd)
('a, 'pdb, 's) updater  = 'a * 'pdb Pads.pd -> 'a * 'pdb Pads.pd
flatten      : ('a,'pdb,(string * string) list) consumer
pretty_print : ('a,'pdb, string) consumer
summarize    : ('a,'pdb, summary -> summary) consumer
to_xml       : ('a,'pdb, xml list) consumer
decompress   : ('a,'pdb,in_channel) producer
generate     : ('a,'pdb, seed) producer
from_xml     : ('a,'pdb, xml list) producer
clean : ('a,'pdb,unit) updater
```

Fig. 11. Classes of generic functions

must define. The user of the generic function uses the functor `MakeTyrep` to produce a representation of the PADS/ML type suitable for use with that generic function.

An apparent disadvantage of this functorized approach is that a given type representation can only be applied to one generic function – the one corresponding to the type constructor for which it was instantiated. However, this limitation is not as restrictive as it might seem. The type constructor at which a type representation is instantiated can be far more general than a single generic function and can encompass a family of functions using the extra type parameter 's. For example, Figure 11 shows how to rewrite the function types in Figure 5 in terms of only three generic function classes: consumers, producers, and updaters.

4   Case Studies

Converting ad hoc data to XML is only one of many possible applications of our generic function framework. In this section, we discuss two other uses of the framework.

4.1   PADX/ML

In previous work [FFGM06], we reported on our experience designing and implementing PADX, a system for querying large-scale PADS data sources with XQuery [Kat04], a standardized query language for XML. PADX synthesizes and extends two existing systems: PADS/C and Galax [FSC⁺03]. With PADX, an analyst writes a PADS description of her ad hoc data, and the PADS/C compiler produces two software artifacts: an XML Schema that specifies the virtual XML view of the corresponding PADS data and a customized library for viewing it as XML. The resulting library is linked with the Galax query engine, permitting the analyst to query ad hoc data sources using XQuery.

We were pleased with PADX's functionality. The unified system gave us a standard, high-performance engine for querying ad hoc data without having to build one from scratch. We were frustrated, however, by the implementation and its limitations. We made substantial modifications to the PADS/C compiler to generate PADX's software artifacts, which required 1050 lines of Standard-ML, 2117 lines of C, and 350 lines of OCAML. The generated libraries were large, *e.g.,* the library for the Sirius description [FG05] was more than 7000 lines of C and used C macros extensively, making the code hard to understand and debug. Most significantly, the changes only supported PADX and were incomplete: PADX can map from PADS data to XML but not vice versa.

Using the generic tool framework, the implementation of PADX/ML is more complete, simpler, and more flexible than that of PADX. The PADX/ML consumer tool maps PADS/ML representations and parse descriptors into values in Galax's abstract XML data model (XDM) (*i.e.,* sequences of elements and XML scalar values), and the PADX/ML producer tool does the inverse, enabling the output of XQuery expressions to be represented as PADS data. Together, the tools are implemented in only 884 lines of OCAML.

The PADX consumer yields a completely lazy tree, which permits the Galax query engine to cope with large-scale data more efficiently. Each XML element in Galax's XDM roughly corresponds to a node in the consumer's lazy tree. The consumer is lazy "all the way down", that is, the consumer does not parse a PADS element in a data source until its corresponding node in the XDM is forced. This laziness is important to query performance. For some queries, Galax can produce query plans that access a virtual XML source sequentially using memory bounded by the query size, not the data size. This optimization is only possible if the underlying data source is itself lazy.

The PADX producer maps values in the Galax XDM into PADS/ML. Given a producer specialized on a type and an XML value in the Galax XDM, the producer simply performs a pattern match on the XML value to map it into the corresponding PADS/ML value. When a match fails, a parse-descriptor header is returned, indicating a syntax error. To apply a producer, however, requires knowing the correspondence between an XML value and an extant, unparameterized PADS/ML type. This correspondence can be recovered by validating an XML value with respect to any PADS/ML-generated XML Schema, as each XML Schema type corresponds one-to-one with a PADS/ML type. If validation succeeds, the XML value is labelled with its corresponding XML Schema type. The compiler produces a meta-data table that given an XML Schema type name selects a specialized producer for the corresponding PADS/ML type.

We did make one modification to the PADS/ML compiler for PADX to generate the XML Schema for a PADS/ML specification. A generic type-consumer tool would avoid this problem, by permitting computation over any PADS/ML type, just like the generic value-consumer tool permits computation over the representations and parse descriptors of any PADS/ML value. No technical issue prevents us from providing a generic type-consumer tool, but it is not yet implemented.

4.2 Harmony

In our second case study, we use our generic infrastructure with the Harmony synchronization framework [PBF+]. An instance of Harmony takes as inputs two *replicas* containing data to be synchronized, an *archive* representing their last synchronized state, and a *schema* describing the set of well-formed replicas. Harmony's synchronization algorithm merges non-conflicting changes made to each replica relative to the archive and subject to the constraints expressed in the schema, and produces as outputs maximally-synchronized replicas (and an updated archive). Harmony instances exist for synchronizing browser bookmarks, calendars, address books, and structured documents.

```
{Section={indent={""},
        start_cmd={elt1={version={}},
                  elt2={"12.0"={}}}}}
```

Fig. 12. Cisco config command `version 12.0` encoded as an unordered tree

To simplify the synchronization algorithm—in particular, the task of aligning and identifying the common data in each replica—Harmony's internal data model is unordered trees and not a richer model like XML. Working with unordered trees makes synchronization simpler, but introduces a "last-mile problem"—most data is not stored as unordered trees. Therefore, before the replicas can be processed using Harmony they need to be parsed, and likewise after synchronization, the updated replicas must be serialized to their original formats. Harmony currently relies on a collection of custom "viewers"—i.e., parsers and corresponding pretty printers—for a variety of on-disk formats (XML, CSV, iCalendar, and Palm Datebook) to bridge this gap. These viewers are not ideal, however, being tedious to write and difficult to maintain. Moreover, every new format requires its own custom viewer. A better solution is to use a generic tool to generate a viewer from a PADS description.

We have implemented generic tools for the unordered tree data model analagous to the `to_xml` and `from_xml` tools for XML. The generic consumer takes a PADS representation of a data value and yields a Harmony tree. The generic producer maps a Harmony tree back to a PADS representation. The representation of a data value as an unordered tree is determined by its type: base type values are represented as trees with a single child whose label encodes the value; records are represented as trees with a child for every field; a value belonging to a variant type is represented as a tree with a single child whose label is the tag; and lists are represented using a cons-cell encoding. Figure 12 shows how the Cisco line from the earlier example is represented as an unordered tree (writing "{" for internal tree nodes and "=" for subtrees).

These generic tools provide effective conduits between arbitrary on-disk representations of ad hoc data described in PADS and Harmony's internal data model. We plan to use them to build Harmony instances for several new data formats in the near future.

5   Discussion

Our generic programming framework combines two existing techniques: Yang's theoretical account of type-indexed values and their encoding in ML-like languages using the ML module system [Yan98], and Hinze's framework for generic programming using Haskell's type classes [Hin04]. We compare our work to these approaches in turn.

We make a number of improvements to Yang's original presentation. First, his theoretical encoding requires first-class polymorphism, which at the time was only available in the ML module system. Now that OCAML provides first-class polymorphism within records, his encoding can be expressed in a significantly more lightweight manner. Second, we have generalized his theoretical encoding to support the definition of generic functions based on other generic functions. Finally, Yang did not support user-defined recursive types, which we address using techniques based on Hinze's work.

While Yang's work showed how to implement generics in OCAML, Hinze's work is the most closely related in terms of the interface it provides to users and generic function developers. The essential difference between Hinze's framework and our own is that Hinze's solution works for Haskell, while ours is for OCAML. This difference manifests itself most notably in that Hinze uses Haskell's type classes to parameterize over type constructors, and so he manages type representations implicitly as dictionaries. We use OCAML's module system for parameterization and our type representations must be passed explicitly, which provides more control over instantiation at the price of some syntactic overhead. An important practical but less essential difference is that we have adapted our system for use with PADS/ML, incorporating parse descriptors and requiring tools to implement a case for constrained types.

The "scrap-your-boilerplate" series of papers [LP03, LP04, LP05] presents another approach to generic programming in HASKELL. Recently, members of the Gallium project have added support for similar functionality to OCAML with the new camlp4 system [cam]. We refer readers to the SYB papers for a full comparison of SYB to other generic-programming approaches, including this one.

Shortly before this paper was ready for publication, Yallop [Yal07] and Karvonen [Kar07] published works on generic programming in ML. Due to lack of time to fully review their work, we offer only basic comparisons. Yallop's work uses camlp4 – an OCAML preprocessor – to extend OCaml with a deriving construct, similar to that found in Haskell. As Yallop points out in his conclusion, while this approach offers a convenient way to use the generic functions, it does not address the challenge of writing new generic functions, which is exactly the goal of the current work. Karvonen's work is more closely related in that it supports generic programming within ML itself, rather than in a preprocessor. However, Karvonen is working within the confines of Standard ML, which lacks recursive values and first-class polymorphism. Hence, the challenges he faces are somewhat different, as is his resulting solution.

The most direct contributions of the present work are both related to PADS/ML: the extension of PADS/ML's support for third-party development of type-directed tools and the description of two non-trivial tools built using this extension. However, both of these contributions have broader relevance. The latter, because PADX/ML and extended Harmony provide compelling examples of the applicability of generic programming techniques to real-world challenges. The former, because the generic programming framework that we present is relevant to OCAML developers in general, not just those interested in PADS/ML.

Acknowledgments

We would like to thank the anonymous reviewers for their helpful comments on the paper and its organization.

References

[cam]   Camlp4 - Gallium,
           http://brion.inria.fr/gallium/index.php/Camlp4
[Con]   Gene Ontology Consortium. Gene ontology project,
           http://www.geneontology.org

[FFGM06]   Fernández, M., Fisher, K., Gruber, R., Mandelbaum, Y.: PADX: Querying large-scale ad hoc data with XQuery. In: PLAN-X (2006)

[FG05]   Fisher, K., Gruber, R.: PADS: A domain-specific language for processing ad hoc data. In: PLDI (2005)

[FGK⁺07]   Nathan Foster, J., Greenwald, M.B., Kirkegaard, C., Pierce, B.C., Schmitt, A.: Exploiting schemas in data synchronization. Journal of Computer and System Sciences 73(4) (June 2007)

[FSC⁺03]   Fernández, M.F., Siméon, J., Choi, B., Marian, A., Sur, G.: Implementing XQuery 1.0: The Galax experience. In: VLDB, pp. 1077–1080 (2003)

[Hin04]   Hinze, R.: Generics for the masses. In: ICFP (2004)

[Kar07]   Karvonen, V.A.J.: Generics for the working ml'er. In: ML Workshop (2007)

[Kat04]   Katz, H. (ed.): XQuery from the experts. Addison-Wesley, Reading (2004)

[LP03]   Lämmel, R., Peyton Jones, S.: Scrap your boilerplate: a practical design pattern for generic programming. In: TLDI (2003)

[LP04]   Lämmel, R., Peyton Jones, S.: Scrap more boilerplate: reflection, zips, and generalised casts. In: ICFP (2004)

[LP05]   Lämmel, R., Peyton Jones, S.: Scrap your boilerplate with class: extensible generic functions. In: ICFP (2005)

[Man06]   Mandelbaum, Y.: The Theory and Practice of Data Description. PhD thesis, Princeton University (September 2006)

[MFW⁺07]   Mandelbaum, Y., Fisher, K., Walker, D., Fernandez, M., Gleyzer, A.: PADS/ML: A functional data description language. In: POPL (2007)

[MHS⁺05]   Mandelbaum, R., Hirata, C.M., Seljak, U., Guzik, J., Padmanabhan, N., Blake, C., Blanton, M.R., Lupton, R., Brinkmann, J.: Systematic errors in weak lensing: application to SDSS galaxy-galaxy weak lensing. Mon. Not. R. Astron. Soc. 361, 1287–1322 (2005)

[PBF⁺]   Pierce, B.C., Bohannon, A., Foster, J.N., Greenwald, M.B., Khanna, S., Kunal, K., Schmitt, A.: Harmony: A synchronization framework for heterogeneous tree-structured data, http://www.seas.upenn.edu/~harmony/

[Yal07]   Yallop, J.: Practical generic programming in ocaml. In: ML Workshop (2007)

[Yan98]   Yang, Z.: Encoding types in ML-like languages. In: ICFP (1998)

Matchete: Paths through the Pattern Matching Jungle

Martin Hirzel[1], Nathaniel Nystrom[1], Bard Bloom[1], and Jan Vitek[1,2]

[1] IBM Watson Research Center, 19 Skyline Drive, Hawthorne, NY 10532, USA
{hirzel,nystrom,bardb,jvitek}@us.ibm.com
[2] Purdue University, Dpt. of Computer Science, West Lafayette, IN 47907, USA

Abstract. Pattern matching is a programming language feature for selecting a handler based on the structure of data while binding names to sub-structures. By combining selection and binding, pattern matching facilitates many common tasks such as date normalization, red-black tree manipulation, conversion of XML documents, or decoding TCP/IP packets. Matchete is a language extension to Java that unifies different approaches to pattern matching: regular expressions, structured term patterns, XPath, and bit-level patterns. Matchete naturally allows nesting of these different patterns to form composite patterns. We present the Matchete syntax and describe a prototype implementation.

Keywords: Pattern matching, regular expressions, XPath, binary data formats, Java.

1   Introduction

Recognizing patterns in data is a recurrent problem in computer science. Many programming languages and systems provide syntax for pattern matching. Functional programming languages emphasize matching over data types, and support defining functions as sequences of cases over the structure of their parameters. String-oriented languages such as AWK or Perl come with builtin support for pattern matching with a powerful regular expression language. XML processing systems often support extracting sub-structures from a document. Finally, some languages support matching of bit-level data to extract patterns in network packets or binary data streams. While pattern matching constructs differ in terms of syntax, data types, type safety, and expressive power, they share the common characteristic of being able to conditionally deconstruct input data and bind variables to portions of their input. This paper is a step towards a unified pattern matching construct for the Java programming language. Our experimental compiler, called Matchete, supports the different flavors of pattern matching mentioned above as well as user-defined patterns.

Below is a simple example that illustrates the expressive power of Matchete. The method findAge() expects a list of strings containing a name and an age, encoded as a sequence of letters followed by a seqence of digits. It traverses the list until it finds a value matching its name argument. If found, it converts the associated age to an integer and returns it. This function showcases a number of features of Matchete. The match statement extracts the value from a List object. A nested pattern specifies a regular expression and at the same time performs string comparison against the value of name. Its age field is implicitly converted from a String to a primitive int.

P. Hudak and D.S. Warren (Eds.): PADL 2008, LNCS 4902, pp. 150–166, 2008.

```
int findAge(String name, List l) {
  match(l) {
    cons~(/([a-zA-Z]+) ([0-9]+)/(name, int age), _): return age;
    cons~(_, List tail): return findAge(name, tail);
  }
  return -1;
}
```

Matchete's contribution is a seamless and expressive integration of the major flavors of pattern matching with a straightforward syntax and semantics. This should be contrasted with many recent efforts that focus on a particular pattern matching style, for example, functional-style patterns in an object-oriented language [5,19,20]. In Matchete, functional-style term patterns, Perl-style regular expressions, XPath expressions, and Erlang-style bit-level patterns can contain one another, and use the same small set of primitive patterns at the leaves. Matchete is a minimal extension to Java, adding only one new statement, one new declaration, and one new kind of expression to the base language. We have implemented a fully functional prototype and have validated the applicability of Matchete by a number of small case studies. The Matchete prototype compiler performs no optimizations, we leave this to future work.

2   Related Work

Structured term pattern matching is a central feature of functional programming languages. In languages such as ML [22] or Haskell [17], instances of algebraic data types can be constructed and deconstructed using the same constructors. The simplicity and elegance of the approach is tied to having a relatively simple data model in which the definition of a data type suffices to automatically define constructors that can be inverted to deconstructors. Object oriented languages introduce abstract data types, and even where constructors could be automatically inverted, this would violate encapsulation and interact poorly with inheritance. A number of recent works have investigated extensions to object-oriented languages that allow pattern matching over abstract data types. Views are implicit coercions between data types that are applied during pattern matching [27]. Active patterns [26] for F# generalize views to functions that deconstruct values into an option type—either Some values if the input value can be deconstructed or None. Active patterns can be used just like regular structural pattern matching on data types. Scala's extractors [5] are a form of active patterns for objects. PLT Scheme's match form allows adding new pattern matching macros, which can be used to support other kinds of pattern matching by supplying an expansion to the primitive matching forms [29]. Tom is a preprocessor that adds structured term pattern matching to Java, C, and Eiffel [23]. OOMatch [25] and JMatch [20] are Java extensions. OOMatch allows pattern declaration in method parameters and resembles Matchete in its treatment of extractors. JMatch provides invertible methods and constructors, which serve to deconstruct values during pattern matching, and also support iteration and logic programming.

String pattern matching is a central feature of text-processing languages such as SNOBOL [12] and Perl [28]. While the Java standard library provides an API for Perl-style regular expressions, which are familiar to many programmers, this API can be awkward to use and leads to code that is considerably more verbose than an equivalent Perl program. Matchete addresses this shortcoming by integrating Perl regular expressions directly in the language.

Bit-level data manipulation has traditionally been the domain of low-level languages such as C. Some recent work takes a type-based approach for parsing bit-level data [1,4,7]. The Erlang programming language, on the other hand, allows specifying bit-level patterns directly. Erlang's patterns are widely used for network protocols, and are optimized [14]. Matchete follows the Erlang approach.

XML pattern matching comes in two flavors: XPath expressions and semi-structured terms. XPath expressions are paths through the tree representation of an XML document that specify sets of nodes [3]. XPath is the primary matching mechanism of XSLT, and Matchete supports XPath directly. Several recent languages treat XML as semi-structured terms [2,8,15,16,18,19,21]. These languages support patterns similar to structured term patterns in functional languages, in some cases augmented by Kleene closure over sibling tree nodes. Matchete also supports structured term patterns.

What sets Matchete apart from this previous work is that it integrates XPath and structured term matching with each other and with Perl-style regular expressions and bit-level patterns.

3   The Matchete Language

Matchete extends Java with a match statement with the following syntax:

MatchStatement ::= match (*Expression*) { *MatchClause** }
MatchClause   ::= *MatchPattern* : *Statement*

A match requires an *Expression* (the subject of the match) and zero or more *Match-Clauses*. Each *MatchClause* has the form *MatchPattern* : *Statement*, where the *MatchPattern* guards the execution of the *Statement* (or handler), and may make some bindings available for the handler. The syntax deliberately resembles that of the Java switch statement, with three important differences: there is no need to write case before each clause, each handler consists of a single statement (which may be a block), and the break keyword is not used to prevent fall-through. This last difference is motivated by software engineering concerns (it is a common mistake to forget a break), and by the need to provide a well-defined scope for variables bound by patterns.

A common beginner's exercise in functional languages is to write a recursive function mult that multiplies the elements of a list. List multiplication has a simple recursive definition: multiply the first element with the result of multiplying the rest of the list. For example, mult([2, 3]) = 2*mult([3]) = 2*3*mult([]). The last factor, mult([]), requires a base case: for an empty list the function returns 1, the multiplicative identity. Of course, if any number in the list is zero, the entire product will be zero and the rest of the list need not be evaluated.

Fig. 1 shows the Matchete definition of mult. The match statement matches the parameter ls against two clauses. The first clause handles the case when the value at the head of the list is zero. The second clause extracts the head of the list, h, and the tail of the list, t, and multiplies h by the result of recursively calling mult on t. If the list

```
1  int mult(IntList ls) {
2    match (ls) {
3      cons˜(0, _): return 0;
4      cons˜(int h, IntList t): return h * mult(t);
5    }
6    return 1;
7  }
```

Fig. 1. List multiply in Matchete

is empty, neither clause matches, and `mult` returns 1. The method `cons˜()` is a user-defined deconstructor of the `IntList` class that extracts the head and the tail of a list.

This example illustrates four kinds of patterns: wildcard (_ matches anything), values (0 matches the integer zero), binders (`int h` matches any integer and binds it to h), and deconstructor patterns (`cons˜()` matches composite data, extracts its parts, and delegates said parts to nested patterns).

3.1 Evaluation Order

Matchete defines a deterministic order of evaluation for patterns. A match statement evaluates match clauses sequentially in textual order until a clause succeeds. Each clause evaluates patterns sequentially in textual order until either a pattern fails, or control reaches the handler statement.

Each pattern, whether simple or composite, operates on a *subject*. The expression on which the match statement operates becomes the subject for the outermost pattern of each match clause. Composite patterns provide subjects for their children (nested patterns) to match on. Consider the following clause where the outer `cons˜` supplies its two nested patterns with subjects:

```
cons˜(1, cons˜(int x, IntList y)): print("1::"+x+"::"+y);
```

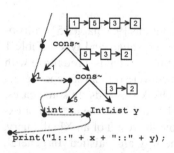

Fig. 2. Evaluation order

Each pattern also has a unique *successor*. The successor of a pattern is the next pattern to run if the match has been successful through the given pattern. In other words, each pattern determines whether its successor runs, or whether to branch to the next clause, if any. The successor of the last pattern in a match clause is the handler.

Fig. 2 illustrates match statement evaluation order: composite patterns have solid edges to child patterns (nesting edges), and each pattern has a dotted edge to its successor (branching edges). Subjects flow along nesting edges, bindings flow along successor edges. Nesting edges are labeled with subjects flowing from parent to child patterns. For example, if the match statement operates on the list [1,5,3,2], that list becomes the subject of the outermost pattern. Each parent pattern extracts subjects for its children to match on. In this case, the number 1 flows to the left child, and the sublist [5,3,2] flows to the right child. Successor edges chain all patterns in the nesting tree in a preorder depth-first traversal. This means that pattern matches are attempted in textual order, left-to-right. If a pattern succeeds, it branches to its successor, otherwise, it branches out of the current match clause. The successor of the last pattern is the handler, in this case, the print statement.

3.2 Type Conversions

Because there can be a mismatch between the type of the data under consideration and the most convenient type for manipulating that data in the handler, Matchete provides support for automatic type conversions. For example, Java programs may store boxed Integer values, yet in order to perform arithmetic, these must be unboxed. Matchete will do the unboxing for the programmer as part of pattern matching. Likewise, XML DOM trees contain text nodes, which the handler may want to manipulate as strings. Pattern matching also makes a branching decision, and it is often convenient to consider the type in that decision. For example, catch clauses in Java try/catch statements perform a limited form of pattern matching, converting the subject (an exception object) to the type of the catch clause (a subclass of Throwable) if the appropriate subclass relationship holds.

Table 1. Type conversions during pattern matching. Object, String, and Integer are defined in package java.lang, while Node and NodeList are defined in package org.w3c.dom.

Subject	Target type	Constraints
obj → RefType		obj instanceof RefType
obj → Node		obj instanceof NodeList and obj.getLength()==1
obj → String		obj instanceof Node and obj.getNodeValue()!=null
obj → PrimitiveType		obj is a boxed object assignment convertible to PrimitiveType
obj → PrimitiveType		obj instanceof String and T.parse$T$(obj) succeeds
prim → String		(always succeeds, using the toString method of the box type)
prim → PrimitiveType		prim assignment convertible to PrimitiveType

Matchete augments Java's type conversions and promotions [9, Chapter 5] with so-called *matching conversions*, defined as a relation between values and types. Table 1 gives these conversion rules. For example, if the subject of a match is a reference with static type Object, say the string literal "42", it can be converted to a reference target of type String provided that the dynamic instanceof check succeeds. In some cases, the conversion may involve multiple steps to get from the subject to the target. For example, NodeList → Node → String → int starts from the result of an XPath query, and converts it to an int if all the constraints along the way are satisfied. In general, Matchete attempts conversions in the order in which Table 1 enumerates them, and the conversion succeeds if it reaches the target type.

3.3 Primitive Patterns

Matchete has three kinds of primitive patterns which can be used at the leaves of a match clause.

Wildcard Patterns   ::=   _

The wildcard pattern, written _, is a catch-all that always matches. Formally, every occurence of the wildcard pattern is distinct and can match against any Java value.

Value Patterns   ::=   *Expression*

It is often convenient to check whether a subject has a particular value. In general, value patterns match against arbitrary Java expressions. A value pattern match first checks whether the type of the subject can be converted to the type of the expression. If so, it checks for equality using == (for primitive types or null) or equals() (for reference types). If both the conversion and the comparison succeed, the value pattern branches to its successor, otherwise it fails.

Binder Patterns   ::=   *Modifiers Type Identifier Dimensions*[?]

Composite patterns extract parts of the subject and bind them to names, so that the handler statement can refer to them directly. This binding is performed by binder patterns. For example, the mult function uses the binder pattern int x to bind the head of the list to a new local variable x for the handler. In general, a binder pattern match succeeds if the type of the subject can be converted to the type of the expression. Binder patterns look like variable declarations, with modifiers (e.g., final), a type, an identifier, and an optional dimensions for array types. The binding is visible in all successors in the same match clause.

3.4   Composite Patterns

A composite pattern is one that has nested sub-patterns, which may themselves be composite or primitive. Each composite pattern, regardless of kind, first decides whether or not to invoke the nested patterns, and if yes, supplies them with subjects. If the composite pattern and everything nested inside of it succeed, it invokes its successor. For example, the root node of Fig. 2 is a composite pattern. It first checks that its subject is a non-empty list. If so, it extracts parts of the list, and supplies them as subjects to its children. If all succeed, the handler runs.

Deconstructor Patterns   ::=   *Identifier* ˜ (*PatternList*)

Deconstructor patterns allow Matchete to match structured terms of user-defined data types and thus program in a style reminiscent of functional programming. One notable difference is that deconstructor patterns invoke user-defined methods that decouple data extraction from the implementation of the data type, preserving encapsulation. A pattern list is simply a comma-separated list of match patterns:

$$PatternList ::= MatchPattern \left(, MatchPattern\right)^{*} \mid Empty$$

Semantically, the deconstructor pattern first checks whether the subject has a deconstructor method with the given identifier, for example, cons in Fig. 1. If yes, it calls subject.method (). The method either returns the subjects for nested patterns, or reports a failure. If there was no failure and the number of subjects matches the length of the *PatternList*, the deconstructor pattern branches to the first nested pattern. Matching proceeds as usual following the rules from Section 3.1.

```
1  class IntList {
2    private int head; private InList tail;
3    public IntList(int h, IntList t){ head = h; tail = t; }
4    public cons˜(int h, IntList t){ h = head; t = tail; }
5  }
```

Fig. 3. List declaration with deconstructor

Deconstructor methods have syntax and semantics that differ from normal Java methods. Syntactically, deconstructors are denoted by the presence of a tilde between their name and their argument list. They have no declared return type.

Declaration   ::+= ... | Deconstructor
Deconstructor ::=   Modifiers Identifier ˜ (ParameterList) ThrowsClause⁷ Block

Semantically, the arguments of a deconstructor are *out* parameters which must be assigned to in the body. The deconstructor can use a `fail;` statement to exit early and report failure. Fig. 3 is an example where class `IntList` has two private fields, a constructor, and a deconstructor (Line 4). In this case, the deconstructor is the inverse of the constructor, it assigns the fields into output parameters for use as subjects in nested matches. The current version of Matchete has no notion of exhaustive matches or unreachable clauses. Considering that deconstructors are user-defined this seems difficult.

Array Patterns   ::=   *ArrayType { PatternList }*
Array patterns are a special case of deconstructor patterns for Java arrays. For example, the pattern `int[]{1, x, int y}` matches an array of three elements if the first element is 1 and the second element has the same value as variable `x`, and binds the third element to a fresh variable `y`. The syntax of array patterns resembles that of array constructors. In general, an array pattern first checks whether the subject is an array of the appropriate length, then invokes nested patterns on extracted elements. Matching proceeds as usual following the rules from Section 3.1.

Regular Expression Patterns   ::=   */ RegExpLiteral / (PatternList)*
Perl excels at extracting data from plain text. This can be attributed to the tight integration of regular expression pattern matching in the syntax. Regular expressions are a fundamental concept from language theory that has phenomenal practical success, because they concisely describe string matches that can be implemented efficiently. For instance, consider the regular expression pattern `/([0-9]+)\.([0-9]+)/ (_, int frac)`. The slashes delimit a regular expression that matches a sequence of digits followed by a decimal point followed by more digits. Parentheses, (...), inside the regular expression capture groups of characters to extract. The parentheses on the right contain a list of nested patterns, which operate on the groups captured by the regular expression on the left. On success, this pattern binds `frac` to the digits after the decimal point.

Regular expression patterns first convert the subject to a string, then match it as specified by the `java.util.regex` package. If this succeeds and produces the correct number of results, the pattern invokes its nested patterns, providing the results as subjects. Matching proceeds as usual following the rules from Section 3.1.

XPath Patterns   ::=   < *XPathLiteral* > (*PatternList*)

XML is a widely-used data interchange format, and XPath is a pattern matching mechanism on the tree representation of an XML document. XPath is widely used because it facilitates common data manipulation tasks through a simple tree query language. An XPath query specifies a path in the tree of XML nodes in a fashion similar to how file name paths in most operating systems specify paths in the tree of directories. The subject of the match is a node, and the result is a set of nodes. Matchete supports XPath patterns. For example, <bibliography/article > (NodeList nodes) extracts the set of all article grandchildren that are children of bibliography children of the subject.

A Matchete XPath pattern converts the subject to a Node or InputSource, then queries it as specified by the javax.xml.xpath package. If this throws any exception, it catches that exception and the match fails, otherwise, it supplies the resulting NodeList as the subject to nested patterns. Matching proceeds as usual following the rules from Section 3.1.

Bit-Level Patterns   ::=   [[(0 | 1 | (*MatchPattern* : *Expression*))*]]

When communicating with low-level network and hardware interfaces, programs need to manipulate data at the level of raw bits. Writing code that does that by hand with shifts and masks is time-consuming and error-prone. However, this problem resembles other typical pattern tasks, in that it requires branching (depending on tag bits) and binding (extracting sequences of payload bits and storing them in variables). Matchete supports matching at the bit-level using patterns such as

```
[[ (0xdeadbeef : 32) 10 (byte x: 6) (int y: x) (int z: 24 - x) ]]
```

This example extracts the first 32 bits, converts them to an integer, and matches them against the the nested integer value pattern 0xdeadbeef. On success, it matches literal bits 1 and 0, then a group of 6 bits, which it binds using the nested binder pattern byte x. Next, it extracts a group of x bits into y, and a group of $24 - x$ bits into z.

Bit-level patterns consist of two kinds of sub-patterns: literal 0 or 1 for matching individual bits, and groups in parentheses for matching subsequences of bits. Each group has the syntax (*MatchPattern* : *Expression*), where the expression specifies a bit width, the number of bits to use as the subject of the nested pattern. The width expression can be any Java expression producing an int, including literals, variables, or arithmetic expressions. The subject for the nested pattern is the group of bits converted to the smallest primitive type that will hold it.

Besides patterns for bit-level deconstruction, Matchete also has expressions for bit-level construction, whose syntax is similar:

PrimaryExpression ::+= ... | *BitLevelExpression*
BitLevelExpression ::=   [[(0 | 1 | (*Expression* : *Expression*))*]]

Parameterized Patterns   ::=   *Identifier* (*Expression*) ~ (*PatternList*)

Parameterized patterns are Matchete's extension mechanism: they allow users to implement new kinds of patterns for use in match statements. For example, the following code uses a parameterized pattern where the parameter is a regular expression string, instead of using the built-in RegExp syntax:

```
1   matchete.Extractor re = myLibrary.RegExp();
2   match(subject) {
3     re("([a-zA-Z]+)␣([0-9]+)")˜(name, int age): handler(age);
4   }
```

Line 1 creates an extractor and stores it in variable re. Matchete implements Line 3 by first making the call

```
re.extract(subject, "([a-zA-Z]+)␣([0-9]+)")
```

That call returns an *extraction* (a tuple of subjects), and Matchete matches the extraction against the nested patterns (in this case, the value pattern name and the binder pattern int age). If all succeeds, Matchete executes the handler.

To support an additional pattern matching mechanism in Matchete, the user needs to implement two matchete library interfaces:

```
interface Extractor{ Extraction extract(Object subject, Object pattern); }
interface Extraction{ int size(); Object get(int i); }
```

In the earlier example, myLibrary.RegExp was a class that implements the Extractor interface, and "([a-zA-Z]+) ([0-9]+)" was passed in as the pattern parameter. In general, the pattern parameter can be anything, such as an SQL query, a fileglob, a boolean predicate, or a scanf format. A parameterized pattern in a match statement leads to an extractor call, which returns an extraction, and Matchete matches the extraction against nested patterns. Matching proceeds as usual following the rules from Section 3.1.

3.5 Deconstructors, Extractors, and Parameterized Patterns

Matchete's deconstructor patterns and parameterized patterns are similar in that both invoke a user-defined pattern matching method. For deconstructors, that method is an instance method of the subject. For parameterized patterns, that method is a method of a separate extractor object. Deconstructors are part of the design of a data type, whereas parameterized patterns serve to wrap a pattern matching library that operates on existing types such as strings.

Other languages supported user-defined pattern matching methods before Matchete. The Scala language supports extractors, which are objects with a user-defined unapply method [5]. For example, if the name cons refers to an extractor object, then the pattern cons(...) calls cons.unapply(subject) and uses the return values in nested patterns. The F# language supports active patterns, which are first-class functions [26]. They work similarly to Scala extractors, but furthermore, can take additional input parameters, similar to parameterized patterns in Matchete.

Matchete gives a slightly different design point than Scala and F#. It relies less on functional language features, and integrates with more other flavors of pattern matching.

3.6 Summary

Table 2 summarizes Matchete's syntax. The additions are limited to a new kind of statement (*MatchStatement*), one new kind of declaration (*Deconstructor*), and one new kind of expression (*BitLevelExpression*). The syntax and semantics of these are described

Table 2. Matchete syntax. Literals are set in monospace fonts, non-terminals in italics. The syntax for RegExpLiteral and XPathLiteral is checked by `java.util.regex` and `javax.xml.xpath`.

Nonterminal	Parsing Expression
Statement	::+= ... | *MatchStatement*
Declaration	::+= ... | *Deconstructor*
PrimaryExpression	::+= ... | *BitLevelExpression*
MatchStatement	::= `match` (*Expression*) { *MatchClause** }
MatchClause	::= *MatchPattern* : *Statement*
MatchPattern	::= *WildcardPattern* | *BitLevelPattern* | *ArrayPattern*
	| *BinderPattern* | *DeconstructorPattern* | *ParameterizedPattern*
	| *RegExpPattern* | *XPathPattern* | *ValuePattern*
ArrayPattern	::= *ArrayType* { *PatternList* }
BinderPattern	::= *Modifiers Type Identifier Dimensions*$^?$
BitLevelExpression	::= `[[` (`0`|`1`| (*Expression* : *Expression*))* `]]`
BitLevelPattern	::= `[[` (`0`|`1`| (*MatchPattern* : *Expression*))* `]]`
DeconstructorPattern	::= *Identifier* ˜ (*PatternList*)
Deconstructor	::= *Modifiers Identifier* ˜ (*ParameterList*) *ThrowsClause*$^?$ *Block*
ParameterizedPattern	::= *Identifier* (*Expression*) ˜ (*PatternList*)
PatternList	::= *MatchPattern* (, *MatchPattern*)* | *Empty*
RegExpPattern	::= / *RegExpLiteral* / (*PatternList*)
ValuePattern	::= *Expression*
WildcardPattern	::= _
XPathPattern	::= < *XPathLiteral* > (*PatternList*)

earlier in this section. Composite patterns are those where *MatchPattern* occurs in the right hand side of the grammar rule. By using the general *MatchPattern* non-terminal instead of any specific kind of pattern, all formalisms are pluggable into each other at the syntactic level. Pluggability at the semantic level is accomplished by the evaluation order rules from Section 3.1 and the type conversion rules from Section 3.2.

4 Examples

Red–black trees. Fig. 4 shows part of a Matchete implementation of red–black trees [13,24]. The `balance` method uses the `T˜` deconstructor to disassemble a node into its components, and then reassembles black interior nodes so that the data structure invariant is maintained: each red node must have two black children.

TCP/IP packet headers. Fig. 5 shows bit-level patterns used to recognize TCP/IP packets. The packet header contains the length of the header itself in 32-bit words (Line 5), and the length of the entire packet in bytes (Line 7). The header consists of a fixed 5-word (20-byte) section and an optional variable-length `options` field (Line 18). The `options` length is computed by subtracting the fixed 5-word length from the header length field. If the header length is less than 5 words, the packet is malformed and the pattern match will fail. Similarly, the length of the packet *payload* (Line 19) is a function of the extracted length and header length.

```
1   class Node {
2     static final int R = 0, B = 1;
3
4     int color;
5     Node left, right;
6     int value;
7
8     Node(int c, Node l, int v, Node r) {
9       color = c; left = l; value = v; right = r;
10    }
11
12    T~(int c, Node l, int v, Node r) {
13      c = color; l = left; v = value; r = right;
14    }
15
16    Node balance() {
17      match (this) {
18        T~(B,T~(R,T~(R,Node a,int x,Node b),int y,Node c),int z,Node d):
19          return new Node(R, new Node(B,a,x,b), y, new Node(B,c,z,d));
20        T~(B,T~(R,Node a,int x,T~(R,Node b,int y,Node c)),int z,Node d):
21          return new Node(R, new Node(B,a,x,b), y, new Node(B,c,z,d));
22        T~(B,Node a,int x,T~(R,T~(R,Node b,int y,Node c)),int z,Node d):
23          return new Node(R, new Node(B,a,x,b), y, new Node(B,c,z,d));
24        T~(B,Node a,int x,T~(R,Node b,int y,T~(R,Node c,int z,Node d))):
25          return new Node(R, new Node(B,a,x,b), y, new Node(B,c,z,d));
26      }
27      return this;
28    }
29  }
```

Fig. 4. Red–black tree balancing

5 The Matchete Compiler

We implemented a compiler that translates Matchete source code into Java source code. The result can then be compiled with a regular Java compiler to Java bytecode, and executed on a Java virtual machine together with the Matchete runtime library.

5.1 Background: Rats! and xtc

The Matchete parser is generated by *Rats!*, a packrat parser generator [11]. *Rats!* has a module system for grammars, which permits Matchete to reuse and extend the Java grammar without copy-and-paste. Instead, the Matchete grammar simply includes the Java grammar as a module, changes it with rule modifications, and adds new rules only for new language features. As *Rats!* is scannerless (i.e., it does not separate lexing from parsing), Matchete needs to recognize new tokens only in match clauses without perturbing the Java syntax.

```
1   class IPDumper {
2     void dumpPacket(byte[] b) {
3       match (b) {
4         [[ (4: 4) /* version 4 */
5            (byte headerLength: 4)
6            (int TOS: 8)
7            (int length: 16)
8            (int identification: 16)
9            (byte evil: 1)
10           (byte doNotFragment: 1)
11           (byte moreFragmentsFollow: 1)
12           (int fragmentOffset: 13)
13           (int ttl: 8)
14           (int protocol: 8)
15           (int headerChecksum: 16)
16           (byte[] srcAddr: 32)
17           (byte[] dstAddr: 32)
18           (byte[] options: ((headerLength-5)*32))
19           (byte[] payload: (length-headerLength*4)*8) ]]: {
20           System.out.println("Source_address:_" + dotted(srcAddr));
21           System.out.println("Destination_address:_" + dotted(dstAddr));
22         }
23         _: System.out.println("bad_header");
24       }
25     }
26     String dotted(byte[] a) {
27       return a[0] + "." + a[1] + "." + a[2] + "." + a[3];
28     }
29   }
```

Fig. 5. TCP/IP packet header parsing

Matchete uses libraries from the **xtc** eXTensible C toolkit [10], which includes semantic analyzers for Java and C. Analyzers are visitors that traverse abstract syntax trees with dynamic dispatch, which permits the Matchete compiler to reuse and extend the Java analyzer without copy-and-paste. Instead, the Matchete semantic analyzer is simply a subclass of the Java analyzer, and defines additional visit methods for the new grammar productions. **xtc** also includes support for synchronized traversal of symbol tables. This permits Matchete to populate the symbol table during semantic analysis, then automatically push and pop the same scopes for the same nodes during code generation. One feature of **xtc** that was particularly helpful in writing the Matchete compiler is the support for concrete syntax, which generates abstract syntax tree snippets from parameterized stencils. This facilitated generation of the boilerplate code required to use, for example, the java.util.regexp and javax.xml.xpath APIs.

5.2 Type Checking

The Matchete compiler statically checks the semantic rules of Java as specified in the Java Language Specification [9]. This includes checking Java code nested inside of new Matchete constructs, such as value patterns, handler statements, deconstructor bodies, and width expressions of bit-level patterns. Type checking of regular Java code is facilitated by Matchete's language design. For example, binder patterns declare the type of the bound variable, which gets used for type-checking the handler statement.

5.3 Translation

The Matchete compiler is a prototype that demonstrates the existence of a straightforward translation from Matchete to Java. It performs no optimizations, we leave that to future work.

```
1   static int mult(IntList ls) {
2     boolean matchIsDone=false;
3     if (matchete.Runtime.hasDeconstructor(ls , "cons")) {
4       final Object[] subject1= matchete.Runtime.deconstruct(ls, "cons");
5       if (null!=subject1 && 2==subject1.length) {
6         final Object subject2=subject1[0];
7         if (matchete.Runtime.convertible(subject2, Integer.TYPE)
8             && 0==matchete.Runtime.toInt(subject2)) {
9           matchIsDone=true;
10          return 0;
11        }
12      }
13    }
14    if (!matchIsDone && matchete.Runtime.hasDeconstructor(ls, "cons")) {
15      final Object[] subject3=matchete.Runtime.deconstruct(ls, "cons");
16      if (null!=subject3 && 2==subject3.length) {
17        final Object subject4=subject3[0];
18        if (matchete.Runtime.convertible(subject4, Integer.TYPE )) {
19          int h=matchete.Runtime.toInt(subject4);
20          final Object subject5=subject3[1];
21          if (null==subject5 || subject5 instanceof IntList) {
22            IntList t=(IntList) subject5;
23            matchIsDone=true;
24            return h * mult(t);
25          }
26        }
27      }
28    }
29    return 1;
30  }
```

Fig. 6. Code generated for example from Fig. 1

After parsing and type checking, the Matchete compiler has a Matchete abstract syntax tree (AST) with type annotations and a symbol table. Next, it transforms this AST into a Java AST. Finally, it turns the Java AST into Java source code. The resulting Java code calls the `matchete.Runtime` library for services implementing common tasks, in particular, dynamic type conversions. As illustrated in Fig. 2, a match consists of a sequence of patterns, each one determining whether its successor runs. The successor order follows a preorder depth-first traversal of the AST. During code generation, each pattern AST node turns into an if-statement around the code generated for its successor. To generate this structure, the code generator simply traverses patterns in reverse order, plugging each pattern into its predecessor as it creates them.

Fig. 6 shows the code generated for the Matchete code in Fig. 1. The outermost if-statements (Lines 3–13 and 14–28) correspond to the match clauses in Lines 3 and 4 of Fig. 1. They communicate with each other using a synthesized boolean variable `matchIsDone`. This code illustrates the translation of deconstructor patterns (Lines 3–5 and 15–17), value patterns (Lines 7–8), the wildcard pattern (no `if` clause required, cf. Fig. 1), and binder patterns (Lines 18–19 and 21–22). The result of deconstructor patterns get used by multiple children, not just the immediate successor (Lines 17 and 20). Deconstructor patterns are currently implemented with reflection, but we intend to use static types to invoke deconstructors directly. The scope of bindings from binder patterns extends over all their successors. For example, variable `h` declared on Line 19 is in scope for the handler in Line 24. Note that code generation for value and binder patterns requires type analysis: for example, Line 7 checks whether *subject2* is convertible to the type of a value expression. In this case, the value is 0, so the type is obviously `int`. But in general, value patterns can contain arbitrary Java expressions, including calls and arithmetic, so finding their type requires a type checking phase in the compiler.

A deconstructor $p\tilde{} (T_1 x_1, \ldots, T_n x_n)$ translates to a method p with no formal parameters. The deconstructor parameters are translated to local variables of the generated method, and the bindings in the deconstructor body are translated to assignments to these variables. The method returns an `Object` array initialized with the deconstructor parameters. A `fail;` statement compiles to `return null;`.

As another example of how the compiler translates composite patterns, consider this XPath pattern for bibliography data: `<.//author/text()>(NodeList authors)`. Fig. 7 shows the Java code that the Matchete compiler generates for this pattern. It

```
1  XPath evaluator = XPathFactory.newInstance().newXPath();
2  try {
3    final Object nodeList = (NodeList) evaluator.evaluate(
4        ".//author/text()",(Node)subject, XPathConstants.NODESET);
5    if (null == nodeList || nodeList instanceof NodeList) {
6      NodeList authors = (NodeList) nodeList;
7      /* successor code */
8    }
9  } catch (XPathExpressionException e) { /* do nothing */ }
```

Fig. 7. Code generated for an XML query

delegates the actual evaluation of the XPath expression to standard Java libraries. Unlike other pattern types, XPath patterns detect match failure by catching an exception. The exception prevents successor patterns from executing, and the empty catch block allows control to reach the next match clause, or the end of the match statement if this pattern was in the last match clause.

6 Discussion

One tradeoff we faced when we designed Matchete was how tightly to integrate each kind of pattern matching mechanism. Both regular expressions and XPaths are examples of loosely integrated pattern matching mechanisms. They are integrated, since they can nest and be nested in patterns of other kinds. But they could be more tightly integrated. For example, the regular expression /([0-9]+) \.([0-9]+)/ (int x, int y) specifies groups twice: once in the regular expression on the left, and then again in the nested binder patterns on the right. A tight integration would combine the two, so that programmers do not have to rely on counting and ordering to correlate them. The advantage of loose integration is that it does not alter the familiar syntax of the existing matching mechanism, and it allows the implementation to reuse feature-rich optimized libraries.

An example of tight integration is bit-level patterns in Matchete. A syntactic argument for tight integration is that when the different matching mechanisms resemble each other, programmers can amortize their learning curve. On the other hand, tight integration puts the full burden of the implementation on the host language vendor.

At the other end of the spectrum is no integration. For example, Matchete does not directly support file name patterns as used in shells or makefiles. Matchete focuses on covering the most important kinds of matches: on typed structured data (deconstructor), on bit data (bit-level), on semistructured data (XPath), and on text (RegExp). But it leaves out variations of these kind of matches, such as file name patterns. Instead, it provides an extension mechanism (parameterized patterns).

Matchete has to strike a balance between static and dynamic typing. The arguments for and against either are a subject of hot debate and beyond the scope of this paper. But no language design can avoid decisions on this. Matchete's decisions are summarized in Section 3.2 and Table 1. Pattern matching in Matchete is mostly dynamically typed. This felt natural, since patterns are often used to overcome a data representation mismatch. However, it reduces optimization opportunities, which is why Matchete adds hints that can allow compilers to determine types statically in many cases. One advantage of demonstrating pattern matching with little reliance on types is that it is more applicable to dynamically typed host languages—Matchete features could easily be transferred from Java to a scripting language. Note that Matchete pattern matches are strongly typed: when they would violate types, patterns quietly fail instead.

The combination of dynamic typing and source-to-source translation raises concerns about ease of debugging Matchete code. When a match statement does not work as the programmer expected, they need to pinpoint the defect. Matchete uses functionality provided with xtc to inject SMAPs [6] into class files, which allow Java debuggers such as Eclipse or Jdb to work at the level of the original Matchete source code.

7 Conclusions

This paper has introduced Matchete, an extension to the Java programming language with a pattern matching construct that integrates data structure deconstruction, string and bit-level manipulation, and XML queries. Our experience with Matchete suggests that the ability to mix and match different kinds of pattern expressions is powerful and leads to compact and elegant code. The prototype compiler is adequate as a proof of concept, but we are actively working on optimizing the generated code.

Acknowledgements

Robert Grimm and the anonymous reviewers gave helpful feedback on the writing. Mukund Raghavachari, Igor Peshansky, and John Field participated in many of the early design discussions. Robert Grimm supplied the *Rats!* and xtc infrastructure, and Byeongcheol "BK" Lee contributed source-level debugging support to it.

References

1. Back, G.: DataScript: A specification and scripting language for binary data. In: Batory, D., Consel, C., Taha, W. (eds.) GPCE 2002. LNCS, vol. 2487, Springer, Heidelberg (2002)
2. Benzaken, V., Castagna, G., Frisch, A.: CDuce: An XML-centric general-purpose language. In: International Conference on Functional Programming (ICFP) (2003)
3. Clark, J., DeRose, S.: XML path language (XPath) version 1.0. W3C recommendation, W3C (November 1999), http://www.w3.org/TR/1999/REC-xpath-19991116
4. Diatchki, I.S., Jones, M.P., Leslie, R.: High-level views on low-level representations. In: International Conference on Functional Programming (ICFP) (2005)
5. Emir, B., Odersky, M., Williams, J.: Matching objects with patterns. In: Ernst, E. (ed.) ECOOP 2007. LNCS, vol. 4609, Springer, Heidelberg (2007)
6. Field, R.: JSR 45: Debugging Support for Other Languages, http://jcp.org
7. Fisher, K., Gruber, R.: PADS: A domain-specific language for processing ad hoc data. In: Programming Language Design and Implementation (PLDI) (2005)
8. Gapeyev, V., Pierce, B.C.: Regular object types. In: Cardelli, L. (ed.) ECOOP 2003. LNCS, vol. 2743, Springer, Heidelberg (2003)
9. Gosling, J., Joy, B., Steele, G., Bracha, G.: The Java Language Specification, 2nd edn. Addison-Wesley, Reading (2000)
10. Grimm, R.: xtc (eXTensible C), http://cs.nyu.edu/rgrimm/xtc/
11. Grimm, R.: Better extensibility through modular syntax. In: Programming Language Design and Implementation (PLDI) (2006)
12. Griswold, R., Poage, J.F., Polonsky, I.P.: The Snobol 4 Programming Language. Prentice-Hall, Englewood Cliffs (1971)
13. Guibas, L.J., Sedgewick, R.: A dichromatic framework for balanced trees. In: Foundations of Computer Science (FOCS) (1978)
14. Gustafsson, P., Sagonas, K.: Efficient manipulation of binary data using pattern matching. Journal on Functional Programming (JFP) (2006)
15. Harren, M., Raghavachari, M., Shmueli, O., Burke, M.G., Bordawekar, R., Pechtchanski, I., Sarkar, V.: XJ: Facilitating XML processing in Java. In: International World Wide Web Conferences (WWW) (2005)

16. Hosoya, H., Pierce, B.: XDuce: A statically typed XML processing language. Transactions on Internet Technology (TOIT) (2001)
17. Hudak, P., Peyton Jones, S.L., Wadler, P., Boutel, B., Fairbairn, J., Fasel, J.H., Guzmán, M.M., Hammond, K., Hughes, J., Johnsson, T., Kieburtz, R.B., Nikhil, R.S., Partain, W., Peterson, J.: Report on the programming language Haskell, a non-strict, purely functional language. SIGPLAN Notices 27(5), R1–R164 (1992)
18. Kirkegaard, C., Møller, A., Schwartzbach, M.I.: Static analysis of XML transformations in Java. IEEE Transactions on Software Engineering (TSE) (2004)
19. Lee, K., LaMarca, A., Chambers, C.: HydroJ: Object-oriented pattern matching for evolvable distributed systems. In: Object-Oriented Programming, Systems, Languages and Applciations (OOPSLA) (2003)
20. Liu, J., Myers, A.C.: JMatch: Iterable abstract pattern matching for Java. In: Dahl, V., Wadler, P. (eds.) PADL 2003. LNCS, vol. 2562, Springer, Heidelberg (2002)
21. Meijer, E., Beckman, B., Bierman, G.M.: LINQ: Reconciling objects, relations, and XML in the .NET framework. In: SIGMOD Industrial Track (2006)
22. Milner, R., Tofte, M., Harper, R., MacQueen, D.: The Definition of Standard ML (Revised). MIT Press, Cambridge (1997)
23. Moreau, P.-E., Ringeissen, C., Vittek, M.: A pattern matching compiler for multiple target languages. In: Hedin, G. (ed.) CC 2003 and ETAPS 2003. LNCS, vol. 2622, Springer, Heidelberg (2003)
24. Okasaki, C.: Purely Functional Data Structures. Cambridge University Press, Cambridge (1998)
25. Richard, A.J.: OOMatch: Pattern matching as dispatch in Java. Master's thesis, University of Waterloo (2007)
26. Syme, D., Neverov, G., Margetson, J.: Extensible pattern matching via a lightweight language extension. In: International Conference on Functional Programming (ICFP) (2007)
27. Wadler, P.: Views: A way for pattern matching to cohabit with data abstraction. In: Principles of Programming Languages (POPL) (1987)
28. Wall, L.: Programming Perl. O'Reilly (1990)
29. Wright, A.K.: Pattern matching for Scheme. The match special form is part of PLT Scheme's MzLib library (1996)

Parser Combinators for Ambiguous Left-Recursive Grammars

Richard A. Frost[1], Rahmatullah Hafiz[1], and Paul Callaghan[2]

[1] School of Computer Science, University of Windsor, Canada
richard@uwindsor.ca
[2] Department of Computer Science, University of Durham, U.K.

Abstract. Parser combinators are higher-order functions used to build parsers as executable specifications of grammars. Some existing implementations are only able to handle limited ambiguity, some have exponential time and/or space complexity for ambiguous input, most cannot accommodate left-recursive grammars. This paper describes combinators, implemented in Haskell, which overcome all of these limitations.

Keywords: Parser combinators, ambiguity, left recursion, functional programming, natural-language parsing.

1 Introduction

In functional programming, higher order functions called parser combinators can be used to build basic parsers and to construct complex parsers for nonterminals from other parsers. Parser combinators allow parsers to be defined in an embedded style, in code which is similar in structure to the rules of the grammar. As such, implementations can be thought of as executable specifications with all of the associated advantages. In addition, parser combinators use a top-down parsing strategy which facilitates modular piecewise construction and testing.

Parser combinators have been used extensively in the prototyping of compilers and processors for domain-specific languages such as natural language interfaces to databases, where complex and varied semantic actions are closely integrated with syntactic processing. However, simple implementations have exponential time complexity and inefficient representations of parse results for ambiguous inputs. Their inability to handle left-recursion is a long-standing problem. These shortcomings limit the use of parser combinators especially in applications with large and complex grammars.

Various techniques have been developed by others to address some of these shortcomings. However, none of that previous work has solved all of them.

The parser combinators that we present here are the first which can be used to create executable specifications of ambiguous grammars with unconstrained left-recursion, which execute in polynomial time, and which generate compact polynomial-sized representations of the potentially exponential number of results for highly ambiguous input.

P. Hudak and D.S. Warren (Eds.): PADL 2008, LNCS 4902, pp. 167–181, 2008.

The combinators are based on an algorithm developed by Frost, Hafiz and Callaghan (2007). That algorithm combines memoization with existing techniques for dealing with left recursion. The memotables are modified to represent the potentially exponential number of parse trees in a compact polynomial sized representation using a technique derived from (Kay 1980) and (Tomita 1986). A novel technique is used to accommodate indirect as well as direct left recursion.

This paper has three objectives: 1) To make the algorithm of Frost, Hafiz and Callaghan known to a wider audience beyond the Computational Linguistics community. In particular by the functional and logic programming communities both of which have a long history of creating parsers as executable specifications (using parser combinators and Definite Clause Grammars respectively), 2) to introduce a library of parser combinators for immediate use by functional programmers, and 3) to illustrate how a declarative language facilitates the incremental implementation of a complex algorithm. Note that extension to include semantics will be straightforward, and that this work can be seen as an important step towards combinators that support general attribute grammars.

As example use of our combinators, consider the following ambiguous grammar from Tomita (1986). The nonterminal s stands for sentence, np for noun-phrase, vp for verbphrase, det for determiner, pp for prepositional phrase, and prep for preposition. This grammar is left recursive in the rules for s and np.

```
s    ::= np vp | s pp       np   ::= noun | det noun | np pp
pp   ::= prep np            vp   ::= verb np
det  ::= "a"   | "the"      noun ::= "i"  | "man" | "park" | "bat"
verb ::= "saw"              prep ::= "in" | "with"
```

The Haskell code below defines a parser for the above grammar using our combinators term, <+>, and *>.

```
data Label = S | ... | PREP
s    = memoize S    $ np *> vp <+> s *> pp
np   = memoize NP   $ noun <+> det *> noun <+> np  *> pp
pp   = memoize PP   $ prep *> np
vp   = memoize VP   $ verb *> np
det  = memoize DET  $ term "a"  <+> term "the"
noun = memoize NOUN $ term "i"<+>term "man"<+>term "park" <+> term "bat"
verb = memoize VERB $ term "saw"
prep = memoize PREP $ term "in" <+> term "with"
```

The next page shows the "prettyprinted" output when the parser function s is applied to "i saw a man in the park with a bat". The compact representation corresponds to the several ways in which the whole input can be parsed as a sentence, and the many ways in which subsequences of it can be parsed as nounphrases etc. For example, the entry for NP shows that nounphrases were identified starting at positions 1, 3, 6, and 9. Some of which were identified as spanning positions 3 to 5, 8, and 11. Two were found spanning positions 3 to 11. The first of which consists of a NP spanning 3 to 5 followed by a PP spanning 5 to 11. (We define a span from x to y as consuming terminals from x to y - 1.)

```
NOUN [1 ->[2 ->[Leaf "i"]]
     ,4 ->[5 ->[Leaf "man"]]
     ,7 ->[8 ->[Leaf "park"]]
     ,10->[11->[Leaf "bat"]]]
DET  [3 ->[4 ->[Leaf "a"]]
     ,6 ->[7 ->[Leaf "the"]]
     ,9 ->[10->[Leaf "a"]]]
NP   [1 ->[2 ->[SubNode NOUN (1,2)]]
     ,3 ->[5 ->[Branch [SubNode DET  (3,4) , SubNode NOUN (4,5)]]
          ,8 ->[Branch [SubNode NP   (3,5) , SubNode PP   (5,8)]]
          ,11->[Branch [SubNode NP   (3,5) , SubNode PP   (5,11)]
               ,Branch [SubNode NP   (3,8) , SubNode PP   (8,11)]]]
     ,6 ->[8 ->[Branch [SubNode DET  (6,7) , SubNode NOUN (7,8)]]
          ,11->[Branch [SubNode NP   (6,8) , SubNode PP   (8,11)]]]
     ,9 ->[11->[Branch [SubNode DET  (9,10), SubNode NOUN (10,11)]]]]
PREP [5 ->[6 ->[Leaf "in"]]
     ,8 ->[9 ->[Leaf "with"]]]
PP   [8 ->[11->[Branch [SubNode PREP (8,9), SubNode NP (9,11)]]]
     ,5 ->[8 ->[Branch [SubNode PREP (5,6), SubNode NP (6,8)]]
          ,11->[Branch [SubNode PREP (5,6), SubNode NP (6,11)]]]]
VERB [2 ->[3 ->[Leaf "saw"]]]
VP   [2 ->[5 ->[Branch [SubNode VERB (2,3), SubNode NP (3,5)]]
          ,8 ->[Branch [SubNode VERB (2,3), SubNode NP (3,8)]]
          ,11->[Branch [SubNode VERB (2,3), SubNode NP (3,11)]]]]
S    [1 ->[5 ->[Branch [SubNode NP  (1,2), SubNode VP (2,5)]]
          ,8 ->[Branch [SubNode NP  (1,2), SubNode VP (2,8)]
               ,Branch [SubNode S   (1,5), SubNode PP (5,8)]]
          ,11->[Branch [SubNode NP  (1,2), SubNode VP (2,11)]
               ,Branch [SubNode S   (1,5), SubNode PP (5,11)]
               ,Branch [SubNode S   (1,8), SubNode PP (8,11)]]]]
```

Parsers constructed with our combinators have $O(n^3)$ worst case time complexity for non-left-recursive ambiguous grammars (where n is the length of the input), and $O(n^4)$ for left recursive ambiguous grammars. This compares well with $O(n^3)$ limits on standard algorithms for CFGs such as Earley-style parsers (Earley 1970). The increase to n^4 is due to expansion of the left recursive nonterminals in the grammar. Experimental evidence suggests that typical performance is closer to $O(n^3)$, possibly because few subparsers are left recursive and hence the $O(n^3)$ term predominates. Experimental evaluation involved four natural-language grammars from (Tomita 1986), four variants of an abstract highly-ambiguous grammar, and a medium-size natural-language grammar with 5,226 rules. The potentially-exponential number of parse trees for highly-ambiguous input are represented in polynomial space as in Tomita's algorithm.

We begin with background material followed by a detailed description of the Haskell implementation. Experimental results, related work, and conclusions are given in sections 4, 5 and 6. Formal proofs of termination and complexity, and the code of the initial Haskell implementation, are available at:

cs.uwindsor.ca/~richard/PUBLICATIONS/APPENDICES_HASKELL.html

2   Background

2.1   Top Down Parsing and Memoization

Top-down parsers search for parses using a top-down expansion of the grammar rules. Tokens are consumed from left to right. Inclusive choice is used to accommodate ambiguity by expanding all alternative right-hand-sides of grammar rules. Simple implementations do not terminate for left-recursive grammars, and have exponential time complexity with respect to the length of the input for non-left-recursive ambiguous grammars.

The problem of exponential time complexity in top-down parsers constructed as sets of mutually-recursive functions has been solved by Norvig (1991). His technique is similar to the use of dynamic programming and state sets in Earley's algorithm (1970), and tables in the CYK algorithm of Cocke, Younger and Kasami. The key idea is to store results of applying a parser p at position j in a memotable and to reuse results whenever the same situation arises. It can be implemented as a wrapper function **memoize** which can be applied selectively to component parsers.

2.2   The Need for Left Recursion

Left-recursion can be avoided by transforming the grammar to a weakly equivalent non-left-recursive form (i.e. to a grammar which derives the same set of sentences, but does not generate the same set of parse trees). Such transformation has two disadvantages: 1) it is error prone, especially for non-trivial grammars, and 2) the loss of some parses (as illustrated in the example in (Frost et al 2007)) complicates the integration of semantic actions, especially in NLP.

2.3   An Introduction to Parser Combinators

The details in this description have been adapted to our approach, and are limited to recognition. We extend the technique to parsers later. Assume that the input is a sequence of tokens $input$, of length $\#input$ the members of which are accessed through an index j. Recognizers are functions which take an index j as argument and which return a set of indices. Each index in the result set corresponds to a position at which the parser successfully finished recognizing a sequence of tokens that began at position j. An empty result set indicates that the recognizer failed to recognize any sequence beginning at j. The result for an ambiguous input is a set with more than one element. This use of $indices$ instead of the more conventional subsequence of input is a key detail of the approach: we need the positions to index into the memotables.

A recognizer **term** 'x' for a terminal 'x' is a function which takes an index j as input, and if j is less than $\#input$ and if the token at position j in the input corresponds to the terminal 'x', it returns a singleton set containing $j + 1$, otherwise it returns the empty set. The **empty** recognizer is a function which always succeeds returning a singleton set containing the current position.

A recognizer for alternation p|q is built by combining recognizers for p and q, using the combinator <+>. When the composite recognizer is applied to index j, it applies p to j, applies q to j, and subsequently unites the resulting sets.

A composite recognizer corresponding to a sequence of recognizers p q on the right hand side of a grammar rule, is built by combining those recognizers using the parser combinator *>. When the composite recognizer is applied to an index j, it first applies p to j, then it applies q to each index in the set of results returned by p. It returns the union of these applications of q. The combinators term, empty, <+> and *> are defined (in functional pseudo code) as follows:

$$
term \quad t \quad j = \begin{cases} \{\} & , j \geq \#input \\ \{j+1\} & , j^{th} \text{ element of } input = t \\ \{\} & , \text{otherwise} \end{cases}
$$

$$
empty \quad j = \{j\}
$$

$$
(p \quad \texttt{<+>} \quad q) \quad j = (p \quad j) \quad \cup \quad (q \quad j)
$$

$$
(p \quad \texttt{*>} \quad q) \quad j = \bigcup(map \quad q \quad (p \quad j))
$$

The combinators can be used to define composite mutually-recursive recognizers. For example, the grammar s ::= 'x' s s | empty can be encoded as s = (term 'x' *> s *> s) <+> empty. Assuming the input is "xxxx", then:

```
(empty <+> term 'x')    2 => {2,3}
(term 'x' *> term 'x') 1 => {3}

  s 0  => {4, 3, 2, 1, 0}
```

The last four values in the result for s 0 correspond to proper prefixes of the input being recognized as an s. The result 4 corresponds to the case where the whole input is recognized as an s. Note that we have used sets in this explanation to simplify later development of the combinators.

3   The Combinators

3.1   Preliminaries

The actual implementation of the combinators *> and <+> for plain recognizers in Haskell is straightforward, and makes use of a library for Sets of Ints. An excerpt is given below. In this fragment and the ones that follow, we make some simplifications to ease presentation of the key details. Full working code is available from the URL given in Section 1. We omit details of how we access the input throughout this paper, treating it as a constant value.

```
type Pos    = Int
type PosSet = IntSet
type R      = Pos -> PosSet
```

```
(<+>)          :: R -> R -> R
p <+> q        = \r -> union (p r) (q r)
(*>)           :: R -> R -> R
p *> q         = \r -> unions $ map q $ elems $ p r
parse          :: R -> PosSet
parse p        = p 0
```

In the following we develop the combinators `*>` and `<+>` incrementally, by adding new features one at a time in each subsection. We begin with memoization, then direct left recursion, then indirect left recursion, then parsing (to trees). The revised definitions accompany new types which indicate a particular version of the combinator. The modifications to `<+>` are omitted when they are reasonably straightforward or trivial.

3.2 Memoizing Recognizers

We modify the combinators so that a memotable is used during recognition. At first the table is empty. During the process it is updated with an entry for each recognizer that is applied to a position. Recognizers to be memoized are labelled with values of a type chosen by the programmer. These labels usually appear as node labels in resulting parse trees, but more generality is possible, e.g. to hold limited semantic information. We require only that these labels be enumerable, i.e. have a unique mapping to and from `Ints`, a property that we use to make table lookups more efficient by converting label occurrences internally to `Ints` and using the optimized `IntMap` library.

The memotable is a map of memo label and start position to a result set. The combinators are lifted to the monad level and the memotable is the state that is threaded through the parser operations, and consulted and/or updated during the `memoize` operation. We use a standard state monad:

```
type ILabel  = Int
type RM memoLabel = Pos -> StateM (State memoLabel) PosSet
data StateM s t = State {unState:: s -> (t, s)}
type State nodeName = IntMap (IntMap PosSet)
(*>) :: RM l -> RM l -> RM l
p *> q = \r -> do end_p  <- p r
                  end_qs <- mapM q (elems end_p)
                  return $ unions end_qs
```

The `memoize` function makes the decision regarding reuse of results. It is implemented as a "wrapper" around other parsers, hence any sub-parser can be memoized. The function checks whether an entry exists in the memotable for the given parser label and position, returning the stored result if yes, otherwise it runs the parser and stores the results before returning them. `update_table` adds the new information to the table. Note that the update effect is to "overwrite" the previous information. The `insertWith...insert` combination merges into the outer table (`insertWith`) a new inner table that discards (`insert`) any previous entry for that label and start position. This is necessary to update the stored information as (left) recursion unwinds (see section 3.3):

```
memoize :: Enum l => l -> RM l -> RM l
memoize e_name parser pos
 = do mt <- get
      case lookupT i_name pos mt of
         Just res -> return res
         Nothing  -> do res <- parser pos
                        modify (update_table res)
                        return res
   where
     i_name = fromEnum e_name
     update_table :: PosSet -> State l -> State l
     update_table res = insertWith (\_ prev -> insert pos res prev)
                                   i_name (singleton pos res)
```

3.3   Accommodating Direct Left Recursion

To accommodate direct left recursion, we use "left-rec counts" c_{ij} denoting the number of times a recognizer r_i has been applied to an index j. For non-left-recursive recognizers c_{ij} will be at most one. For left-recursive recognizers, c_{ij} is increased on recursive descent. Application of a recognizer r_i to an index j is curtailed whenever c_{ij} exceeds the number of unconsumed tokens of the input plus 1. At this point no parse is possible (other than spurious parses from cyclic grammars — which we want to curtail anyway.) As an illustration, consider the following portion of the search space being created during the parse of two remaining tokens on the input (where N, P and Q are nodes in the parse search space corresponding to nonterminals. A, B and C are nodes corresponding to terminals or nonterminals):

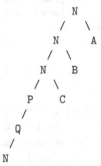

The last call of the parser for N should be curtailed owing to the fact that, irrespective of what A, B, and C are, either they must require at least one input token, or else they must rewrite to empty. If they all require a token, then the parse cannot succeed. If any rewrite to empty, then the grammar is cyclic (N is being rewritten to N). The last call should be curtailed in either case.

Curtailing a parse when a branch is longer than the length of the remaining input is incorrect as this can occur in a correct parse if recognizers are rewritten into other recognizers which do not have "token requirements to the right". Also, we curtail the recognizer when the left-rec count exceeds the number of unconsumed tokens *plus 1*. The plus 1 is necessary for the case where the recognizer rewrites to empty on application to the end of the input.

This curtailment test is implemented by passing a "left-rec context" down the invocation tree. The context is a frequency table of calls to the memoized parsers encountered on the current chain.

```
type L_Context = [(ILabel, Int)]
type LRM memolabel = L_Context -> RM memolabel
```

Only *> and memoize need to be altered beyond propagating the information downwards. memoize checks before expanding a parser p to see if it has been called more than there are tokens left in the input, and if so, returns an empty result, otherwise continues as before though passing a context updated with an extra call to p. The alteration to *> controls what context should be passed to q: the current context should only be passed when p has consumed no tokens, i.e. has done nothing to break the left-recursive chain.

```
(*>) :: LRM l -> LRM l -> LRM l
p *> q = \ctxt r -> do end_p <- p ctxt r
                       let pass_ctxt e | e == r    = ctxt
                                       | otherwise = []
                       end_qs<-mapM (\e-> q (pass_ctxt e) e)(elems end_p)
                       return $ unions end_qs
memoize :: Enum l => l -> LRM l -> LRM l
memoize e_name p ctxt pos
  = do mt <- get
       case lookupT i_name pos mt of
            Just res -> return res
            Nothing  | depth_cutoff i_name ctxt >
                                     (length_input - pos + 1) -> empty
                     | otherwise -> do
                                    .. p (increment i_name ctxt) pos ..
    where i_name = fromEnum e_name
          depth_cutoff i e = case lookup i e of Nothing -> 0
                                                Just fe -> fe
```

Notice what happens when unwinding the left-recursive calls. At each level, memoize runs the parser and adds the results to the table for the given label and start position. This table update, as mentioned earlier, overwrites previous information at the start position, and therefore the table always contains the "best results so far". Note that the algorithm accommodates cyclic grammars. It terminates for such grammars with information being stored in the memotable which can be subsequently used to identify cycles.

3.4   Accommodating Indirect Left Recursion

We begin by illustrating how the method above may return incomplete results for grammars containing indirect left recursion. Consider the following grammar, and subset of the search space, where the left and right branches represent the expansions of the first two alternate right-hand-sides of the rule for the nonterminal S, applied to the same position on the input:

```
S ::= S ..| Q | P | x                      S
P ::= S ..                           /      +      \
Q ::= T                           S ..              Q
T ::= P                            |                |
                                  S ..              T
                                   |                |
                                   P                P
                                   |                |
                                  S ..            S ..
                                   |
                          curtail S
```

Suppose that the branch for the left alternative is expanded before the right branch during the search, and that the left branch is curtailed due to the left-rec count for S exceeding its limit. The results stored for P on recursive ascent of the left branch is an empty set. The problem is that the later call of P on the right branch should not reuse the empty set of results from the first call of P as they are incomplete with respect to the position of P on the right branch (i.e. if P were to be reapplied to the input in the context of the right branch, the results would not necessarily be an empty set.) This problem is a result of the fact that, on the left branch, S caused curtailment of the results for P as well as for itself.

Our solution to this problem is as follows: 1) Pass left-rec contexts downwards as in subsection 3.3. 2) Generate the reasons for curtailment when computing results. For each result we need to know if the subtrees contributing to it have been curtailed through any left-rec limit, and if so, which recognizers caused the curtailment. 3) Store results in the memotable together with a subset of the current left-rec context corresponding to those recognizers that caused the curtailment at the current position, and 4) Whenever a stored result is being considered for reuse, the left-rec-context of that result is compared with the left-rec-context of the current node in the parse space. The result is only reused if, for each recognizer in the left-rec context of the result, the left-rec-count is smaller than or equal to the left-rec-count in the current context. This ensures that a result stored for application P of a recognizer at index j is only reused by a subsequent application P' of the same recognizer at the same position, if the left-rec context for P' would constrain the result more, or equally as much, as it had been constrained by the left-rec context for P at j. If there were no curtailment, the left-rec context of a result would be empty and that result can be reused anywhere irrespective of the current left-rec context.

This strategy extends the recognizer return type to include a set of labels that caused curtailments during that parse. Note that we only collect information about curtailment for the current position, so only collect results from q in the case where p consumed no input, i.e. where the endpoint of p is the same as the starting position.

```
type CurtailingNTs  = IntSet
type UpResult       = (CurtailingNTs, PosSet)
type State nodeName = IntMap (IntMap (L_Context,UpResult))
type CLRM memoLabel = L_Context -> Pos
```

```
                                   -> StateM (State memoLabel) UpResult

(*>) :: CLRM l -> CLRM l -> CLRM l
p *> q = \ctxt r -> do (cut,end_p) <- p ctxt r
                       let pass_ctxt e | e == r    = ctxt
                                       | otherwise = []
                           merge_cuts e prev new
                                       | e == r    = union prev new
                                       | otherwise = prev
                           join (prev_cut, prev_result) e
                           = do (new_cut, result) <- q (pass_ctxt e) e
                                return ( merge_cuts e prev_cut new_cut
                                       , union prev_result result )
                       end_qs <- foldM join (cut, empty) end_p
                       return end_qs
```

The function `<+>` is modified to merge information from the subparsers:

```
(<+>) :: CLRM l -> CLRM l -> CLRM l
(p <+> q) inp cc  = do (cut1,m) <- p inp cc
                       (cut2,n) <- q inp cc
                       return ( union cut1 cut2 , union m n )
```

When retrieving results, `memoize` compares the current context with the pruned stored context. Reuse is only allowed if every label in the stored context appears in the current context and is not less constrained in the current context. Otherwise, the parser is run further in the current context to compute the results that were curtailed (and hence missing) in the earlier call.

```
pruneContext :: CurtailingNTs -> L_Context -> L_Context
pruneContext rs ctxt = [nc | nc@(n,c) <- ctxt, n 'member' rs]
canReuse :: L_Context -> L_Context -> Bool
canReuse current stored
 = and [ or [ cc >= sc | (cn,cc) <- current, sn == cn ]
       | (sn,sc) <- stored ]
```

3.5   Building Parse Trees

Turning a recogniser into a parser is straightforward. A set of endpoints now becomes a map of endpoints to lists of trees that end at that point. The memotable type is altered to contain this new information: it stores tree results with their curtail set and a relevant L_context. The tree type is shown below.

```
data Tree l = Empty | Leaf Token | Branch [Tree l]  | ...
type ParseResult memoLabel = [(Int, [Tree memoLabel])]
type UpResult memoLabel = (CurtailingNTs, ParseResult memoLabel)
data Stored memoLabel = Stored { s_stored   :: UpResult memoLabel
                               , s_context :: L_Context
                               , s_results :: [(Int, Tree memoLabel)]}
type State memoLabel = IntMap (IntMap (Stored memoLabel))
type P memoLabel
    = L_Context -> Pos -> StateM (State memoLabel) (UpResult memoLabel)
```

term parsers now return a list of leaf values with suitable endpoints. The empty parser returns an empty tree. Alternative parses from <+> are merged by appending together the lists of trees ending at the same point. The maps are held in ascending endpoint order to give this operation an $O(n)$ cost.

Sequences require *> to join all results of p with all results of q, forming new branch nodes in the tree, and merging the resulting maps together. The former is achieved with addP which combines a particular result from p with all subsequent results from q, and with addToBranch which merges lists of trees from both the left and the right into a new list of trees. Notice that this operation is a cross-product: it must pair each tree from the left with each tree on the right. Tree merging or packing is done by concatenating results at the same endpoint.

```
addP :: [[Tree l]] -> ParseResult l -> ParseResult l
addP left_result right_output
= [ (re , addToBranch left_result right_results)
                    | (re , right_results) <- right_output ]
addToBranch :: [[Tree l]] -> [[Tree l]] -> [[Tree l]]
addToBranch lts rts = [r ++ l | l <- lts, r <- rts]
```

The memoize function handles the rest of tree formation, both labelling and introducing sharing to avoid an exponential number of trees. Labelling attaches the memo label to the tree result. Sharing replaces the computed list of results with a single result that contains sufficient information to find the original list which will be stored in the memo table. This single result is then returned to higher parsers as a 'proxy' for the original list. To avoid recomputation, we also store the proxy in the memotable to be retrieved by subsequent parser lookups. This technique avoids exponential blow-up of the number of results propagated by parsers. An example of the resulting compact representation of parse trees has been given in Section 1.

It is important to note that the combinators support addition of semantics. The extension from trees to semantic values is straightforward via an "applicative functor" interface, e.g. with operator (<*>) :: P (a -> b) -> P a -> P b. A monadic interface may also be defined.

Test Set	#Input	#Parses	Our method				Tomita's method			
			G1	G2	G3	G4	G1	G2	G3	G4
Tomita's	19	346			0.02				4.79	
sent. set 1	26	1,464			0.03				8.66	
Tomita's	22	429	0.02	0.02	0.03	0.03	2.80	6.40	4.74	19.93
sent. set 2	31	16,796	0.02	0.02	0.05	0.08	6.14	14.40	10.40	45.28
	40	742,900	0.02	0.06	0.08	0.09	11.70	28.15	18.97	90.85

Fig. 1. Informal comparison with Tomita's results (timings in seconds)

4   Experimental Results

To provide evidence of low-order polynomial costs, we conducted a small scale evaluation with respect to: a) Four practical natural-language grammars (Tomita 1986, Appendix F, pages 171 to 184); b) Four variants of an abstract highly ambiguous grammar from Aho and Ullman (1972); and c) A medium size NL grammar for an Air Travel Information System maintained by Carroll (2003).

Our Haskell program was compiled using the Glasgow Haskell Compiler 6.6. We used a 3GHz/1Gb PC. The performance reported is the "MUT time" as generated in GHC runtime statistics, which is an indication of the time spent doing useful computation. It excludes time spent in garbage collection. We also run with an initial heap of 100Mb and do not fix an upper limit to heap size (apart from the machine's capacity).

Note that the grammars we have tested are inherently expensive owing to the dense ambiguity, and this is irrespective of which parsing method is used.

4.1   Tomita' Grammars

The grammars used were: G1 (8 rules), G2 (40 rules), G3 (220 rules), and G4 (400 rules) (Tomita 1986). We used two sets of input: a) the two most-ambiguous inputs from Tomita's sentence set 1 (page 185 App. G) of lengths 19 and 26 which we parsed with G3 (as did Tomita), and b) three inputs of lengths 4, 10, and 40, with systematically increasing ambiguity, from Tomita's sentence set 2.

Figure 1 shows our times and those recorded by Tomita for his algorithm, using a DEC-20 machine (Tomita 1986, pages 152 and 153 App. D). Clearly there can be no direct comparison against years-old DEC-20 times. However, we note that Tomita's algorithm was regarded, in 1986, as being at least as efficient as Earley's and viable for natural-language parsing using machines that were available at that time. The fact that our algorithm is significantly faster on current PCs supports the claim of viability for NL parsing.

4.2   Highly Ambiguous Abstract Grammars

We defined parsers for four variants of a highly-ambiguous grammar introduced by Aho and Ullman (1972): an unmemoized non-left–recursive parser s, a memoized version ms, a memoized left–recursive version sml, and a memoized left–recursive version with one sub-component also memoized smml:

```
s    =                    term 'x' *> s  *> s    <+> empty
sm   = memoize SM   $ term 'x' *> sm *> sm    <+> empty
sml  = memoize SML  $ sml  *> sml *> term 'x' <+> empty
smml = memoize SMML $ smml *> (memoize SMML' $ smml *> term 'x') <+>empty
```

We chose these four grammars as they are highly ambiguous. The results in figure 2 show that our algorithm can accommodate massively ambiguous input involving the generation of large and complex parse forests. '*' denotes memory overflow and '-' denotes timings less than 0.005 seconds.

Input Length	No. of parses	s	sm	sml	smml
6	132	1.22	-	-	-
12	208,012	*	-	-	0.02
24	1.289e+12		0.08	0.13	0.06
48	1.313e+26		0.83	0.97	0.80

Fig. 2. Timings for highly-ambiguous grammars (time in seconds)

4.3 ATIS – A Medium Size NL Grammar

Here, we used a modified version of the ATIS grammar and test inputs generated by Carroll (2003), who extracted them from the DARPA ATIS3 treebank.

Our modifications include adding 634 new rules and 66 new nonterminals in order to encode the ATIS lexicon as CFG rules. The resulting grammar consists of 5,226 rules with 258 nonterminals and 991 terminals. Carroll's test input set contains 98 natural language sentences of average length 11.4 words. An example sentence is *"i would like to leave on thursday morning may fifth before six a.m."*.

Times to parse ranged from <1 second for the 5 shortest inputs, to between 12 and 19 seconds for the 5 longest inputs. The average time was 1.88 seconds. Given that our Haskell implementation is in an early stage of development, these results suggest that it may be possible to use our algorithm in applications involving large grammars.

5 Related Work

Our combinators implement the algorithm of Frost, Hafiz and Callaghan (2007). The relationship of that algorithm to work by others on left recursion is discussed in detail in their paper. The following is a brief summary: As in Shiel (1976), the algorithm passes information to parsers which is used in curtailment. The information passed is similar to the cancellation sets used by Nederhof and Koster (1993). The algorithm uses the memoization technique of Norvig (1991) to achieve polynomial complexity with parser combinators, as do Frost (1994), Johnson (1995), and Frost and Hafiz (2006). Note that Ford (2002) has also used memoization in functional parsing, but for constrained grammars. Lickman accommodates left-recursion using fixed points (1995), based on an unpublished idea by Wadler, but he does not address the problem of exponential complexity. Johnson (1995) integrates a technique for dealing with left recursion with memoization. However, the algorithm on which we base our combinators differs from Johnson's $O(n^3)$ approach in the technique that we use to accommodate left recursion. Also, the algorithm facilitates the construction of compact representations of parse results whereas Johnson's appears to be very difficult to extend to do this. As in Frost and Hafiz (2006) the algorithm integrates "left-recursion counts" with memoization, and defines recognizers as functions which take an index as argument and which return a set of indices. The algorithm is an improvement in that it can accommodate indirect as well as direct left recursion and can be used to create parsers in addition to recognizers.

Extensive research has been carried out on parser combinators. A comprehensive overview of that work can be found in (Frost 2006). Our approach owes much to that work. In particular, our combinators and motivation for their use follows from Burge (1975) and Fairburn (1986). Also, we use Wadler's (1985) notion of failure as an empty list of successes, and many of the ideas from Hutton and Meijer (1995) on monadic parsing.

6   Concluding Comments

We have developed a set of parser combinators which allow modular and efficient parsers to be constructed as executable specifications of ambiguous left-recursive grammars. The accommodation of left recursion greatly increases what can be done in this approach, and removes the need for non-expert users to painfully rewrite and debug their grammars to avoid left recursion. We believe that such advantages balance well against any reduction in performance, especially when an application is being prototyped, and in those applications where the additional time required for parsing is not a major factor in the overall time required when semantic processing, especially of ambiguous input, is taken into account. Experimental results indicate that the combinators are feasible for use in small to medium applications with moderately-sized grammars and inputs. The results also suggest that with further tuning, they may be used with large grammars.

Future work includes proof of correctness, analysis w.r.t. grammar size, improvements for very large grammars, detailed comparison with other combinators systems such as Parsec, reduction of reliance on monads in order to support some form of "on-line" computation, comparison with functional implementations of GLR parsers, and extension of the approach to build modular executable specifications of attribute grammars.

Acknowledgements

The authors would like to thank the referees for their careful reviews, constructive criticisms, and helpful suggestions. Richard Frost and Rahmatullah Hafiz thank the Natural Sciences and Engineering Research Council of Canada (NSERC), and the Government of Ontario, respectively, for their support.

References

1. Aho, A.V., Ullman, J.D.: The Theory of Parsing, Translation, and Compiling, vol. I: Parsing. Prentice-Hall, Englewood Cliffs (1972)
2. Burge, W.H.: Recursive Programming Techniques. Addison-Wesley, Reading (1975)
3. Carroll, J.: Efficiency in large-scale parsing systems – parser comparison (2003), http://informatics.sussex.ac.uk/research/nlp/carroll/elsps.html
4. Earley, J.: An efficient context-free parsing algorithm. Communications of the ACM 13(2), 94–102 (1970)

5. Fairburn, J.: Making form follow function: An exercise in functional programming style. Cambridge Comp. Lab. Technical Report No. 89 (1986)
6. Ford, B.: Packrat parsing: Simple, powerful, lazy, linear time. In: ICFP, pp. 36–47 (2002)
7. Frost, R.A.: Realization of natural language interfaces using lazy functional programming. ACM Comp. Surv. 38(4) Article 11 (2006)
8. Frost, R.A.: Using memoization to achieve polynomial complexity of purely functional executable specifications of non-deterministic top-down parsers. SIGPLAN Notices 29(4), 23–30 (1994)
9. Frost, R.A., Hafiz, R., Callaghan.: Modular and efficient top-down parsing for ambiguous left-recursive grammars. In: Proc. of the Tenth Int. Conf. on Parsing Technologies, pp. 109–120. ACL Press (2007)
10. Frost, R.A., Hafiz, R.: A new top-down parsing algorithm to accommodate ambiguity and left recursion in polynomial time. SIGPLAN Notices 42(5), 46–54 (2006)
11. Hutton, G., Meijer, E.: Monadic parser combinators. J. of Functional Programming 8(4), 437–444 (1995)
12. Johnson, M.: Squibs and discussions: Memoization in top-down parsing. Computational Linguistics 21(3), 405–417 (1995)
13. Kuno, S.: The augmented predictive analyzer for context-free languages — its relative efficiency. Communications of the ACM 9(11), 810–823 (1966)
14. Lickman, P.: Parsing With Fixed Points. Master's Th., Oxford (1995)
15. Nederhof, M.J., Koster, C.H.A.: Top-down parsing for left-recursive grammars. Technical Report 93–10. Research Institute for Declarative Systems, Department of Informatics, Faculty of Mathematics and Informatics, Katholieke Universiteit, Nijmegen (1993)
16. Norvig, P.: Techniques for automatic memoization with applications to context-free parsing. Computational Linguistics 17(1), 91–98 (1991)
17. Shiel, B.A.: Observations on context-free parsing. Technical Reports TR 12–76, Center for Research in Computing Technology, Aiken Computational Laboratory, Harvard University (1976)
18. Tomita, M.: Efficient Parsing for Natural Language: A Fast Algorithm for Practical Systems. Kluwer Academic Publishers, Boston, MA (1986)
19. Wadler, P.: How to replace failure by a list of successes. In: Jouannaud, J.-P. (ed.) Functional Programming Languages and Computer Architecture. LNCS, vol. 201, pp. 113–128. Springer, Heidelberg (1985)

DCGs + Memoing = Packrat Parsing but Is It Worth It?

Ralph Becket and Zoltan Somogyi

NICTA and
Department of Computer Science and Software Engineering
The University of Melbourne, 111 Barry Street, Parkville
Victoria 3010, Australia
{rafe,zs}@csse.unimelb.edu.au

Abstract. Packrat parsing is a newly popular technique for efficiently implementing recursive descent parsers. Packrat parsing avoids the potential exponential costs of recursive descent parsing with backtracking by ensuring that each production rule in the grammar is tested at most once against each position in the input stream. This paper argues that (a) packrat parsers can be trivially implemented using a combination of definite clause grammar rules and memoing, and that (b) packrat parsing may actually be significantly *less* efficient than plain recursive descent with backtracking, but (c) memoing the recognizers of just one or two nonterminals, selected in accordance with Amdahl's law, can sometimes yield speedups. We present experimental evidence to support these claims.

Keywords: Mercury, parsing, packrat, recursive descent, DCG, memoing, tabling.

1 Introduction

Recursive descent parsing has many attractions: (a) it is simple to understand and implement; (b) all the features of the implementation language are available to the parser developer; (c) complex rules can be implemented easily (for instance, longest match, or A not followed by B); (d) parsing rules may if necessary depend on 'state' such as the current contents of the symbol table; and (e) higher order rules may be used to abstract away common grammatical features (e.g. comma-separated lists).

However, recursive descent parsing requires backtracking for grammars that aren't LL(1) and, in the worst case, that backtracking may lead to exponential complexity. Consider the grammar in figure 1. Assuming a top-down, left-to-right, recursive descent strategy, matching the non-terminal "a" against the input string "xxxzzz" involves testing all possible length six expansions of a before succeeding.

Packrat parsing ensures linear complexity for such grammars by testing each production rule at most once against each position in the input stream. This

P. Hudak and D.S. Warren (Eds.): PADL 2008, LNCS 4902, pp. 182–196, 2008.
© Springer-Verlag Berlin Heidelberg 2008

```
a  ::=  b | c
b  ::=  'x' d 'y'
c  ::=  'x' d 'z'
d  ::=  a | epsilon
```

Fig. 1. A grammar with pathological recursive descent behaviour: a, b, c, d are non-terminals; 'x', 'y', 'z' are terminals; epsilon matches the empty string

is typically done by incrementally constructing a table mapping each *(non-terminal, input position)* pair to *unknown, failed,* or a number n where parsing succeeded consuming n input tokens. (In practice the 'succeeded' entries may also contain other information, such as abstract syntax tree representations of the matched input fragment.) Figure 2 gives an example of a packrat table being filled out.

				Input position			
	1	2	3	4	5	6
a	6_{-15-}	4_{-11-}	2_{-7-}	$failed_{-3-}$		
b	$failed_{-13-}$	$failed_{-9-}$	$failed_{-5-}$	$failed_{-1-}$		
c	6_{-14-}	4_{-10-}	2_{-6-}	$failed_{-2-}$		
d		4_{-12-}	2_{-8-}	0_{-4-}		

Fig. 2. Filling out a packrat table matching non-terminal a from figure 1 against "xxxzzz". Blank entries denote *unknown,* 'failed' denotes a non-match, numbers denote successful parsing consuming that number of input tokens, and –subscripts– show the order in which entries were added.

Packrat parsing has recently been made popular by packages such as Pappy (Bryan Ford's Haskell package [2]) and Rats! (Robert Grimm's Java package [3]).

There are two key problems with the packrat approach. First, the table can consume prodigious amounts of memory (the Java parser generated by Pappy requires up to 400 bytes of memory for every byte of input). Second, it cannot easily be extended to handle contextual information, such as the current line number. Another, perhaps less significant, problem is that the packrat table cannot be used for nondeterministic grammars.

In this paper, we describe an alternative approach to packrat parsing that can avoid these problems. First, section 2 shows that recursive descent parsers can be constructed quite easily in Mercury [8] using Definite Clause Grammars [6]. Section 3 goes on to show how Mercury DCG parsers can be trivially converted into packrat parsers by memoing the recognition predicates of all the nonterminals, and that being selective about what to memo has its advantages. Section 4 gives some interesting performance results, comparing the Mercury approach with Robert Grimm's Rats! packrat parser generator. Section 5 concludes with a discussion of the relative merits of packrat parsers and plain DCG parsers.

2 Definite Clause Grammars

Logic programming languages such as Prolog and Mercury have built-in support for coding recursive descent parsers in the form of definite clause grammars (DCGs). The Mercury syntax of a DCG rule is

```
H --> B.
```

where H is the head of the rule (the non-terminal) and B is its body. The syntax for the body is

```
B   ::=  [x1, ..., xn]
     |   B1, B2
     |   ( if B1 then B2 else B3 )
     |   B1 ; B2
     |   { G }
```

Body terms match as follows: [x1, ..., xn] succeeds iff the next n items of input unify with x1 to xn respectively (these items are consumed by the match); B1, B2 matches B1 followed by B2; (if B1 then B2 else B3) matches either B1, B2, or just B3 in the case that B1 does not match at the current position; B1 ; B2 matches either B1 or B2; { G } succeeds iff the ordinary Mercury goal G succeeds. A body item not B is syntactic sugar for (if B then { false } else { true }), where the goal true always succeeds and the goal false always fails.

The compiler uses a simple source-to-source transformation to convert DCG rules into ordinary Mercury. Every DCG rule becomes a predicate with two extra arguments threaded through, corresponding respectively to the representation of the input remaining before and after matching. Figure 3 shows the transformation algorithm.

By way of an example, the following DCG rule nat matches natural numbers (as in Prolog, Mercury variable names start with an upper case letter, while predicate names and function symbols start with a lower case letter):

```
nat    --> digit, digits.
digit  --> [X], { char.is_digit(X) }.
digits --> ( if digit then digits else { true } ).
```

char.is_digit is a predicate in the Mercury standard library; it succeeds iff its argument is a character between '0' and '9'. Note that the last rule implements longest match.

Transform   H --> B   into   H(S0, S) :- <<B, S0, S>>   where

```
<<[x1, ..., xn],    S0, S>> = S0 = [x1, ..., xn | S]
<<(C1, C2),         S0, S>> = some [S1] (<<C1, S0, S1>>,
                                          <<C2, S1, S >>)
<<( if C then T           = some [S1] ( if  <<C, S0, S1>>
        else E ), S0, S>>             then <<T, S1, S >>
                                      else <<E, S0, S >> )
<<(D1 ; D2),        S0, S>> = (<<D1, S0, S>> ; <<D2, S0, S>>)
<<{ G }             S0, S>> = G, S = S0
```

Fig. 3. Transforming DCG rules into plain Mercury. S0, S1, S are input stream states.

DCGs are very flexible: rules can take arguments and compute results. The following version of **nat** returns the number matched as an integer:

```
nat(N)       --> digit(D), digits(D, N).
digit(D)     --> [X], { char.digit_to_int(X, D) }.
digits(M, N) -->
     ( if digit(D) then digits(10 * M + D, N) else { N = M } ).
```

Here, **digits** takes M (the numeric value of the digits read so far) as a parameter and computes N (the numeric value of the entire digit sequence matched by the nonterminal) as the result. **char.digit_to_int(X, D)** succeeds iff X is a digit, unifying D with its integer value.

Negation can allow for elegant disambiguation between rules:

```
integer(S, I) --> sign(S), nat(I), not frac_part(_F).
real(S, I, F) --> sign(S), nat(I), frac_part(F).
frac_part(F)  --> ['.'], digit(D), frac(100.0, float(D)/10.0, F).
```

```
frac(M, F0, F) --> ( if    digit(D)
                     then frac(M * 10.0, F0 + float(D) / M, F)
                     else { F = F0 } ).
sign(S)        --> ( if ['-'] then { S = -1 } else { S = 1 } ).
```

The pattern **not frac_part(_F)** succeeds iff **frac_part(_F)** fails, hence the **integer** rule only matches natural numbers that are not followed by a fractional part. Without this negated pattern, **integer** would match the initial part of the lexeme of every **real** number.

Higher order DCG rules can be used to abstract out common grammatical patterns, such as these:

```
optional(P, X) -->
     ( if P(Y) then
```

```
            { X = yes(Y) }
        else
            { X = no }
        ).

    zero_or_more(P, List) -->
        ( if P(Head) then
            zero_or_more(P, Tail),
            { List = [Head | Tail] }.
        else
            { List = [] }
        ).

    one_or_more(P, [Head | Tail]) -->
        P(Head),
        zero_or_more(P, Tail).

    comma_separated_list(P, [Head | Tail]) -->
        P(Head),
        zero_or_more(comma_followed_by(P), Tail).

    comma_followed_by(P, X) -->
        [','],
        P(X).
```

(In each of these cases P must be a DCG rule computing a single result.)

Using these higher order rules is quite simple. For example, one can match a comma-separated list of natural numbers just by calling by calling `comma_separated_list(nat, Nats)`.

3   Using Memoing to Create Packrat Parsers

The Mercury compiler provides extensive support for several forms of tabled evaluation. Memoing is one of these forms. When a memoized predicate is called, it looks up its call table to see whether it has been called with these arguments before. If not, it enters the input arguments in the call table, executes as usual, and then records the output arguments of each answer. On the other hand, if the predicate *has* been called with these input arguments before, it returns the answers from the call's answer table directly, *without* executing the predicate's code.

To memoize a Mercury predicate or function one need only add the appropriate pragma. For example:

```
:- pragma memo(nat/3, <attributes>).
:- pragma memo(integer/4, <attributes>).
:- pragma memo(real/5, <attributes>).
```

The first argument of the memo pragma is the *name/arity* pair identifying the predicate to be memoized. For DCG rules the arity component is that of the Mercury predicate resulting from the DCG transformation of figure 3, which adds two extra arguments to the DCG rule.

The second argument to the memo pragma is a list of attributes controlling the memoization transformation. Valid attributes are:

- allow_reset tells the compiler to generate a predicate that the user can call to clear the predicate's memo table.
- statistics tells the compiler to keep statistics about all the accesses to the predicate's memo table, and to generate a predicate that user code can call to retrieve these statistics.
- specified([...]) tells the compiler how to construct the call table. The list should contain one element for each predicate argument. If the argument is an input argument, this element can be value, addr or promise_implied.
  - value tells the compiler to table the full value of the argument. If the term bound to this argument at runtime contains n function symbols, this will take $O(n)$ time and can create $O(n)$ new nodes in the call tree, so it can be slow.
  - addr tells the compiler to table only the address of the argument, which uses only constant time and space. The downside is that while equal addresses imply equal values, nonequal addresses do *not* imply unequal values. Therefore if any arguments are tabled by address, two calls in which the values of all input arguments are equal may nevertheless not be recognized as being the same call, leading to the unnecessary recomputation of some previously stored answers.
  - promise_implied asserts that the corresponding argument need not be stored or looked up in the call table, because the user promises its value to be a function of the values of the other input arguments.

  If the argument is an output argument, the corresponding element should be output.
- fast_loose tells the compiler to table all input arguments by address; it is equivalent to a longer specified([...]) annotation.

For parsing applications, asking for all input arguments to be tabled by address is almost always optimal.

Memoizing all the rules in a DCG parser essentially converts a recursive descent parser into a packrat parser. The memoized predicates generated by the Mercury compiler employ hash tables with separate chaining. Tables start small, but are automatically expanded when their load factors exceed a threshold. They therefore have $O(1)$ expected lookup times, the same order as packrat tables. Since hash tables are more complex than mere 2D arrays, their constant factor is higher, but in practice, the hash table approach may well be superior. This is because packrat tables will nearly always be sparsely populated, so the hash tables probably occupy less memory and are therefore likely to be more memory-system friendly — one would expect significantly less paging when parsing any sizeable amount of input. Of course, the packrat table can be compressed, as in [4], but that erodes, eliminates, or even reverses the constant factor advantage. Furthermore, it is a *specialized* optimization; with memoed DCGs, any optimization of the memo tables is of *general* use. The more general memoing mechanism has two further advantages: it works for parsing nondeterministic grammars, and, more importantly, it supports parameterized parsing rules, such as `comma_separated_list`.

4   Performance Evaluation

To see how memoized DCG parsers perform compared to packrat parsers, we need both kinds of parsers for the same language, preferably a language with lots of programs available as test data. We implemented a parser for the Java language to allow comparison with results published for other packrat parsers (e.g. [2], [3]).

4.1   Parser Structure

Our implementation is an almost direct transliteration of the grammar provided in Sun's Java Language Specification (Second Edition) which can be found on-line at `http://java.sun.com/docs/books/jls/second_edition/html/syntax.doc .html`. (Section 3 of that document specifies the lexical structure of identifiers, primitive literals and so on). We did the translation into Mercury done by hand (although doing so automatically would not have been hard were it not for the occasional error in Sun's published grammar, such as the handling of `instanceof` expressions). We did not take advantage of any opportunities for optimization.

We implemented a rule from Sun's grammar such as

```
BlockStatement ::= LocalVariableDeclarationStatement
               |  ClassOrInterfaceDeclaration
               |  [Identifier :] Statement
```

as the Mercury DCG predicate

```
block_statement -->
    ( if local_variable_declaration_statement then
        []
    else if class_or_interface_declaration then
        []
    else
        optional(label), statement
    ).

label -->
    identifier,
    punct(":").
```

[] is the DCG equivalent of a no-op goal and the grammatical convenience [Identifier :] is replaced with a higher order call to one of the predicates we showed in section 2. The higher order argument of that call representing the identifier-colon pattern could have been an anonymous lambda-expression, but making it a separate named predicate (label) is more readable.

The reason why the predicate is only a recognizer (i.e. it doesn't return anything useful like a parse tree) is to remove any differences in the parse tree construction process as a source of unwanted variability in our comparison with the Rats! packrat parser generator. Since Rats! views nonterminals as being defined by an *ordered* list of productions, which stops looking for parses using later productions after finding a parse using an earlier production, this code also replaces the apparent nondeterminism of the original grammar with a deterministic if-then-else chain. In the absence of code to build parse trees, the identity of the production that matches a nonterminal like block_statement doesn't matter anyway. Adapting the implementation to also construct an abstract syntax tree would simply require an extra parameter in each DCG predicate's argument list, together with some simple code in each production to compute its value. In fact, the definition of optional in section 2 assumes that we are building parse trees; if we are not, we need to use this simplified definition instead:

```
optional(P) -->
   ( if P then [] else [] ).
```

4.2   Experimental Setup

Our test load consisted of the 735 largest Java source files taken from a randomly chosen large Java program, the Batik SVG toolkit. (More source files would have exceeded the 20 Kbyte limit on the length of command line argument vectors.) The input files range in size from a few hundred lines to more than 10,000 lines; they total more than 900,000 lines and 9.6 Mbytes.

To evaluate packrat parsing, we used the xtc Java parser generated with the Rats! optimizing packrat parser generator (version 1.12.0, released on 18 July 2007). We took the grammar specification from the Rats! web site, so it should match the version used in Grimm's paper [4]. We ran the generated parser both with and without the Java optimization option (-Xms20m) recommended by Grimm, which starts the system with a 20 Mb memory allocation pool. The startup times were nontrivial either way, so figure 4 reports not just the time taken by each version to parse the test load, but also the time taken by each version on the null load (a single empty file), and the difference between them. The figures represent user time in seconds; they were obtained by averaging the times from 22 runs.

We also tried to test a packrat parser generated by Pappy, but we could not get it to work.

To evaluate DCG parsing and memoing, we wrote a script that could take a template Java parser written in Mercury and create several hundred different versions of it. These versions varied along the following dimensions.

Input representation. There are several possible ways to represent the input and the current position of the parser in it. We tested five of these.

chars: the state is a list of the characters remaining in the input.

single: the state is a triple: a string giving the entire contents of the input file, the length of that string, and the current offset.

global: the state is just an integer, the current offset. The input string and its length are stored in global variables, and accessed using impure foreign language code.

pass1: the state is just an integer, the current offset, but the input string and its length are passed around to every recognition predicate as a pair in one extra input argument.

pass2: the state is just an integer, the current offset, but the input string and its length are passed around to every recognition predicate as two separate extra input arguments.

The chars approach increases the size of the input to be parsed eight-fold (it uses one eight-byte cons cell per character), while the single approach requires allocating a three-word cell on the heap for every character match, so these should be slower than the other three.

All these alternatives assume that the entire input is available when parsing starts. For non-interactive applications, this is ok. Interactive applications can use other representations; they will probably be slower, but interactive applications typically don't care about that, since in such systems the user is usually by far the slowest component.

Mercury backend. The Mercury compiler can generate either low level C code that is effectively assembler [8] or high level C code that actually uses C constructs such as functions, local variables, while loops and so on [5].

Memoed predicates. The parser has 92 recognition predicates, and we could memo an arbitrary subset of these predicates. We ran tests with all recognition predicates memoed, with no predicates memoed, and 92 versions each with a single predicate memoed. Based on preliminary results, we also selected four versions with two or three interesting predicates memoed.

None of the Mercury versions had measurable startup times, so we don't report them. We also don't have room to report timing results for all versions of the Mercury parser, so figure 5 reports only a selection. (The full set of raw data are available from the Mercury web site, right next to this paper.) The figures represent user time in seconds; they were obtained by averaging the times from 22 runs. For each of the ten possible combinations of backend and input representation, we present times for three out of the 98 variations along the memoized predicates that we explored:

best: the best time from all the versions we tested;

none: the time with no predicates memoed (equivalent to pure recursive descent parsing);

all: the time with all predicates memoed (equivalent to packrat parsing).

Parser version	Null load	Test load	Difference
unoptimized	0.56s	7.54s	6.98s
optimized	0.52s	6.92s	6.40s

Fig. 4. Times for Rats! packrat parser

Backend	Input	Best	None memoed	All memoed
high level C	chars	3.56s	4.60s (1.29, 77th)	14.08s (3.96, 98th)
high level C	single	3.38s	4.14s (1.22, 77th)	13.44s (3.98, 98th)
high level C	global	1.30s	1.34s (1.03, 16th)	10.63s (8.18, 98th)
high level C	pass1	1.35s	1.36s (1.01, 2nd)	10.66s (7.90, 98th)
high level C	pass2	1.24s	1.24s (1.00, 2nd)	10.65s (8.59, 98th)
low level C	chars	5.01s	5.03s (1.00, 2nd)	16.58s (3.31, 98th)
low level C	single	4.76s	5.01s (1.05, 4th)	15.94s (3.35, 98th)
low level C	global	1.82s	1.90s (1.04, 65th)	12.89s (7.08, 98th)
low level C	pass1	1.87s	1.92s (1.02, 13th)	13.18s (7.05, 98th)
low level C	pass2	2.13s	2.29s (1.08, 85th)	13.71s (6.44, 98th)

Fig. 5. Times for Mercury DCG parser

The **none** and **all** columns also contain the ratio between the time in that column and the best time, and its position in the list of all the 98 times along the "memoed predicates" dimension from best to worst.

Rats! emits parser code in Java whereas the Mercury compiler emits C code (compiled with `gcc`), which makes this aspect something of an apples to oranges performance comparison.

The Java compiler we used was build 2.3 of IBM's J9 suite (released April 2007). The Mercury compiler we used was version `rotd-2007-08-18`; the generated C code was compiled with gcc 3.4.4 (20050314). The test machine was a PC with a 2.4 GHz Pentium IV CPU with 512 Kb of cache, 512 Mb of main memory, running Linux kernel version 2.6.8-2.

4.3   Performance Analysis

There are two main kinds of observations we can make about the performance data in figures 4 and 5: comparisons between packrat parsing using Rats! and memoed DCG parsing using Mercury, and comparisons among the various versions of memoed DCG parsing using Mercury. We start with the latter.

It is clear from figure 5 that memoing all recognition predicates is never a good idea. For every combination of the other dimensions (backend and input representation), memoing everything was *always* the worst possible choice in the "memoed predicates" dimension. The raw data also shows that it was always worst by a very wide margin. This effect is so strong that we would be very surprised if memoing everything turned out *not* to be the worst choice (from a similar range of possibilities) for any other grammar.

Figure 5 also shows that memoing nothing, i.e. using a plain recursive descent parser, is usually quite close to being the optimal choice. In several cases it is separated from the best choice by less time than the typical measurement error.

With the low level C backend and using "global" as the input representation, the speeds of the best 65 versions are all within 4% of each other. This shows that for most predicates, memoing just that predicate and nothing else is likely to have only an insignificant effect. again often within measurement error. Our raw data confirms that the trend also holds for the other nine rows of figure 5, though in those the clustering is slightly looser.

However, there are some predicates whose memoing leads to significant effects. For example, memoing the recognizer for the `punct` nonterminal (whose definition is `punct(Punct) --> match_string(Punct), whitespace`) always leads to significant slowdowns. In each row, it leads to one of the three worst times in that row, the only worse choices (amongst the ones we tested) being memoing everything and memoing `punct` *and* two other predicates. On the other hand, memoing the recognizer for the `modifiers_opt` nonterminal almost always lead to speedups; the version with only this predicate memoed was the fastest version for four of the ten rows, and was second, third and fifth fastest respectively in three other rows.

As it happens, the recognizer predicate for `punct` is called very frequently, but in more than 95% of cases it fails immediately, so a call to the recognizer typically does very little. On the other hand, `modifiers_opt` looks for zero or more occurrences of `modifier`, which requires looking for any one of eleven keywords, so even in the typical case where none of these is present, it requires a nontrivial amount of work to recognize this fact.

`punct` and `modifiers_opt` are also at opposite ends of the scale when it comes to the cost of memoing. `modifiers_opt` has no input apart from the current input position, and so (for every one of the input representations we tested) checking whether we have already looked for this nonterminal at this position requires only a single hash table lookup.[1] On the other hand, `punct` also has another input, the string to be matched. Computing the string's hash value requires scanning it, and comparing the probe string with a hash slot's occupant requires scanning it again (at least in the case of a hit), so the table lookup will take significantly more than twice as long for `punct` as for `modifiers_opt`. (Using the address of a string as its hash value could speed this up, but Mercury doesn't yet support tabling strings by their addresses; we are in the process of fixing this.)

These observations are a simple consequence of Amdahl's law [1]. The effect on performance of memoing a recognizer predicate depends on

1. the fraction of the runtime of the parser that the predicate accounts for,
2. the ratio of the time taken to execute the recognizer predicate's body compared to the time taken to perform the table lookup that could avoid that execution, and

---

[1] With the pass1 and pass2 input representations, the extra arguments are always the same, so we specify `promise_implied` to ensure that these arguments are not memoed. This is OK, since we always reset all tables when switching from one file to another.

3. the probability that the table lookup fails, so you have to execute the predicate body anyway.

The first point is the reason why memoing most predicates doesn't have a measurable impact. If a predicate accounts for only a small part of the execution time, memoing it can't have more than a small effect either, in which case not memoing it is better since it does not waste any space (in memory, or more importantly, *in the cache*) on the memo table. However, the key point is the second one: if the table lookup takes at least as long as executing the predicate body, then *memoing will yield a slowdown, not a speedup*, even if almost all lookups are hits. Pure recognizers are particularly vulnerable to this effect. Adding code to build ASTs and/or to evaluate semantic predicates to the bodies of nonterminals will reduce the relative if not the absolute costs of tabling.

Comparing the performance of the Rats!-generated packrat parser in figure 4 with the performance of the the all-memoed Mercury DCG parser in figure 5 is very difficult because the difference between packrat parsing (including all the optimizations applied by Rats!) and memoed DCG parsing is confounded by other differences, chiefly in how the parsers' executables are generated (Rats! generates Java, whereas Mercury generates C). If Rats! is ever modified to generate C, or if the Mercury compiler's Java backend is ever completed, this confounding factor would be removed.

Grimm reports [4] that the set of 17 optimizations performed by Rats! (some of which rely on the presence of hand-written annotations) yield a cumulative speedup of a factor of 8.9. That was on a different machine and on a different test load, but by nevertheless applying that factor to the data in figure 4, we can estimate (*very* roughly) that a totally unoptimized packrat parser in Java would take 50 to 60 seconds on our load on our test machine (6.4s $* 8.9 = 56.96$s). At 16.58 seconds, even the slowest Mercury DCG parser is significantly faster than that. While some of this is almost certainly due to the Java vs C difference, part of it is probably due to differences in how the two systems manage their tables. Likewise, all ten versions of a plain Mercury DCG parser with no memoing are much faster than the fully optimized Rats! generated packrat parser.

The best parser generated by Rats! (the one with all optimizations applied, which avoids memoing many nonterminals) is a factor of 8.9 faster than the worst Rats! parser (the one with no optimizations applied, which memoes all nonterminals). In most rows of figure 5, the difference between the best and worst versions is smaller than that. That tells us that Rats! is tapping some sources of speedup that we don't. This is not surprising, given that section 8 of [4] gives a long list of optimizations that we haven't even tried to apply, even though they would be worthwhile. However, the fact that we get speedups in the factor of 3 to factor of 8 range by simply not memoing anything, and some slight speedups beyond that by carefully selecting one or two predicates to memo, shows that with this single optimization (memoing almost nothing) we are also tapping an important source of speedup that Rats! doesn't.

Rats! actually has an optimization that reduces the set of memoed nonterminals, and figure 4 of [4] shows that of the 17 optimizations applied by Rats, this one gets one of the two biggest speedups (almost a factor of 2). However, our data shows that memoing even fewer nonterminals can yield even bigger speedups.

We think the Rats! technique of starting off by memoing all nonterminals, and then applying heuristics to choose some nonterminals to *not* be memoed, is approaching the problem from the wrong end. We think the right approach is to start by memoing nothing, and then applying heuristics to choose some nonterminals to *be* memoed. Rats! uses heuristics based on properties of the grammar. We think that while these have their place, it is much more important to pay attention to Amdahl's law and memo a nonterminal only if the expected speedup due to this step is (a) positive and (b) nontrivial, i.e. likely to be measurable.

The best way to estimate the expected speedup is via feedback from a profiler that can record the program's overall execution time, the average time to execute each nonterminal's predicate, the average time to table the arguments of that predicate, and the average hit rate of each table. In the absence of such feedback, the system can either try to estimate that information from the structure of the grammar (this approach has had some success in other contexts, e.g. granularity analysis), or ask the programmer to annotate the predicates that should be tabled. Running a few experiments with different sets of annotations doesn't take very long (figure 5 is based on several thousand such experiments, all driven by a single script), and in fact may be *less* work than annotating all the "transient" nonterminals in a Rats! parser specification.

Of course, adopting no memoing as the default approach means abandoning the linear time guarantee of packrat parsing; with few or no nonterminals memoed, large chunks of the input may in theory be scanned an exponential number of times. However, we don't think this is a problem. First, as many others have noted [7], exponential behavior just doesn't seem to happen in practice anyway. Second, the linear time guarantee always had problems. Tabling everything consumes main memory at a high rate, and so risks starting thrashing, thus dropping the program from DRAM speed to disk speed. While a theoretician may say the performance is still linear, that won't prevent complaints from users. The fact that many languages nowadays (including Java and Mercury) include a garbage collector (which must scan the tables at least once in a while, but won't be able to recover memory from them) just makes this even worse. Given these facts, we think that in the absence of a genuine need for a guaranteed linear upper bound, focusing just on the expected case makes much more sense.

5   Discussion and Conclusion

The PEGs (parsing expression grammars) that underlie packrat parsers and DCGs (definite clause grammars) have very similar expressive power. While PEGs usually require support from a specialized tool, DCGs can be implemented directly in a general purpose programming language. This brings some advantages, for example the ability to use higher order code to abstract away common patterns and the ability to use standard tools such as debuggers and profilers. In this paper, we have shown another of these advantages, which is that if the host language has support for memoization, then *any* DCG parser can be turned into a packrat parser simply by memoizing the predicates implementing the production rules. This is by far the simplest way to construct a packrat parser: it uses a general purpose language feature, it handles the arguments representing the current offset in the input the same way as any other arguments (such as those representing a symbol table), and doesn't even require any new implementation effort.

However, while it is trivial to turn any DCG parser into a packrat parser, our data shows that this is almost always a performance loss, not a win. Our data shows that not memoing any predicates is consistently *much* faster than memoing *all* predicates, and that memoing nothing is in fact usually pretty close to optimal. While generalizing from a sample of one (the Java grammar) is always dangerous, we believe this result is very likely to hold for the grammar of any programming language, since these tend to have only relatively few ambiguous components. (Grammars for natural languages can be expected to have much more pervasive ambiguity.) Most predicates don't contribute significantly to the parser's runtime, so tabling them just adds overhead in both space and time. For memoing to yield a benefit, the memoed predicate must contribute significantly to the runtime of the parser, and the average running time of one of its invocations multiplied by the hit rate of the table (the expected savings), must exceed the time taken by the tabling operations themselves (the cost). We propose that this be the chief consideration in deciding what predicates to memo in a recursive descent parser. This consideration is so important that respecting it, and tabling only a minimal set of predicates (usually only one, sometimes none) leads to a parser that is significantly faster than the one generated by Rats!, even though the Rats! applies a whole host of other optimizations we don't.

The best of both worlds would be a system that respected Amdahl's law in choosing what to memo but also applied all the other optimizations applied by Rats!. Some of them (e.g. factoring out common prefixes that occur in the conditions of a chain of if-then-elses) are generic enough that it makes sense to add them to the implementations of general purpose programming languages such as Mercury. Some (e.g. turning the code that recognizes `public | private | protected` from a chain of if-then-elses into a decision tree) are specific to parsers, and thus are appropriate only for a parser generator. The same is true for Rats!'s support for left-recursive productions.

References

1. Amdahl, G.: Validity of the single processor approach to achieving large scale computing capabilities. In: Proceedings of the AFIPS Spring Join Computer Conference, Atlantic City, New Jersey, pp. 483–485 (1967)
2. Ford, B.: Packrat parsing: Simple, powerful, lazy, linear time. In: Proceedings of the Seventh ACM SIGPLAN International Conference on Functional Programming, Pittsburgh, Pennsylvania, pp. 36–47 (2002)

3. Grimm, R.: Practical packrat parsing. New York University Technical Report, Dept. of Computer Science, TR2004-854 (2004)
4. Grimm, R.: Better extensibility through modular syntax. In: Proceedings of the ACM SIGPLAN 2006 Conference on Programming Language Design and Implementation, Ottawa, Canada, pp. 38–51 (2006)
5. Henderson, F., Somogyi, Z.: Compiling Mercury to high-level C code. In: Horspool, R.N. (ed.) CC 2002 and ETAPS 2002. LNCS, vol. 2304, Springer, Heidelberg (2002)
6. Perreira, F., Warren, D.: Definite clause grammars for language analysis — a survey of the formalism and a comparison with augmented transition networks. Artificial Intelligence 13, 231–278 (1980)
7. Redziejowski, R.: Parsing expression grammar as a primitive recursive-descent parser with backtracking. Fundamenta Informaticae 79(1-4), 513–524 (2007)
8. Somogyi, Z., Henderson, F., Conway, T.: The execution algorithm of Mercury: an efficient purely declarative logic programming language. Journal of Logic Programming 29(1-3), 17–64 (1996)

An Improved Continuation Call-Based
Implementation of Tabling

Pablo Chico de Guzmán[1,2], Manuel Carro[1], Manuel V. Hermenegildo[1,2],
Cláudio Silva[3], and Ricardo Rocha[3]

[1] School of Computer Science, Univ. Politécnica de Madrid, Spain
pchico@clip.dia.fi.upm.es, {mcarro,herme}@fi.upm.es
[2] Depts. of Comp. Science and Electr. and Comp. Eng., Univ. of New Mexico, USA
herme@cs.unm.edu
[3] DCC-FC & LIACC, University of Porto, Portugal
ccaldas@dcc.online.pt, ricroc@dcc.fc.up.pt

Abstract. Tabled evaluation has been proved an effective method to
improve several aspects of goal-oriented query evaluation, including termination and complexity. Several "native" implementations of tabled
evaluation have been developed which offer good performance, but many
of them require significant changes to the underlying Prolog implementation, including the compiler and the abstract machine. Approaches based
on program transformation, which tend to minimize changes to both the
Prolog compiler and the abstract machine, have also been proposed, but
they often result in lower efficiency. We explore some techniques aimed
at combining the best of these worlds, i.e., developing an extensible implementation which requires minimal modifications to the compiler and
the abstract machine, and with reasonably good performance. Our preliminary experiments indicate promising results.

Keywords: Tabled logic programming, Implementation, Performance,
Program transformation.

1 Introduction

Tabling [4,19,20] is a resolution strategy which tries to *memoize* previous calls
and their answers in order to improve several well-known shortcomings found
in SLD resolution. It brings some of the advantages of bottom-up evaluation to
the top-down, goal-oriented evaluation strategy. In particular, evaluating logic
programs under a tabling scheme may achieve termination in cases where SLD
resolution does not (because of infinite loops —for example, the tabled evaluation of bounded term-size programs is guaranteed to always terminate). Also,
programs which perform repeated computations can be greatly sped up. Program declarativeness is also improved since the order of clauses and goals within
a clause is less relevant, if at all. Tabled evaluation has been successfully applied in many fields, such as deductive databases [13], program analysis [5,21],
reasoning in the semantic Web [24], model checking [11], and others.

P. Hudak and D.S. Warren (Eds.): PADL 2008, LNCS 4902, pp. 197–213, 2008.
© Springer-Verlag Berlin Heidelberg 2008

In all cases the advantages of tabled evaluation stem from checking whether calls to *tabled predicates*, i.e., predicates which have been marked to be evaluated using tabling, have been made before. Repeated calls to tabled predicates consume answers from a table, they suspend when all stored answers have been consumed, and they fail when no more answers can be generated. However, the advantages are not without drawbacks. The main problem is the complexity of some (efficient) implementations of tabled resolution, and a secondary issue is the difficulty in selecting which predicates to table in order not to incur in undesired slow-downs.

Two main categories of tabling mechanisms can be distinguished: *suspension-based* and *linear* tabling mechanisms. In suspension-based mechanisms the computation state of suspended tabled subgoals has to be preserved to avoid backtracking over them. This is done either by *freezing* the stacks, as in XSB [16], by copying to another area, as in CAT [7], or by using an intermediate solution as in CHAT [8]. Linear tabling mechanisms maintain a single execution tree where tabled subgoals always extend the current computation without requiring suspension and resumption of sub-computations. The computation of the (local) fixpoint is performed by repeatedly looping subgoals until no more solutions can be found. Examples of this method are the linear tabling of B-Prolog [22,23] and the DRA scheme [9].

Suspension-based mechanism have achieved very good performance results but, in general, deep changes to the underlying Prolog implementation are required. Linear mechanisms, on the other hand, can usually be implemented on top of existing sequential engines without major modifications but their efficiency is affected by subgoal recomputation. One of our theses is that it should be possible to find a combination of the best of both worlds: a suspension-based mechanism that is reasonably efficient and does not require complex modifications to the compiler or underlying Prolog implementation, thus contributing to its maintainability an making it easier to port it to other Prolog systems. Also, we would like to avoid introducing any overhead that would reduce the execution speed for SLD execution.

Our starting point is the *Continuation Call Mechanism* presented by Ramesh and Chen in [14]. This approach has the advantage that it indeed does not need deep changes to the underlying Prolog machinery. On the other hand it has shown up to now worse efficiency than the more "native" suspension-based implementations. Our aim is to analyze the bottlenecks of this approach, explore variations thereof, and propose solutions in order to improve its efficiency while keeping tabling-related changes clearly separated from the basic WAM implementation. While the approach may not necessarily be significantly simpler than other (native) approaches, we will argue that it does allow a more modular design which reduces and isolates in separate modules the changes made to the underlying WAM. This hopefully will make it easier to maintain the implementation of both tabling and the WAM itself, as well as adapting the tabling scheme and code to other Prolog systems.

In more concrete terms, and in the spirit of [14], the implementation we will propose tries to be non intrusive and change only minimally the initial WAM, moving the low-level tabling data structures either to the Prolog level or to external modules. Other systems, like Mercury [18], also implement tabling using external modules and program transformation, so as not to change the compiler and runtime system. Despite these similarities, the big differences in the base language make the implementation technically very different also.

2 Tabling Basics

We now sketch how tabled evaluation works from a user point of view (more details can be found in [4,16]) and briefly describe the continuation call mechanism implementation technique proposed in [14], on which we base our work.

2.1 Tabling by Example

We use as running example the program in Figure 1, taken from [14], whose purpose is to determine reachability of nodes in a graph We ignore for now the :- tabled path/2 declaration (which instructs the compiler to use tabled execution for the designated predicate), and assume that SLD resolution is to be used. Then, a query such as ?- path(a, N). may never terminate if, for example, edge/2 represents a cyclic graph.

Adding the :- tabled declaration forces the compiler and runtime system to distinguish the first occurrence of a tabled goal (the *generator*) and subsequent calls which are identical up to variable renaming (the *consumers*). The generator applies resolution using the program clauses to derive answers for the goal. Consumers *suspend* the current execution path (using implementation-dependent means) and start execution on a different branch. When such an alternative branch finally succeeds, the answer generated for the initial query is inserted in a table associated with the original goal. This makes it possible to reactivate suspended calls and to continue execution at the point where they were stopped. Thus, consumers do not use SLD resolution, but obtain instead the answers from the table where they were inserted previously by the producer. Predicates not marked as tabled are executed following SLD resolution, hopefully with (minimal or no) overhead due to the availability of tabling in the system.

2.2 The Continuation Call Technique

The continuation call technique [14] implements tabling by a combination of program transformation and side effects in the form of insertions into and retrievals from a table which relates calls, answers, and the continuation code to be executed after consumers read answers from the table. We will now sketch how the mechanism works using the path/2 example (Figure 1). The original code is transformed into the program in Figure 2 which is the one actually executed.

Roughly speaking, the transformation for tabling is as follows: a bridge predicate for path/2 is introduced so that calls to path/2 made from regular Prolog

```
                           path(X, Y):- slg(path(X, Y)).

                           slg_path(path(X, Y), Id):-
                              edge(X, Y),
:- tabled path/2.             slgcall(Id, [X], path(Y, Z), path_cont).
                           slg_path(path(X, Y), Id):-
path(X, Z):-                  edge(X, Y),
   edge(X, Y),                answer(Id, path(X, Y)).
   path(Y, Z).
path(X, Z):-               path_cont(Id, [X], path(Y, Z)):-
   edge(X, Z).               answer(Id, path(X, Z)).
```

Fig. 1. A sample program   **Fig. 2.** The program in Figure 1 after being transformed for tabled execution

execution do not need to be aware of the fact that path/2 is being tabled. The call to the slg/1 primitive will ensure that its argument is executed to completion and will return, on backtracking, all the solutions found for the tabled predicate. To this end, slg/1 starts by inserting the call in the answer table and generating an identifier for it. Control is then passed to a new, distinct predicate: in this case, slg_path/2.[1] slg_path/2 receives in the first argument the original call to path/2 and in the second one the identifier generated for the parent call, which is used to relate operations on the table with this initial call. Each clause of slg_path/2 is derived from a clause of the original path/2 predicate by:

- Adding an answer/2 primitive at the end of each clause resulting from a transformation and which is not a *bridge* to call a continuation predicate. answer/2 is responsible for checking for redundant answers and executing whatever continuations (see the following item) there may be associated with that call identified by its first argument.
- Instrumenting recursive calls to path/2 using the slgcall/4 primitive. If the term passed as an argument (i.e., path(X, Y)) is already in the table, slgcall/4 creates a new consumer which consumes answers from the table. Otherwise, the term is inserted in the table with a new call identifier and execution follows using the slg_path/2 program clauses to derive new answers. In the first case, path_cont/3 is recorded as (one of) the continuation(s) of path(X, Y) and slgcall/4 fails. In the second case path_cont/3 is only recorded as a continuation of path(X, Y) if the tabled call cannot be completed. The path_cont/3 continuation will be called from answer/2 after inserting a new answer or erased upon completion of path(X, Y).
- The body of path_cont/3 encodes what remains of the clause body of path/2 after the recursive call. It is constructed in a similar way to slg_path/2, i.e., applying the same transformation as for the initial clauses and calling slgcall/4 and answer/2 at appropriate times.

---

[1] The distinct name has been created for simplicity by prepending slg_ to the predicate name –any safe means of constructing a unique predicate symbol can be used.

```
answer( callid  Id , term Answer) {
  insert  Answer in answer table
  If  (Answer ∉ answer table)
    for  each  continuation  call  C
      of  tabled  call  Id  {
        call (C) consuming Answer;
    }
  return FALSE;
}
```

Fig. 3. Pseudo-code for `answer/2`

```
slgcall ( callid  Parent, term Bindings,
          term Call, term CCall) {
  Id = insert  Call  into answer table;
  if  (Id . state  == READY) {
    Id . state  = EVALUATING;
    call  the transformed  clause  of  Call;
    check  for  completion;
  }
  consume answers for  Id;
  if  (Id . state  != COMPLETE)
    add a new continuation
      call (CCall,  Bindings)  to  Id;
  return FALSE;
}
```

Fig. 4. Pseudo-code for `slgcall/4`

The second argument of `slgcall/4` and `path_cont/3` is a list of bindings needed to recover the environment of the continuation call. Note that, in the program in Figure 1, an answer to a query such as `?- path(X, Y)` may need to bind variable `X`. This variable does not appear in the recursive call to `path/2`, and hence it does not appear in the `path/2` term passed on to `slgcall/4` either. In order for the body of `path_cont/3` to insert in the table the answer corresponding to the initial query, variable `X` (and, in general, any other necessary variable) has to be passed down to `answer/2`. This is done with the list `[X]`, which is inserted in the table as well and completes the environment needed for the continuation `path_cont/3` to resume the previously suspended call.

A safe approximation of the variables which should appear in this list is the set of variables which appear in the clause before the tabled goal and which are used in the continuation, including the `answer/2` primitive if there is one in the continuation —this is the case in our example. Variables appearing in the tabled call itself do not need to be included, as they will be passed along anyway.

Recovering a previous execution environment is an important operation in tabled execution. Other approaches to this end are the use of forward trail and freeze registers of SLG-WAM [16], which involves using lower-level mechanisms. The continuation call approach, which performs several tabling operations at the Prolog level through program transformation and can *a priori* be expected to be somewhat slower, has, however, the nice property that the implementation does not need to change the underlying WAM machinery, which helps its adaptation it to different Prolog systems. On the other hand, the table management is usually, and for efficiency reasons, written using some lower-level language and accessed using a suitable interface.

The pseudo-code for `answer/2` and `slgcall/4` is shown in Figures 3 and 4, respectively. The pseudo-code for `slg/1` is similar to that of `slgcall/4` but, instead of consuming answers, they are returned on backtracking and it finally fails when all the stored answers have been exhausted. The program transformation and primitives try to complete subgoals as soon as possible, failing whenever new answers are found. Thus, they implement the so-called *local scheduling* [16].

Checking for completion: The completion detection algorithm (see [17] for more details) is similar to that in the SLG-WAM. We just provide a sketch here. Completion is checked for in the execution of the `slgcall/4` primitive after exhausting all alternatives for the subgoal call at hand and resuming all of its consumers. To do that, we use two auxiliary fields in the table entry corresponding to every subgoal, `SgFr_dfn` and `SgFr_dep`, to quickly determine whether such a subgoal is a leader node. The `SgFr_dfn` field reflects the order in which the subgoals being evaluated were called. New subgoal frames are numbered incrementally as they are created, adding one to the `SgFr_dfn` of the previous (youngest) subgoal, whose frame is always pointed to by the global variable `SF_TOP`. `SgFr_dep` holds the number of the older call on which it depends, which is initialized with the same number as `SgFr_dfn`, meaning that initially no dependencies exist. If P_1, a tabled subgoal already inserted in the table, is called from the execution of another tabled subgoal, P_2, the `SgFr_dep` field of the table entry of P_2 is updated with the value of `SgFr_dep` field of P_1, meaning P_2 depends on P_1. When checking for completion, and using this information from the table entries, a subgoal can quickly determine whether it is a leader node. If `SgFr_dfn` = `SgFr_dep`, then we know that during its evaluation no dependencies to older subgoals have appeared and thus the *Strongly Connected Component* (SCC) including the subgoals starting from the table entry referred to by `SF_TOP` up to the current subgoal can be completed. On the other hand, if `SgFr_dep` < `SgFr_dfn`, we cannot perform completion. Instead, we must propagate the current dependency to C, the subgoal call that continues the evaluation. To do that, the `SgFr_dep` field is copied to `SgFr_dep` field of C, and completion can be performed only when the computation reaches the subgoal that does not depend on older subgoals.

Issues in the Continuation Call Mechanism: We have identified two performance-related issues when implementing the technique sketched in the previous section. The first one is rather general and related to the heavy use of the interface between C and Prolog (in both directions) that the implementation makes, which adds an overhead which cannot be neglected.

The second one is the repeated copying of continuation calls. Continuation calls (which are, in the end, Prolog predicates with an arbitrarily long list of variables as an argument) are completely copied from Prolog memory to the table for every consumer found. Storing a pointer to these structures in memory is not enough, since `slg/1` and `slgcall/4` fail immediately after associating a continuation call with a tabled call in order to force the program to search for more solutions and complete the tabled call. Therefore, the data structures created during forward execution may be removed on backtracking and not be available when needed. Reconstructing continuations as Prolog terms from the data stored in the table when they are resumed to consume previously stored answers is necessary. This can also clearly have a negative impact on performance.

Finally, an issue found with the implementation we started with [15] (which is a version of [14] in Yap Prolog) is that it did not allow backtracking over Prolog predicates called from C, which makes it difficult to implement other scheduling strategies. Since this shortcoming may appear also in other C interfaces, it is a clear candidate for improvement.

3   An Improvement over the Continuation Call Technique

We now propose some improvements to the different limitations of the original design and implementation that we discussed in Section 2.2. In order to measure execution times, we are taking the implementation described in [15] to be close enough to that described in [14] in order to be used as a basis for our developments. It is also an implementation of high quality whose basic components (e.g., tables based on tries, following [12]) are similar to those in use in current tabling systems. This implementation was ported to Ciao, where the rest of the development was performed. In what follows this initial port to Ciao will be termed the "baseline implementation."

3.1   Using a Lower-Level Interface

Calls from C to Prolog were initially performed using a relatively high-level interface similar to those commonly found in current state of the art logic programming systems: operations to create and traverse Prolog terms appear to the programmer as regular C functions, and details of the internal data representation are hidden to the programmer. This interface imposed a noticeable overhead in our implementation, as the calls to C functions had to allocate environments, pass arguments, set up Prolog environments to call Prolog from C, etc.

In order to make our implementation as fast as possible, a possibility is to integrate all the C code into the WAM and try to avoid altogether costly format conversions, etc. However, as mentioned before, we preferred to make as few changes as possible in the WAM. Therefore we chose to use directly lower-level operations and take advantage of facilities (e.g., macros) initially designed to be internally used by the WAM. While this in principle makes porting more involved, the fact is that the facilities provided in C interfaces for Prolog and the internal WAM operations are typically quite related and similar, since they all provide an interface to an underlying architecture and data representation which is common to many Prolog implementations.

Additionally, the code which constructs Prolog terms and performs calls from C is the same regardless of the program being executed and its complexity is certainly manageable. Therefore, we decided to skip the programmer interface and call directly macros available in the engine implementation. That was not a difficult task and it sped the execution up by a factor of 2.5 on average.

3.2   Calling Prolog from C

A relevant issue in the continuation call technique (and, possibly, in other cases) is the use of a C-to-Prolog interface to call Prolog goals from C — e.g., when continuations, which have been internally stored, have to be resumed, as done by slgcall/4 and answer/2. We wanted to design a solution which relied as little as possible on non-widely available characteristics of C-to-Prolog interfaces (to simplify porting the code), but which kept the efficiency as high as possible.

The general solution we have adopted is to move calls to continuations from the C level to the Prolog level by returning them as a term, using an extra argument in our primitives, to be called from Prolog. This is possible since continuations are rewritten as separate, unique predicates which therefore have an entry point accessible from Prolog. If several continuations have to be called, they can be returned and invoked one at a time on backtracking,[2] and fail when there is no pending continuation call. New continuations generated during program execution can be destructively inserted at the end of the list of continuations transparently to Prolog. Additionally, this avoids using up C stack space due to repeated Prolog → C → Prolog → ... calls, which may exhaust the C stack. Moreover, the C code is somewhat simplified (e.g., there is no need to set up a Prolog environment to be used from C) which makes using a lower-level, faster interface less of a burden.

3.3   Freezing Continuation Calls

In this section we sketch some proposals to reduce the overhead associated with the way continuation calls are handled in the original continuation call proposal.

Resuming consumers: Our starting point saves a binding list in the table to reinstall the environment of consumers when they have to be resumed. This is a relatively non-intrusive technique, but it requires copying terms back and forth between Prolog and the table where calls are stored. Restarting a consumer needs to construct a term whose first argument is the new answer (which is stored in the heap), the second one is the identifier of the tabled goal (an atomic item), and third one a list of bindings (which may be arbitrarily large). If the list of bindings has N elements, constructing the continuation call requires creating $\approx 2N + 4$ heap cells. If a continuation call is resumed often and N is high, the efficiency of the system can degrade quickly.

The technique we propose constructs continuation calls on the heap as regular Prolog terms. As these continuations are later recovered through a unique call identifier, and each continuation is unified with a new, fresh variable (CCall in resume_ccalls/4, Figure 7), full unification or even pattern matching are unnecessary, and resuming a continuation is a constant time operation.

However, the fragment of code which constructs the continuation call performs backtracking to continue exploring pending branches. This will remove the constructed call from the heap. Protecting that term is needed to make it possible to construct it only once and reuse it later. A feasible and simple solution is to freeze continuation calls in a memory area which is not affected by backtracking.

---

[2] This exploits being able to write non-deterministic predicates in C. Should this feature not be available, a list of continuations can always be returned instead which will be traversed on backtracking using member/2.

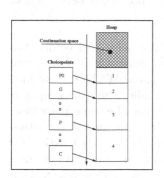

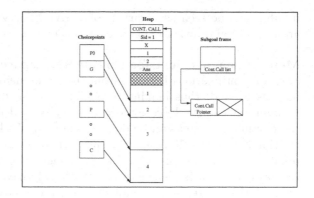

Fig. 5. Initial state   **Fig. 6.** Frozen continuation call

This will in principle make the aforementioned problem disappear. Selecting a brand new area will, however, bring additional issues as some WAM instructions would have to be changed in order to take it into account: for example, variable binding direction is commonly determined using the addresses of variables (in addition to their tags) so that younger variables point to older variables in order to save trailing. One easy way to reconcile existing WAM machinery with this continuation call area is to reserve part of the heap for it. This makes the usual WAM assumptions to hold and exactly the same WAM instructions can be used to construct and traverse data structures both in the regular heap and in the continuation call area. Therefore, regarding forward execution and backtracking, only minimal changes (e.g., the initialization of the **H** pointer, and selecting the right read/write heap pointer when dealing with the regular heap or the continuation call zone) have to be introduced.

Figure 5 shows the state of the choicepoint stack and heap (both assumed to grow downwards) before freezing a continuation call. Figure 6 shows the continuation call (C, [X,1,2], Ans) frozen at the beginning of the heap, where it is unaffected by backtracking as the WAM execution started with the **H** pointer placed just after the continuation call zone. In order to recover the continuation calls, a new field is added to the table pointing to a (Prolog) list whose elements, in turn, point to every continuation found so far for a given tabled goal.

This makes freezing a continuation call require some extra time in order to copy it on the heap. However, resuming a continuation is a constant time operation. Other systems, like CHAT or SLG-WAM, spend some extra time while preparing a consumer to be resumed, as they need to record bindings in a forward trail in order to later reinstall them. In our case, when the continuation is to be executed, the list of bindings carried with it is unified with the variables in its body, implementing essentially the same functionality as the forward trail.

In a previous paper [6] we presented a preliminary version of this technique where the heap was frozen by manipulating the contents of some choicepoints, in what can be seen as a variant of CHAT. The work presented herein works around several drawbacks in that approach.

Memory management for continuation space: As mentioned before, the area for continuations is taken from the same memory zone where the general heap is located, thus making it possible to use the same WAM instructions without any change. In case more memory is needed, reallocating the heap and the continuation area can be done simultaneously, keeping the same placement relation between both. As data inside both areas has the same format, adjusting pointers can be done using memory management routines already existing for the regular WAM implementation, which only have to be updated to take into account the existence of a gap of unused memory between the continuation call and regular heap areas. Additionally, sliding the heap within its zone to make room for more heap or for more continuations amounts only to readjusting pointers by a constant amount.

Frozen continuations are, in principle, only reachable from the table structure, which makes them candidates to be (wrongly) removed in case of garbage collection. A possible solution which needs almost no change to the garbage collector is to link a Prolog list L from some initial, dummy choice point. Each element in L points to the continuation list of a generator, which makes all the continuations reachable by the garbage collector, and therefore protected. When a generator is completed all of its answers are already stored in the trie, and its continuations are no longer needed. Removing the pointer from L to this list of unneeded continuations will make garbage collection reclaim their space. In order to adjust the pointers from table entries to the continuations when these are reallocated after a garbage collection, each element of L includes a pointer back to the corresponding table entry which can be used to quickly locate which pointers have to be updated in the table entries. A new routine has to be added to the garbage collector to perform this step.

Avoiding trail management to recover a continuation call state: The same term T corresponding to a continuation call C can be used several times to generate multiple answers to a query. This is in general not a problem as answers are in any case saved in a safe place (e.g., the answer table), and backtracking would undo the bindings to the free variables in T. There is, however, a particular case which needs special measures. When a continuation call C_1, identical to C, is resumed within the scope of C, and it is going to read a new answer, the state of T has to be reset to its frozen initial state. Since C_1 is using the same heap term T as C, we say that C_1 is a *reusing* call.

The solution we present tries to eliminate the need for treating reusing calls as a special case of a continuation call. Reusing calls appear because our baseline implementation resumes continuations when new answers are found, just when we could be in the scope of an identical continuation call. But resumptions can be delayed until the moment in which we are going to check for completion (in the generator) and then the continuation calls with unconsumed answers can be resumed. Following this approach there are no reusing calls because a new continuation call is never resumed within the scope of another continuation call and we do not need to do any trail management.

New tabling primitives and translation for path/2: Figure 7 shows the new program transformation we propose for the path/2 program in order to take into account the ideas in the previous sections. Variables Pred, CCall, and F will contain goals built in C but called from Prolog (Section 3.2). The third and fourth arguments of resume_ccalls/4 implement a trick to create a choicepoint with *dummy* slots which will be used to store pointers to the next continuation to execute and to the generator whose continuations we are resuming. Creating such a slot in this way, at the source level, avoids having to change the structure of choicepoints and how they are managed in the abstract machine.

In the clause corresponding to path/2, the primitive slg/1 shown in Figure 2 is now split into slgcall/3, execute_generator/2, and consume_answer/2. slgcall/3 tests whether we are in a generator position. In that case, it constructs a new goal from the term passed as first argument (the term slg_path/2 will be constructed in this case). This goal is returned in variable Pred, which will be called later. Otherwise, the goal true will be returned.

This new goal is always passed to execute_generator/2 which executes it. If it is true it will succeed, and the execution will continue with consume_answer/2. However, slg_path/2 is ensured to ultimately fail (because the solutions to the tabled predicate are generated by storing answers into the table and failing in answer/2), so that the "else" part of execute_generator/2 is taken. There, consumers are resumed before checking for completion and consume_answer/2 returns, on backtracking, each of the answers found for path(X, Y).

slg_path/2 is similar to path/2 but it does not have to return all solutions on backtracking, as consume_answer/2 does. Instead, it has to generate all possible solutions and save them: new_ccall/5 inserts a new continuation if the execution of path(Z,Y) is not complete. Otherwise, it uses path_cont_1 as the main functor of a goal whose arguments are answers consumed from the table. This goal is returned in F and immediately called. In this particular case the (recursive) call to path/2 is the last goal in the recursive clause (see Figure 1), and therefore the continuation directly inserts the answer in the table.

Finally, answer/2 does not resume continuations anymore to avoid reusing calls, since resume_ccalls/4 resumes all the continuations of the tabled call identified by Sid and its dependent generators before checking for completion.

3.4   Freezing Answers

When resume_ccalls/4 is resuming continuation calls, answers found for the tabled calls so far are used to continue execution. These answers are, in principle, stored in the table (i.e., answer/2 inserted them), and they have to be constructed on the heap so that the continuation call can access them and proceed with execution.

The ideas in Section 3.3 can be reused to freeze the answers and avoid the overhead of building them again. As done with the continuation calls, a new

```
path(X,Y) :-                              slg_path (path(X, Y), Sid ) :-
    slgcall (path(X, Y), Sid, Pred),          edge(X, Y),
    execute_generator (Pred,Sid ),            answer(path(X, Y), Sid ).
    consume_answer(path(X, Y), Sid).
                                          path_cont_1(path(X, Y), Sid, [Z]) :-
slg_path (path(X, Y),Sid) :-                  answer(path(Z, Y), Sid ).
    edge(X, Z),
    slgcall (path(Z, Y), NSid, Pred),     execute_generator (Pred,Sid) :-
    execute_generator (Pred,NSid),            (
    new_ccall (Sid, NSid, [X],                    call (Pred) ->
              path_cont_1, F),                    true
    call (F).                                 ;
                                              resume_ccalls (Sid ,CCall ,0,0),
                                              call (CCall)
                                              ).
```

Fig. 7. New program transformation for right-recursive definition of `path/2`

field is added to the table pointing to a (Prolog) list which holds all the answers found so far for a tabled goal. This list will be traversed for each of the consumers of the corresponding tabled call. In spite of this freezing operation, answers to tabled goals are additionally stored in the table. There are two reasons for this: the first one is that when some tabled goal is completed, all the answers have to be accessible from outside the derivation tree of the goal. The second one is that the table makes checking for duplicate answers faster.

3.5   Repeated Continuation Calls

Continuation calls could be duplicated in a table entry, which forces an unnecessary recomputation when new answers are found. This problem can also show up in other *suspension-based* tabling implementations and it can degrade the efficiency of the system. As an example, if the program in Figure 7 is executed against a graph with duplicate `edge/2` facts, duplicate continuation calls will be created, as `edge(X, Z)` in the body of `slg_path/2` can match two identical facts and return two identical bindings which will make `new_ccall/4` to insert two identical continuations. Since we traverse the new continuations to copy them in the heap, we can check for duplicates before storing them without having to pay an excessive performance penalty. As done with answers, a trie structure is used to check for duplicates in an efficient manner.

4   Performance Evaluation

We have implemented the proposed techniques as an extension of the Ciao system [1]. Tabled evaluation is provided to the user as a loadable *package* that provides the new directives and user-level predicates, performs the program transformations, and links in the low-level support for tabling. We have implemented

Table 1. Terse description of the benchmarks used

lchain X	Left-recursive path program, unidimensional graph.
lcycle X	Left-recursive path program, cyclic graph.
rchain X	Right-recursive path program (this generates more continuation calls), unidimensional graph.
rcycle X	Right-recursive path program, cyclic graph.
rcycleR X	Right-recursive path program, cyclic graph with repeated edges.
rcycleF X	Like rcycle 256, but executing `fib(20,_)` before `edge/2` goals.
numbers X	Find arithmetic expressions which evaluate to some number N using all the numbers in a list L.
numbers Xr	Same as above, but all the numbers in L are all the same (this generates a larger search space).
atr2	A parser for Japanese.

Table 2. Speed comparison of three Ciao implementations

Benchmark	Ciao + Ccal (baseline)	Lower C interf.	Ciao + CC
lchain 1,024	7.12	2.85	1.89
lcycle 1,024	7.32	2.92	1.96
rchain 1,024	2,620.60	1,046.10	557.92
rcycle 1,024	8,613.10	2,772.60	1,097.26
numbers 5	1,691.00	781.40	772.10
numbers 5r	3,974.90	1,425.48	1,059.93

and measured three variants: the first one is based on a direct adaptation of the implementation presented in [15], using the standard, high-level C interface. We have also implemented a second variant in which the lower-level and simplified C interface is used, as discussed in Sections 3.1 and 3.2. Finally, a third variant, which we call CC (Callable Continuations), incorporates the proposed improvements to the model discussed in Sections 3.3 and 3.4.

We evaluated the impact of this series of optimizations by using some of the benchmarks in Table 1. The results are shown in Table 2, where times are given in milliseconds. Lowering the level of the C interface and improving the transformation for tabling and the way calls are performed have a clear impact. It should also be noted that the latter improvement seems to be specially relevant in non-trivial programs which handle data structures (the larger the data structures are, the more re-copying we avoid) as opposed to those where little data management is done. On average, we consider the version reported in the rightmost column to be the implementation of choice among those we have developed, and this is the one we will refer to in the rest of the paper.

Table 3 tries to determine how the proposed implementation of tabling compares with state-of-the-art systems —namely, the latest available versions of XSB, YapTab, and B-Prolog, at the time of writing. In this table we provide, for several benchmarks, the raw time (in milliseconds) taken to execute them using tabling and, when possible, SLD resolution. Measurements have been made on Ciao-1.13, using the standard, unoptimized bytecode-based compilation, and with the CC extensions loaded, as well as in XSB 3.0.1, YapTab 5.1.1, and B-Prolog 7.0. All the executions were performed using local scheduling and disabling garbage collection; in the end this did not impact execution times very much. We used `gcc 4.1.1` to compile all the systems, and we executed them on a machine with Fedora Core Linux, kernel 2.6.9, and an Intel Xeon processor.

Analyzing the behavior of the `rcycle X` benchmark, which is an example of almost pure tabling evaluation, we observe that our asymptotic behavior is similar to other tabling approaches. If we multiply X by N, the resulting time for all of the systems (except YapTab) is multiplied by approximately $2N$. YapTab does not follow the same behavior, and, while we could not find out exactly the reason, we think it is due to YapTab *on-the-fly* creating an indexing table which selects the right `edge/2` clause in constant time, while other implementations spend more time performing a search.

B-Prolog, which uses a linear tabling approach, is the fastest SLG resolution implementation for `rcycle X`, since there is no recomputation in that benchmark. However, efficiency suffers if a costly predicate has to be recomputed: this is what happens in `rcycleF`, where we added a call to a predicate calculating the 20th Fibonacci number before each of the calls to `edge/2` in the body of `path/2`. This is a (well-known) disadvantage of linear tabling techniques which does not affect suspension-based approaches. It has to be noted, however, that current versions of B-Prolog implement an optimized variant of its original linear tabling mechanism [22] which tries to avoid reevaluation of looping subgoals. The impact of recomputation is, therefore, not as important as it may initially seem. Additionally, in our experience B-Prolog is already a very fast SLD system, and its speed seems to carry on to SLG execution, which makes it, in our experiments, the fastest SLG system in absolute terms, except when unneeded recomputation is performed.

The ideas discussed in Section 3.5 show their effectiveness in the `rcycleR 2048` benchmark, where duplicating the clauses of `edge/2` produces repeated consumers. While B-Prolog is affected by a factor close to 2, and XSB and YapTab by a factor of 1.5, the Ciao+CC implementation is affected only by a factor of a 5% because it does not add repeated consumers to the tabled evaluation.

In order to compare our implementation with XSB, we must take into account that XSB is somewhat slower than Ciao when executing programs using SLD resolution —at least in those cases where the program execution is large enough to be really significant (between 1.8 and 2 times slower for these nontrivial programs). This is partly due to the fact that XSB is, even in the case of SLD execution, prepared for tabled resolution, and thus the SLG-WAM has an additional overhead (reported to be around 10% [16]) not present in other Prolog systems and also presumably that the priorities of their implementors were understandably more focused on the implementation of tabling. However, XSB executes tabling around 1.8 times faster than our current implementation, confirming, as expected, the advantages of the native implementation, since we perform some operations at the Prolog level.

Table 3. Comparing Ciao+CC with XSB, YapTab, and B-Prolog

Program	Ciao+CC		XSB		YapTab		B-Prolog	
	SLD	Tabling	SLD	Tabling	SLD	Tabling	SLD	Tabling
rcycle 256	-	70.57	-	36.44	-	59.95	-	26.02
rcycle 512	-	288.14	-	151.26	-	311.47	-	103.16
rcycle 1,024	-	1,097.26	-	683.18	-	1,229.86	-	407.95
rcycle 2,048	-	4,375.93	-	3,664.02	-	2,451.67	-	1,596.06
rcycleR 2,048	-	4,578.50	-	5,473.91	-	3,576.31	-	2,877.60
rcycleF 256	-	1,641.95	-	2,472.61	-	1,023.77	-	2,023.75
numbers 3r	1.62	1.39	3.61	1.91	1.87	1.08	1.46	1.13
numbers 4r	99.74	36.13	211.08	51.72	108.08	29.16	83.89	22.07
numbers 5r	7,702.03	1,059.93	16,248.01	1,653.82	8,620.33	919.88	6,599.75	708.40
atr2	-	703.19	-	581.31	-	278.41	-	272.55

Although this lower efficiency is obviously a disadvantage of our implementation, it is worth noting that, since our approach does not introduce changes neither in the WAM nor in the associated Prolog compiler, the speed at which non-tabled Prolog is executed remains unchanged. In addition to this, the modular design of our approach gives better chances of making it easier to port to other systems. In our case, executables which do not need tabling have very little tabling-related code, as the data structures (for tries, etc.) are created as dynamic libraries, loaded on demand, and only stubs are needed in the regular engine. The program transformation is taken care of by a *package* (a plugin for the Ciao compiler) [2] which is loaded and active only at compile time.

In non-trivial benchmarks like numbers Xr, which at least in principle should reflect more accurately what one might expect in larger applications, execution times are in the end somewhat favorable to Ciao+CC when comparing with XSB. This is probably due to the faster raw speed of the basic engine in Ciao but it also implies that the overhead of the approach to tabling used is reasonable after the proposed optimizations. In this context it should be noted that in these experiments we have used the baseline, bytecode-based compilation and abstract machine. Turning on global analysis and using optimizing compilers [3,10] can further improve the speed of the SLD part of the computation.

The results are also encouraging to us because they appear to be another example supporting the "Ciao approach:" start from a fast and robust, but extensible LP-kernel system and then include additional characteristics by means of pluggable components whose implementation must, of course, be as efficient as possible but which in the end benefit from the initial base speed of the system.

We have not analyzed in detail the memory consumption behavior of the continuation call technique, as we are right now working on improving it. However, since we copy the same part of the heap CAT does, but using a different strategy, and we eventually (as generators are completed) get rid of the data structures corresponding to the frozen continuation calls, we foresee that our memory consumption should currently be in the same range as that of CAT.

5   Conclusions

We have reported on the design and efficiency of some improvements made to the continuation call mechanism of Ramesh and Chen. While, as expected, we cannot achieve using just these techniques the same level of performance during tabled evaluation as the natively implemented approaches our experimental results show that the overhead is essentially a reasonable constant factor, with good scaling and convergence characteristics. We argue that this is a useful result since the proposed mechanism is still easier to add to an existing WAM-based system than implementing other approaches such as the SLG-WAM, as it requires relatively small changes to the underlying execution engine. In fact, almost everything is implemented within a fairly reusable C library and using a Prolog program transformation. Our main conclusion is that using an external module for implementing tabling is a viable alternative for adding tabled evaluation to Prolog systems, especially if coupled with the proposed optimizations. It is also an approach that ties in well with the modular approach to extensions which is an integral part of the design of the Ciao system.

Acknowledgments

This work was funded in part by the IST program of the European Commission, FP6 FET project IST-15905 *MOBIUS*, by the Spanish Ministry of Education and Science (MEC) project TIN2005-09207-C03   *MERIT-COMVERS* and by the Government of the Madrid Region (CAM) Project S-0505/TIC/0407 *PROME-SAS*. Manuel Hermenegildo is also funded in part by the Prince of Asturias Chair in Information Science and Technology at the U. of New Mexico, USA and the IMDEA-Software Institute, Madrid, Spain. Cláudio Silva and Ricardo Rocha were partially funded by project Myddas (POSC/EIA/59154/2004). Ricardo Rocha was also funded by project STAMPA (PTDC/EIA/67738/2006).

References

1. Bueno, F., Cabeza, D., Carro, M., Hermenegildo, M., López-García, P., Puebla, G. (eds.): The Ciao System. Ref. Manual (v1.13). Technical report, C. S. School (UPM) (2006), http://www.ciaohome.org
2. Cabeza, D., Hermenegildo, M.: The Ciao Modular, Standalone Compiler and Its Generic Program Processing Library. In: Special Issue on Parallelism and Implementation of (C)LP Systems. Electronic Notes in Theoretical Computer Science, vol. 30(3), Elsevier, North Holland (2000)
3. Carro, M., Morales, J., Muller, H.L., Puebla, G., Hermenegildo, M.: High-Level Languages for Small Devices: A Case Study. In: Flautner, K., Kim, T. (eds.) Compilers, Architecture, and Synthesis for Embedded Systems, pp. 271–281. ACM Press / Sheridan (October 2006)
4. Chen, W., Warren, D.S.: Tabled Evaluation with Delaying for General Logic Programs. Journal of the ACM 43(1), 20–74 (1996)
5. Dawson, S., Ramakrishnan, C.R., Warren, D.S.: Practical Program Analysis Using General Purpose Logic Programming Systems – A Case Study. In: Proceedings of PLDI 1996, pp. 117–126. ACM Press, New York, USA (1996)

6. Chico de Guzmán, P., Carro, M., Hermenegildo, M., Silva, C., Rocha, R.: Some Improvements over the Continuation Call Tabling Implementation Technique. In: CICLOPS 2007, ACM Press, New York (2007)
7. Demoen, B., Sagonas, K.: CAT: The Copying Approach to Tabling. In: Palamidessi, C., Meinke, K., Glaser, H. (eds.) ALP 1998 and PLILP 1998. LNCS, vol. 1490, pp. 21–35. Springer, Heidelberg (1998)
8. Demoen, B., Sagonas, K.F.: Chat: The copy-hybrid approach to tabling. Practical Applications of Declarative Languages, 106–121 (1999)
9. Guo, H.-F., Gupta, G.: A Simple Scheme for Implementing Tabled Logic Programming Systems Based on Dynamic Reordering of Alternatives. In: International Conference on Logic Programming, pp. 181–196 (2001)
10. Morales, J., Carro, M., Hermenegildo, M.: Improving the Compilation of Prolog to C Using Moded Types and Determinism Information. In: Jayaraman, B. (ed.) PADL 2004. LNCS, vol. 3057, pp. 86–103. Springer, Heidelberg (2004)
11. Ramakrishna, Y.S., Ramakrishnan, C.R., Ramakrishnan, I.V., Smolka, S.A., Swift, T., Warren, D.S.: Efficient Model Checking Using Tabled Resolution. In: Grumberg, O. (ed.) CAV 1997. LNCS, vol. 1254, pp. 143–154. Springer, Heidelberg (1997)
12. Ramakrishnan, I.V., Rao, P., Sagonas, K.F., Swift, T., Warren, D.S.: Efficient tabling mechanisms for logic programs. In: ICLP, pp. 697–711 (1995)
13. Ramakrishnan, R., Ullman, J.D.: A survey of research on deductive database systems. Journal of Logic Programming 23(2), 125–149 (1993)
14. Ramesh, R., Chen, W.: A Portable Method for Integrating SLG Resolution into Prolog Systems. In: Bruynooghe, M. (ed.) International Symposium on Logic Programming, pp. 618–632. MIT Press, Cambridge (1994)
15. Rocha, R., Silva, C., Lopes, R.: On Applying Program Transformation to Implement Suspension-Based Tabling in Prolog. In: Dahl, V., Niemelä, I. (eds.) ICLP 2007. LNCS, vol. 4670, pp. 444–445. Springer, Heidelberg (2007)
16. Sagonas, K., Swift, T.: An Abstract Machine for Tabled Execution of Fixed-Order Stratified Logic Programs. ACM Transactions on Programming Languages and Systems 20(3), 586–634 (1998)
17. Silva, C.: On Applying Program Transformation to Implement Tabled Evaluation in Prolog. Master's thesis, Faculdade de Ciências, Universidade do Porto (January 2007)
18. Somogyi, Z., Sagonas, K.: Tabling in Mercury: Design and Implementation. In: Van Hentenryck, P. (ed.) PADL 2006. LNCS, vol. 3819, pp. 150–167. Springer, Heidelberg (2005)
19. Tamaki, H., Sato, M.: OLD resolution with tabulation. In: Third International Conference on Logic Programming, London. LNCS, pp. 84–98. Springer, Heidelberg (1986)
20. Warren, D.S.: Memoing for logic programs. Communications of the ACM 35(3), 93–111 (1992)
21. Warren, R., Hermenegildo, M., Debray, S.K.: On the Practicality of Global Flow Analysis of Logic Programs. In: Fifth International Conference and Symposium on Logic Programming, pp. 684–699. MIT Press, Cambridge (1988)
22. Zhou, N.-F., Sato, T., Shen, Y.-D.: Linear Tabling Strategies and Optimizations. Theory and Practice of Logic programming (accepted for publication 2007), http://arxiv.org/abs/0705.3468v1
23. Zhou, N.-F., Shen, Y.-D., Yuan, L.-Y., You, J.-H.: Implementation of a linear tabling mechanism. Journal of Functional and Logic Programming 2001(10) (October 2001)
24. Zou, Y., Finin, T., Chen, H.: F-OWL: An Inference Engine for Semantic Web. In: Hinchey, M.G., Rash, J.L., Truszkowski, W.F., Rouff, C.A. (eds.) FAABS 2004. LNCS (LNAI), vol. 3228, pp. 238–248. Springer, Heidelberg (2004)

Scheduling Light-Weight Parallelism in ArTCoP

J. Berthold[1], A. Al Zain[2], and H.-W. Loidl[3]

[1] Fachbereich Mathematik und Informatik
Philipps-Universität Marburg, D-35032 Marburg, Germany
berthold@mathematik.uni-marburg.de
[2] School of Mathematical and Computer Sciences
Heriot-Watt University, Edinburgh EH14 4AS, Scotland
ceeatia@macs.hw.ac.uk
[3] Institut für Informatik, Ludwig-Maximilians-Universität München, Germany
hwloidl@tcs.ifi.lmu.de

Abstract. We present the design and prototype implementation of the scheduling component in ArTCoP (architecture transparent control of parallelism), a novel run-time environment (RTE) for parallel execution of high-level languages. A key feature of ArTCoP is its support for deep process and memory hierarchies, shown in the scheduler by supporting light-weight threads. To realise a system with easily exchangeable components, the system defines a *micro-kernel*, providing basic infrastructure, such as garbage collection. All complex RTE operations, including the handling of parallelism, are implemented at a separate system level. By choosing *Concurrent Haskell as high-level system language*, we obtain a prototype in the form of an executable specification that is easier to maintain and more flexible than conventional RTEs. We demonstrate the flexibility of this approach by presenting *implementations of a scheduler for light-weight threads* in ArTCoP, based on GHC Version 6.6.

Keywords: Parallel computation, functional programming, scheduling.

1 Introduction

In trying to exploit the computational power of parallel architectures ranging from multi-core machines to large-scale computational Grids, we are currently developing a new parallel runtime environment, ArTCoP, for executing parallel Haskell code on such complex, hierarchical architectures. Central to the design of ArTCoP is the concept of *deep memory and deep process hierarchies*. The system uses different control mechanisms at different levels in the hierarchy. Thus, data access and presence of parallelism can be transparent to the language level. For the memory management this provides a choice of using explicit data distribution or virtual shared memory. For the process management this means that units of computation are very light-weight entities, and we explicitly control the scheduling of these units. In this paper we focus on the scheduling component of the system.

P. Hudak and D.S. Warren (Eds.): PADL 2008, LNCS 4902, pp. 214–229, 2008.

Our modular design defines a minimal *micro-kernel*. More complex operations are implemented in a high-level system language (Concurrent Haskell) outside this kernel. As a result, this design provides an *executable specification* and all code presented in this paper has been tested in the context of a modified runtime-environment (RTE) of the Glasgow Haskell Compiler (GHC) Version 6.6.

Immediate benefits of this design are the ease of prototyping and of replacing key components of the RTE — issues of particular importance in complex parallel systems such as *computational grids* [6], incorporating thousands of machines on a global scale. Supporting such global architectures, as well as emerging multi-core machines, requires support for deep memory and process hierarchies, which use different implementations, depending on the underlying architecture or other system features. Additionally the system needs to be *adaptive* in the sense that it dynamically adapts its behaviour to dynamically changing characteristics of the parallel machine.

In this sense, ArTCoP provides a generic and adaptive system for parallel computation, combining features of our existing parallel RTEs for GpH [19] and Eden [2,3]. We present a *prototype implementation* of key concepts in such a system in the form of an executable specification, amenable to formal reasoning. We arrive at a system with a clear modular design, separating basic components by their functionality and employing a hierarchy with increasing levels of abstraction. The micro-kernel of this system is accessed via a narrow interface, and most of the coordination of the system is realised in a functional language. We demonstrate the flexibility of the system by refining a simple scheduler and adding sophisticated work distribution policies.

2   Related Work

Work in the 80s on high-level languages for system-level programming mainly focused on how to implement O/S concepts in a functional [8,14,18] or logic [17] style. Most of these systems introduce specific primitives to deal with non-determinism, whereas later approaches either insisted on maintaining deterministic behaviour [9] or used special data structures to control interactions between concurrent threads (such as MVars in Concurrent Haskell [15]). Early implementations of functional operating systems are NEBULA [11] and KAOS [20]. More recent functional systems are Famke [21] and Hello [4].

An early system that uses a micro-kernel (or substrate) approach in the RTE, is the Scheme-based Sting [10] system. Sting defines a coordination layer on top of Scheme, which is used as computation language. Genericity is demonstrated by directly controlling concurrency and processor abstractions, via Scheme-level policy managers, responsible for scheduling, migration etc. This general framework supports a wide range of features, such as (first-order) light-weight threads, thread pre-emption, and asynchronous garbage collection. Common paradigms for synchronisation (e.g. master-slave parallelism, barrier communication etc) are implemented at system level and demonstrate the possibility to easily define application-optimised synchronisation patterns. However, since Sting uses

Scheme as a system level language, it lacks the clear separation of pure and impure constructs at system level as offered by Haskell. We also consider the static type safety for system level code, provided by Haskell, an advantage.

Most closely related to our high-level language approach to O/S design is [7]. It defines a Haskell interface to low-level operations and uses a hardware monad to express stateful computations. It focuses on safety of system routines, using its own assertion language and Haskell's strong type system. This interface has been used to code entire O/S kernels (House, Osker) directly in Haskell, reporting satisfying performance. In contrast to this proof-of-concept approach, we want to improve maintainability by realising the more complex RTE routines in Haskell, but still keeping a micro-kernel implemented in a low-level language.

Another related project, the Manticore [5] system, targets parallelism at multiple levels, and enables the programmer to combine task and data parallelism. Manticore's computation language is a subset of ML, a strict functional language. The compiler and runtime system add NESL-like support for parallel arrays and tuples, and a number of scheduling primitives. Similar in spirit to our approach, only a small kernel is implemented in low-level C; other features are implemented in external modules, in an intermediate ML-like language of the compiler. A prototype implementation is planned for the end of 2007, and aims to be a testbed for future Manticore implementations and language design. As opposed to ArTCoP's genericity in coordination support, Manticore explicitly restricts itself to shared-memory multi-core architectures, and does not support networked computing, nor location-awareness and monitoring features.

The Famke system [21] is implemented in Clean and explores the suitability of Clean language features such as dynamic types and uniqueness typing for O/S implementation. Using these features type-safe mobile processes and concurrency are implemented. The latter uses a first class continuation approach and implements scheduling at system level.

Most recently Peng Li et al [13] have presented a micro-kernel (substrate) based design for the concurrent RTE of GHC, including support for software transactional memory (STM). This complements our work, which focuses on control of parallelism, and we intend to combine the design of our interface with that currently produced for GHC.

3 Design Aims of a Generic Runtime-Environment

3.1 Simplest Kernel

ArTCoP aims to provide support for parallel programming from the conceptual, language designer perspective. A major goal of its design is to explore how many of the coordination tasks can be specified at higher levels of abstraction, and to identify the minimal and most general runtime support for parallel coordination. Therefore, major parts of the RTE are implemented in a high-level language. Following a functional paradigm has the advantage that specifications can more or less be executed directly and that it facilitates theoretical reasoning such as correctness proofs.

3.2   Genericity

Our study concentrates on identifying and structuring the general requirements of parallel coordination, with the only assumption that concurrent threads are executing a functionally specified computation, explicitly or implicitly coordinated by functional-style coordination abstractions.

The genericity we aim at is two-fold: By providing only very simple actions as primitive operations, our system, by design, is not tied to particular languages. We avoid language-specific functionality whenever possible, thus ArTCoP supports a whole spectrum of coordination languages. Secondly, the coordination system can be used in combination with different computation engines, and is not restricted to a particular virtual machine. Furthermore, this coordination makes minimal assumptions on the communication between processing elements (PEs). ArTCoP thus concentrates *key aspects of parallelism* in one place, without being tied to a certain parallelism model.

3.3   Multi-level System Architecture

High-level parallel programming manifests a critical trade-off: providing operational control of the execution while abstracting over error-prone details. In our system, we separate these different concerns into different levels of a multi-level system architecture. As shown in Figure 1, ArTCoP follows the concept of a *micro-kernel*, proven useful in the domain of operating system design.

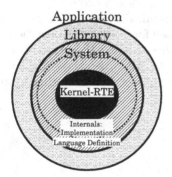

Fig. 1. Layer view of ArTCoP

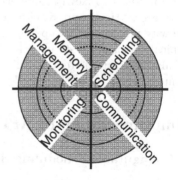

Fig. 2. Component view of ArTCoP

At *Kernel level*, the most generic support for parallelism is implemented. The system offers explicit asynchronous data transfer between nodes, means to start and stop computations, as well as ways to retrieve machine information at runtime. Operations at this level are very simple and general. *System Modules* build on the kernel to restrict and combine the basic actions to higher-level constructs, i.e. the constructs of a proper parallel functional language. The runtime support is necessarily narrowed to a special model at this level. The implemented parallel coordination language is nothing else but the interface of the system level modules. At *Library level* and *Application level*, concrete algorithms, or higher-order functions for common parallel algorithmic patterns (called skeletons [16]) can be encoded using the implemented language.

Focusing more on functionality and modularity, the kernel can be divided vertically into four interacting components, as shown in Figure 2: Parallel subtasks are created and sent to other processing elements (PEs) for parallel execution by the *scheduling* component, which controls the local executing units. Explicit *communication* between several scheduler instances on different PEs is needed to coordinate and monitor the parallel execution. The *memory management* component is responsible for (de-)allocating dynamic data and distributing it over the available machines, interacting in this task with the communication component. Explicit message passing is possible, but not mandatory for data communication, and it is possible to implement a shared address space instead. In order to decide which PE is idle and suitable for a parallel job, static and dynamic system information is provided by a *monitoring component*.

3.4 High Level Scheduler Control

The key issue in efficiently using a wide-area network infrastructure for parallel computations is to control the parallel subtasks that contribute to the overall program, and to *schedule* the most suitable task for execution, depending on the current machine load and connectivity (whereas efficiently combining them is an algorithmic issue). Likewise, modern multicore CPUs will often expose uneven memory access times and synchronisation overhead. Parallel processes must be placed with minimal data dependencies, optimised for least synchronisation, and dynamically consider system load and connectivity. ArTCoP aims to be a common framework for different coordination concepts. Adaptive scheduling support will thus be specified in the *high-level language* and not in the runtime system.

4   Implementation of ArTCoP

4.1 Configurable Scheduling Support

We propose a parallel RTE which allows system programmers and language designers to define appropriate scheduling control at the system level in Haskell. In our parallel system the scheduler is a monadic Haskell function using an internal scheduler state, and *monitors* all computations on one machine. Subtasks are activated and controlled by a separate manager thread, which can take into account properties of the subtask and static and dynamic machine properties. The scheduler thread runs concurrently to the controlled computations and relies on a low-level round-robin scheduler inside the RTE. To specify it, we use the state monad and features of Concurrent Haskell, combining stateful and I/O-actions by a monad transformer [12]. We briefly summarise main features and notation in Fig. 3.

Monads and Concurrency in Haskell Monads, in one sentence, are Haskell's way to hide side-effects of a computation. If a computation is not referentially transparent, e.g. depends on externals (IO) or a system State, it can be mathematically described as a *monadic* evaluation. Likewise for side-effecting constructs, those which modify an *external* "state".

The IO monad in Haskell implements user interaction, and also encapsulates the nondeterministism of Concurrent Haskell: forking and killing threads, yielding (to the scheduler), and synchronised communication via MVars. The monad State encapsulates and provides controlled and ordered access to an arbitrary state As a (contrived) example, we define some functions which modify a simple counter, or run stateful counting actions.

```
data Counter = Counter Int Int    -- data type Int x Int (and constructor)

-- modifiers, stateful action on Counter
inc,dec,reset :: State Counter ()
-- modify the state by a given function (lambda-notation)
inc = modify (\(Counter n accesses) -> Counter (n+1)(accesses+1))
dec = modify (\(Counter n accesses) -> Counter (n-1)(accesses+1))
reset = do (Counter _ accesses) <- get  -- read the state
           put (Counter 0 (accesses+1)) -- set sth. as the new state
```

Do-notation, as shown in reset, is an intuitive notation for composing monadic actions, and for binding new names to returned values for subsequent use.

Modern Haskell implementations come with a rich set of hierarchically organised libraries, which provide these general monad operations, and specifics to certain monads, e.g. for the State monad, to elegantly program and run complex stateful computations. Exemplified here: evalState runs a stateful computation, sequence_ sequences several monadic actions (all return the void type ()).

```
countTo :: Int -> Counter -- run stateful computation on start state,
countTo m = evalState      --    and return final state
            (sequence_ (replicate m inc ++ [reset])) -- actions
            (Counter 0 0)                             -- start state
```

Monad transformers [12] can be used to combine two monads, in our case the IO and the State monad. IO actions are embedded into the combined monad by liftIO.

Fig. 3. Summary: Monads and Concurrency in Haskell

Parallel tasks in a coordination language implemented by ARTCoP will appear as a new type of job at library level. Haskell's type system allows to specify the respective scheduler for a certain kind of parallelism by overloading instances of a *type class* named ScheduleJob. The internal scheduler state type depends on the concrete job type and forms another type class which provides a start state and a termination check. A third type class ScheduleMsg relates Jobs and State to messages between the active units and provides a message processing function. Table 1 summarises the overloaded functions in the scheduler classes. A trivial default scheduler schedule is provided (shown in Fig. 4), which only starts the main computation, repeatedly checks for termination, and returns the final scheduler state upon termination.

Table 1. Overview of class funtions (implemented at system level)

`type StateIO s a = StateT s IO a`	type alias combining State and IO monad
`class ScheduleState st where`	
`startSt         :: st`	the initial state of the scheduler
`killAllThreads  :: StateIO st ()`	shutdown function
`checkTermination :: StateIO st Bool`	check state, return whether to stop
`checkHaveWork   :: StateIO st Bool`	check state, return whether any local work available
`class ScheduleJob job st	job -> st where`	
`runJobs  :: [job] -> IO st`	run jobs with default start state
`schedule :: [job] -> StateIO st st`	schedule jobs, return final state
`forkJob  :: job -> StateIO st ()`	fork one job, modify state accordingly
`class ScheduleMsg st msg	st -> msg where`	
`processMsgs:: [msg] -> StateIO st Bool`	process a set of message for the scheduler, modify state accordingly. Return `True` immediately if a global stop is requested.

```
runJobs jobs = evalStateT (schedule jobs) startSt
schedule (job:jobs) = do forkJob job
                         schedule jobs
schedule [] = do liftIO kYield                -- pass control
             term <- checkTermination     -- check state
             if term then get          -- return final state
             else schedule ([]::[job]) -- repeat
```

Fig. 4. Default scheduler

Thus, language designers do not deal with runtime system code, but simply define the scheduling for such jobs at the system level. As a simple example, every machine could control a subset of the jobs, running one instance of the scheduler. To model this behaviour, only a few simple operations need to be hard-wired into the kernel. The basic kernel support can be grouped into scheduler control, communication, and system information. All primitive operations provided by the kernel (indicated by the leading k), and their types, are shown in Table 2. For the example, the Kernel has to provide the number of available PEs (kNoPe), and must support spawning asynchronous jobs on other PEs (kRFork), namely a scheduler instance which runs the jobs assigned to the local PE.

4.2 Explicit Communication

If additional jobs are created dynamically, they may be transmitted to a suitable PE, and received and activated by its scheduling loop. The scheduler instances may also exchange *requests* for additional work and receive jobs as their answers. This model requires communication between the scheduler instances. The kernel supplies an infrastructure for explicit message passing between any two running

Table 2. Overview of primitive operations (provided by the kernel)

Functionality at Kernel Level (primitive operations)	
`kRFork :: PE -> IO() -> IO()`	start a remote computation
`kFork :: IO() -> IO ThreadId`	start a local thread (Conc. Haskell)
`kYield :: IO()`	pass control to other threads (Conc. Haskell)
`kOpenPort:: IO( ChanName' [a],[a])`	open a stream inport at receiver side, return port handle and placeholder
`kSend:: ChanName' [a] -> a -> IO()`	basic communication primitive, send an element of type a to a receiver (a port handle)
`kThisPe,kNoPe :: IO Int`	get own node's ID / no. of nodes
`kThreadInfo :: ThreadId -> IO ThreadState`	get current thread state (Runnable, Blocked, Terminated)
`kPEInfo :: Int -> IO InfoVector`	info about a node in the system (cpu speed, latency, load, location etc)

threads. It relies on typed *stream channels*, created from Haskell by `kOpenPort`, and managed by the kernel internally. A `kOpenPort` returns a placeholder for the stream, and a Haskell port representation to be used by senders for `kSend`. Sending data by `kSend` does not imply any evaluation; data has to be explicitly evaluated to the desired degree prior to sending.

Stream communication between all scheduler instances, and startup synchronisation, are easy to build on this infrastructure. The scheduler may also receive messages from the locally running threads (e.g. to generate new jobs), which can be sent via the same stream. Language designers define suitable message types, accompanied by an instance declaration which provides the message processing function in the class `ScheduleMsg`.

```
instance ScheduleJob MyJob MySchedulerState where
    schedule (j:js) = do forkJob j
                         mapM_ addToPool js
                         schedule ([]::[MyJob])
    schedule empty = do stop <- do { ms <- receiveMsgs ; processMsgs ms }
                        term <- checkTermination
                        if (term || stop)
                           then do { killAllThreads; get }
                           else do work <- checkHaveWork
                                   if (not work)
                                      then sendRequest
                                      else liftIO kYield
                                   schedule empty
```

Fig. 5. Scheduler for a parallel job-pool

Figure 5 sketches a scheduler for such a language, assuming the existence of a globally managed job pool. If an instance runs out of work, it will send a request. It will eventually receive an answer, and the next call to processMsgs will activate the contained job. This example enables reasoning about appropriate workload distribution and the consequences and side conditions, while the scheduling loop itself remains small and concise. All essential functionality is moved from the scheduling loop into separate functions, e.g. we leave completely unspecified how jobs are generated and managed in the job pool, and how a scheduler instance decides that it needs work (in checkHaveWork). All these aspects can be defined in helper functions, allowing a clear, structured view on the scheduling implemented.

4.3 Monitoring Information

Programmable scheduling support at system level requires knowledge about static and dynamic system properties at runtime. Our system kernel is geared towards adaptive techniques developed for GRIDGUM 2, GpH on computational Grids [1], and provides the necessary information. For location awareness, we have kNoPe for the total number of PEs in the parallel system, and kThisPe for the own PE. Another primitive, peInfo :: PE -> IO InfoVector returns a vector of data about the current system state of one PE. This information is continuously collected by the kernel and held in local tables *PEStatic* and *PEDynamic*.

Load information at system level: A list of load information represented in a Haskell data structure PEInfo is a self-suggesting component of the scheduler state in many cases. The concrete selection, postprocessing and representation of system information (provided by the kernel) depends on how the scheduler at system level wants to use the information. An example of a Haskell type PEInfo is shown in Fig. 6. It includes selected components of the scheduler state: the number of threads controlled by the local scheduler, and how many sparks (potential parallel computations) it holds.

```
data PEInfo = PE { runQ_length :: Int, noOfSparks  :: Int ,   -- system
                   clusterId  :: Int , clusterPower:: Double,
                   cpuSpeed :: Int   , cpuLoad :: Double,     -- kernel
                   latency  :: Double, pe_ip   :: Int32,
                   timestamp:: ClockTime }
startup :: StateIO s ()
startup = do infos <- buildInfos --  startup, returns initial [PEInfo]
             let ratios = zipWith (\lat str -> fromIntegral str / lat)
                                   (map latency infos) (map cpuSpeed infos)
                 myVote = fromJust (findIndex (== maximum ratios) ratios)
             votes <- allGather myVote
             setMainPE (1 + hasMostVotes votes)
```

Fig. 6. System level code related to load information

As exemplified in the figure, the scheduler can do arbitrary computations on PEInfo structures. For instance, to start the computation on a "strong" machine with good connectivity, all PEs could *elect* the main PE by a strength/latency ratio. Each PE votes for a relatively strong neighbour, where neighbourhood is a function of latency, varying for different electing PEs. A collective (synchronising) message-passing operation allGather is easily expressed using explicit communication. Referential transparency guarantees that all PEs will then compute the same value without further synchronisation.

5   Hierarchical Task Management and Adaptive Load Distribution

5.1   Hierarchical Task Management

We now embed the scheduler of the GUM RTE [19], which implements the GpH parallel extension of Haskell, into the generic framework presented in the previous section. In short, GUM provides two concepts going beyond the design of the simple scheduler in the previous section:

- *hierarchical task management*, distinguishing between potential parallelism ("sparks") and realised parallelism ("threads"); the former can be handled cheaply and is the main representation for distributing load; the latter, representing computation, is more heavy-weight and fixed to a processor;
- *adaptive load distribution*, which uses information on latency and load of remote machines when deciding how to distribute work;

We will see that, in this high-level formulation of the scheduler, the code modifications necessary to realise these two features are fairly simple. Hereafter, we first describe how to model the hierarchical task management in GUM. These changes only affect the scheduling component. In tuning load distribution, we then interact with the monitoring and communication components.

First we specify the machine state in the GUM RTE, consisting of: *a)* a *thread pool* of all threads; these are active threads controlled by the scheduler, each with its own stack, registers etc; *b)* a *spark pool* of all potential parallel tasks; these are modeled as pointers into the heap; *c)* *monitoring information* about load on other PEs; this information is kept, as a partial picture, in tables on each processor;

We model this data structure as a triple:

```
data GumState = GSt Threadpool Sparkpool [PEInfo]
type Sparkpool  = [GumJob]
type Threadpool = [ThreadId]
```

and we make GumState an instance of ScheduleState.

The code for the GUM scheduler is summarised in Figure 7. The arguments to schedule are jobs to be executed. These jobs are forked using a kernel routine, and added to the thread pool (forkJob). The case of an empty argument list

```
instance ScheduleJob GumJob GumState where
 runJobs jobs = evalStateT (initLoad >> (schedule jobs)) startSt
 forkJob (GJ job) =   do tid <- liftIO (kFork job)
                           modify (addThread tid)
 schedule (j:js) = do { forkJob j ; schedule js }
 schedule empty  = do
   (runThrs, blThrs) <- updateThreadPool      -- update and
    term <- checkTermination                  -- (1) check local state
   if term
      then do { bcast GSTOP ; get } -- finished
      else do localWork <- if runThrs > 0    -- (2) local work available?
                             then return True  -- yes: runnable thread
                             else activateSpark -- no: look for spark
               stop <- if localWork
                          then do reqs <- readMs
                                     processMsgs reqs
                          else do sendFish   -- (3) get remote work
                                     waitWorkAsync
               if stop then do { killAllThreads; get } -- finished
                          else do liftIO kYield  -- (4) run some threads
                                     schedule empty
-- essential helper functions:
activateSpark :: StateIO GumState Bool -- tries to find local work
sendFish :: StateIO GumState ()          -- sends request for remote work
waitWorkAsync :: StateIO GumState Bool -- blocks on receiving messages

updateThreadPool :: StateIO GumState (Int,Int)
updateThreadPool = do
    (GSt threads sps lds) <- get
    tStates <- liftIO (mapM kThreadInfo threads)
    let list = filter (not . isFinished . snd) (zip threads tStates )
        blocked = length (filter (isBlocked . snd) list)
        runnable = length (filter (isRunnable . snd) list)
    put (GSt (map fst list) sps lds)
    return (runnable, blocked)
```

Fig. 7. GUM scheduler

describes how the scheduler controls the machine's workload. First the scheduler checks for termination (1). Then the scheduler checks the thread pool for runnable tasks, otherwise it tries to activate a local spark (2). If local work has been found, it will only read and process messages. The handlers for these messages are called from processMsgs, which belongs to the communication module. If no local work has been found, a special FISH message is sent to search for remote work (3). Finally, it yields execution to the micro-kernel, which will execute the next thread (4) unless a stop message has been received, in which case the system will be shut down. The thread pool is modeled as a list of jobs, and `updateThreadPool` retrieves the numbers of runnable and blocked jobs.

The above mechanism will work well on closely connected systems but, as measurements show, it does not scale well on Grid architectures. To address shortcomings of the above mechanism on wide-area networks, we make modifications to the thread management component for better load balancing, following concepts of the adaptive scheduling mechanism for computational Grids [1]. The key concept in these changes is *adaptive load distribution*: the behaviour of the system should adjust to both the static configuration of the system (taking into account CPU speed etc.) and to dynamic aspects of the execution, such as the load of the individual processors. One of the main advantages of our high-level language approach to system-level programming is the ease with which such changes can be made. The functions of looking for remote work (`sendFish` and its counterpart in `processMsgs`) and picking the next spark (`activateSpark`) are the main functions we want to manipulate in tuning scheduling and load balancing for wide-area networks. Note that by using index-free iterators (such as `filter`) we avoid dangers of buffer-overflow. Furthermore, the clear separation of stateful and purely functional code makes it easier to apply equational reasoning.

5.2   Adaptive Load Distribution Mechanisms

The adaptive load distribution deals with: *startup, work locating,* and *work request handling,* and the key new policies for adaptive load distribution are that work is only sought from relatively heavily loaded PEs, and preferably from local cluster resources. Additionally, when a request for work is received from *another cluster*, the receiver may add more than one job if the sending PE is in a "stronger" cluster. The necessary static and dynamic information is either provided by the kernel, or added and computed at system level, and propagated by attaching load information to every message between PEs (as explained in Section 4.3).

Placement of the main computation. During startup synchronisation, a suitable PE for the main computation is selected, as already exemplified in Section 4.3. GridGum 2 starts the computation in the 'biggest' cluster, i.e. the cluster with the largest sum of CPU speeds over all PEs in the cluster, a policy which is equally easy to implement.

Work Location Mechanism. The Haskell code in Figure 8 shows how the target PE for a FISH message is chosen adaptively by `choosePE`. A ratio between CPU speed and load (defined as `mkR`) is computed for all PEs in the system. Ratios are checked against the local ratio `myRatio`, preferring nearby PEs (with low latency, sorted first), to finally target a nearby PE which recently exposed higher load than the sender. This policy avoids single hot spots in the system, and decreases the amount of communication through high-latency communication, which improves overall performance.

```
data GumMsg = FISH [PEInfo] Int -- steal work, share PEInfo on the way
            | SCHEDULE [PEInfo] GumJob -- give away work (+ share PEInfo)
            | GSTOP
            | ... other (system) messages...
sendFish:: StateIO GumState ()
sendFish = do infos <- currentPEs -- refresh PE information
              me <- liftIO kThisPe
              pe <- choosePe me
              liftIO (kSend pe ( FISH infos me ))

 -- good neighbours for work stealing: low latency, highly loaded
choosePe :: Int -> StateIO GumState (ChanName' [GumMsg])
choosePe me = do
  (GSt _ _ lds ) <- get
  let mkR pe = (fromIntegral (cpuSpeed pe)) / (cpuLoad pe)
      rList  = [ ((i,mkR pe), latency pe) -- compute 'ratio'
               | (i,pe) <- zip [1..] lds ]   -- keep latency and PE
      cands  = filter ((< myRatio) . snd) -- check for high load
               (map fst                   -- low latencies first
               (sortBy (\a b -> compare (snd a) (snd b)) rList))
      myRatio  = (snd . fst) (rList!!(me-1))
  if null cands  then return (port 1)    -- default: main PE
                 else return (port ((fst . head) cands))
```

Fig. 8. GRIDGUM 2 Work location algorithm

Work Request Handling Mechanism. To minimise high-latency communications between different clusters, the work request handling mechanism tries to send multiple sparks in a SCHEDULE message, if the work request has originated from a cluster with higher relative power (see Figure 9). The relative power of a cluster is the sum of the speed-load ratios over all cluster elements. If the originating cluster is weaker or equally strong, the FISH message is served as usual. In Figure 9, after updating the dynamic information (1), the sender cluster is compared to the receiver cluster (2), and a bigger amount of sparks is retrieved and sent if appropriate (3). In this case the RTE temporarily switches from passive to active load distribution.

6 Conclusions

We have presented the scheduling component in ARTCoP, a hierarchical runtime-environment (RTE) for parallel extensions of Haskell, which has been implemented on top of GHC Version 6.6. Using a *micro-kernel* approach, most features of the RTE, such as scheduling, are implemented in Haskell, which enables rapid prototyping of easily replaceable modules. Thus we can support both *deep memory and deep process hierarchies*. The latter is discussed in detail by

```
instance ScheduleMsg GumState GumMsg where
   processMsgs ((FISH infos origin):rest) = do processFish infos origin
                                                processMsgs rest
   processMsgs ((SCHEDULE ...)      :rest) = ...

processFish :: [PEInfo] -> Int -> StateIO GumState ()
processFish infos orig = do
      updatePEInfo infos             -- update local dynamic information (1)
      me <- liftIO kThisPe
      if (orig == me) then return () --  my own fish: scheduler will retry
        else do
          new_infos <- currentPEs     -- compare own and sender cluster (2)
          let info   = new_infos!!(orig-1)
              myInfo = new_infos!!(me-1)
              amount = if (clusterPower info > clusterPower myInfo)
                         then noOfSparks myInfo `div` 2  -- stronger: many
                         else 1                     -- weak or the same: one
          sparks <- getSparks amount True       -- get a set of sparks (3)
          case sparks of
          []    -> do target <- choosePe me      -- no sparks: forward FISH
                      liftIO (kSend target (FISH new_infos orig))
          some -> liftIO (sequence_ -- send sequence of SCHEDULE messages
                    (map ((kSend (port orig)).(SCHEDULE new_infos)) some))
```

Fig. 9. GRIDGUM 2 work request handling algorithm

presenting a scheduler for light-weight tasks. The former is ongoing work in the form of defining a virtual shared memory abstraction. Considering the daunting complexity of global networks with intelligent, automatic resource management, modular support for such deep hierarchies will gain increasing importance. In particular, we are interested in covering the whole range of parallel architectures, from multi-core, shared-memory systems to heterogeneous, wide-area networks such as Grid architectures.

As one general result, we can positively assess the suitability of this class of languages for system level programming. Realising computation patterns as index-free iterator functions avoids the danger of buffer-overflows, and the absence of pointers eliminates a frequent source of errors. In summary, the language features that have proven to be most useful are: higher-order functions, type classes and stateful computation free of side effects (using monads).

Our prototype implementation realises all code segments shown in the paper, using the GHC RTE as micro-kernel, and Concurrent Haskell as a system-level programming language. This prototype demonstrates the feasibility of our micro-kernel approach. The different variants of the scheduler, specialised to several parallel Haskell implementations, show the flexibility of our approach.

While we cannot present realistic performance figures of this implementation yet, we are encouraged by related work reporting satisfying performance for O/S modules purely written in Haskell [7] and by recent performance results from a micro-kernel-structured RTE for Concurrent Haskell [13]. We plan to combine our (parallel) system with this new development by the maintainers of GHC and to further extend the features of the parallel system.

References

1. Al Zain, A.D., Trinder, P.W., Loidl, H-W., Michaelson, G.: Managing Heterogeneity in a Grid Parallel Haskell. Scalable Computing: Practice and Experience 7(3), 9–26 (2006)
2. Berthold, J.: Towards a Generalised Runtime Environment for Parallel Haskells. In: Bubak, M., van Albada, G.D., Sloot, P.M.A., Dongarra, J.J. (eds.) ICCS 2004. LNCS, vol. 3038, p. 297. Springer, Heidelberg (2004)
3. Berthold, J., Loogen, R.: Parallel coordination made explicit in a functional setting. In: IFL 2006. LNCS, vol. 4449, pp. 73–90. Springer, Heidelberg (2007)
4. Biagioni, E., Fu, G.: The Hello Operating System,
   http://www2.ics.hawaii.edu/~esb/prof/proj/hello/
5. Fluet, M., Ford, N., Rainey, M., Reppy, J., Shaw, A., Xiao, Y.: Status Report: The Manticore Project. In: Proceedings of the ACM SIGPLAN Workshop on ML, Freiburg, Germany, pp. 15–24 (October 2007)
6. Foster, I., Kesselman, C., Tuecke, S.: The anatomy of the Grid: Enabling scalable virtual organizations. International Journal of High Performance Computing Applications 15(3), 200–222 (2001)
7. Hallgren, T., Jones, M.P., Leslie, R., Tolmach, A.P.: A Principled Approach to Operating System Construction in Haskell. In: ICFP 2005. Conf. on Functional Programming, Tallinn, Estonia, September 26–28, pp. 116–128. ACM Press, New York (2005)
8. Henderson, P.: Purely Functional Operating Systems. In: Functional Programming and its Applications, Cambridge University Press, Cambridge (1982)
9. Holyer, I., Davies, N., Dornan, C.: The Brisk Project: Concurrent and Distributed Functional Systems. In: Glasgow Workshop on Functional Programming, Electronic Workshops in Computing, Ullapool, Scotland, Springer, Heidelberg (1995)
10. Jagannathan, S., Philbin, J.: A Customizable Substrate for Concurrent Languages. In: PLDI 1992. Conf. on Programming Language Design and Implementation, pp. 55–67. ACM Press, New York (1992) (ACM SIGPLAN Notices 27(7))
11. Karlsson, K.: Nebula, a Functional Operating System. Technical report, Chalmers University (1981)
12. King, D.J., Wadler, P.: Combining Monads. Technical report, University of Glasgow (1993)
13. Peng Li, A.T., Marlow, S., Peyton Jones, S.: Lightweight Concurrency Primitives for GHC. In: Haskell Workshop, Freiburg, Germany, pp. 107–118 (2007)
14. Perry, N.: Towards a Functional Operating System. Technical report, Dept. of Computing, Imperial College, London, UK (1988)
15. Peyton Jones, S.L., Gordon, A., Finne, S.: Concurrent Haskell. In: POPL 1996. Symp on Principles of Programming Languages, ACM Press, New York (1996)
16. Rabhi, F.A., Gorlatch, S. (eds.): Patterns and Skeletons for Parallel and Distributed Computing. Springer, Heidelberg (2002)

17. Shapiro, E.: Systems Programming in Concurrent Prolog. In: POPL 1984. Symp. on Principles of Programming Languages, Salt Lake City, Utah (1984)
18. Stoye, W.R.: A New Scheme for Writing Functional Operating Systems. Technical Report 56, Computer Lab, Cambridge University (1984)
19. Trinder, P.W., Hammond, K., Mattson, J.S., Partridge, A.S., Peyton Jones, S.L.: GUM: A Portable Parallel Implementation of Haskell. In: PLDI 1996. Conf. on Programming Language Design and Implementation, Philadelphia, pp. 79–88 (1996)
20. Turner, D.: Functional Programming and Communicating Processes. In: de Bakker, J.W., Nijman, A.J., Treleaven, P.C. (eds.) PARLE. LNCS, vol. 259, pp. 54–74. Springer, Heidelberg (1987)
21. van Weelden, A., Plasmeijer, R.: Towards a Strongly Typed Functional Operating System. In: Peña, R., Arts, T. (eds.) IFL 2002. LNCS, vol. 2670, pp. 45–72. Springer, Heidelberg (2003)

Towards a High-Level Implementation of Execution Primitives for Unrestricted, Independent And-Parallelism

Amadeo Casas[1], Manuel Carro[2], and Manuel V. Hermenegildo[1,2]

[1] Depts. of Comp. Science and Electr. and Comp. Eng., Univ. of New Mexico, USA
{amadeo, herme}@cs.unm.edu
[2] School of Comp. Science, Univ. Politécnica de Madrid, Spain and IMDEA-Software
{mcarro, herme}@fi.upm.es

Abstract. Most efficient implementations of parallel logic programming rely on complex low-level machinery which is arguably difficult to implement and modify. We explore an alternative approach aimed at taming that complexity by raising core parts of the implementation to the source language level for the particular case of and-parallelism. We handle a significant portion of the parallel implementation at the Prolog level with the help of a comparatively small number of concurrency-related primitives which take care of lower-level tasks such as locking, thread management, stack set management, etc. The approach does not eliminate altogether modifications to the abstract machine, but it does greatly simplify them and it also facilitates experimenting with different alternatives. We show how this approach allows implementing both restricted and unrestricted (i.e., non fork-join) parallelism. Preliminary experiments show that the performance sacrificed is reasonable, although granularity control is required in some cases. Also, we observe that the availability of unrestricted parallelism contributes to better observed speedups.

Keywords: Parallelism, Virtual Machines, High-level Implementation.

1   Introduction

The wide availability of multicore processors is finally making parallel computers mainstream, thus bringing a renewed interest in languages and tools to simplify the task of writing parallel programs. The use of declarative paradigms and, among them, logic programming, is considered an interesting approach for obtaining increased performance through parallel execution on multicore architectures, including multicore embedded systems. The high-level nature of these languages allows coding in a style that is closer to the application and thus preserves more of the original parallelism for automatic parallelizers to uncover. Their amenability to semantics-preserving automatic parallelization is also due, in addition to this high level of abstraction, to their relatively simple semantics,

P. Hudak and D.S. Warren (Eds.): PADL 2008, LNCS 4902, pp. 230–247, 2008.

and the separation between the control component and the declarative specification. This makes it possible for the evaluator to execute some operations in any order (including in parallel), without affecting the meaning of the program. In addition, logic variables can be assigned a value at most once, and thus it is not necessary to check for some types of flow dependencies or to perform single statement assignment (SSA) transformations, as done with imperative languages. At the same time, the presence of dynamic data structures with "declarative pointers" (logical variables), irregular computations, or complex control makes the parallelization of logic programs a particularly interesting case that allows tackling complex parallelization-related challenges in a formally simple and well-understood context [14].

Parallel execution of logic programs has received considerable attention and very significant progress has been made in the area (see, e.g., [11] and its references). Two main forms of parallelism have been exploited: *Or-parallelism* (Aurora [22] and MUSE [2]) parallelizes the execution of different clauses of a predicate (and their continuations) and is naturally applicable to programs which perform search. *And-parallelism* refers to the parallel execution of different goals in the resolvent. It arises naturally in different kinds of applications (independently of whether there is implicit search or not), such as, e.g., divide-and-conquer algorithms. Systems like &-Prolog [16], DDAS [27] and others have exploited and-parallelism, while certain combinations of both and- and or-parallelism have been exploited by e.g. &ACE [24], AKL [20], and Andorra [26].

The basic ideas of the &-Prolog model have been adopted by many other systems (e.g., &ACE and DDAS). It consists of two components: a parallelizing compiler which detects the possible runtime dependencies between goals in clause bodies and annotates the clauses with expressions to decide whether parallel execution can be allowed at runtime, and a run-time system that exploits that parallelism. The run-time system is based on an extension of the original WAM architecture and instruction set, and was originally implemented, as most of the other systems mentioned, on shared-memory multiprocessors, although distributed implementations were also taken into account. We will follow the same overall architecture and assumptions herein, and concentrate as well on (modern) shared-memory, multicore processors.

These models and their implementations have been shown very effective at exploiting parallelism efficiently and obtaining significant speedups. However, most of them are based on quite complex, low-level machinery which makes implementing and maintaining these systems inherently hard. In this paper we explore an alternative approach that is based on raising some components to the source language level and keeping at low level only selected operations related to, e.g., thread handling and locking. We expect of course a performance impact, but hope that this division of concerns will make it possible to more easily explore variations on the execution schemes. While doing this, another objective of our proposal is to be able to easily exploit unrestricted and-parallelism, i.e., parallelism that is not restricted to fork-join operations.

2   Classical Approaches to And-Parallelism

In goal-level and-parallelism, a key issue is which goals to select for parallel execution in order to avoid situations which lead to incorrect execution or slow-down [19,14]. Not only errors but also significant inefficiency can arise from the simultaneous execution of computations which depend on each other since, for example, this may trigger more backtracking than in the sequential case. Thus, goals are said to be independent if their parallel execution will not perform additional search and will not produce incorrect results. Very general notions of independence have been developed, based on constraint theory [10]. However for simplicity we discuss only those based on variable sharing.

In *Dependent and-parallelism (DAP)* goals are executed in parallel even if they share variables, and the competition to bind them has to be dynamically dealt with using notions such as sequencing bindings from producers to consumers. Unfortunately this usually implies substantial execution overhead. In *Strict Independent and-parallelism (SIAP)* goals are allowed to execute in parallel only when they do not share variables, which guarantees the correctness and no-slowdown. *Non-strict independent and-parallelism (NSIAP)* is a significant extension, also guaranteeing the no-slowdown property, in which goals are parallelized even if they share variables, provided that at most one goal binds a shared variable or the goals agree in the possible bindings for shared variables. Compile-time tools have been devised and implemented to statically detect cases where this holds, thus making the runtime machinery lighter and faster. Undetermined cases can, if deemed advantageous, be checked at runtime.

Another issue is whether any restrictions are posed on the patterns of parallelization. For example, *Restricted and-parallelism (RAP)* constrains parallelism to (nested) fork-join operations. In the &-Prolog implementation of this model conjunctions which are to be executed in parallel are often marked by replacing the sequential comma (,/2) with a parallelism operator (&/2).

In this paper we will focus on the implementation of IAP and NSIAP parallelism, as both have practically identical implementation requirements. Our objective is to exploit both restricted and unrestricted, goal-level and-parallelism.

Once a method has been devised for selecting goals for parallel execution, an obviously relevant issue is how to actually implement such parallel execution. One usual implementation approach used in many and-parallel systems (both for IAP [16,24] and for DAP [27]) is the *multi-sequential, marker model* introduced by &-Prolog [13]. In this model parallel goals are executed in different *abstract machines* which run in parallel. In order to preserve sequential speed, these abstract machines are extensions of the sequential model, usually the Warren Abstract Machine (WAM) [29,1], which is the basis of most efficient sequential implementations. Herein we assume for simplicity that each (P)WAM has a parallel thread (an "agent") attached and that we have as many threads as processors. Thus, we can refer interchangeably to WAMs, agents, or processors.

p(X, Y, Z) :- q(X), r(X, Y) & s(X, Z).

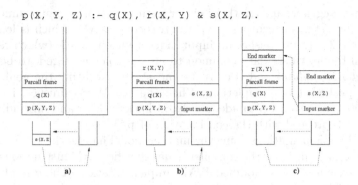

Fig. 1. Sketch of data structures layout using the marker model

Within each WAM, sequential fragments appear in contiguous stack sections exactly as in the sequential execution.[1] The new data areas are [16]:

Goal List: A shared area onto which goals that are ready to execute in parallel are pushed. WAMs can pick up goals from other WAMs' (or their own) goal lists. Goal list entries include a pointer to the environment where the goal was generated and to the code starting the goal execution, plus some additional control information.

Parcall Frames: They are created for each parallel conjunction and hold the necessary data for coordinating and synchronizing the parallel execution of the goals in the parallel conjunction.

Markers: They separate stack sections corresponding to different parallel goals. When a goal is picked up by an agent, an *input marker* is pushed onto the choicepoint stack. Likewise, an *end marker* is pushed when a goal execution ends. These are linked to ensure that backtracking will happen following a logical (i.e., not physical) order.

Figure 1 sketches a possible stack layout for a program such as:

$$p(X, Y, Z) :- q(X), r(X, Y) \& s(X, Z).$$

with query p(X, Y, Z). We assume that X will be ground after calling q/1. Different snapshots of the stack configurations are shown from left to right. Note that in the figure we are intermixing parcall frames and markers in the same stack. Some actual implementations have chosen to place them in different parts of the available data areas.[2]

When the first WAM executes the parallel conjunction r(X, Y) & s(X, Z), it pushes a parcall frame onto its stack and a goal descriptor onto its goal stack for the goal s(X, Z) (i.e., a pointer to the WAM code that will construct this call in

---

[1] In some proposals this need not be so: This can actually be relaxed: *continuation markers* [28] allow sequential execution to spread over non-contiguous sections. We will not deal with this issue here.

[2] For example, in &ACE parcall frames are pushed onto a separate stack and their slots are allocated in the heap, to simplify memory management.

the argument registers and another pointer to the appropriate environment), and it immediately starts executing r(X, Y). A second WAM, which is looking for jobs, picks s(X, Z) up, pushes an input marker into its stack (which references the parcall frame, where data common to all the goals is stored, to be used in case of *internal failure*) and constructs and starts executing the goal. An end marker is pushed upon completion. When the last WAM finishes, it will link the markers (so as to proceed adequately on backtracking and unwinding), and execution will proceed with the continuation of p/3.

Classical implementations using the marker model handle the &/2 operator at the abstract machine level: the compiler issues specific WAM instructions for &/2, which are executed by a modified WAM implementation. These modifications are far from trivial, although relatively isolated (e.g., unification instructions are usually not changed, or changed in a generic, uniform way).

As mentioned in the introduction, one of our objectives is to explore an alternative implementation approach based on raising components to the source language level and keeping at low level only selected operations. Also, we would like to avoid modifications to the low-level compiler. At the same time, we want to be able to easily exploit unrestricted and-parallelism, i.e., parallelism that is not restricted to fork-join operations. These two objectives are actually related in our approach because, as we will see in the following section, we will start by decomposing the parallelism operators into lower-level components which will also allow supporting unrestricted and-parallelism.

3   Decomposing And-Parallelism

It has already been reported [6,5] that it is possible to construct the and-parallel operator &/2 using more basic yet meaningful components. In particular, it is possible to implement the semantics of &/2 using two end-user operators, &>/2 and <&/1, defined as follows:[3]

- G &> H   schedules goal G for parallel execution and continues with the code after G &> H. H is a *handler* which contains (or *points to*) the state of goal G.
- H <&   waits for the goal associated with H (G, in the previous item) to finish. At that point all bindings G could possibly generate are ready, since G has reached a solution. Assuming goal independence between G and the calls performed while G was being executed, no binding conflicts will arise.

G &> H ideally takes a negligible amount of time to execute, although the precise moment in which G actually starts depends on the availability of resources (primarily, free agents/processors). On the other hand, H <& suspends until the associated goal finitely fails or returns an answer. It is interesting to note that

---

[3] We concentrate on forward execution here. See Section 4.5 for backtracking behavior. Also, although exception handling is beyond our current scope, exceptions uncaught by a parallel goal surface at the corresponding <&/1, where they can be captured.

the approach shares some similarities with the concept of *futures* in parallel functional languages. A future is meant to hold the return value of a function so that a consumer can wait for its complete evaluation. However, the notions of "return value" and "complete evaluation" do not make sense when logic variables are present. Instead, H <& waits for the moment when the producer goal has completed execution, and the "received values" (a tuple, really) will be whatever (possibly partial) instantiations have been produced by such goal.

With the previous definitions, the &/2 operator can be expressed as:

A & B :- A &> H, call(B), H <&.

(Actual implementations will of course expand A & B at compile time using the above definition in order not to pay the price of an additional call and the meta-call. The same can be applied to &> and <&.) However, these two new operators can additionally be used to exploit more and-parallelism than is possible with &/2 alone [9]. We will just provide some intuition by means of a simple example (an experimental performance evaluation is included in Section 5.)[4]

Consider predicate p/3 defined as follows:

p(X,Y,Z) :- a(X,Z), b(X), c(Y), d(Y,Z).

whose (strict) dependencies (assuming that X,Y,Z are free and do not share on entry) are shown in Figure 2. A classical fork-join parallelization is shown in Figure 3, while an alternative (non fork-join) parallelization using the new operators is shown in Figure 4. We assume here that solution order is not relevant.

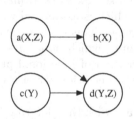

Fig. 2. Dep. graph for p/3

It is obvious that it is always possible to parallelize programs using &>/2 and <&/1 and obtain the same parallelism as with &/2 (since &/2 can be defined in terms of &>/2 and <&/1). The converse is not true. Furthermore, there are cases (as in Figure 4) where the parallelizations allowed by &>/2 and <&/1 can be expected to result in shorter execution times, for certain goal execution times [9]. In our example, the annotation in Figure 3 misses the possible parallelism between the subgoals c/1 and b/1, which the code in Figure 4 allows: c/1 is scheduled at the beginning of the execution, and it is waited for in Hc <&, just after b/1 has been scheduled for parallel execution.

In addition to &>/2 and <&/1, we propose specialized versions in order to obtain additional functionality or more efficiency. In particular, &!>/2 and <&!/1 are intended to be equivalent to &>/2 and <&/1, respectively, but only for single-solution, non-failing goals, where there is no need to anticipate backtracking during forward execution. These primitives allow the parallelizer to flag goals that analysis has detected to be deterministic and non-failing (see [18]), and this can result in important simplifications in the implementation.

---

[4] Note that the &>/2 and <&/1 operators do not replace the fork-join operator &/2 at the language level due to its conciseness in cases in which no extra parallelism can be exploited with &>/2 and <&/1.

```
p(X, Y, Z):-                    p(X, Y, Z) :-
    a(X, Z) & c(Y),                 c(Y) &> Hc,
    b(X) & d(Y, Z).                 a(X, Z),
                                    b(X) &> Hb,
                                    Hc <&,
                                    d(Y, Z),
                                    Hb <&.
```

Fig. 3. Nested fork-join annotation   **Fig. 4.** Using the new operators

4   Sketch of a Shared Memory Implementation

Our proposed implementation divides responsibilities among several layers. User-level parallelism and concurrency primitives intended for the programmer and parallelizers are at the top and written in Prolog. Below, goal publishing, searching for available goals, and goal scheduling are written at the Prolog level, relying on some low-level support primitives for, e.g., locking or low-level goal management, with a Prolog interface but written in C.

In our current implementation for shared-memory multiprocessors, and similarly to [16], agents wait for work to be available, and execute it if so. Every agent is created as a thread attached to an (extended) WAM stack set. Sequential execution proceeds as usual, and coordination with the rest of the agents is performed by means of shared data structures. Agents make new work available to other agents (and also to itself) through a *goal list* which is associated with every stack set and which can be consulted by all the agents. This is an instance of the general class of *work-stealing* scheduling algorithms, which date back at least to Burton and Sleep's [4] research on parallel execution of functional programs and Halstead's [12] implementation of Multilisp, and the original &-Prolog abstract machine [13,16], for logic programs.

In the following subsections we will introduce the library with the (deterministic) low-level parallelism primitives and we will present the design (and a sketch of the actual code, simplified for space reasons) of the main source-level algorithms used to run deterministic, non-failing goals in parallel. We will conclude with some comments on the execution of nondeterministic goals in parallel.

4.1   Low-Level Parallelism Primitives

The low-level layer has been implemented as a Ciao library ("apll") written in C which provides basic mechanisms to start threads, wait for their completion, push goals, search for goals, access to O.S. locks, etc. Most of these primitives need to refer to an explicit goal and need to use some information related to its state (whether it has been taken, finished, etc.). Hence the need to pass them a **Handler** data structure which abstracts information related to the goal at hand.

The current (simplified) list of primitives follows. Note that this is not intended to be a general-purpose concurrency library (such as those available in Ciao and other Prolog systems —in fact, very little of what should appear in such a generic library is here), but a list of primitives suitable for efficiently implementing at a higher-level different approaches to exploiting independent and-parallelism. We are, for clarity, adding explicitly the library qualification.

apll:push_goal(+Goal,+Det,-Handler) atomically creates a unique *handler* (an opaque structure) associated to Goal and publishes Goal in the goal list for any agent to pick it up. Handler will henceforth be used in any operation related to Goal. Det describes whether Goal is deterministic or not.

apll:find_goal(-Handler) searches for a goal published in some goal list. If one exists, Handler is unified with a handler for it; the call fails otherwise, and it will succeed at most once per call. Goal lists are accessed atomically so as to avoid races when updating them.[5]

apll:goal_available(+Handler) succeeds if the goal associated to Handler has not been picked up yet, and fails otherwise.

apll:retrieve_goal(+Handler,-Goal) unifies Goal and the goal initially associated to Handler.

apll:goal_finished(+Handler) succeeds if the execution state of the goal associated to Handler is finished, and fails otherwise.

apll:set_goal_finished(+Handler) sets to finished the execution state of the goal associated to Handler.

apll:waiting(+Handler) succeeds when the execution state of the agent which published the goal associated to Handler is suspended and fails otherwise.

Additionally, a set of locking primitives is provided to perform synchronization and to obtain mutual exclusion at the Prolog level. Agents are synchronized by using two different locks:[6] one which is used to ensure mutual exclusion when dealing with shared data structures (i.e., when adding new goals to the list), and another one which is used to synchronize the agent waking up when <&/1 is waiting for either more work to be available, or the execution of a goal picked up by some other agent to finish. Both can be accessed with specific (*_self) predicates to specify the ones belonging to the calling agent. Otherwise, they are accessed through a goal Handler, and then the locks accessed are those belonging to the agent which created the goal that Handler refers to (i.e., its *creator*).

apll:suspend suspends the execution of the calling thread.

apll:release(+Handler) releases the agent which created Handler (which could have suspended itself with the above described predicate).

apll:release_some_suspended_thread selects one out of any suspended threads and resumes its execution.

apll:enter_mutex(+Handler) attempts to enter mutual exclusion by using the lock of the agent associated to Handler, in order to access its shared variables.

apll:enter_mutex_self same as above, with the agent's own mutex.

---

[5] Different versions exist of this primitive which can be used while implementing different goal scheduling strategies.

[6] Note that both locks are local to the thread, i.e., they are not global locks.

apll:exit_mutex(+Handler) *signals* the lock in the realm of the agent associated to Handler in order to exit mutual exclusion.

apll:exit_mutex_self same as above with the calling thread.

The following sections will clarify how these primitives are intended to be used.

4.2   High-Level Goal Publishing

Based on the previous low-level primitives, we will develop the user-level ones. We will describe a particular strategy (which is the one used in our experiments) in which idle agents are suspended and resumed depending on the availability of work, instead of continuously looking for tasks to perform.

A call to &!>/2 (or &>/2 if the goal is nondeterministic) publishes the goal in the goal list managed by the agent, which makes it available to other agents. Figure 5 shows the (simplified) Prolog code

```
Goal &!> Handler :-
    apll:push_goal(Goal,det,Handler),
    apll:release_some_suspended_thread.
```

Fig. 5. Publishing a (deterministic) parallel goal

implementing this functionality (again, the code shown can be expanded in line but is shown as a meta-call for clarity). First, a pointer to the goal generated is inserted in the goal list, and then a signal is broadcast to let suspended agents know that new work is available. As we will see later, the agent receiving the signal will resume its execution, pick up the new parallel goal, and start its execution.

After executing Goal &!> H, H will hold the state of Goal, which can be inspected both by the thread which publishes Goal and by any thread which picks up Goal to execute it. Therefore, in some sense, H takes the role of the *parcall frame* in [16], but it goes to the heap instead of being placed in the environment. Threads can communicate and synchronize through H in order to consult and update the state of Goal. This is especially important when executing H <&!.

4.3   Performing Goal Joins

Figure 6 provides code implementing <&!/1 (the deterministic version of <&/1). First, the thread needs to check whether the goal has been picked up by some other agent, using apll:goal_available/1. If this is not the case, then the publishing agent executes it locally, and <&!/1 succeeds trivially. Note that mutual exclusion is requested with apll:enter_mutex_self/0 in order to avoid incorrect concurrent accesses to (shared) data structures related to goal management.

If the goal has been picked up by another agent and its execution has finished, then <&!/1 will automatically succeed (note that mutual exclusion is entered again in order to safely check the goal status). In that case, the bindings made during goal execution are, naturally, available, since we are dealing with a shared-memory implementation. If the goal execution has not finished yet then the thread will search for more work in order to keep itself busy, and it will only

```
H <&! :-                              perform_other_work(H) :-
    apll:enter_mutex_self,                apll:enter_mutex_self,
    (                                     (
        apll:goal_available(H) ->             apll:goal_finished(H) ->
        apll:retrieve_goal(H,Goal),           apll:exit_mutex_self
        apll:exit_mutex_self,             ;
        call(Goal)
    ;                                         find_goal_and_execute,
        apll:exit_mutex_self,                 perform_other_work(H)
        perform_other_work(H)             ).
    ).
```

Fig. 6. Goal join with continuation

```
find_goal_and_execute :-
    apll:find_goal(Handler),
    apll:exit_mutex_self,
    apll:retrieve_goal(Handler,Goal),
    call(Goal),                           create_agents(0) :- !.
    apll:enter_mutex(Handler),            create_agents(N) :-
    apll:set_goal_finished(Handler),          N > 0,
    (                                         conc:start_thread(agent),
        apll:waiting(Handler) ->              N1 is N - 1,
        apll:release(Handler)                 create_agents(N1).
    ;
        true
    ),
    apll:exit_mutex(Handler).             agent :-
find_goal_and_execute :-                      apll:enter_mutex_self,
    apll:exit_mutex_self,                     find_goal_and_execute,
    apll:suspend.                            agent.
```

Fig. 7. Finding a parallel goal and executing it   **Fig. 8.** Creating parallel agents

suspend if there is definitely no work to perform at the moment. This ensures that overall efficiency is kept at a reasonable level, as we will see in Section 5. We want to note, again, that this process is protected from races when accessing shared variables by using locks for mutual exclusion and synchronization.

Figure 7 shows the code for find_goal_and_execute/0, which searches for work in the system. If a goal is found, the executing thread will retrieve and execute it, ensure mutual exclusion on the publishing agent data structures (where the handler associated to the goal resides), mark the goal execution as finished and resume the execution of the publishing agent, if it was suspended. In that case, the publishing agent (suspended in eng_suspend/0) will check which situation applies after resumption and act accordingly after recursively invoking the predicate perform_other_work/1. If no goal was available for execution, find_goal_and_execute/0 will suspend waiting for more work to be created.

4.4 Agent Creation

Agents are generated using the `create_agents/1` predicate (Figure 8) which launches a number of O.S. threads using the `start_thread/0` predicate imported from a generic concurrency library (thus the `conc` prefix used, again, for clarity). Each of these threads executes the `agent/0` code, which continuously either executes work in the system and looks for more work when finished, or sleeps when there is nothing to execute. We assume for simplicity that agent creation is performed at system startup or just before starting a parallel execution. Higher-level predicates are however provided in order to manage threads in a more flexible way. For instance, `ensure_agents/1` makes sure that a given number of executing agents is available. In fact, agents can be created lazily, and added or deleted dynamically as needed, depending on machine load. However, this interesting issue of thread throttling is beyond the scope of this paper.

4.5 Towards Non-determinism

For simplicity we have left out of the discussion and also of the code the support for backtracking, which clearly complicates things. We have made significant progress in our implementation towards supporting backtracking so that, for example, the failure-driven top level is used unchanged and memory is recovered orderly at the end of parallel executions. However, completing the implementation of backtracking is still the matter of current work.

There are interesting issues both at the design level and also at the implementation level. An interesting point at the design level is for example deciding whether backtracking happens when going over `&>/2` or `<&/1` during backward execution. Previous work [6,5] leaned towards the latter, which is also probably easier to implement; however, there are also reasons to believe that the former may in the end be more appropriate. For example, in parallelized loops such as:

p([X|Xs]):- b(X) &> Hb, p(Xs), Hb <&.

spawning `b(X)` and keeping the recursion local and not the other way around is important because task creation is the real bottleneck. However, the solution order is not preserved if backtracking occurs at `<&/1`, but it is if backtracking occurs at `&>/2`. Note that in such loops the loss of last call optimization (LCO) is only of relative importance, since if there are several solutions to either `b/1` or `p/1`, LCO could not be applied anyway, and a simple program transformation (to store handlers in an accumulating parameter) can recover it if necessary.

At the implementation level, avoiding the "trapped goal" and "garbage slots" problems [17] is an issue to solve. One approach under consideration to this end is to move trapped stack segments (sequential sections of execution) to the top of the stack set in case backtracking is needed from a trapped section. Sections which become empty can be later compacted to avoid garbage slots. In order to express this at the Prolog level, we foresee the need of additional primitives, still the subject of further work, to manage stack segments as first-class citizens.

Another fundamental idea in the approach that we are exploring is not to create markers explicitly, but use instead, for the same purpose, standard choice

Table 1. Benchmarks for restricted and unrestricted IAP

AIAKL	Simplified *AKL* abstract interpreter.	**Hamming**	Calculates *Hamming* numbers.
Ann	Annotator for and-parallelism.	**Hanoi**	Solves *Hanoi* puzzle.
		MergeSort	Sorts a 10000 element list.
Boyer	Simplified version of the *Boyer-Moore* theorem prover.	**MMatrix**	Multiplies two 50×50 matrices.
Deriv	Symbolic derivation.	**Palindrome**	Generates a palindrome of 2^{14} elements.
FFT	Fast Fourier transform.	**QuickSort**	Sorts a 10000 element list.
Fibonacci	Doubly recursive *Fibonacci*.	**Takeuchi**	Computes *Takeuchi*.
FibFun	Functional *Fibonacci*.	**WMS2**	A work scheduling program.

points built by creating alternatives (using alternative clauses) directly in the control code (in Prolog) that implements backtracking.

5   Experimental Results

We now present performance results obtained after executing a selection of well-known benchmarks with independent and-parallelism. As mentioned before, we have implemented the proposed approach in Ciao [3], an efficient system designed with extension capabilities in mind. All results were obtained by averaging ten runs on a state-of-the-art multiprocessor, a Sun Fire T2000 with 8 cores and 8 Gb of memory. While each core is capable of running 4 threads in parallel, and in theory up to 32 threads could run simultaneously on this machine, we only show speedups up to 8 agents. Our experiments (see the later comments related to Figure 10) show that speedups with more than 8 threads stop being linear even for completely independent computations (i.e., 32 totally independent threads do not really speed up as if 32 independent processors were available), as threads in the same core compete for shared resources such as integer pipelines. Thus, beyond 8 agents, it is hard to know whether reduced speedups are due to our parallelization and implementation or to limitations of the machine.

Although most of the benchmarks we use are quite well-known, Table 1 provides a brief description. Speedups appear in Tables 2 (which contains only programs parallelized using restricted [N]SIAP, as in Figure 3) and 3 (which additionally contains unrestricted IAP programs, as in Figure 4). The speedups are with respect to the sequential speed on one processor of the original, unparallelized benchmark. Therefore, the columns tagged *1* correspond to the slowdown coming from executing a parallel program in a single processor. Benchmarks with a *GC* suffix were executed with granularity control with a suitably chosen threshold and benchmarks with a *DL* suffix use difference lists and require NSIAP for parallelization. All the benchmarks in the tables were automatically parallelized using CiaoPP [18] and the annotation algorithms described in [9] (*TakeuchiGC* needed however some unfolding in order to uncover and allow exploiting more parallelism using the new operators, as discussed later).

Table 2. Speedups for restricted IAP

Benchmark	Number of processors								
	Seq.	1	2	3	4	5	6	7	8
AIAKL	1.00	0.97	1.77	1.66	1.67	1.67	1.67	1.67	1.67
Ann	1.00	0.98	1.86	2.65	3.37	4.07	4.65	5.22	5.90
Boyer	1.00	0.32	0.64	0.95	1.21	1.32	1.47	1.57	1.64
BoyerGC	1.00	0.90	1.74	2.57	3.15	3.85	4.39	4.78	5.20
Deriv	1.00	0.32	0.61	0.86	1.09	1.15	1.30	1.55	1.75
DerivGC	1.00	0.91	1.63	2.37	3.05	3.69	4.21	4.79	5.39
FFT	1.00	0.61	1.08	1.30	1.63	1.65	1.67	1.68	1.70
FFTGC	1.00	0.98	1.76	2.14	2.71	2.82	2.99	3.08	3.37
Fibonacci	1.00	0.30	0.60	0.94	1.25	1.58	1.86	2.22	2.50
FibonacciGC	1.00	0.99	1.95	2.89	3.84	4.78	5.71	6.63	7.57
Hamming	1.00	0.93	1.13	1.52	1.52	1.52	1.52	1.52	1.52
Hanoi	1.00	0.67	1.31	1.82	2.32	2.75	3.20	3.70	4.07
HanoiDL	1.00	0.47	0.98	1.51	2.19	2.62	3.06	3.54	3.95
HanoiGC	1.00	0.89	1.72	2.43	3.32	3.77	4.17	4.41	4.67
MergeSort	1.00	0.79	1.47	2.12	2.71	3.01	3.30	3.56	3.71
MergeSortGC	1.00	0.83	1.52	2.23	2.79	3.10	3.43	3.67	3.95
MMatrix	1.00	0.91	1.74	2.55	3.32	4.18	4.83	5.55	6.28
Palindrome	1.00	0.44	0.77	1.09	1.40	1.61	1.82	2.10	2.23
PalindromeGC	1.00	0.94	1.75	2.37	2.97	3.30	3.62	4.13	4.46
QuickSort	1.00	0.75	1.42	1.98	2.44	2.84	3.07	3.37	3.55
QuickSortDL	1.00	0.71	1.36	1.95	2.26	2.76	2.96	3.18	3.32
QuickSortGC	1.00	0.94	1.78	2.31	2.87	3.19	3.46	3.67	3.75
Takeuchi	1.00	0.23	0.46	0.68	0.91	1.12	1.32	1.49	1.72
TakeuchiGC	1.00	0.88	1.61	2.16	2.62	2.63	2.63	2.63	2.63

It can be deduced from the results that in several benchmarks the *natural* parallelizations produce small granularity. This, understandably, impacts our implementation since a sizable part of it is written in Prolog, which implies additional overhead in the preparation and execution of parallel goals. Thus, it is not possible to perform a fair comparison of the speedups obtained with respect to previous (lower-level) and-parallel systems. The overhead implied by the proposed approach produces comparatively low performance on a single processor and in some cases with very fine granularity, such as Boyer and Takeuchi, speedups are shallow (below 2×) even over 8 processors. In these examples execution is dominated by the sequential code of the scheduler and agent management in Prolog. However, even in these cases, setting a granularity threshold based on a measure of the input argument size [21] much better results can be obtained. Figure 11 depicts graphically the impact of granularity control in some benchmarks. Annotating the parallelized program to take into account granularity measures based on the size of the input arguments, and finding out the optimal threshold for a given platform, can be done automatically in many cases [21,23].

Table 3 shows a different comparison: some programs have traditionally been executed under IAP using the restricted (nested fork-join) annotations, and can

Table 3. Speedups for both restricted and unrestricted IAP

Benchmark	Parallelism	Number of processors								
		Seq.	1	2	3	4	5	6	7	8
FFTGC	Restricted	1.00	0.98	1.76	2.14	2.71	2.82	2.99	3.08	3.37
	Unrestricted	1.00	0.98	1.82	2.31	3.01	3.12	3.26	3.39	3.63
FibFunGC	Restricted	1.00	1.00	1.00	1.00	1.00	1.00	1.00	1.00	1.00
	Unrestricted	1.00	0.99	1.95	2.89	3.84	4.78	5.71	6.63	7.57
Hamming	Restricted	1.00	0.93	1.13	1.52	1.52	1.52	1.52	1.52	1.52
	Unrestricted	1.00	0.93	1.15	1.64	1.64	1.64	1.64	1.64	1.64
TakeuchiGC	Restricted	1.00	0.88	1.61	2.16	2.62	2.63	2.63	2.63	2.63
	Unrestricted	1.00	0.88	1.62	2.39	3.33	4.04	4.47	5.19	5.72
WMS2	Restricted	1.00	0.99	1.01	1.01	1.01	1.01	1.01	1.01	1.01
	Unrestricted	1.00	0.99	1.10	1.10	1.10	1.10	1.10	1.10	1.10

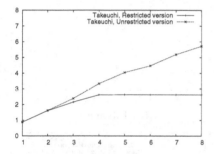

Fig. 9. Restricted and unrestricted IAP versions of *Takeuchi*

Fig. 10. *Fibonacci* with gran. control vs. maximum speedup in real machine.

be annotated for parallelism using the more flexible &>/2 and <&/1 operators, as in Figures 3 and 4. In some cases those programs obtain little additional speedup, but, interestingly, in other cases the gains are very relevant. An interesting example is the *Takeuchi* function which underwent a manual (but mechanical) transformation involving an *unfolding* step, which produced a clause where non-nested fork-join [15] can be taken advantage of, producing a much better speedup. This can be clearly seen in Figure 9. Note that the speedup curve did not seem to stabilize even when the 8 processor mark was reached.

The *FibFun* benchmark is also an interesting case. A definition of Fibonacci was written in Ciao using the functional package [8] which implements a rich functional syntactic layer via compilation to the logic programming kernel. The automatic translation into predicates does not produce however the same Fibonacci program that programmers usually write (input parameters are calculated right before making the recursive calls), and it turns out that it cannot be directly parallelized using existing order-preserving annotators and restricted IAP. On the other hand it can be automatically parallelized (including the translation from functional to logic programming notation) using the unrestricted operators.

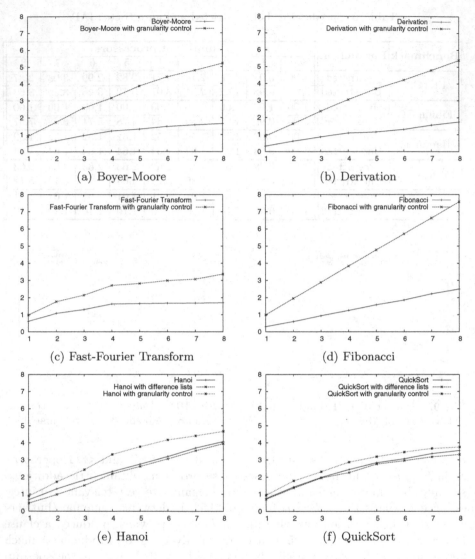

Fig. 11. Speedups for some selected benchmarks with and without granularity control

Despite our observation that the T2000 cannot produce linear speedups beyond 8 processors even for independent computations, we wanted to try at least a Prolog example using as many threads as natively available in the machine, and compare its speedup with that of a C program generating completely independent computations. Such a C program provides us with a practical upper bound on the attainable speedups. The results are depicted in Figure 10 which shows both the ideally parallel C program and a parallelized Fibonacci running on our implementation. Interestingly, the speedup obtained is only marginally worse than the best possible one. In both curves it is possible to observe a sawtooth shape, presumably caused by tasks filling in a row of units in all cores and starting to use up additional thread units in other cores, which happens at 1×8, 2×8, and 3×8 threads.

6   Conclusions

We have presented a new implementation approach for exploiting and-parallelism in logic programs with the objectives of simpler machinery and more flexibility. The approach is based on raising the implementation of some components to the source language level by using more basic high-level primitives than the fork-join operator and keeping only some relatively simple operations at a lower level. Our preliminary experimental results show that reasonable speedups are achievable with this approach, although the additional overhead, at least in the current implementation, makes it necessary to use granularity control in many cases in order to obtain good results. In addition, recent compilation technology and implementation advances [7,25] provide hope that it will eventually be possible to recover a significant part of the efficiency lost due to the level at which parallel execution is expressed. Finally, we have observed that the availability of unrestricted parallelism contributes in practice to better observed speedups. We are currently working on improving the implementation both in terms of efficiency and of improved support for backtracking. We have also developed simultaneously specific parallelizers for this approach, which can take advantage of the unrestricted nature of the parallelism which it can support [9].

Acknowledgments. This work was funded in part by the IST program of the European Commission, FP6 FET project IST-15905 *MOBIUS*, by the Ministry of Education and Science (MEC) project TIN2005-09207-C03 *MERIT-COMVERS* and by the Madrid Regional Government CAM project S-0505/TIC/0407 *PROMESAS*. Manuel Hermenegildo and Amadeo Casas were also funded in part by the Prince of Asturias Chair in Information Science and Technology at UNM.

References

1. Ait-Kaci, H.: Warren's Abstract Machine, A Tutorial Reconstruction. MIT Press, Cambridge (1991)
2. Ali, K.A.M., Karlsson, R.: The Muse Or-Parallel Prolog Model and its Performance. In: 1990 North American Conference on Logic Programming, pp. 757–776. MIT Press, Cambridge (1990)
3. Bueno, F., Cabeza, D., Carro, M., Hermenegildo, M., López-García, P., Puebla, G. (Eds.): The Ciao System. Ref. Manual (v1.13). Technical report, C. S. School (UPM) (2006), http://www.ciaohome.org
4. Burton, F.W., Sleep, M.R.: Executing functional programs on a virtual tree of processors. In: Functional Programming Languages and Computer Architecture, pp. 187–195 (October 1981)
5. Cabeza, D.: An Extensible, Global Analysis Friendly Logic Programming System. PhD thesis, Universidad Politécnica de Madrid (UPM), Facultad Informatica UPM, 28660-Boadilla del Monte, Madrid-Spain (August 2004)

6. Cabeza, D., Hermenegildo, M.: Implementing Distributed Concurrent Constraint Execution in the CIAO System. In: Proc. of the AGP 1996 Joint Conference on Declarative Programming, pp. 67–78 (July 1996)
7. Carro, M., Morales, J., Muller, H.L., Puebla, G., Hermenegildo, M.: High-Level Languages for Small Devices: A Case Study. In: Flautner, K., Kim, T. (eds.) Compilers, Architecture, and Synthesis for Embedded Systems, pp. 271–281. ACM Press/Sheridan (October 2006)
8. Casas, A., Cabeza, D., Hermenegildo, M.: A Syntactic Approach to Combining Functional Notation, Lazy Evaluation and Higher-Order in LP Systems. In: Hagiya, M., Wadler, P. (eds.) FLOPS 2006. LNCS, vol. 3945, Springer, Heidelberg (2006)
9. Casas, A., Carro, M., Hermenegildo, M.: Annotation Algorithms for Unrestricted Independent And-Parallelism in Logic Programs. In: LOPSTR 2007. 17th International Symposium on Logic-based Program Synthesis and Transformation, The Technical University of Denmark, Springer, Heidelberg (2007)
10. de la Banda, M.G., Hermenegildo, M., Marriott, K.: Independence in CLP Languages. ACM Transactions on Programming Languages and Systems 22(2), 269–339 (2000)
11. Gupta, G., Pontelli, E., Ali, K., Carlsson, M., Hermenegildo, M.: Parallel Execution of Prolog Programs: a Survey. ACM Transactions on Programming Languages and Systems 23(4), 472–602 (2001)
12. Halstead, R.H.: MultiLisp: A Language for Concurrent Symbolic Computation. ACM TOPLAS 7(4), 501–538 (1985)
13. Hermenegildo, M.: An Abstract Machine for Restricted AND-parallel Execution of Logic Programs. In: Shapiro, E. (ed.) Third International Conference on Logic Programming. LNCS, vol. 225, pp. 25–40. Springer, Heidelberg (1986)
14. Hermenegildo, M.: Parallelizing Irregular and Pointer-Based Computations Automatically: Perspectives from Logic and Constraint Programming. Parallel Computing 26(13–14), 1685–1708 (2000)
15. Hermenegildo, M., Carro, M.: Relating Data–Parallelism and (And–) Parallelism in Logic Programs. The Computer Languages Journal 22(2/3), 143–163 (1996)
16. Hermenegildo, M., Greene, K.: The &-Prolog System: Exploiting Independent And-Parallelism. New Generation Computing 9(3,4), 233–257 (1991)
17. Hermenegildo, M., Nasr, R.I.: Efficient Management of Backtracking in AND-parallelism. In: Shapiro, E. (ed.) Third International Conference on Logic Programming. LNCS, vol. 225, pp. 40–55. Springer, Heidelberg (1986)
18. Hermenegildo, M., Puebla, G., Bueno, F., López García, P.: Integrated Program Debugging, Verification, and Optimization Using Abstract Interpretation (and The Ciao System Preprocessor). Science of Computer Programming 58(1–2), 115–140 (2005)
19. Hermenegildo, M., Rossi, F.: Strict and Non-Strict Independent And-Parallelism in Logic Programs: Correctness, Efficiency, and Compile-Time Conditions. Journal of Logic Programming 22(1), 1–45 (1995)
20. Janson, S.: AKL. A Multiparadigm Programming Language. PhD thesis, Uppsala University (1994)
21. López-García, P., Hermenegildo, M., Debray, S.K.: A Methodology for Granularity Based Control of Parallelism in Logic Programs. Journal of Symbolic Computation, Special Issue on Parallel Symbolic Computation 21(4–6), 715–734 (1996)
22. Lusk, E., et al.: The Aurora Or-Parallel Prolog System. New Generation Computing 7(2,3) (1990)

23. Mera, E., López-García, P., Puebla, G., Carro, M., Hermenegildo, M.: Combining Static Analysis and Profiling for Estimating Execution Times. In: Hanus, M. (ed.) PADL 2007. LNCS, vol. 4354, pp. 140–154. Springer, Heidelberg (2006)
24. Pontelli, E., Gupta, G., Hermenegildo, M.: ACE: A High-Performance Parallel Prolog System. In: International Parallel Processing Symposium, pp. 564–572. IEEE Computer Society Technical Committee on Parallel Processing, IEEE Computer Society, Los Alamitos (1995)
25. Santos-Costa, V.: Optimising Bytecode Emulation for Prolog. In: Nadathur, G. (ed.) PPDP 1999. LNCS, vol. 1702, pp. 261–277. Springer, Heidelberg (1999)
26. de Morais Santos-Costa, V.M.: Compile-Time Analysis for the Parallel Execution of Logic Programs in Andorra-I. PhD thesis, University of Bristol (August 1993)
27. Shen, K.: Overview of DASWAM: Exploitation of Dependent And-parallelism. Journal of Logic Programming 29(1–3), 245–293 (1996)
28. Shen, K., Hermenegildo, M.: Flexible Scheduling for Non-Deterministic, And-parallel Execution of Logic Programs. In: Fraigniaud, P., Mignotte, A., Robert, Y., Bougé, L. (eds.) Euro-Par 1996. LNCS, vol. 1124, pp. 635–640. Springer, Heidelberg (1996)
29. Warren, D.H.D.: An Abstract Prolog Instruction Set. TR 309, SRI International (1983)

Hierarchical Master-Worker Skeletons

Jost Berthold, Mischa Dieterle, Rita Loogen, and Steffen Priebe

Philipps-Universität Marburg, Fachbereich Mathematik und Informatik
Hans Meerwein Straße, D-35032 Marburg, Germany
{berthold,dieterle,loogen,priebe}@informatik.uni-marburg.de

Abstract. Master-worker systems are a well-known and often applicable scheme for the parallel evaluation of a pool of tasks, a *work pool*. The system consists of a master process managing a set of worker processes. After an initial phase with a fixed amount of tasks for each worker, further tasks are distributed in reply to results sent back by the workers. As this setup quickly leads to a bottleneck in the master process, the paper investigates techniques for hierarchically nesting the basic master-worker scheme. We present implementations of hierarchical master-worker skeletons, and how to automatically calculate parameters of the nested skeleton for good performance.

Nesting master-worker systems is nontrivial especially in cases where new tasks are dynamically created from previous results (typically breadth-or depth-first tree search algorithms). We discuss how to handle dynamically growing pools in a hierarchy and present a declarative implementation for nested master-worker systems with dynamic task creation.

The skeletons are experimentally evaluated with two typical test programs. We analyse their runtime behaviour and the effects of different hierarchies on runtimes via trace visualisations.

1 Introduction

Parallelising an algorithm implemented as a functional program starts by identifying a set of largely independent evaluations. These *tasks* have to be assigned to nodes of a parallel computer, to gain high speedups by simultaneous evaluation. If the tasks are *regular* and their *number* is statically known, mapping them to the parallel nodes is trivial. The everyday situation, however, faces us with *irregular* tasks of varying and unknown complexity. The *static* task distribution should be replaced by a *dynamic* one.

The *master-worker* scheme is a parallel skeleton for a task pool with dynamic task distribution. A master process distributes tasks to a set of subordinate worker processes, and collects the results. Many-to-one communication enables the master to evenly supply a new task to each worker every time it sends back a result. Worker idle-time in the period between sending a result and receiving a new task can

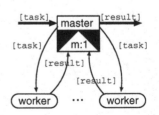

Fig. 1. Master-worker scheme

P. Hudak and D.S. Warren (Eds.): PADL 2008, LNCS 4902, pp. 248–264, 2008.

be avoided by pre-assigning a configurable amount (*prefetch*) of tasks to all workers. The prefetch parameter determines the behaviour of the skeleton, between a completely dynamic (prefetch 1) and a completely static distribution (prefetch $\geq \frac{\text{no. of tasks}}{\text{no. of workers}}$).

So far, we have assumed a statically fixed task pool, which, in essence, results in a parallelised map function with dynamic assignment. Again, more realistic are *dynamic* settings where results might imply additional new tasks at runtime. This changes the scene completely: Tasks are not only irregular and of unknown number, but also carry an unknown 'task productivity'. This weakens the influence of the prefetch parameter.

A master-worker scheme essentially relies on a double functionality of the master process: it is responsible for collecting (possibly large) results, and it emits new tasks to idle workers. When a large number of workers is used, the single master process quickly becomes a bottleneck which paralyses the whole scheme. On the other hand, using more coarse-grained work requests, and consequently tasks, would restrict the dynamic adaption to the workload. As a remedy, we conceptually investigate techniques to nest the basic master-worker skeleton in a *master-worker hierarchy*. The master process at the top distributes tasks to several lower submasters, each of which manages a (smaller) worker set of its own, or possibly another level of submasters in a deeper hierarchy.

The hierarchical master-worker system as a whole is tree-shaped, with worker processes at the leaves and submasters as the inner nodes. The optimal hierarchy layout depends on the nature of the tasks, and on the number and performance of processing elements (PEs). The basic skeleton mechanism of tasks and requests remains the same at all tree levels, but at higher levels of the tree, skeleton parameters and distribution policies have to be adjusted to achieve good performance. In the case of a dynamic task pool, another question we investigate is whether submasters at one level should forward new tasks to upper levels, or keep them for their own worker set. A simple hierarchical scheme for master-worker systems has been presented in [7]. While we concentrate on the hierarchies, the focus of [7] has been a modified master process, which enables a transformation of the dynamically evolving task queue considering global information.

The paper is organised as follows: Section 2 presents non-hierarchical and hierarchical master-worker skeletons for a static task pool; the essential mechanism for nesting the basic skeleton, and how to automatically compute suitable skeleton parameters. In Section 3, we extend the skeleton for the case of dynamic task sets, and show the more complex nesting mechanisms needed for this skeleton variant. Each section includes experiments with an example application, discussing the behaviour for different hierarchy layouts and prefetch values. Section 4 discusses related work, Section 5 concludes.

2   Static Task Pools

In this section, we consider master-worker systems with a *static* task pool, i.e. no tasks are created during processing. The task pool is a list of tasks which can also

```
mw :: (Trans t, Trans r) => Int -> Int -> (t -> r) -> [t] -> [r]
mw n prefetch wf tasks = ress
  where (reqs, ress) =  (unzip . merge) (spawn workers inputs)
        -- workers    :: [Process [t] [(Int,r)]]
        workers    =  [process (zip [i,i..] . map wf) | i <- [0..n-1]]
        inputs     =  distribute n tasks (initReqs ++ reqs)
        initReqs   =  concat (replicate prefetch [0..n-1])

-- task distribution according to worker requests
distribute :: Int -> [t] -> [Int] -> [[t]]
distribute np tasks reqs = [taskList reqs tasks n | n<-[0..np-1]]
    where taskList (r:rs) (t:ts) pe | pe == r   = t:(taskList rs ts pe)
                                    | otherwise =   taskList rs ts pe
          taskList _       _      _ = []
```

Fig. 2. Eden master-worker skeleton with a static task pool

be provided as a stream, the total number of tasks does not have to be known in advance. System termination depends, however, on closing this task stream.

2.1   The Basic Master-Worker Skeleton

We perform our experiments in the parallel Haskell extension Eden [4] which allows to specify many different variants of the general master-worker schemes in an elegant and concise way. Figure 2 shows the Eden implementation of the basic master-worker skeleton. The task pool `tasks` is distributed to n worker processes, which, for each task, apply the worker function `wf` and return a pair consisting of the worker number and the result of the task evaluation to the master process, i.e. the process evaluating `mw`. The worker numbers are interpreted as requests for new tasks. The master uses a function `distribute` to send tasks to the workers according to the (n*prefetch) requests initially created and the ones received from the workers.[1] Care must be taken that `distribute` is *incremental*, i.e. it can deliver partial result lists without the need to evaluate requests not yet available. The skeleton uses the following Eden functions:

- `process ::(Trans a, Trans b) => (a -> b) -> Process a b`
  wraps a function into a *process abstraction* which shifts function evaluation to a remote processing element. The `Trans` context ensures the existence of internal communication functions.
- `spawn :: [Process a b] -> [a] -> [b]`
  starts *processes* on remote machines eagerly.
- `merge :: [[r]] -> [r]`
  nondeterministically merges a set of streams into a single one.

---

[1] Because the input for Eden processes is evaluated by concurrent threads in the generator process, separate threads for each worker evaluate the local function `tasklist`.

An additional merge phase would be necessary to restore the initial task order for the results. This can be accomplished by adding tags to the task list, and passing results through an additional function `mergeByTags` (not shown) which merges the result streams from all workers (each sorted by tags, thus less complex than a proper sorting algorithm). We will not go into further details.

In the following, we will investigate the properties and implementation issues of hierarchical master-worker skeletons. As proclaimed in the introduction, this should enable us to overcome the bottleneck in the master when too many workers must be served.

2.2   Nesting the Basic Master-Worker Skeleton

To simplify the nesting, the basic skeleton `mw` is modified in such a way that it has the same type as its worker function. We therefore assume a worker function `wf :: [t] -> [r]`, and replace the expression (`map wf`) in the worker process definition with `wf`. This leads to a slightly modified version of `mw`, denoted by `mw'` in the following. An elegant nesting scheme (taken from [7]) is defined in Figure 3. The parameters specify the branching degrees and prefetch values per level, starting with the root parameters. The length of the parameter lists determines the depth of the generated hierarchical system.

```
mwNested :: (Trans t, Trans r) =>
            [Int] -> [Int] ->   -- branching degrees/prefetches per level
            ([t] -> [r]) ->     -- worker function
            [t] -> [r]          -- tasks, results
mwNested ns pfs wf = foldr fld wf (zip ns pfs)
   where fld :: (Trans t, Trans r) =>
               (Int,Int) -> ([t] -> [r]) -> ([t] -> [r])
         fld (n,pf) wf = mw' n pf wf
```

Fig. 3. Static nesting with equal level-wise branching

The nesting is achieved by folding the zipped branching degree and prefetches lists, using the proper worker function, of type `[t] -> [r]`, as the starting value. The folding function `fld` corresponds to the `mw'` skeleton applied to the branching degree and prefetch value parameters taken from the folded list and the worker function produced by folding up to this point.

The parameters in the nesting scheme above allow to freely define tree shape and prefetch values for all levels. As the `mw` skeleton assumes the same worker function for all workers in a group, it generates a regular hierarchy, one cannot define different branching or prefetch within the same level. It is possible to define a version of the static nestable work pool which is even more flexible (not considered here), yet more simple skeleton interfaces are desirable, to provide access to the hierarchical master-worker at different levels of abstraction. We can define an interface that automatically creates a regular hierarchy with reasonable parameters for a given number of available processing elements.

```
mwNest :: (Trans t, Trans r) =>
          Int -> Int -> Int -> Int -> (t -> r) -> [t] -> [r]
mwNest depth level1 np basepf f tasks
   = let nesting = mkNesting np depth level1
     in mwNested nesting (mkPFs basepf nesting) (map f) tasks
```

In this version, the parameter lists are computed from a given base prefetch, nesting depth and top-level branching degree by auxiliary functions. These fewer parameters provide simple control of the tree size and shape, and prefetch adjusted to the task granularity.

Auxiliary function `mkNesting` computes a regular nesting scheme from the top-level branching degree `level1` and the nesting `depth`, which appropriately maps to `np`, the number of processing elements (PEs) to use. It calculates the branching list for a hierarchy, where all intermediate levels are binary. The number of workers per group depends on the number of remaining PEs, rounded up to make sure that all PEs are used. Please note that this possibly places several worker processes on the same PE. Workers sharing the same PE will appear as slow workers in the system, but this should be compensated by the dynamic task distribution unless the prefetch is too high.

$$
l_d = \left\lceil \frac{\overbrace{np - l_1 \cdot (2^{d-1} - 1)}^{\text{total \# subm.s}}}{\underbrace{l_1 \cdot 2^{d-2}}_{\text{\# lowest subm.s}}} \right\rceil \Rightarrow \text{Branching list: } \underbrace{l_1 : 2 : 2 : \ldots : l_d}_{d \text{ levels}}
$$

A central problem for the usage of the nested scheme is the choice of appropriate prefetch values per level, specified by the second parameter. A submaster with m workers requiring prefetch p should receive a prefetch of at least $m \cdot p$ tasks to be able to supply p initial tasks to its child processes. Given a worker (leaf) prefetch of `pf` and a branching list $[l_1, ..., l_{d-1}, l_d]$, this leads to the following minimum prefetch at the different levels:

$$
\left[\prod_{j=k}^{d-1} l_j * pf \mid k \in [1 \ldots d-1] \right] = [(l_2 \cdot l_3 \cdot l_4 \cdot pf), (l_3 \cdot l_4 \cdot pf), (l_4 \cdot pf), pf]
$$

A reserve of one task per child process is added to this minimum, to avoid the submaster running out of tasks, since it directly passes on the computed prefetch amount to its children. The list of prefetch values is computed by a `scanr1`.

2.3   Experimental Results

We have tested the presented nesting scheme with different branching and prefetch parameters, with an application that calculates a Mandelbrot set

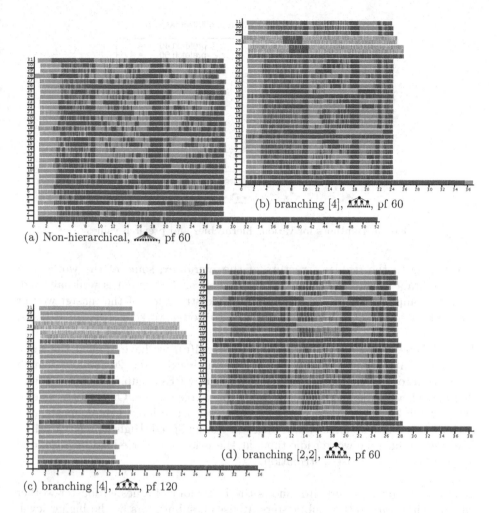

(a) Non-hierarchical, ⛰, pf 60

(b) branching [4], ⛰⛰, pf 60

(c) branching [4], ⛰⛰, pf 120

(d) branching [2,2], ⛰⛰, pf 60

Fig. 4. Mandelbrot traces, with different nesting and varying prefetch

visualisation of 5000 × 5000 pixels. All experiments use a Beowulf cluster of the Heriot-Watt University Edinburgh, 32 Intel P4-SMP nodes at 3 GHz with 512 MB RAM and Fast Ethernet. The *timeline diagrams* in Figure 4 visualise the process activity over time for program runs with different nesting and prefetch. Blocked processes are red (dark), and active/runnable processes green/yellow (light).

Flat vs. Hierarchical Master-worker System. The hierarchical system shows better runtime behaviour than the flat, i.e. non-hierarchical version. Although fewer PEs are available for worker processes, the total runtimes decrease substantially. Figure 4(a) shows a trace of the non-hierarchical master-worker scheme. Many worker processes are blocked most of the time. In a hierarchical version with a single additional level comprising four submasters, shown in (b), workers finish

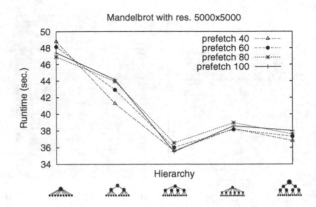

Fig. 5. Runtimes for various hierarchies and prefetch values

faster. Due to the regular structure of the hierarchy, some of the workers in the last branch share the same PE. Nevertheless, the system is well-balanced, but not completely busy. The dynamic task distribution of the master-worker inherently compensates load imbalance due to slower workers or irregular tasks.

Load Balance and Prefetch Values. In Figure 4(c), we have applied the same nesting as in (b), but we increased the prefetch value to 120. Small prefetch values lead to very good load balancing, especially PEs occupied by several (and therefore slow) workers do not slow down the whole system. On the other hand, low prefetch lets the workers run out of work sooner or later. Consequently, it is better to correlate prefetch values with the worker speed. Higher prefetch values (like 120) reduce the worker idle time, at the price of a worse load balance, due to the almost static task distribution.

Depth vs. Breadth. Figure 4(d) shows the behaviour of a nested master-worker scheme with *two* levels of submasters. It uses 2 submasters at the higher level, each serving two submasters. From our experiments, we cannot yet identify clear pros and cons of employing *deeper* hierarchies. Comparing runs with one and two additional submaster-levels, runtime and load balancing behaviour are almost the same, the advantage of the one-level hierarchy in Figure 4(b) remains rather vague. As shown in Figure 5, a broad flat hierarchy reveals the best total runtimes. However, the submasters will as well become bottlenecks when serving more and more child processes. Therefore, deeper hierarchies will be advantageous on bigger clusters with hundreds of machines.

Garbage Collection and Post-Processing. Another phenomenon can be observed in traces (a), (b) and (d): If the prefetch is small, relatively short inactivity at the tree root can make the whole system run out of work and lead to global inactivity. In this case, the reason are garbage collections in the master process, which make all the submasters and workers run out of tasks. The effect is intensified by higher top-level branching, and compensated by higher prefetch (c).

Additional experiments have shown that the bottleneck in the master process is mainly caused by the size of the result data structures, collected and stored in the master's local heap. This causes the long post-processing phases that can be observed in our traces. Moreover, since new requests are processed together with the result values, request processing is slowed down in the master processes. Using the same setup as in the previous experiments but replacing worker results with empty lists, the master has no problems to keep all workers busy, even with small prefetch values and no hierarchy.

2.4   Result Hierarchies

The hierarchy throttles the flow of results and thus helps shorten the post-processing phases. Therefore, the hierarchical master-worker skeletons show better total runtimes, as shown in Figure 5. The skeleton can further be optimised by decoupling result and request communication. Results may be much larger and hence more time consuming to be sent than simple requests of type Int. When requests are sent concurrently and directly to the master, they can be received and processed faster, speeding up work distribution. This, however, applies only if the master is not too busy collecting results.

In this section, we consider a skeleton which collects the results hierarchically to unload the master, but sends requests and tasks *directly* from the master to the workers. The inner processes of the process tree collect the results from their child processes, but also serve as additional workers. The result streams of inner workers are merged with the collected ones, and forwarded to their parent process. To speed up the work distribution, we additionally separate the task distributor functionality of the master from its collector role (also proposed in [6]), which is only a minor change to the

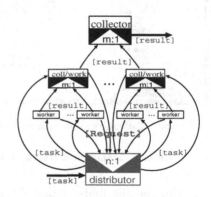

Fig. 6. Result-hierarchical scheme with separation of distributor and collector

previous result-hierarchical skeleton. The result-collecting master creates a distributor process and redirects the direct connections between master and workers to exchange tasks and results. The resulting process structure is depicted in Figure 6.

Figure 7 shows traces for the non-hierarchical skeleton with concurrent request handling, with and without a separate distributor process, and a variant which collects results in a hierarchy, with 4 submasters. As shown in trace (a), concurrent request handling alone does not improve the skeleton performance.

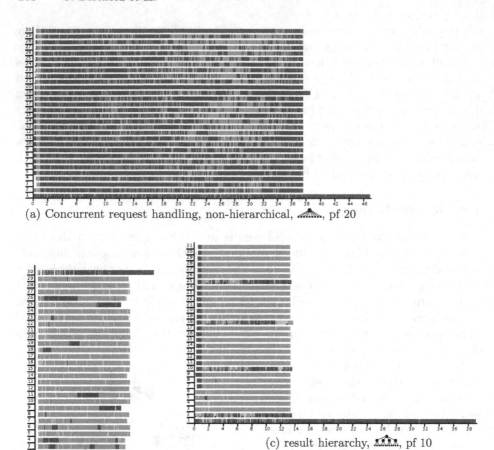

(a) Concurrent request handling, non-hierarchical, ⛰⛰⛰, pf 20

(c) result hierarchy, ⛰⛰⛰, pf 10

(b) separate distributor, non-hierarchical ⛰⛰⛰, pf 20

Fig. 7. Mandelbrot traces, different result-hierarchical skeletons

Separating the distributor (trace (b), top bar shows distributor) already creates an almost steady workload for the workers, but exposes the same long post-processing. A result hierarchy (trace (c), without separate distributor) shortens the post-processing phase to some extent, while keeping the same positive effect on worker load.

3   Dynamic Creation of New Tasks

Except for some problems consisting of independent tasks which are trivial to parallelise, e.g. mandelbrot, ray tracing and other graphical problems, many problems deliver tasks containing inherent data dependencies. Thus, the task pool is not completely known initially, or it depends on other calculation results to be fully defined. This is the case when the problem space is built hierarchically, as a tree structure or following other, more complex, patterns.

3.1 The Dynamic Master-Worker Skeleton

The elementary master-worker skeleton can easily be extended to enable the dynamic creation of additional tasks within the worker processes. In the version shown in Figure 8, the worker processes deliver a list of new tasks with each result, and the master simply adds the new tasks to its task queue. A straightforward extension would be to let the master filter or transform the task queue, considering global information (main point of investigation in [7]).

```
mwDyn :: (Trans t, Trans r) => Int -> Int -> (t -> (r,[t])) -> [t] -> [r]
mwDyn n prefetch wf initTasks = finalResults
 where -- identical to static task pool except for the type of workers
        (reqs, ress) =  (unzip . merge) (spawn workers inputs)
        workers      =  [process (zip [i,i..] . map wf) | i <- [0..n-1]]
        inputs       =  distribute n tasks (initReqs ++ reqs)
        initReqs     =  concat (replicate prefetch [0..n-1])
        -- additions for task queue management and termination detection
        tasks        =  initTasks ++ newTasks
        initNumTasks =  length initTasks
        (finalResults, newTasks) = tdetect ress initNumTasks

-- task queue control for termination detection
tdetect :: [(r,[t])] -> Int -> ([r], [t])
tdetect ((r,[]):ress) 1     = ([r], []) -- final result
tdetect ((r,ts):ress) numTs = (r:moreRes, ts ++ moreTs)
  where (moreRes, moreTs) = tdetect ress (numTs-1+length ts)
```

Fig. 8. Eden master-worker skeleton with a dynamic task pool

The static task pool version terminates as soon as all the tasks have been processed. With dynamic task creation, explicit termination detection becomes necessary, because the task list contains a reference to potential new tasks. In the skeleton shown in Figure 8, a function tdetect keeps track of the current number of tasks in process. It is essential that the result list is extracted via tdetect and that the evaluation of this function is driven by the result stream. As long as new tasks are generated, the function is recursively called with an updated task counter, initialised to the length of the skeleton input.[2] As soon as the result of the last task arrives, the system terminates by closing the tasks list and, via distribute, the input streams of the worker processes.

---

[2] The reader might notice that the initial task list now has to have fixed length. This skeleton cannot be used in a context where the input tasks arrive as a stream.

3.2   Nesting the Dynamic Task Pool Version

It would be possible to apply the simple nesting scheme from Section 2 to the dynamic master-worker skeleton mwDyn. However, newly created tasks would always remain in the lower submaster-worker level because the interface of mwDyn only passes results, but not tasks, to upper levels. For nesting, the dynamic master-worker scheme mwDyn has to be generalised to enable a more sophisticated task management within the submaster nodes.

Each submaster receives a task stream from its master and a result stream including new tasks from its workers. It has to produce task streams for its workers and a result stream including new tasks for its master (see Figure 9). Sending back all dynamically generated tasks is a waste of bandwidth, when they might be needed in the local subtree. A portion of the generated new tasks can be kept locally, but surplus tasks must be passed up to the next level. Furthermore, sending a result should *not* automatically be interpreted as a request for a new task, since tasks kept locally

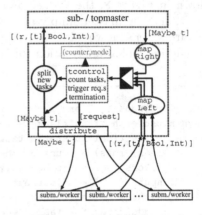

Fig. 9. Submaster functionality in the dynamic master-worker hierarchy

can compensate for solved tasks. Finally, global information about tasks in process is needed at the top-level, to decide when to terminate the system. The Eden code for the submaster in Figure 10 shows the necessary changes:

- The input stream for submasters and workers has type Maybe t, where the value Nothing serves as a termination signal, propagated downwards from the top level.
- The output stream of submasters (and workers) now includes information about the number of tasks kept locally, and a Bool flag, indicating the request for a new task, leading to type [(r,[t],Bool,Int)].
- The incoming list initTasks for submasters is a stream, which has to be *merged* with the stream of worker answers, and processed by a central control function tcontrol. The origin of each input to tcontrol is indicated by tags Left (worker answers) and Right (parent input), using the Haskell sum type Either (Int,(r,[t],Bool,Int)) (Maybe t)
- All synchronisation is concentrated in the task control function tcontrol. It both controls the local task queue, passes new requests to distribute, and propagates results (and a portion of generated tasks) to the upper levels.

The heart of the dynamic master-worker hierarchy is the function tcontrol, shown in Figure 11. It maintains two counters: one for the amount of tasks

```
mwDynSub :: (Trans t, Trans r) =>
            Int -> Int -> ([Maybe t] -> [(r,[t],Bool,Int)])
            -> [Maybe t] -> [(r,[t],Bool,Int)]
mwDynSub n pf wf initTasks = finalResults where
  fromWorkers  = spawn workers inputs
  -- worker     :: [Process [Maybe t] [(Int,(r,[t],Bool,Int))]]
  workers      = [process (zip [i,i..] . wf) | i <- [0..n-1]]
  inputs       = distribute n tasks (initReqs ++ reqs)
  initReqs     = concat (replicate pf [0..n-1])
  -- task queue management
  ctrlInput = merge (map Right initTasks : map (map Left) fromWorkers)
  (finalResults, tasks, reqs) = tcontrol (n*pf+n) (False,0,0) ctrlInput
```

Fig. 10. Eden submaster for nested dynamic master-worker skeleton

that have been generated and passed up to this submaster, to decide whether a request must be sent up, and the overall task count in the subtree below.

Tasks sent by the parent are simply enqueued in the local task queue. Tasks generated by workers are split into a part that is kept local, and a part that is passed upwards. The nested task pools can be seen as a system of interdependent *buffers*, and both buffer-underruns and buffer-overruns will spoil the skeleton performance. This is relatively easy for a static task list: the exchange of tasks and results between different buffers is limited, and the prefetch parameter defines the maximum buffer size. In the extension for dynamically growing task

```
tcontrol _ (_,_,0) ((Right Nothing):_)   -- from above, final termination
= ([],repeat Nothing,[])
tcontrol pf (even,local,numTs) ((Right (Just t)):ress) -- task from above
= let (moreRes, moreTs, reqs) = tcontrol pf (even, local ,numTs+1) ress
    in (moreRes, (Just t):moreTs, reqs)
-- from i below, (result, new tasks, flag, no. of retained tasks)
tcontrol pf (even,local,numTs) ((Left (i,(r,ts,wantNew,tBelow))):ress)
= let (localTs,fatherTs,evenAct) = split numTs pf ts even
          newLocal = length localTs + local
            - if wantNew && not newTasksForMe then 1 else 0
          newNumTs = numTs-1 + length localTs + tBelow
          (moreRes, moreTs, reqs)
            = tcontrol pf (evenAct, newLocal, newNumTs) ress
          newreqs = if wantNew then i:reqs else reqs
          newTasksForMe = local + length localTs == 0 && wantNew
    in ((r, fatherTs, newTasksForMe, heldBelow + lenlocalTs):moreRes,
            (map Just localTs) ++ moreTs, newreqs)
```

Fig. 11. Control function for submaster of Figure 10

pools, more sophisticated policies are needed instead of mechanically forwarding new tasks and requests.

To achieve a roughly even level of tasks in each submaster, the task pool size is limited by two thresholds (sometimes called low and high watermark [3]). When too few tasks are locally generated, additional new tasks must be requested from the upper level, while all surplus tasks must be forwarded to upper levels. In our version, tcontrol emits requests when all self-generated tasks have been assigned, thereby trying to maintain its initial local task buffer size, given by the prefetch parameter. The split function decides how many tasks to hold in the subtree below a submaster. If a sufficient amount of self-generated tasks fills the subtree below the node (overall task count numTs), all generated tasks are forwarded to the upper level. The split function we use (not shown) splits generated tasks one half each, until the total task count exceeds the double prefetch for the whole subtree below. Different heuristics can be configured by exchanging the split function, and minor changes in tcontrol.

The top-level master in the nesting scheme for a dynamic task pool works similar to the submasters we have described, but of course cannot forward tasks to the outside. A separate top-level master has to be defined.

```
topMaster :: (Trans t, Trans r) =>
        Int -> Int -> ([Maybe t] -> [(r,[t],Bool,Int)]) -> [t] -> [r]
```

Besides termination detection, the former tdetect function now takes the role of tcontrol in the submaster processes, also incorporating the more sophisticated request handling we have introduced in the tcontrol function. Further changes are the adaption of the worker function to the Maybe type interface and the termination signal Nothing for all submasters upon termination.

3.3   Experimental Results

The skeletons that support dynamic task creation have been tested with a special test application: a program which computes all satisfying variable assignments for a particular logical formula (i.e. it is a specialised SAT problem solver). Tasks are incomplete variable assignments, and the workers successively assign a value to a new variable and partially evaluate the result. An assignment that already yields false is immediately discarded, true results are counted, yet unspecified results are new tasks returned to the level above.

The test program runs the satisfiability check for a formula which disjoins *all* conjunctions of n logical variables where k variables are negated (yielding $\binom{n}{k}$ disjoint monoms). In the underlying *search tree* of the SAT problem, each node has at most two child nodes, but for particular formulas, many subproblem nodes in the search tree can immediately be discarded. Using a formula of 200 variables and 1 negation tests the skeleton behaviour for such a broad sparse tree. Especially with sparse search trees, it is challenging for the load balancing strategy to evenly fill the process hierarchy with tasks, avoiding idle times. Many tasks can be discarded early, but the test for 200 variables is complex. In contrast, a test with negated 8 variables out of 16 shows the performance for a dense tree

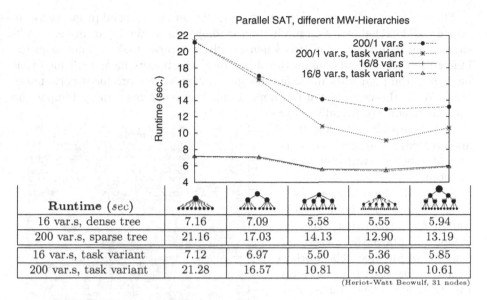

Runtime (sec)					
16 var.s, dense tree	7.16	7.09	5.58	5.55	5.94
200 var.s, sparse tree	21.16	17.03	14.13	12.90	13.19
16 var.s, task variant	7.12	6.97	5.50	5.36	5.85
200 var.s, task variant	21.28	16.57	10.81	9.08	10.61

(Heriot-Watt Beowulf, 31 nodes)

Fig. 12. Experiments using skeletons for dynamic task pool

with very small tasks. Runtimes have been compared for the basic skeleton, for hierarchies with one level of two, four and six submasters, and for a binary hierarchy with two levels.

Flat vs. Hierarchical Skeleton: In general, variants of hierarchical master-worker schemes perform better than the non-hierarchical skeleton in our test runs. However, when testing a formula with only 16 variables, tasks are numerous, but very simple. For this variant, hierarchical skeletons yield smaller runtime gains.

Depth vs. Breadth: The runtime comparison in Figure 12 shows that, in our setup of 31 machines, broader hierarchies with only one level perform better than the binary two-level hierarchy. The variant with 6 submasters yields the best results, whether sparse or dense decision trees. Measurements with a simplified test procedure, where tasks are checked very quickly using additional knowledge about the tested formula, confirm this result: The performance of the skeleton with two-level nesting is slightly worse than for the one-level nestings. Of course, this result again has to be qualified for bigger clusters.

Prefetch and Forwarding Policy: Prefetch values have little influence on performance (or trace appearance) for this test program, since there are relatively few tasks in the beginning anyway and many of the generated tasks are held close to the processing units. Higher prefetch values only lead to "bundled" working and idle phases instead of a more steady workload. Using higher prefetches, we also observed periods of global inactivity, again caused by garbage collections of the top-level master.

The partition policy for tasks returned by workers is a crucial property for an even global load balance. Our minimum threshold, the prefetch parameter, is self-suggesting: requests are emitted when locally generated tasks cannot keep the buffer filled. For the maximum threshold, our experiments have confirmed that increasing the high watermark for the split policy hardly produces perfomance gains. While the very existence of a maximum threshold has principal impact on the load balance (especially in our setup where only few new tasks are created), it is not necessary to add another parameter to the skeleton.

Figure 13 shows a trace for a program run using the best skeleton in our experiment, with six submasters above the leaves, on a sparse decision tree. The workers expose a slow startup phase, since the (relatively few) tasks must first be propagated in all branches. Tasks are well distributed among the different submaster branches, leading to an even workload among the worker processes. Even though some PEs are reserved as submasters, the remaining workers outperform the non-hierachical skeleton close to factor 2.

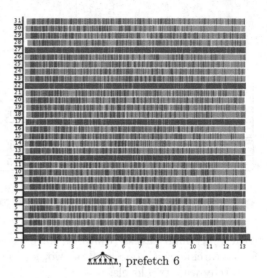

, prefetch 6

Fig. 13. Trace for SAT solver (200/1 var.)

4   Related Work

The commonly used master-worker scheme with a single master managing a set of workers is a well-known scheme which has been used in many different languages [1]. Modifications of this scheme are however more rare, and we are not aware of general hierarchical master-worker schemes like ours.

Driven by the insight that the propagation of messages is expensive in a master-worker scheme, Poldner and Kuchen [6] present a variant where the master is divided into a task distributor (*dispatcher*) and a result *collector*. As described in 2.4, we extended this variant to a skeleton with a hierarchy of collectors and only one distributor. In order to save communication, the dispatcher of Poldner and Kuchen applies a *static* task distribution, and they argue that for a large number of tasks, a roughly even load balance can be expected. However, this contradicts one basic idea of dynamic master-worker skeletons: the intention to balance not only task irregularity, but also potential differences in worker performance.

In [5], Poldner and Kuchen investigate skeletons for branch & bound problems. A centralized master-worker skeleton is compared to a set of distributed workers connected by a bidirectional ring, without a central master. Distributed workers can establish load balance using a supply-driven or a demand-driven mechanism. In addition to the load balancing problem, the paper addresses branch & bound-specific requirements like fast propagation of updated bounds, and distributed termination detection. In the experiments with two branch & bound algorithms, the distributed skeleton with demand-driven load balancing shows best performance, due to the reduced communication need.

Hippold and Rünger describe *task pool teams* [2], a programming environment for SMP clusters that is explicitly tailored towards irregular problems with strong inter-task dependences. The scheme comprises a set of task pools, each running on its own SMP node, and interacting via explicit message passing. Dynamic task creation by workers, task migration, and distributed task pools with a task stealing mechanism are possible. Locality can be exploited to hold global data on the SMP nodes, while communication between nodes is used for task migration, remote data access, and global synchronisation.

Various load balancing strategies for divide-and-conquer algorithms are discussed by Nieuwpoort et al., in [8]. The authors experiment with different techniques to exchange tasks between autonomous worker processes, in the context of WAN-connected clusters (hierachical wide-area systems). Aside from special optimisations to handle different network properties, a basic distinction is made between task *pushing* and *stealing* approaches. Demand-driven work stealing strategies are generally considered advantageous, but must take into account the high latency connections in question. The work pushing strategy speculatively (and blindly) forwards tasks to *random* peers when the amount of local tasks exceeds a prefetch threshold. Contrary to the randomised, or purely demand-driven, task distribution in this work, our skeletons are always based on task-request cycles, and concentrate surplus tasks at higher levels.

5 Conclusions

We have given a series of functional implementations of the parallel master-worker scheme. The declarative approach enables a clear conceptual view of the skeleton nesting we have developed.

Starting with a very compact version of the standard scheme, we have given implementations for skeleton nesting, to shift the administrative load to a whole hierarchy of (sub-)masters. The hierarchies have been elegantly expressed as foldings over the modified basic scheme. In the case of a dynamically growing task pool, a termination detection mechanism is needed. Nesting this skeleton is far more complex and needs special code for submasters, especially an appropriate task forwarding policy in the submaster processes.

As our tests show, master-worker hierarchies generally speed up runtime and keep workers busier, avoiding the bottleneck of a flat skeleton. Hierarchy layout and suitable prefetch values, however, have to be chosen carefully, depending on the target architecture and problem characteristics. Our experiments show the importance of suitable task distribution and task forwarding policies, which we have described and discussed in detail.

We have presented implementations and experiments with a range of hierarchical master-worker variants, and we will continue investigations on some open topics. As ongoing work, we will develop distributed work pools, like the one proposed by Poldner and Kuchen in [5], and compare them to our master-worker hierarchies.

Acknowledgements. We greatly appreciate the opportunity to conduct runtime experiments on the Beowulf cluster of the Heriot-Watt University in Edinburgh.

References

1. Danelutto, M., Pasqualetti, F., Pelagatti, S.: Skeletons for Data Parallelism in P^3L. In: Lengauer, C., Griebl, M., Gorlatch, S. (eds.) Euro-Par 1997. LNCS, vol. 1300, pp. 619–628. Springer, Heidelberg (1997)
2. Hippold, J., Rünger, G.: Task Pool Teams: A Hybrid Programming Environment for Irregular Algorithms on SMP Clusters. Concurrency and Computation: Practice and Experience 18, 1575–1594 (2006)
3. Loidl, H.-W.: Load Balancing in a Parallel Graph Reducer. In: Hammond, K., Curtis, S. (eds.) SFP 2001 — Scottish Functional Programming Workshop, Bristol, UK. Trends in Functional Programming, vol. 3, pp. 63–74 (2001) (Intellect)
4. Loogen, R., Ortega-Mallén, Y., Peña-Marí, R.: Parallel Functional Programming in Eden. Journal of Functional Programming 15(3), 431–475 (2005)
5. Poldner, M., Kuchen, H.: Algorithmic skeletons for branch & bound. In: Filipe, J., Shishkov, B., Helfert, M. (eds.) ICSOFT (1), pp. 291–300. INSTICC Press (2006)
6. Poldner, M., Kuchen, H.: Scalable farms. In: Joubert, G.R., Nagel, W.E., Peters, F.J., Plata, O.G., Tirado, P., Zapata, E.L. (eds.) ParCo 2005. Parallel Computing: Current & Future Issues of High-End Computing, Jülich, Germany. NIC Series, vol. 33, pp. 795–802 (2006)
7. Priebe, S.: Dynamic Task Generation and Transformation within a Nestable Workpool Skeleton. In: Nagel, W.E., Walter, W.V., Lehner, W. (eds.) Euro-Par 2006. LNCS, vol. 4128, pp. 615–624. Springer, Heidelberg (2006)
8. van Nieuwpoort, R.V., Kielmann, T., Bal, H.E.: Efficient load balancing for wide-area divide-and-conquer applications. In: PPoPP 2001. Proceedings of the eighth ACM SIGPLAN symposium on Principles and practices of parallel programming, pp. 34–43. ACM Press, New York (2001)

High-Level Multi-threading Programming in Logtalk

Paulo Moura[1], Paul Crocker[1], and Paulo Nunes[2]

[1] Dep. of Computer Science, University of Beira Interior
6201-001 Covilh, Portugal
Phone: +351 275319891; Fax: +351 275319899
pmoura@di.ubi.pt, crocker@di.ubi.pt
[2] Polytechnic Institute of Guarda
6301-559 Guarda, Portugal
Phone: +351 271220120; Fax: +351 271220150
pnunes@ipg.pt

Abstract. Logtalk, an object oriented logic programming language, provides experimental support for multi-threading programming with selected back-end Prolog compilers. By making use of core, low-level Prolog predicates that interface with operating-system native threads, Logtalk provides a high-level set of directives and predicates that allows programmers to easily take advantage of modern multi-processor and multi-core computers without worrying about the details of creating, synchronizing, or communicating with threads. Logtalk multi-threading programming features include support for concurrent calls akin to and-parallelism and or-parallelism, non-deterministic thread goals, asynchronous calls, and predicate synchronization. The integration with the Logtalk object-oriented features allows objects to send and receive both synchronous and asynchronous messages and to call local predicates concurrently. Logtalk multi-threading features are orthogonal to object-oriented concepts and can be useful even in the context of plain Prolog.

Keywords: logic-programming, concurrency, threads.

1 Introduction

In recent years, computers supporting multiple processors and multi-core processors have become mainstream. Major players in the hardware business such as Intel, AMD, or IBM provide complete lines of multi-core processors for desktop and portable computers. In fact, nowadays, we have to look hard to buy a single-core personal computer. Coupled with the support for multi-threading applications found on current operating systems, there is a strong incentive to migrate from pure sequential programs to programs that take performance and responsiveness advantages from using multiple threads.

Writing multi-threading applications implies using programming languages that provide the necessary support for thread creation, synchronization, and

P. Hudak and D.S. Warren (Eds.): PADL 2008, LNCS 4902, pp. 265–281, 2008.

communication. One of the most commonly used multi-threading Application Programming Interface (API) is defined by the POSIX standard. The POSIX threads API or, as commonly know, *pthreads*, is a set of C functions dealing with thread management, mutual exclusion, and condition variables[1] [1,2]. Given that most Prolog compilers are implemented in C or C++, pthreads is a common choice for providing core, low-level multi-threading built-in predicate support. However, despite threads being a powerful programming mechanism, it is easy to get into trouble when failing to properly synchronize threads accessing shared resources such as input/output streams and dynamic state. Although there are always tasks where a low-level multi-threading API is necessary, programming scenarios where a simpler, high-level interface is preferred are common. Recently, high level multi-threading programming constructs for imperative languages have become popular. For example, the OpenMP API [3,4] implements high level programming constructs for shared-memory parallel applications, working as a pre-processor for C, C++ and Fortran. Another example is Intel's Threading Building Blocks [5], which provides high-level, task-based parallelism to C++. In the case of Prolog, earlier attempts to automate code parallelization proved difficult due to language semantic issues, e.g. order-dependency between goals. Nevertheless, extensive research [6] has resulted in a number of successful experimental systems, such as e.g. Andorra-I [7] and Muse [8]. These systems suffer from maintenance and portability problems, however, stemming from the complexity of their inner workings. Therefore, we cannot always rely on them for industrial applications. Logtalk [9,10] takes a more pragmatic approach, striving for a simple and minimal set of directives and built-in predicates that allows programmers to easily take advantage of modern multi-processor and multi-core computers without worrying about low-level details of creating, synchronizing, or communicating with threads. Our work is motivated by past experiences with multi-agents systems (mostly using Logtalk with Peter Robinson's Qu-Prolog) and by a current project on the validation of large CAD/CAM data model files [11] where most steps are natural candidates for parallelization due to their independence and being side-effects free. Logtalk multi-threading development is guided by four main goals: (1) simple support for making concurrent calls, mostly for parallelizing independent computations; (2) support for asynchronous calls, where we can start a computing thread, perform some other tasks, and later retrieve the thread goal solutions; (3) simple directives for predicates that need to be synchronized due to side-effects; (4) a portable and robust implementation, capable of running with several back-end Prolog compilers in most operating-systems. Interestingly, these goals are orthogonal to Logtalk object-oriented features. Although objects provides an execution context for our multi-threading predicates and directives, where we take advantage of objects encapsulation and of objects local database, our results can also be applied in the context of plain Prolog (complementing, not replacing, core low-level multi-threading support).

---

[1] Condition variables allow the implementation of notification mechanisms where a thread suspends execution until some condition becomes true.

This paper begins by describing the core support found on current Prolog compilers for multi-threading programming, used as a foundation for our work. Second, the Logtalk multi-threading programming features are presented and discussed. A brief comparison with related work follows. We conclude by discussing the current status of our work. Full documentation, complete code of the examples, and the implementation of the multi-threading features described in this paper are available with the current Logtalk stable distribution. The reader is invited to try out and give feedback on the actual system.

2 Starting Point: Prolog Multi-threading Core Support

Prolog compilers such as SWI-Prolog [12], YAP [13], Qu-Prolog [14,15], BinProlog [16,17], XSB [18,19], or Ciao [20] provide a low-level, comprehensive set of built-in predicates supporting multi-threading programming. Most of these Prolog compilers make use of pthreads or, for some operating systems, of a suitable emulation. A recent ISO standardization proposal [21], started in April 2006, aims to specify a common core of low-level multi-threading programming support based on the semantics of POSIX threads[2]. We have decided to base the Logtalk high-level support for multi-threading programming on this common interface. The current Logtalk version supports multi-threading programming using SWI-Prolog, YAP, and XSB as back-end Prolog compilers; we expect soon to be able to support Qu-Prolog, pending on-going work on the implementation of the current standardization proposal.

The current ISO standardization proposal specifies a comprehensive set of predicates for thread, mutex, and message queue management. It also includes a set of predicates for querying and setting thread creation default options. Most of these options deal with the different per-thread memory areas such as the stacks used by the Prolog implementation. The size of these memory areas is specially relevant for 32-bit architectures. The maximum number of threads we can create before exhausting the memory address space[3] can be severely limited by default size values aimed to cover most cases without the need of hand-tuning. Prolog implementations differ on their memory handling mechanisms. For heavily multi-threaded applications, implementations using *stack-shifters* for keeping default memory sizes small, dynamically expanding memory only when necessary, have an advantage over implementations that allocate large chunks of virtual memory space to simplify memory handling, relying on the operating system virtual memory mechanisms. This is important for a high-level multi-threading API such as the one provided by Logtalk, where it is not desirable to force the programmer to worry about such low-level details as the default thread stack size. Another key feature of the ISO proposal is that threads do not share

---

[2] The standardization group includes so far SWI-Prolog, YAP, Qu-Prolog, XSB, and Ciao developers. Collaboration from other interested parties is most welcome.

[3] Note that we are talking about virtual memory space; actually used memory is often much less.

variables. This feature both constrains and simplifies the Logtalk multi-threading features and their implementation.

3 Logtalk Multi-threading Support: Overview

Logtalk multi-threading programming is supported by a small set of built-in predicates and directives, which can be regarded as a high-level API complementing, not replacing, the core, lower-level API provided by selected Prolog compilers. This high-level API can be split in three groups of predicates and a set of directives. The first group contains a single predicate, `threaded/1`, which supports concurrent calls akin to and-parallelism and or-parallelism. The second group of predicates provide support for asynchronous calls, here interpreted as separating proving a goal from the retrieval of the goal solutions. Two basic predicates are provided, `threaded_call/1` and `threaded_exit/1`, supporting non-deterministic thread goals. From these two predicates, we derive three specialized predicates: `threaded_once/1`, `threaded_ignore/1`, and `threaded_peek/1`. The third group of predicates allows thread synchronization using notifications, which are arbitrary, programmer-defined non-variable terms. Notifications are used as a peer-to-peer mechanism supported by the predicates `threaded_wait/1` and `threaded_notify/1`. The Logtalk multi-threading directives include two object directives, `threaded/0` and `synchronized/0`, and a predicate directive, `synchronized/1`, enabling an object to make multi-threading calls and supporting object and predicate-level synchronization. Logtalk multi-threading predicate calls always take place within the context of an object[4]. Thus, objects are able to send and receive both synchronous and asynchronous messages and to call local predicates concurrently. In the following sections, we provide a detailed account of Logtalk multi-threading support, illustrated with several examples, with an emphasis on the technical aspects of the current implementation.

4 Object Message Queues

Logtalk object message queues are used whenever an object defines predicates that make concurrent calls or asynchronous calls. In order to automatically create and set up an object message queue the `threaded/0` object directive is used:

```
:- threaded.
```

The object message queue is created when the object is compiled and loaded into memory or when created at runtime (the message queue for the pseudo-object *user* is automatically created at Logtalk startup). These message queues are only bounded be available memory and are used internally for storing replies to the threaded calls made from within the objects themselves and for exchanging thread notifications, as we will discuss later. The implicit use of object message

---

[4] When at the Logtalk top-level interpreter, the execution context is the pseudo-object *user*.

queues for storing and exchanging thread results provides a cleaner and simpler alternative to the explicit use of blackboards or the dynamic database, as found on some other systems.

It is tempting to make this directive optional, thus simplifying Logtalk multi-threading programming. In most cases, the Logtalk compiler could simply set up the creation of the object message queue when finding a call to a multi-threading built-in predicate in the body of an object predicate. However, it is always possible to construct new goals at runtime that call the multi-threading built-in predicates. In addition, an object may import a category[5] whose predicates make multi-threading calls (see section 7.3 for an example). Creating the object message queue on the fly is possible but would lead to runtime errors if the back-end Prolog compiler does not support all the core multi-threading features Logtalk relies on. Thus, we choose to make the `threaded/0` object directive mandatory. This allows us to both check at compile time for proper back-end Prolog compiler support and to cope with threaded goals generated at runtime in ways that cannot be anticipated by the Logtalk compiler.

5   Making Concurrent Calls

Logtalk provides a basic multi-threading built-in predicate, `threaded/1`, which supports concurrent calls akin to both and-parallelism and or-parallelism. In this context, and-parallelism and or-parallelism refers to using, respectively, a conjunction of goals and a disjunction of goals as a predicate argument. This built-in predicate is deterministic and opaque to cuts. Each goal in its argument is proved in its own thread (except when the argument is neither a conjunction nor a disjunction of goals, in which case no threads are created for proving it and the predicate is equivalent to the standard Prolog built-in predicate `once/1`). Goals can be calls to local object predicates, messages to *self*, or messages to other objects. Thus, both local predicates and other object methods can be called concurrently.

5.1   And-Parallelism

When the argument is a conjunction of goals, the `threaded/1` predicate call blocks the caller thread until either one of thread goals fails, rises an exception, or all the implicit thread goals succeed. A failure or an exception leads to the immediate termination of the other threads. The *and-parallelism* functionality of the `threaded/1` predicate covers a common programming pattern on multi-threading applications: parallelizing a set of independent computations. Here, independent computations translate to a conjunction of goals with no shared variables. Thus, each goal can be proved in parallel without worrying about synchronizing variable instantiations or suspending a thread goal until a variable is instantiated.

---

[5] Logtalk categories are object building blocks (components), which can be virtually imported (without code duplication) by any object, irrespective of inheritance relations.

Nevertheless, it turns out that forbidding the use of shared variables is over-restrictive and, with care, the programmer can sometimes use shared variables to further improve performance. For example, assume that we want to find all prime numbers in a given interval using two threads. We could write:

```
prime_numbers(N, M, Primes) :-
    M > N,
    N1 is N + (M - N) // 2,
    N2 is N1 + 1,
    threaded((
        prime_numbers(N2, M, [], Acc),
        prime_numbers(N, N1, Acc, Primes)
    )).
```

In this simple example, the two prime_numbers/4 goals in the threaded/1 predicate call share a variable (Acc) that acts as an accumulator, allowing us to avoid a call to an append/3 predicate at the end (which would cancel part of the performance gains of using multi-threading). At a user level, sharing variables meets the expectations of a programmer used to single-threading programming and suggests easy parallelization of single-threaded code by simply wrapping-around goals in threaded/1 predicate calls. At the implementation level, sharing variables between thread goals is problematic as the core Prolog thread creation predicates make a copy of the thread goal, thus loosing variable bindings. When a thread goal terminates, the variable bindings are reconstructed by Logtalk in the process of retrieving the goal solutions. That is, shared variables are only synchronized after thread termination. A failure to synchronize shared variables results in the failure of the threaded/1 call. Depending on how each goal uses the shared variables, their use may lead to other problems. For example, a predicate call may depend on a shared variable being instantiated in order to behave properly. This will not work as the thread goals are independently proved. Safe use of shared variables implies that the individual thread goals do not depend on their instantiation, as in the example above where the shared variable is used only as an accumulator. Research on these cases, which are examples of *non-strict independent and-parallelism*, is described on [22].

5.2   Competing Threads: Reinterpreting Goal Disjunction

The threaded/1 predicate allows a disjunction of goals to be interpreted as a set of *competing* goals, each one running in its own thread. The first thread to terminate successfully leads to the termination of the other threads. Thus, the goals in a disjunction compete for a solution instead of being interpreted as possibly providing alternative solutions. This is useful when we have several methods to compute something, together with several processors or cores available, without knowing a priori which method will be faster or able to converge into a solution. For example, assume that we have implemented several methods for calculating the roots of real functions. We may then write:

```
find_root(Function, A, B, Error, Zero, Method) :-
    threaded((
            bisection::find_root(Function, A, B, Error, Zero),
            Method = bisection
        ;   newton::find_root(Function, A, B, Error, Zero),
            Method = newton
        ;   muller::find_root(Function, A, B, Error, Zero),
            Method = muller
    )).
```

The `threaded/1` call returns both the identifier of the fastest method and its result. Depending on the function and on the initial interval, one method may converge quickly into the function root while other method may simply diverge, never finding it. This is a pattern typical of other classes of algorithms (e.g. graph path-finding methods or matrix eigenvalues calculation methods), making the `threaded/1` predicate useful for a wide range of problems.

It is important to stress that only the first successful goal on a disjunction can lead to the instantiation of variables on the original argument. Thus, we do not need to worry about the representation of multiple bindings of the same variable across different disjunction goals.

The effectiveness of this predicate relies on two factors: (1) the ability to cancel the slower threads once a winning thread completes and (2) the number of cores available. Canceling a thread is not always possible or as fast as desirable as a thread can be in a state where no interrupts are accepted, depending on the computations being performed. Aborting a thread is tricky in most multi-threading APIs, including pthreads. In the worst case scenario, some slower threads may run up to completion. Most current laptop and desktop computers contain two, four, or eight cores, making the possible waste of processing power by slower, non cancelable threads problematic. However, the number of cores per-processor is expected to rise steadily over the next years with each new generation of processors, making the concept of *competitive or-parallelism* presented here an interesting proposal for implementing speculative threading (see e.g. [23]). Thus, the usefulness of the `threaded/1` predicate or-parallelism functionality is both hardware bounded and application-domain dependent.

6   Making Asynchronous Calls

Logtalk provides two basic multi-threading built-in predicates, `threaded_call/1` and `threaded_exit/1`, which allows us to make asynchronous calls and to later retrieve the corresponding results. Paired `threaded_call/1` and `threaded_exit/1` calls must be made from within the same object. An asynchronous call can be either a call to a local object predicate or a message sending call. Being asynchronous, a call to the `threaded_call/1` predicate is always true and results in the creation of a new thread for proving its argument. In addition, no variable binding occurs as a consequence of the call. The thread results (goal success, failure, or exception) are posted to the message queue of the execution context object. A simple example:

```
| ?- threaded_call(sort([3,1,7,4,2,9,8], _)).
yes

| ?- threaded_exit(sort([3,1,7,4,2,9,8], Sorted)).
Sorted = [1,2,3,4,7,8,9]
yes
```

This example shows how a `threaded_exit/1` call picks up the solutions from a `threaded_call/1` with a matching goal argument. When multiple threads run a matching goal, the `threaded_exit/1` call picks up the first thread to add a goal solution to the message queue of the execution context object. Calls to the `threaded_exit/1` predicate block the caller until the object message queue receives the reply to the asynchronous call. Logtalk provides a complementary predicate, `threaded_peek/1`, which may be used to check if a reply is already available without removing it from the object message queue. The `threaded_peek/1` predicate call succeeds or fails immediately without blocking the caller. However, repeated use of this predicate is equivalent to polling a thread queue, which may severely hurt performance.

When using asynchronous calls, the link between a `threaded_exit/1` call and the corresponding `threaded_call/1` call is made using unification. When there are several `threaded_call/1` calls for a matching `threaded_exit/1` call, the connection can potentially be established with any of them. For those cases where this behavior is deemed problematic (e.g. due to goal side-effects), Logtalk provides extended `threaded_call/2` and `threaded_exit/2` built-in predicates that allows the use of call identifier tags. For example:

```
| ?- threaded_call(sort([3,1,7,4,2,9,8], _), Tag1),
     threaded_call(sort([3,1,7,4,2,9,8], _), Tag2).
Tag1 = 1,
Tag2 = 2
yes

| ?- threaded_exit(sort([3,1,7,4,2,9,8], Sorted), 2).
Sorted = [1,2,3,4,7,8,9]
yes
```

Tags work as thread handles and should be regarded as instances of an opaque type. The concept of thread handles can also be found on some Prolog multithreading implementations such as Ciao and on the ISO standardization proposal in the specification of predicate `thread_create/3`.

6.1 Non-deterministic Goals

Asynchronous calls are often deterministic. Typically, they are used for performing some lengthy computation without blocking other aspects of an application. A common example is decoupling an interface from background computing threads. Nevertheless, Logtalk also allows non-deterministic asynchronous calls. The basic idea is that a computing thread suspends itself after providing a solution, waiting for a request for an alternative solution. For example, assuming a `lists` object implementing a `member/2` predicate, we could write:

```
| ?- threaded_call(lists::member(_, [1,2,3])).
yes

| ?- threaded_exit(lists::member(X, [1,2,3])).
X = 1 ;
X = 2 ;
X = 3 ;
no
```

In this case, the `threaded_call/1` and the `threaded_exit/1` calls are made within the pseudo-object *user*, whose message queue is used internally to store computed goal solutions. The implicit thread running the `lists::member/2` goal suspends itself after providing a solution, waiting for the request of an alternative solution; the thread is automatically terminated when the runtime engine detects that further backtracking to the `threaded_exit/1` call is no longer possible.

Supporting non-deterministic thread goals can be tricky as the thread is suspended between requests for alternative solutions: if a new request never occurs, the result could be a zombie thread. The current Logtalk implementation solves this problem by taking advantage of the `call_cleanup/2` built-in predicate found on a growing number of Prolog compilers. This predicate allows us to call a *clean-up* goal as soon as the Prolog runtime detects that a goal is finished because it succeeded or failed deterministically or because its choice-points have been cut[6].

There is one caveat when using the `threaded_exit/1` predicate that a programmer must be aware of, especially when using this predicate within failure-driven loops. When all the solutions have been found (and the thread generating them is therefore terminated), further calls to the predicate will generate an exception as the answering thread no longer exists. Note that failing instead of throwing an exception is not an acceptable solution as it could be misinterpreted as a failure of the thread goal.

For deterministic asynchronous calls, Logtalk provides a `threaded_once/1` built-in predicate that is more efficient when there is only one solution or when you want to commit to the first solution of the thread goal. In this case, the thread created for proving a goal stores the first solution on the message queue of the object making the `threaded_once/1` call and terminates. The solution thus becomes available for later retrieval by a call to the `threaded_exit/1` predicate.

---

[6] This functionality cannot be implemented at the Prolog level, making the availability of this built-in predicate an additional requirement for running Logtalk multi-threading applications with a specific back-end Prolog compiler. Standardization of this predicate is currently being discussed.

6.2 One-Way Asynchronous Calls

The built-in predicate `threaded_ignore/1` allows us to prove a goal in a new thread without caring about the results. For example, assume that we are developing a multi-agent application where an agent may send an *happy birthday* message to another agent. We could simply write:

```
..., threaded_ignore(agent::happy_birthday), ...
```

This call succeeds with no reply of the goal success, failure, or even exception ever being sent back to the message queue object making the call (note that this predicate implicitly implies a deterministic call of its argument).

7 Dealing with Side Effects: Synchronizing Predicate Calls

Proving goals in a multi-threading environment may lead to problems when the goals imply side-effects such as input/output operations or modifications to an object database. For example, if a new thread is started with the same goal before the first one finished its job, we may end up with mixed output, a corrupted database, or unexpected goal failures.

The usual solution for synchronizing calls is to use semaphores, mutexes, or some other similar mechanism. In the case of the multi-threading ISO standardization proposal, a set of built-in predicate for working with mutexes is already specified. We could certainly use them to synchronize predicate calls. However, working at this level, implies naming, locking, and unlocking mutexes. This is a task best performed by the compiler and the language runtime rather than the programmer who should only need to worry about declaring which predicate calls should be synchronized.

In Logtalk, predicates (and grammar rule non-terminals) with side-effects can be simply declared as synchronized by using either the `synchronized/0` object directive or the `synchronized/1` predicate directive. Together, these two directives allows from object-level synchronization to predicate-level synchronization. Proving a query to a synchronized predicate (or synchronized non-terminal) is protected internally by a mutex, thus allowing for easy thread synchronization.

7.1 Object-Level Synchronization

The `synchronized/0` object directive allows us to synchronize all object predicates using the same mutex:

```
:- synchronized.
```

This directive provides the simplest possible synchronization solution; it is useful for small objects where all or most predicates access the same shared resources.

7.2   Predicate-Level Synchronization

When fine-grained synchronization is preferred, the `synchronized/1` predicate directive allows us to synchronize subsets of an object predicates or a single object predicate. For example, the following two directives:

```
:- synchronized([write_buffer/1, read_buffer/1]).
:- synchronized(random/1).
```

will make calls to the `write_buffer/1` and `read_buffer/1` predicates synchronized using the same mutex while the predicate `random/1` will use a different mutex.

7.3   Synchronizing Predicate Calls Using Notifications

Declaring a set of predicates as synchronized can only ensure that they are not executed at the same time by different threads. Sometimes we need to suspend a thread not on a synchronization lock but on some condition that must hold true for a thread goal to proceed. That is, we want a thread goal to be suspended until a condition becomes true instead of simply failing. The built-in predicate `threaded_wait/1` allows us to suspend a predicate execution (running in its own thread) until a notification is received. Notifications are posted using the built-in predicate `threaded_notify/1`. A notification is a Prolog term that a programmer chooses to represent some condition becoming true. Any Prolog term can be used as a notification argument for these predicates. Related calls to the `threaded_wait/1` and `threaded_notify/1` must be made within the same object as its message queue is used internally for posting and retrieving notifications. Each notification posted by a call to the `threaded_notify/1` predicate is consumed by a single `threaded_wait/1` predicate call, i.e. these predicates implement a peer-to-peer mechanism. Care should be taken to avoid deadlocks when two (or more) threads both wait and post notifications to each other.

To see the usefulness of this notification mechanism consider the *dining philosophers* problem [24]: five philosophers sitting at a round table, thinking and eating, each sharing two chopsticks with its neighbors. Chopstick actions (picking up and putting down) can be easily synchronized using a notification such that a chopstick can only be handled by a single philosopher at a time:

```
:- category(chopstick).

    :- public([pick_up/0, put_down/0]).

    pick_up :-
        threaded_wait(available).

    put_down :-
        threaded_notify(available).

:- end_category.
```

There are five chopsticks, therefore we need to define the corresponding five objects. The code of all of them is similar:

```
:- object(cs1,
    imports(chopstick)).

    :- threaded.
    :- initialization(threaded_notify(available)).

:- end_object.
```

Each philosopher is represented by a simple object that specifies the left and right chopsticks. For example:

```
:- object(p2,
    imports(philosopher)).

    left_chopstick(cs2).
    right_chopstick(cs3).

:- end_object.
```

Deadlock is avoided by using the classical solution of exchanging the left and right chopsticks for one of the philosophers.

The full source code of this and other examples of the use of notifications to synchronize threads are provided with the current Logtalk distribution for the interested reader. Common usage patterns are generate-and-test scenarios where size-limited buffers are used for intermediate storage of candidate solutions. In these scenarios, a producer thread needs to suspend when the buffer is full, waiting for the consumer thread to notify it of available spots. Likewise, a consumer thread needs to suspends when the buffer is empty, waiting for the producer thread to notify it that new items are available for consumption.

8   Performance

Preliminary tests show that the performance of Logtalk multi-threading applications scales as expected with the number of threads used, bounded by the number of processing cores. The following table shows the relative speedup as we increase the number of threads in three simple benchmark tests: calculating primes numbers and sorting lists using the merge sort and the quicksort algorithms. The sorting examples allow some degree of scalability by using parametric threaded objects whose parameter is the number of threads to use.

Benchmark · Number of threads	1	2	4
Prime numbers (in the interval [1, 500000])	1.00	1.65	3.12
Merge sort (20000 float random numbers)	1.00	1.87	2.87
Quicksort (20000 float random numbers)	1.00	1.43	1.82

The corresponding multi-threading examples can be found on the current Logtalk distribution. The tests are performed on an Apple MacPro Dual 3.0GHz Dual-Core Intel Xeon 5100 with 2GB of RAM, running MacOS X 10.4.10. The back-end Prolog compiler used was SWI-Prolog 5.6.37. Similar speedups are observed with other Prolog compilers such as YAP and the current development version of XSB. Future work will look into quantifying the performance overhead added by the Logtalk high-level multi-threading predicates when compared with the core Prolog multi-threading predicates.

Use of multi-threading features is interesting for problems where the computation costs surpasses the overhead of thread creation and management. Part of this overhead is operating-system dependent. For example, we found that, on the hardware described above, Linux provide the fastest thread creation and thread join results, followed by Windows XP SP2, and than MacOS X 10.4. For practical applications, experimentation is necessary in order to fine-tune a multi-threading solution given the problem complexity, the number of processing cores, the back-end Prolog compiler, and the operating-system.

9   Related Work

Besides the Prolog compilers currently implementing the ISO standardization proposal, a number of other Prolog compilers provide alternative implementations of multi-threading concepts. Two of these compilers are BinProlog and Ciao Prolog, which we briefly discuss below. A prototype multi-threading version of SICStus Prolog is described in [25]. Outside the scope of Prolog compilers, Erlang [26,27] is one of the best known examples of declarative programming languages supporting concurrent (and distributed) systems.

9.1   BinProlog

BinProlog provides a set of multi-threading built-in predicates, ranging from simple, high-level predicates to lower-level predicates that give increasing control to the programmer. As this paper deals essentially with high-level predicates, two BinProlog predicates stand out. The predicate bg/1 allows a goal to be proved in its own thread. The predicate synchronize/1 uses an implicit mutex to prevent two threads of executing its argument concurrently.

Most BinProlog multi-threading examples use a blackboard for storing and retrieving thread goal results. The programmer must use the blackboard explicitly. In contrast, the use of object message queues by Logtalk for exchanging thread goal results is transparent to the programmer.

BinProlog supports thread synchronizing using *thread guards*. Thread guards, which work as mutexes, can be generated by calling the new_thread_guard/1 predicate and used with the predicates thread_wait/1, thread_notify/1, and thread_notify_all/1. Despite the name similarity, these predicates are quite different from the Logtalk threaded_wait/1 and threaded_notify/1 predicates where notifications are arbitrary non-variable Prolog terms chosen by the programmer.

9.2   Ciao Prolog

Ciao Prolog supports a concept of *engines*, which are used for proving a goal using a separate set of memory areas. These engines can use an operating-system thread for proving a goal, therefore providing support for concurrency. Similar to other Prolog compilers, goals are copied into engine, thus loosing variable bindings. Ciao provides a set of predicates for managing engines that rely on the use of goal identifiers to reference a specific engine. Goal identifiers play a role similar to the thread identifiers found on other Prolog compilers. The Prolog database is shared between threads and is used as the primary means of thread communication and synchronization. Ciao makes use of *concurrent* predicates, which are dynamic predicates that allow thread execution to be suspended until a new clause is asserted. Ciao supports non-deterministic thread goals, providing a `eng_backtrack/2` predicate to backtrack over thread goals. When a thread goal fails, the engine is not automatically terminated; the programmer must explicitly call a `eng_release/1` predicate. This contrasts with Logtalk where a thread is automatically terminated when the thread goal fails. It is possible that the implementation in Ciao of a functionality similar to the one provided by the `call_cleanup/2-3` predicate would also allow transparent engine release.

9.3   SWI-Prolog High-Level Multi-threading Library

Recent SWI-Prolog versions include a new high-level multi-threading library. This library provides two predicates, `concurrent/3` and `first_solution/3`, which provide functionality similar to the Logtalk predicate `threaded/1`. The predicate `concurrent/3` allows easy concurrent execution of a set of goals. The caveats listed in the SWI-Prolog library documentation are basically the same that apply to Logtalk and to every other Prolog compiler making a copy of a goal when using a thread: users of this predicate are advised against using shared goal variables. This seems to be more of a cautious advise for safe use the `concurrent/3` predicate than an implementation limitation (note that both this SWI-Prolog library and Logtalk rely on the same core multi-threading built-in predicates). The predicate `first_solution/3` runs a set of goals concurrently and picks the first one to complete, killing the other threads. This predicate shares with the Logtalk `threaded/1` predicate the same potential thread cancelation problem: a thread may be in a state where no signals are being processed, delaying or preventing thread cancelation. The SWI-Prolog library predicates allows the user to specify a list of options that will be used by the underlying calls to the core `thread_create/3` predicate. Thus, simpler predicates using the default thread creation options are trivial to implement.

9.4   Java Threads

Java includes native support for multi-threading programming. It provides both low- and high-level features for thread creation, communication, and synchronization. Java threads are objects while Logtalk threads run object methods (goals) concurrently. Logtalk allows several threads per object, which translates to a programming model different from Java and other similar languages. While Logtalk allows both object and fine-grained method (predicate) synchronization,

Java synchronization support always translates to object locking.[7] That is, Java uses one lock per object while Logtalk can use one lock per object, one lock per predicate, or one lock per group of predicates. In Java, two synchronized methods cannot be executed at the same time, even if the actions of one method do not need to be synchronized with the other. This limitation may be overcome by using synchronized statements, each one using a different synchronization object. In Logtalk, the programmer only needs to group the predicates that must be synchronized together by using separate synchronization/1 directives. Java supports thread cooperation using the wait(), notify(), and notifyAll() methods; these methods need to be called inside a synchronized block or a synchronized method to avoid deadlock from race conditions, making them cumbersome to use. The Java notifyAll() method allows notification of all waiting threads, something that can be coded but is not built-in in the current version of Logtalk. Logtalk threaded_wait/1 and threaded_notify/1 are arguably simpler, though restricted to peer-to-peer functionality. Logtalk notifications are posted into object message queues and thus are never missed due to race conditions, avoiding a potential source of deadlock.

10 Conclusions and Future Work

Logtalk currently uses a Prolog system as a back-end compiler, including for core multi-threading services. The features described in this paper could be implemented at a lower level, arguably with some performance gains (e.g. by minimizing the overhead of thread creation). The downside would be loosing the broad compatibility of Logtalk with Prolog compilers. Although currently only a small number of Prolog compilers provide the necessary interface to POSIX threads (or a suitable emulation), we expect its number to grow in the future.

Logtalk shares with some Prolog implementations the goal of finding useful high-level multi-threading primitives. Most high-level multi-threading predicates are supported by the same or similar core, low-level features. Therefore, a convergence and cross-fertilization of research results is expected and desirable. For example, Logtalk predicates such as threaded/1 and the synchronized/0-1 directives would be useful even in plain Prolog. Further experimentation and real-world usage will eventually show which high-level multi-threading predicates are worthwhile to implement across systems.

Our current work focus on documenting functionality, developing programming examples, and testing our implementation for robustness and compatibility across Prolog compilers and operating systems. The specification of the multi-threading predicates and directives is considered stable. The Logtalk multi-threading features will soon drop their experimental status to become available for using in production systems.

Work on the ISO draft standard proposal for Prolog multi-threading support [28] is progressing steadily. The current Logtalk implementation uses only a small subset of the proposed thread predicates. An improved implementation

---

[7] In Logtalk, this corresponds to using the synchronization/0 directive.

may be possible using a more complete Prolog interface to POSIX threads. In fact, the major reason for the Logtalk multi-threading features to be classified as experimental is due to the lack of a final standard specification that can be relied on for all the compliance testing necessary for writing robust portable code.

Acknowledgments. We are grateful to Peter Robinson, Jan Wielemaker, Vitor Costa, Terrance Swift, and Rui Marques for their ground work implementing Prolog multi-threading core support and for helpful suggestions and discussions on the subject of this paper. We thank also the anonymous reviewers for their helpful suggestions. This work has been funded by the Fundação para a Ciência e Tecnologia, Portugal, and by the Instituto das Telecomunicações, Portugal.

References

1. ISO/IEC. International Standard ISO/IEC 9945-1:1996. Information Technology–Portable Operating System Interface (POSIX)–Part 1: System Application: Program Interface (API). ISO/IEC (1996)
2. Butenhof, D.R.: Programming with POSIX Threads. Professional Computing Series. Addison-Wesley, Reading (1997)
3. Chandra, R., Dagum, L., Kohr, D., Maydan, D., McDonald, J., Menon, R.: Parallel Programming in OpenMP. Morgan Kaufmann Publishers, Los Altos, CA 94022, USA (2001)
4. OpenMP: Simple, Portable, Scalable SMP Programming, http://openmp.org/
5. Intel Threading Building Blocks, http://threadingbuildingblocks.org/
6. Gupta, G., Pontelli, E., Ali, K., Carlsson, M., Hermenegildo, M.: Parallel Execution of Prolog Programs: A Survey. ACM Transactions on Programming Languages and Systems 23(4), 472602 (2001)
7. Costa, V.S., Warren, D.H.D., Yang, R.: Andorra-I: A Parallel Prolog System that Transparently Exploits both And- and Or-Parallelism. SIGPLAN Not. 26(7), 83–93 (1991)
8. Ali, K., Karlsson, R.: The Muse Or-parallel Prolog model and its performance. In: Proceedings of the 1990 North American conference on Logic programming, pp. 757–776. MIT Press, Cambridge (1990)
9. Moura, P.: Logtalk – Design of an Object-Oriented Logic Programming Language. PhD thesis, Department of Computer Science, University of Beira Interior, Portugal (September 2003)
10. Moura, P.: Logtalk web site, http://logtalk.org/
11. Moura, P., Marchetti, V.: Logtalk Processing of STEP Part 21 Files. In: Etalle, S., Truszczyński, M. (eds.) ICLP 2006. LNCS, vol. 4079, pp. 453–454. Springer, Heidelberg (2006)
12. Wielemaker, J.: Native preemptive threads in SWI-Prolog. In: Palamidessi, C. (ed.) ICLP 2003. LNCS, vol. 2916, pp. 331–345. Springer, Heidelberg (2003)
13. Costa, V.S.: YAP Home Page, http://www.ncc.up.pt/~vsc/Yap/
14. Clark, K.L., Robinson, P., Hagen, R.: Multi-threading and Message Communication in Qu-Prolog. Theory and Practice of Logic Programming 1(3), 283–301 (2001)
15. Robinson, P.: Qu-prolog web site, http://www.itee.uq.edu.au/~pjr/HomePages/QuPrologHome.html

16. Tarau, P.: BinProlog 2006 11.x Professional Edition – Advanced BinProlog Programming and Extensions Guide (2006)
17. Tarau, P.: BinNet Corporation. BinProlog Home Page,
    http://www.binnetcorp.com/BinProlog/
18. The XSB Research Group. The XSB Programmer's Manual: version 3.1 (2007)
19. The XSB Research Group. XSB Home Page, http://xsb.sourceforge.net/
20. Carro, M., Hermenegildo, M.: Concurrency in Prolog Using Threads and a Shared Database. In: International Conference on Logic Programming, pp. 320–334 (1999)
21. Moura, P.(ed.): ISO/IEC DTR 132115:2007 Prolog Multi-threading predicates,
    http://logtalk.org/plstd/threads.pdf
22. Hermenegildo, M.V., Rossi, F.: Strict and Nonstrict Independent And-Parallelism in Logic Programs: Correctness, Efficiency, and Compile-Time Conditions. Journal of Logic Programming 22(1), 1–45 (1995)
23. González, A.: Speculative Threading: Creating New Methods of Thread-Level Parallelization (December 2005), http://www.intel.com/technology/magazine/research/speculative-threading-1205.htm
24. Wikipedia: Dining philosophers problem,
    http://en.wikipedia.org/wiki/Dining_philosophers_problem
25. Eskilson, J., Carlsson, M.: SICStus MT—A Multithreaded Execution Environment for SICStus Prolog. In: Palamidessi, C., Glaser, H., Meinke, K. (eds.) ALP 1998 and PLILP 1998. LNCS, vol. 1490, pp. 36–53. Springer, Heidelberg (1998)
26. Hedqvist, P.: A Parallel and Multithreaded Erlang Implementation. Master's thesis, Uppsala University, Uppsala, Sweden (June 1998)
27. Erlang Home Page, http://www.erlang.org/
28. Hodgson, J.: ISO/IEC/ JTC1/SC22/WG17 Official Home Page,
    http://www.sju.edu/~jhodgson/wg17/wg17web.html

Switched-On Yampa*
Declarative Programming of Modular Synthesizers

George Giorgidze[1] and Henrik Nilsson[2]

[1] School of Computer Science, University of Nottingham, UK
ggg@cs.nott.ac.uk
[2] School of Computer Science, University of Nottingham, UK
nhn@cs.nott.ac.uk

Abstract. In this paper, we present an implementation of a modular synthesizer in Haskell using Yampa. A synthesizer, be it a hardware instrument or a pure software implementation, as here, is said to be *modular* if it provides sound-generating and sound-shaping components that can be interconnected in arbitrary ways. Yampa, a Haskell-embedded implementation of Functional Reactive Programming, supports flexible, purely declarative construction of hybrid systems. Since music is a hybrid continuous-time and discrete-time phenomenon, Yampa is a good fit for such applications, offering some unique possibilities compared to most languages targeting music or audio applications. Through the presentation of our synthesizer application, we demonstrate this point and provide insight into the Yampa approach to programming reactive, hybrid systems. We develop the synthesizer gradually, starting with fundamental synthesizer components and ending with an application that is capable of rendering a standard MIDI file as audio with respectable performance.

Keywords: Functional Reactive Programming, synchronous dataflow languages, hybrid systems, computer music.

1 Introduction

A dynamic system or phenomenon is *hybrid* if it exhibits both continuous-time and discrete-time behaviour at the chosen level of abstraction. Music is an interesting example of a hybrid phenomenon in this sense. At a fundamental level, music is sound: continuous pressure waves in some medium such as air. In contrast, a musical performance has some clear discrete aspects (along with continuous ones): it consists of sequences of discrete notes, different instruments may be played at different points of a performance, and so on.

There exist many languages and notations for describing sound or music and for programming computers to carry out musical tasks. However, they mostly tend to focus on either the discrete or the continuous aspects. Traditional musical notation, or its modern-day electronic derivatives such as MIDI files or

---

* This work is supported by EPSRC grant EP/D064554/1. Thanks to the anonymous referees for many useful suggestions.

P. Hudak and D.S. Warren (Eds.): PADL 2008, LNCS 4902, pp. 282–298, 2008.

domain-specific languages like Haskore [5], focus on describing music in terms of sequences of notes. If we are interested in describing music at a finer level of detail, in particular, what it actually sounds like, options include modelling languages for describing the physics of acoustic instruments, various kinds of electronic synthesizers, or domain-specific languages like Csound [14]. However, the focus of synthesizer programming is the sound of a single note, and how that sound evolves over time. The mapping between the discrete world of notes and the continuous world of sound is hard-wired into the synthesizer, outside the control of the programmer.

Here we take a more holistic approach allowing the description of both the continuous and discrete aspects of music and musical applications; that is, an approach supporting programming of *hybrid* systems. Yampa [4,10], an instance of Functional Reactive Programming (FRP) in the form of a domain-specific language embedded in Haskell, provides the prerequisite facilities. Our basic approach is that of *modular synthesis*. Modular synthesizers were developed in the late 1950s and early 1960s and offered the first programmatic way to describe sound. This was achieved by wiring together sound-generating and sound-shaping *modules* electrically. Yampa's continuous-time aspects serve this purpose very well. Additionally we leverage Yampa's capabilities for describing systems with a highly dynamic structure, thus catering for the discrete aspects of music. In this paper, we illustrate:

- how basic sound-generating and sound-shaping modules can be described and combined into a simple monophonic (one note at a time) synthesizer;
- how a monophonic synthesizer can be constructed from an instrument description contained in a SoundFont file;
- how to run several monophonic synthesizer instances simultaneously, thus creating a polyphonic synthesizer capable of playing Standard MIDI Files.

The resulting application renders the musical score in a given MIDI file using SoundFont instrument descriptions. The performance is fairly good: a moderately complex score can be rendered about as fast as it plays (with buffering). All code is available on-line.[1] In addition to what is described in this paper, the code includes supporting infrastructure for reading MIDI files, for reading SoundFont files, and for writing the result as audio files or streams (.wav).

The contribution of this work lies in the application of declarative hybrid programming to a novel application area, and as an example of advanced declarative hybrid programming. We believe it will be of interest to people interested in a declarative approach to describing music and programming musical applications, to practitioners interested in advanced declarative hybrid programming, and to educationalists seeking interesting and fun examples of declarative programming off the beaten path. The importance of the latter is illustrated by the DrScheme experience, where first-class images and appropriate reactive abstractions have enabled high-school students to very quickly pick up pure functional programming through implementation of animations and games [3].

---

[1] http://www.cs.nott.ac.uk/~ggg

2   Yampa

In the interest of making this paper sufficiently self-contained, we summarize the basics of Yampa in the following. For further details, see earlier papers on Yampa [4,10]. The presentation draws heavily from the Yampa summary in [2].

2.1   Fundamental Concepts

Yampa is based on two central concepts: *signals* and *signal functions*. A signal is a function from time to values of some type:

$$Signal\ \alpha \approx Time \rightarrow \alpha$$

Time is continuous, and is represented as a non-negative real number. The type parameter α specifies the type of values carried by the signal. For example, the type of an audio signal, i.e., a representation of sound, would be *Signal Sample* if we take *Sample* to be the type of the varying quantity.[2]

A *signal function* is a function from *Signal* to *Signal*:

$$SF\ \alpha\ \beta \approx Signal\ \alpha \rightarrow Signal\ \beta$$

When a value of type *SF* α β is applied to an input signal of type *Signal* α, it produces an output signal of type *Signal* β. Signal functions are *first class entities* in Yampa. Signals, however, are not: they only exist indirectly through the notion of signal function.

In order to ensure that signal functions are executable, we require them to be *causal*: The output of a signal function at time t is uniquely determined by the input signal on the interval $[0, t]$. If a signal function is such that the output at time t only depends on the input at the very same time instant t, it is called *stateless*. Otherwise it is *stateful*.

2.2   Composing Signal Functions

Programming in Yampa consists of defining signal functions compositionally using Yampa's library of primitive signal functions and a set of combinators. Yampa's signal functions are an instance of the arrow framework proposed by Hughes [7]. Some central arrow combinators are *arr* that lifts an ordinary function to a stateless signal function, composition ⋙, parallel composition &&&, and the fixed point combinator *loop*. In Yampa, they have the following types:

$$arr\ :: (a \rightarrow b) \rightarrow SF\ a\ b$$
$$(\ggg) :: SF\ a\ b \rightarrow SF\ b\ c \rightarrow SF\ a\ c$$
$$(\&\&\&) :: SF\ a\ b \rightarrow SF\ a\ c \rightarrow SF\ a\ (b, c)$$
$$loop\ :: SF\ (a, c)\ (b, c) \rightarrow SF\ a\ b$$

---

[2] Physically, sound is varying pressure, and it might come about as a result of the varying displacement of a vibrating string, or the varying voltage of an electronic oscillator. Here we abstract from the physics by referring to the instantaneous value of a sound wave as a "sample", as is conventional in digital audio processing.

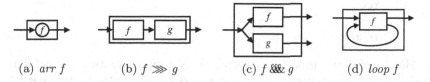

(a) *arr f*   (b) $f \gg g$ (c) $f \;\&\&\&\; g$ (d) *loop f*

Fig. 1. Basic signal function combinators

We can think of signals and signal functions using a simple flow chart analogy. Line segments (or "wires") represent signals, with arrowheads indicating the direction of flow. Boxes represent signal functions, with one signal flowing into the box's input port and another signal flowing out of the box's output port. Figure 1 illustrates the aforementioned combinators using this analogy. Through the use of these and related combinators, arbitrary signal function networks can be expressed.

2.3 Arrow Syntax

Paterson's arrow notation [11] simplifies writing Yampa programs as it allows signal function networks to be described directly. In particular, the notation effectively allows signals to be named, despite signals not being first class values. In this syntax, an expression denoting a signal function has the form:

> **proc** *pat* → **do**
> $pat_1 \leftarrow sfexp_1 \prec exp_1$
> $pat_2 \leftarrow sfexp_2 \prec exp_2$
>   . . .
> $pat_n \leftarrow sfexp_n \prec exp_n$
> $returnA \prec exp$

Note that this is just *syntactic sugar*: the notation is translated into plain Haskell using the arrow combinators.

The keyword **proc** is analogous to the λ in λ-expressions, *pat* and pat_i are patterns binding signal variables pointwise by matching on instantaneous signal values, *exp* and exp_i are expressions defining instantaneous signal values, and $sfexp_i$ are expressions denoting signal functions. The idea is that the signal being defined pointwise by each exp_i is fed into the corresponding signal function $sfexp_i$, whose output is bound pointwise in pat_i. The overall input to the signal function denoted by the **proc**-expression is bound pointwise by *pat*, and its output signal is defined pointwise by the expression *exp*. An optional keyword **rec** allows recursive definitions (feedback loops).

For a concrete example, consider the following:

> $sf = $ **proc** $(a, b) \rightarrow$ **do**
> $(c1, c2) \leftarrow sf1 \;\&\&\&\; sf2 \prec a$
> $d \qquad\;\; \leftarrow sf3 \lll sf4 \prec (c1, b)$

$$\textbf{rec}$$
$$e \leftarrow sf5 \prec (c2, d, e)$$
$$returnA \prec (d, e)$$

Note the use of the tuple pattern for splitting sf's input into two "named signals", a and b. Also note the use of tuple expressions and patterns for pairing and splitting signals in the body of the definition; for example, for splitting the output from $sf1 \; \&\&\& \; sf2$. Also note how the arrow notation may be freely mixed with the use of basic arrow combinators.

2.4   Events and Event Sources

To model discrete events, we introduce the *Event* type:

data *Event a = NoEvent | Event a*

A signal function whose output signal is of type *Event T* for some type T is called an *event source*. The value carried by an event occurrence may be used to convey information about the occurrence. The operator *tag* is often used to associate such a value with an occurrence:

$tag :: Event\ a \to b \to Event\ b$

2.5   Switching

The structure of a Yampa system may evolve over time. These structural changes are known as *mode switches*. This is accomplished through a family of *switching* primitives that use events to trigger changes in the connectivity of a system. The simplest such primitive is *switch*:

$switch :: SF\ a\ (b, Event\ c) \to (c \to SF\ a\ b) \to SF\ a\ b$

The *switch* combinator switches from one subordinate signal function into another when a switching event occurs. Its first argument is the signal function that initially is active. It outputs a pair of signals. The first defines the overall output while the initial signal function is active. The second signal carries the event that will cause the switch to take place. Once the switching event occurs, *switch* applies its second argument to the value tagged to the event and switches into the resulting signal function.

Yampa also includes *parallel* switching constructs that maintain *dynamic collections* of signal functions connected in parallel [10]. We will come back to this when when we discuss how to construct a polyphonic synthesizer.

3   Synthesizer Basics

A modular synthesizer provides a number of sound-generating and sound-shaping modules. By combining these in appropriate ways, various types of sounds can

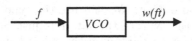

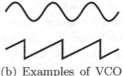

(a) VCO: f is the control voltage that determines the oscillator frequency; w determines the waveform.

(b) Examples of VCO waveforms.

Fig. 2. Voltage Controlled Oscillator (VCO)

be realized, be they sounds that resemble different acoustic instruments such as string or brass, or completely new ones. Such a configuration of modules is known as a *patch*. Non-modular synthesizers are structured in a similar way, except that the the module configuration to a large extend is predetermined. In this section we introduce some basic synthesizer modules, explain their purpose, and implement some simple ones in Yampa.

3.1 Oscillators

An oscillator is what generates the sound in a synthesizer. As it is necessary to vary the frequency in order to play music, some form of dynamic tuning functionality is needed. Traditionally, this was done by constructing electronic oscillators whose fundamental frequency could be determined by a control voltage. Such a circuit is known as a Voltage Controlled Oscillator (VCO): see Fig. 2(a).

There are many choices for the actual waveform of the oscillator, indicated by the function w in Fig. 2(a). Typically w is some simple periodic function, like the ones in Fig. 2(b): sine and sawtooth. However, w can also be a recording of some sound, often an acoustic instrument. The latter kind of oscillator is the basis of so called sample[3]-based or wavetable synthesizers.

As a first example of using Yampa for sound synthesis, let us implement a simple sine wave oscillator with dynamically controllable frequency. The equations for a sine wave with fixed frequency f are simply

$$\phi = 2\pi f t \tag{1}$$
$$s = sin(\phi) \tag{2}$$

However, we want to allow the frequency to vary over time. To obtain the angle of rotation ϕ at a point in time t, we thus have to *integrate* the varying angular frequency $2\pi f$ from 0 to t. We obtain the following equations:

$$\phi = 2\pi \int_0^t f(\tau)\, d\tau \tag{3}$$
$$s = sin(\phi) \tag{4}$$

---

[3] "Sample" is an overloaded term. Depending on context, it can refer either to the sampled, instantaneous value of a signal, or to a recording of some sound. In a digital setting, the latter is a sequence of samples in the first sense.

Let us consider how to realize this. Our sine oscillator becomes a signal function with a control input and an audio output. We will use the type *CV* (for
Control Value) for the former, while the type of the latter is just *Sample* as
discussed in Sect. 2.1. Further, we want to parameterize an oscillator on its
nominal frequency. Thus, our oscillator will become a function that given the
desired nominal frequency f_0 returns a signal function whose output oscillates
at a frequency f that can be adjusted around f_0 through the control input:

oscSine :: *Frequency* → *SF CV Sample*

Following common synthesizer designs, we adopt the convention that increasing the control value by one unit should double the frequency (up one octave),
and decreasing by one unit should halve the frequency (down one octave). If we
denote the time-varying control value by $cv(t)$, we get

$$f(t) = f_0 2^{cv(t)} \tag{5}$$

We can now define *oscSine* by transliterating equations 3, 4, and 5 into Yampa
code:

```
oscSine :: Frequency → SF CV Sample
oscSine f0 = proc cv → do
    let f = f0 * (2 ** cv)
    phi ← integral ≺ 2 * pi * f
    returnA ≺ sin phi
```

Note that time is implied, so unlike the equations above, signals are never explicitly indexed by time.

In traditional synthesizers, there is a second class of oscillators known as Low
Frequency Oscillators (LFO) which are used to generate time-varying control
signals. However, our *oscSine* works just as well at low frequencies. Let us use
two sine oscillators where one modulates the other to construct an oscillator
with a gentle vibrato:

constant 0 ⋙ *oscSine* 5.0 ⋙ *arr* (*0.05) ⋙ *oscSine* 440

Figure 3 illustrates this patch graphically.

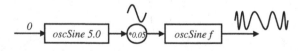

Fig. 3. Modulating an oscillator to obtain vibrato

3.2   Amplifiers

The next fundamental synthesizer module is the variable-gain amplifier. As the gain traditionally was set by a control voltage, such a device is known as a Voltage Controlled Amplifier (VCA). See Fig. 4. VCAs are used to dynamically control the amplitude of audio signals or control signals; that is, multiplication of two signals, where one often is a low-frequency control signal.

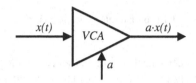

Fig. 4. Voltage Controlled Amplifier (VCA)

An important application of VCAs is to shape the output from oscillators in order to create musical notes with a definite beginning and end. The approach used is to derive a two-level control signal from the controlling keyboard called the *gate* signal. It is typically positive when a key is being pressed and 0 V otherwise. By deriving a second control signal from the keyboard proportional to *which* key is being pressed, feeding this to a VCO, feeding the output from the VCO to the input of a VCA, and finally controlling the gain of the VCA by the gate signal, we have obtained a very basic but usable modular synthesizer patch with an organ-like character: see Fig. 5.

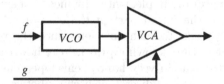

Fig. 5. Basic synthesizer patch: f controls the frequency, g is the gate signal

Since the conceptual operation of a VCA is just multiplication of signals, implementation in Yampa is, of course, entirely straightforward.

3.3   Envelope Generators

When acoustic instruments are played, it often takes a discernable amount of time from starting playing a note until the played note has reached full volume. This is known as the attack. Similarly, a note may linger for a while after the end of the playing action. How the volume of a note evolves over time, its *envelope*, is a very important characteristic of an instrument. In Sect. 3.2, we saw how a patch with an organ-like envelope could be obtained by controlling a VCA with

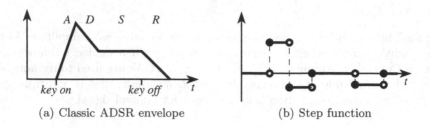

(a) Classic ADSR envelope   (b) Step function

Fig. 6. Envelope generation

the gate signal. To play notes with other types of envelopes, we need to control the VCA with a control signal that mirrors the desired envelope.

An *envelope generator* is a circuit that is designed to allow a variety of musically useful envelopes to be generated. Figure 6(a) shows a classic ADSR envelope. The first phase is the Attack (A). Immediately after a key has been pressed, the control signal grows to its maximal value at a programmable rate. Once the maximal value has been reached, the envelope generator enters the second phase, Decay (D). Here, the control signal decreases until it reaches the sustain level. The third phase is Sustain (S), and the envelope generator will remain there until the key is released. It then enters the fourth phase, Release (R), where the control signal goes to 0. If the key is released before the sustain phase has been reached, the envelope generator will proceed directly to the release phase.

This kind of behaviour is easily programmable in Yampa. An envelope signal with segments of predetermined lengths can be obtained by integrating a step function like the one in Fig. 6(b). Progression to the release phase upon reception of a note-off event is naturally implemented by means of switching from a signal function that describes the initial part of the envelope to one that describes the release part in response to such an event since the release of a key does not happen at a point in time known a priori. Note how the hybrid capabilities of Yampa now start to come in very handy: envelope generation involves both smoothly evolving segments and discrete switching between such segments.

To illustrate, we sketch the implementation of a generalized envelope generator with the following signature:

$$envGen :: CV \rightarrow [(Time, CV)] \rightarrow Maybe\ Int$$
$$\rightarrow SF\ (Event\ ())\ (CV, Event\ ())$$

The first argument gives the start level of the desired envelope control signal. Then follows a list of time and control-value pairs. Each defines a target control level and how long it should take to get there from the previous level. The third argument specifies the number of the segment before which the sustain phase should be inserted, if any. The input to the resulting signal function is the note-off event that causes the envelope generator to go from the sustain phase to the following release segment(s). The output is a pair of signals: the generated envelope control signal and an event indicating the completion of the last release segment. This event will often occur significantly *after* the note-off event and is useful for indicating when a sound-generating signal function should be terminated.

Let us first consider a signal function to generate an envelope with a predetermined shape:

$envGenAux :: CV \rightarrow [(Time, CV)] \rightarrow SF \ a \ CV$
$envGenAux \ l0 \ tls = afterEach \ trs \ggg hold \ r0 \ggg integral \ggg arr \ (+l0)$
   where
    $(r0, trs) = toRates \ l0 \ tls$

The auxiliary function *toRates* converts a list of time and level pairs to a list of time and rate pairs. Given such a list of times and rates, the signal function *afterEach* generates a sequence of events at the specified points in time. These are passed through the signal function *hold* that converts a sequence of events, i.e. a discrete-time signal, to a continuous-time signal. The result is a step function like the one shown in Fig. 6(b). By integrating this, and adding the specified start level, we obtain an envelope signal of the specified shape.

We can now implement the signal function *envGen*. In the case that no sustain segment is desired, this is just a matter pairing *envGenAux* with an event source that generates an event when the final segment of the specified envelope has been completed. The time for this event is obtained by summing the durations of the individual segments:

$envGen \ l0 \ tls \ Nothing = envGenAux \ l0 \ tls \ \&\& \ after \ (sum \ (map \ fst \ tls)) \ ()$

If a sustain segment is desired, the list of time and level pairs is split at the indicated segment, and each part is used to generate a fixed-shape envelope using *envGenAux*. Yampa's *switch* primitive is then employed to arrange the transition from the initial part of the envelope to the release part upon reception of a note-off event:

$envGen \ l0 \ tls \ (Just \ n) =$
   $switch \ (\mathbf{proc} \ noteoff \rightarrow \mathbf{do}$
        $l \leftarrow envGenAux \ l0 \ tls1 \prec ()$
        $returnA \prec ((l, noEvent), noteoff \ `tag` \ l))$
        $(\lambda l \rightarrow envGenAux \ l \ tls2 \ \&\& \ after \ (sum \ (map \ fst \ tls2)) \ ())$
   where
    $(tls1, tls2) = splitAt \ n \ tls$

Note how the level of the generated envelope signal at the time of the note-off event is sampled and attached to the switch event (the construction *noteoff* `tag` *l*). This level determines the initial level of the release part of the envelope to avoid any discontinuity in the generated envelope signal.

3.4   A Simple Modular Synthesizer Patch

Let us finish this synthesizer introduction with a slightly larger example that combines most of the modules we have encountered so far. Our goal is a

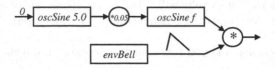

Fig. 7. Vibrato and bell-like envelope

synthesizer patch that plays a note with vibrato and a bell-like envelope (fast attack, gradual decay) in response to events carrying a MIDI note number; i.e., note-on events.

Let us start with the basic patch. It is a function that when applied to a note number will generate a signal function that plays the desired note once:

$$playNote :: NoteNumber \rightarrow SF\ a\ Sample$$
$$playNote\ n = \mathbf{proc}\ \_ \rightarrow \mathbf{do}$$
$$\begin{array}{lll} v & \leftarrow oscSine\ 5.0 & \prec 0.0 \\ s & \leftarrow oscSine\ (toFreq\ n)\prec 0.05 * v \\ (e, \_) & \leftarrow envBell & \prec noEvent \\ returnA\prec e * s \end{array}$$
$$envBell = envGen\ 0.0\ [(0.1, 1.0), (1.5, 0.0)]\ Nothing$$

Figure 7 shows a graphical representation of *playNotes*.

The auxiliary function *toFreq* converts from MIDI note numbers to frequency, assuming equal temperament:

$$toFreq :: NoteNumber \rightarrow Frequency$$
$$toFreq\ n = 440 * (2 ** (((fromIntegral\ n) - 69.0)\ /\ 12.0))$$

Next we need to arrange that to switch into an instance of *playNote* whenever an event carrying a note number is received:

$$playNotes :: SF\ (Event\ NoteNumber)\ Sample$$
$$playNotes = switch\ (constant\ 0.0\ \&\!\&\ identity)$$
$$\qquad\qquad\qquad playNotesRec$$
$$\quad\mathbf{where}$$
$$\qquad playNotesRec\ n =$$
$$\qquad\qquad switch\ (playNote\ n\ \&\!\&\ notYet)\ playNotesRec$$

The idea here is to start with a signal function that generates a constant 0 audio signal. As soon as a first event is received, we switch into *playNotesRec*. This plays the note once. Meanwhile, we keep watching the input for note-on events (except at time 0, when *notYet* blocks any event as *playNotesRec* otherwise would keep switching on the event that started it), and as soon as an event is received we switch again, recursively, into *playNotesRec*, thus initiating the playing of the next note. And so on.

4   A SoundFont-Based Monophonic Synthesizer

The SoundFont format is a standardized way to describe musical instruments. It is a sample-based format, i.e. based on short recordings of actual instruments, but it also provides true synthesizer capabilities through a network of interconnected modules of the kind described in Sect. 3. In this section, we sketch how to turn a SoundFont description into a monophonic synthesizer using Yampa.

4.1   Implementing a Sample-Based Oscillator

We first turn our attention to implementing an oscillator that uses recorded waveforms or samples. A SoundFont file contains many individual samples (often megabytes of data), each a recording of an instrument playing some particular note. Along with the actual sample data there is information about each sample, including the sampling frequency, the fundamental (or *native*) frequency of the recorded note, and loop points. The latter defines a region of the sample that will be repeated to allow notes to be sustained. Thus samples of short duration can be used to play long notes.

In our implementation, data for all the samples is stored in a single array:

type *SampleData* = *UArray SamplePointIndex Sample*
type *SamplePointIndex* = *Word32*

Note that the type *Sample* here refers to an instantaneous sample value, as opposed to an entire recording. Information about individual samples are stored in records of type *SampleInfo*. In addition to the information already mentioned, these also store the start and end index for each sample.

A sample-playing oscillator can now be defined in much the same way as the sine oscillator from Sect. 3.1, the main difference being that the periodic function now is given by table lookup and linear interpolation:

oscSmplAux :: *Frequency* → *SampleData* → *SampleInfo*
    → *SF CV* (*Sample, SamplePointIndex*)
oscSmplAux freq sdta sinf = **proc** *cv* → **do**
    phi ← *integral*≺ *freq* / (*smplFreq sinf*) * (2 ** *cv*)
    let (*n, f*) = *properFraction* (*phi* * *smplRate sinf*)
        p1 = *pos n*
        p2 = *pos* (*n* + 1)
        s1 = *sdta* ! *p1*
        s2 = *sdta* ! *p2*
    returnA≺ (*s1* + *f* * (*s2* − *s1*), *p2*)
    where
        pos n = ...

The local function *pos* converts a sample number to an index by "wrapping around" in the loop region as necessary. In addition to the instantaneous sample value, the oscillator also outputs the current sample index. This enables a smooth

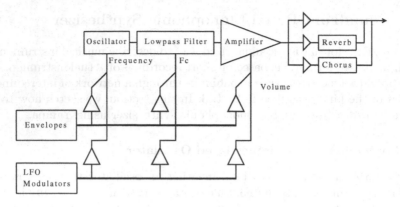

Fig. 8. The SoundFont synthesis model

transition to the release segment of a sample (after the loop region) when a note-off event is received.

Finally, we can define a complete oscillator that takes care of the transition to the release segment on a note-off event through switching from *oscSmplAux* to an oscillator that plays the release segment. We only give the type signature:

$oscSmpl :: Frequency \rightarrow SampleData \rightarrow SampleInfo$
$\rightarrow SF\ (CV, Event\ ())\ Sample.$

4.2   Combining the Pieces

Given the sample-based oscillator, a complete SoundFont synthesizer can be obtained by wiring together the appropriate modules according to the SoundFont synthesis model shown in Fig. 8, just like the simple monophonic synthesizer was constructed in Sect. 3.4. The SoundFont model does include *filters*. While not considered in this paper, filters can easily be realized using Yampa's unit delays [12].

In our case, we also choose to do the MIDI processing at this level. Each monophonic synthesizer is instantiated to play a particular note at a particular MIDI channel at some particular strength (velocity). The synthesizer instance continuously monitors further MIDI events in order to identify those relevant to it, including note-off events to switch to the release phase and any articulation messages like pitch bend. This leads to the following type signature, where the output event indicates that the release phase has been completed and the playing of a note thus is complete:

type $MonoSynth = Channel \rightarrow NoteNumber \rightarrow Velocity$
$\rightarrow SF\ MidiEvent\ (Sample, Event\ ()).$

5   A Polyphonic Synthesizer

In this section, we consider how to leverage what we have seen so far in order to construct a polyphonic synthesizer capable of playing standard MIDI files.

5.1   Dynamic Synthesizer Instantiation

The central idea is to instantiate a monophonic synthesizer in response to every note-on event, and then run it in parallel with any other active synthesizer instances until the end of the played note. Yampa's parallel switching construct [10] is what enables this dynamic instantiation:

$$
\begin{aligned}
pSwitchB :: &\ Functor\ col \Rightarrow \\
&col\ (SF\ a\ b) && \text{-- Initial signal func. collection} \\
&\rightarrow SF\ (a, col\ b)\ (Event\ c) && \text{-- Event source for switching} \\
&\rightarrow (col\ (SF\ a\ b) \rightarrow c \rightarrow SF\ a\ (col\ b)) && \text{-- Signal function to switch into} \\
&\rightarrow SF\ a\ (col\ b)
\end{aligned}
$$

The combinator *pSwitchB* is similar to *switch* described in Sect. 2.5, except that

- a collection of signal functions are run in parallel
- a separate signal function is used to generate the switching event
- the function computing the signal function to switch into receives the collection of subordinate signal functions as an extra argument.

The latter allows signal functions to be *independently* added to or removed from a collection in response to note-on and monosynth termination events, while *preserving* the state of all other signal functions in the collection.

The overall structure of the polyphonic synthesizer is shown in Fig. 9. The signal function *triggerChange* generates a switching event when reconfiguration is necessary (i.e. when adding or removing monosynth instances). The function *performChange* computes the new collection of monosynth instances after a switch. The output signal from the parallel switch is a collection of samples at each point in time, one for every running monosynth instance. This can be

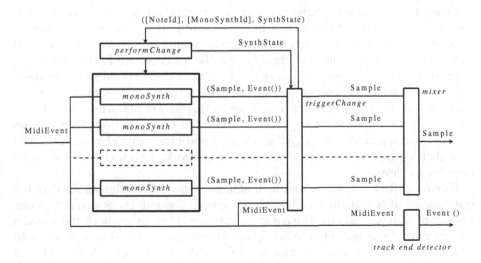

Fig. 9. Overall structure of the polyphonic synthesizer

seen as a collection of audio signals. The signal function *mixer* sums all these samples into a single audio signal.

5.2 Performance

Despite being implemented in a very straightforward (almost naive) way, the performance of the polyphonic synthesizer is reasonable. For example, using modern hardware (1.8 GHz Intel dual core) and compiling using GHC, a moderately complex score like Mozart's *Rondo Alla Turca*, can be rendered as fast as it plays at 22 kHz sampling rate using a SoundFont[4] piano definition. However, an audio buffer is needed between the synthesizer process and the audio player to guard against garbage collection pauses and the like: thus, the *latency* is high.

6   Related Work

Haskore [5] is a language for programming music embedded in Haskell. Its fundamental design resembles traditional musical scores, but as it is an embedding in Haskell, Haskell can be used for "meta programming". Haskore itself does not deal with defining instruments, but see the discussion of HasSound below. Describing musical scores was not our focus in this work. Haskore could clearly be used to that end, being a Haskell embedding just like Yampa. Since our framework provides an interface to MIDI and MIDI files, *any* application capable of generating MIDI could in principle be used as a frontend. However, one could also explore implementing "score-construction" abstraction directly in the Yampa framework. An interesting aspect of that would be that there is no firm boundary between the musical score and the sounds used to perform it. One could also imagine interactive compositions, as Yampa is a reactive programming language.

Csound is a domain-specific language for programming sound and musical scores [14]. Fundamentally, it is a modular synthesizer, enabling the user to connect predefined modules in any conceivable manner. It is possible to extend Csound with new modules, but these have to be programmed in the underlying implementation language: C. Thanks to its extensibility, Csound now provides a vast array of sound generating and sound shaping modules. Obviously, what we have done in this paper does not come close to this level of maturity. However, we do claim that our hybrid setting provides a lot of flexibility in that it both allows the user to implement basic signal generation and processing algorithms as well as higher-level discrete aspects in a single framework, with no hard boundaries between the levels.

HasSound [6] is a domain-specific language embedded in Haskell for defining instruments. It is actually a high-level frontend to Csound: HasSound definitions are compiled to Csound instrument specifications. Therein lies both HasSound's strength and weakness. On the one hand, HasSound readily provides access to lots of very sophisticated facilities from Csound. On the other hand, the end

---

[4] http://www.sf2midi.com/index.php?page=sdet&id=8565

result is ultimately a static Csound instrument definition: one cannot do anything in HasSound that cannot (at least in principle) be done directly in Csound. The approach taken in this paper is, in principle, more flexible.

Low-level audio processing and sound-generation in Haskell has also been done earlier. For example, Thielemann [13] develops an audio-processing framework based on representing signals as co-recursively defined streams. However, the focus is on basic signal processing, not on synthesis applications.

Karczmarczuk [8] presents a framework with goals similar to ours using a stream-based signal representation. Karczmarczuk focuses on musically relevant algorithms and present a number of concise realizations of physical instrument simulations, including the Karplus-Strong model of a plucked string [9], reverb, and filters. He also presents an efficient, delay-based sine oscillator, and does consider how to modulate its frequency by another signal to create vibrato.

However, Karczmarczuk's framework, as far as it was developed in the paper, lacks the higher-level, discrete facilities of Yampa, and the paper does not consider how to actually go about programming the logic of playing notes, adding polyphony[5], etc. Also, the arrow framework offers a very direct and intuitive way to combine synthesizer modules: we dare say that someone familiar with programming modular synthesizers would feel rather at home in the Yampa setting, at least as long as predefined modules are provided. The correspondence is less direct in Karczmarczuk's framework as it stands.

7 Conclusions

FRP and Yampa address application domains that have not been traditionally associated with pure declarative programming. For example, in earlier work we have applied Yampa to video game implementation [2], and others have since taken those ideas much further [1]. In this paper, we have applied Yampa to another domain where pure declarative programming normally is not considered, modular synthesis, arguing that the hybrid aspects of Yampa provides a particularly good fit in that we can handle both low-level signal processing and higher-level discrete aspects, including running many synthesizer instances in parallel to handle polyphony. We saw that Yampa's parallel, collection-based switch construct [10] was instrumental for achieving the latter. We also think that being able to do all of this seamlessly in a single framework opens up interesting creative possibilities.

As it stands, our framework is mainly a proof of concept. Nevertheless, we feel that the Yampa style of programming is immediately useful in an educational context as it makes it possible to implement interesting examples from somewhat unexpected domains in an intuitive, concise, and elegant manner, thus providing an incentive to learn pure declarative programming. We note that others have had similar experiences with related approaches [3].

---

[5] Summing a fixed number of streams to play more than one note is, of course, straightforward. But polyphonic performance requires independent starting and stopping of sound sources.

References

1. Cheong, M.H.: Functional programming and 3D games. In: BEng thesis, University of New South Wales, Sydney, Australia (November 2005)
2. Courtney, A., Nilsson, H., Peterson, J.: The Yampa arcade. In: Haskell 2003. Proceedings of the 2003 ACM SIGPLAN Haskell Workshop, Uppsala, Sweden, pp. 7–18. ACM Press, New York (2003)
3. Felleisen, M.: Personal communication and on-line lecture notes (June 2007), http://www.ccs.neu.edu/home/matthias/HtDP/Prologue/book.html
4. Hudak, P., Courtney, A., Nilsson, H., Peterson, J.: Arrows, robots, and functional reactive programming. In: Jeuring, J., Peyton Jones, S.L. (eds.) AFP 2002. LNCS, vol. 2638, pp. 159–187. Springer, Heidelberg (2003)
5. Hudak, P., Makucevich, T., Gadde, S., Whong, B.: Haskore music notation - an algebra of music. Journal of Functional Programming 6(3), 465–483 (1996)
6. Hudak, P., Zamec, M., Eisenstat, S.: HasSound: Generating musical instrument sounds in Haskell. NEPLS talk, Brown University. Slides (October 2005), http://plucky.cs.yale.edu/cs431/HasSoundNEPLS-10-05.ppt
7. Hughes, J.: Generalising monads to arrows. Science of Computer Programming 37, 67–111 (2000)
8. Karczmarczuk, J.: Functional framework for sound synthesis. In: Hermenegildo, M.V., Cabeza, D. (eds.) PADL 2005. LNCS, vol. 3350, pp. 7–21. Springer, Heidelberg (2005)
9. Karplus, K., Strong, A.: Digital synthesis of plucked string and drum timbres. Computer Music Journal 7(2), 43–55 (1983)
10. Nilsson, H., Courtney, A., Peterson, J.: Functional reactive programming, continued. In: Haskell 2002. Proceedings of the 2002 ACM SIGPLAN Haskell Workshop, Pittsburgh, Pennsylvania, USA, pp. 51–64. ACM Press, New York (2002)
11. Paterson, R.: A new notation for arrows. In: Proceedings of the 2001 ACM SIGPLAN International Conference on Functional Programming, Firenze, Italy, pp. 229–240 (September 2001)
12. Smith, J.O.: Introduction to Digital Filters, August 2006 edn. CCRMA (May 2006), http://ccrma.stanford.edu/~jos/filters06/
13. Thielemann, H.: Audio processing using Haskell. In: DAFx 2004. Proceedings of the 7th International Conference on Digital Audio Effects, Naples, pp. 201–206 (2004)
14. Vercoe, B.: The Canonical Csound Reference Manual. MIT Media Lab (2007)

Model-Based Testing of Thin-Client Web Applications and Navigation Input

Pieter Koopman, Peter Achten, and Rinus Plasmeijer

Software Technology, Nijmegen Institute for Computing and Information Sciences,
Radboud University Nijmegen, The Netherlands
{pieter, P.Achten, rinus}@cs.ru.nl

Abstract. More and more software systems use a browser as the universal graphical user interface. As a consequence these applications inherit browser navigation as part of their interface. Typical browser actions are the use of the back- and forward-button and the cloning of windows. Browser navigation is difficult to deal with because it has effects that are noticed indirectly by the application logic. It is easy to forget or misunderstand the consequences of this aspect in the construction of a program. Hence, testing the correct behavior of the application is very desirable, preferably with an automatic model-based test tool. For this kind of model-based testing a specification including browser navigation is needed. We introduce a transformation to lift the specification of a program without browser navigation to one with browser navigation. This reduces the specification effort considerably. The distinguishing feature of our method is that it allows the test engineer to specify only the exceptions to the general rule. We show how this lifting of specifications is used for some examples and how errors are found in real web applications. The described system builds on the model-based test tool G∀ST.

1 Introduction

Equipping software systems with an HTML-based browser interface has many advantages: the interface becomes platform independent, the look and feel is familiar to new users, and it is often less work to implement a browser based GUI instead of some traditional GUI library. Moreover, the new application obtains browser navigation (cloning of windows and the possibility to go back and forward between previous states of the GUI) for free. The browsers provide this new GUI navigation without any help from the web application by maintaining a stack of previous pages. The possibility to review previous states in the interaction can be very convenient for the user. It is even possible to go to a previous page and give a new input in that state of the GUI to investigate several options or to undo mistakes.

A consequence of using a browser as GUI is that the application, and hence its state, becomes divided between the browser (handling rendering and browser navigation) and the web application (handling the events and all other interfaces of the program) on the server. In thick-clients the browser handles even a larger

P. Hudak and D.S. Warren (Eds.): PADL 2008, LNCS 4902, pp. 299–315, 2008.

part of the application by executing (Java) scripts, but that is outside the scope of this paper. We focus on thin client web applications. By returning to a previous page the current part of the state stored at the client site is replaced by a previous version as well. Since the web application at the server is unaware of this browser navigation, the part of the state stored at the server is unaffected. Whether some part of the state should be changed on browser navigation is problem dependent. Parts of the state representing actions or objects in the real world, like purchases in a web shop, can usually not be undone by the user. Hence these parts of the state should not be changed by going to a previous page, this is achieved by storing them on the server. Other parts of the state, like the contents of the basket in a web shop, can safely be changed by browser navigation and hence should be stored in the page. Storing some part of the state at the wrong place is usually harmless without browser navigation, but using browser navigation reveals the problem, see also [4]. Hence, it is desirable to include browser navigation in the tests of software with a web interface.

In this paper we extend our approach for model-based testing of web applications [6] to the additional behavior imposed by browser navigation. A web application to be tested is modeled by an extended state machine. The test system automatically determines conformance between the web application and its model by generating inputs. The corresponding output is checked by the test system using the model. Many other existing models used for testing browser navigation, like [1], cover only the input elements available in the web-page and are not able to check the correctness of the new page obtained.

The effects of browser navigation on the models needed for testing are severe. Even if the original implementation under test, iut, can be adequately modeled by a *finite* state machine, an *infinite* state machine is needed for testing with browser navigation buttons. Each state in the model without browser navigation has to be replaced by an unbounded number of states where the difference between those states is the history of previous pages reachable with the back-button and the forward-button. It would be tedious if the behavior corresponding to this browser directed navigation must be specified for each and every system. Fortunately the behavior is very similar, but not necessarily identical, for most web applications. This enables us to define a *model transformer* that adds default behavior for the back and forward-button to each state in the model. We have chosen to take the model where all state information is local in the current web page as the default. This default corresponds to the browsing of simple old fashioned web-pages. If other behavior is required for specific states or inputs, the test engineer has to specify only the exceptions to the default behavior.

The organization of this paper is as follows. Section 2 rephrases testing of thin-client web applications in order to make this paper more self contained. In section 3 we elaborate on the special behavior associated with the back- and forward-button. Section 4 introduces a general model transformer to turn a model of a web application without browser navigation into a model with default behavior for the back- and forward-button. This is illustrated by two simple examples, for the first one (section 4.1) the automatic transformation does everything wanted, for the second example (section 4.2) exceptions of the default behavior are specified. Other forms of browser navigation are briefly touched in section 5. In section 6 we discuss related work. Finally we draw conclusions.

2 Model Based Testing of Thin Client Web Applications

In this paper we use the automatic model-based test tool G∀ST [5]. G∀ST uses functions in the functional programming language Clean[1] [8] as specification. Distinguishing features of G∀ST are the fully automatic generation of tests, their execution and the generation of verdicts. Input generation for arbitrary types can be derived automatically using generic programming as well as specified explicitly by the test engineer.

Reactive systems such as web applications are modeled with an Extended State Machine, ESM. An individual transition is written as $s \xrightarrow{i/o} t$, where s is the source state, t is the target state, i is the input value, and o the associated output. An ESM is similar to a Mealy Finite State Machine, FSM, but can have an infinite number of states, inputs and outputs. Moreover, an ESM can be *nondeterministic*, i.e. there can be multiple transitions for each state and input. Sometimes the output determines the target state, but there exist also systems with transitions $s \xrightarrow{i/o} t_1$ and $s \xrightarrow{i/o} t_2$ for some s, i and o with $t_1 \neq t_2$. From a single source state s there exist two (or more) transitions with identical labels (input and output), but different target states. An ESM used as specification in model-based testing can be nondeterministic for two reasons. Either the system specified is nondeterministic, or the system is deterministic but there is incomplete state information in the specification. Consider for instance the purchase of an item from a webstore. If the goods in stock are unknown in the specification, the model has to allow the response to situation where the item is in stock as well as the situation where the item is not available. The webstore itself will be deterministic; if the item is available it will be sold. The specification of this transition in model-based testing however, must be nondeterministic due to the incomplete state information. Such a situation with incomplete state information in the specification is common in model-based testing.

A specification is *partial* if there is a combination of a reachable state and a valid input that does not occur in any of the specified transitions. The conformance relation defined in section 2.1 states that any behavior of the system under test is allowed if the specification does not cover the current state and input. Since anything is allowed, testing such a transition is useless. G∀ST is able to handle these partial specifications.

For the specification of a web application the state can be freely chosen by the test engineer. The type HtmlInput represents input elements in a web-page like: buttons, links, drop-down lists and edit-boxes. One can use any desired type for

---

[1] See http://www.st.cs.ru.nl/papers/2007/CleanHaskellQuickGuide.pdf for the main differences between Clean and Haskell.

inputs in the model if one provides an instance of the class `transInput i :: i →` `HtmlInput` for that type. Using a tailor made type instead of `HtmlInput` is convenient in the generation of test data. For instance, the test engineer can construct a data type to generate only integers values between 0 and 10, and define an instance of `transInput` that puts these values in the desired edit-box. The output is always an element of type `Html`. This type is an abstract syntax tree for HTML-code rather than a textual representation. We reuse the type for HTML from the iData toolkit [7], Clean's tool for generic web-page generation.

For the specification of the output of a web application we do not want to specify the HTML after each input completely. That would be much too detailed and restrictive. Instead of modeling a single transition $s \xrightarrow{i/o} t$ by a tuple (s, i, o, t) and the entire specification δ_r by a set of tuples $\delta_r \subseteq S \times I \times O^* \times S$, we use a function. This specification function δ_F takes the current state and input as argument and yields a function that takes the output of the web application as argument and yields the set of allowed target states. In this way, the output can be used to determine the target states. Instead of a single function, δ_F yields a list of functions. Hence, the type of the specification is $\delta_F(s, i) \in S \times I \to \mathbb{P}(O^* \to \mathbb{P}S)$. In this representation the empty set conveniently models partial specifications. The set of functions is convenient in the composition and transformation of specifications as shown below. Moreover, in this representation it is much easier to determine the set of inputs that are allowed in a state s (the init defined below) then in a representation of the specification as a function δ_F of type $S \times I \to O^* \to \mathbb{P}S$). Mathematically these types of specifications are equivalent, but for a test system the first version is much more convenient. Finally, this representation makes it easier to mix it with the existing specification format used by G∀ST where one specifies the combinations of outputs and target states $S \times I \to \mathbb{P}(O^* \times S)$.

A specification of the form $S \times I \to \mathbb{P}(O^* \times S)$ is similar to a classical Mealy machine were the output function $S \times I \to \mathbb{P}(O^*)$ and state transition function $S \times I \to \mathbb{P}S$ are joined to a single function. Classical Mealy machines are deterministic, i.e. these functions have types $S \times I \to O^*$ and $S \times I \to S$. Moreover, classical Mealy machines handle finite state machines, that is the sets S, I, and O should be finite. For a nondeterministic specification it is essential to join the output and transition function to a single specification function in order to make the connection between outputs and target state on nondeterministic transitions. Using functions of type $S \times I \to \mathbb{P}(O^* \to \mathbb{P}S)$ for the specification instead of functions yielding a list of tuples has as advantage that is is possible to use a small function as specification instead of a very long list of tuples. In the specification of a web application the type O represents the HTML-pages allowed. In general one does not want to specify the produced output of a web application until the last bit of the HTML output. Details like the background color of the page are usually completely irrelevant and one does not want to specify those particulars. Listing all allowed outputs would at least be nasty and annoying. In such situations a function of type $S \times I \to \mathbb{P}(O^* \to \mathbb{P}S)$ is much more convenient, the functions $O^* \to \mathbb{P}S$ can implement a predicate over the produced HTML. Of course it is still possible to model a finite state machine in this representation. If the web application at hand should be a finite state machine, we can still test it as a finite state machine. In general the web application is modeled as an ESM, which shows richer behavior.

For a single transition our specification reads: $s \xrightarrow{i/o} t \Leftrightarrow \exists f \in \delta_F(s,i) \wedge t \in f(o)$. For web applications the functions f yielded by $\delta_F(s,i)$ are predicates over the HTML output of the web application. Such a predicate typically verifies some key aspects of a web-page, like the availability of buttons and specific text fields. We show some examples in section 4.1.

Although technically superfluous, it turns out to be convenient to have the possibility to specify one additional predicate P relating the output and target state in each and every transition. This predicate checks whether the combination of HTML and target state is well formed[2]. That is $s \xrightarrow{i/o} t \Leftrightarrow \exists f \in \delta_F(s,i) \wedge t \in f(o) \wedge P(o,t)$.

The set of inputs allowed in a state s is $\mathsf{init}(s) \equiv \{i | \delta_F(s,i) \neq \emptyset\}$. A *trace* is a sequence of inputs and associated outputs from some start state. The empty trace connects a state to itself: $s \xRightarrow{\epsilon} s$. A trace $s \xRightarrow{\sigma} t$ can be extended with a transition $t \xrightarrow{i/o} u$ to the trace $s \xRightarrow{\sigma;i/o} u$. If we are not interested in the target state we write $s \xrightarrow{i/o} \equiv \exists t.s \xrightarrow{i/o} t$ or $s \xRightarrow{\sigma} \equiv \exists t.s \xRightarrow{\sigma} t$. All traces from state s are: $\mathsf{traces}(s) = \{\sigma | s \xRightarrow{\sigma}\}$. All reachable states after a trace σ from state s are: $s \, \mathsf{after}\, \sigma \equiv \{t | s \xRightarrow{\sigma} t\}$. We overload traces, init, and after for sets of states instead of a single state by taking the union of the individual results. When the transition function, δ_F, to be used is not clear from the context, we add it as subscript to the operator.

2.1 Conformance

Here the implementation under test, iut, is a web application. The iut is modeled as a black box transition system. One can observe its traces, but not its state. The iut and its specification need not have identical input output behavior in all situations to say that the web application conforms to the specification.

Conformance of the iut to the specification spec is defined as:

$$\mathsf{iut\ conf\ spec} \equiv \forall \sigma \in \mathsf{traces}_{\mathsf{spec}}(s_0), \forall i \in \mathsf{init}(s_0\ \mathsf{after}_{\mathsf{spec}}\ \sigma), \forall o \in O^*.$$

$$(t_0\ \mathsf{after}_{\mathsf{iut}}\ \sigma) \xrightarrow{i/o} \Rightarrow (s_0\ \mathsf{after}_{\mathsf{spec}}\ \sigma) \xrightarrow{i/o}$$

Here s_0 is the initial state of spec. The initial state of the iut, t_0, is generally not known. The iut is in this abstract state when we select its url for the first time. Intuitively the conformance relation reads: if the specification allows input i after trace σ, then the observed output of the iut should be allowed by the specification. If spec does not specify a transition for the current state and input, anything is allowed.

---

[2] In the implementation this function is able to yield an error message if the combination of output and target state is invalid, rather than having a plain boolean as result.

For the specification spec it is perfectly legal to be partial. That is nothing is specified about the behavior for some state and input combinations. The interpretation in the conformance relation is that all behavior of the iut is allowed. Since everything is allowed, it makes no sense to test this.

The iut cannot refuse inputs. In every state the iut should give some response to any input. This response can be an error message or an empty sequence. During testing for conformance only inputs occurring in the specification after a valid trace will be applied.

This conformance relation is very similar to Tretmans ioco (Input Output Conformance) relation. The original ioco relation [9] handles conformance of labeled transition systems (LTS). The essential difference between a LTS (as used in the ioco relation) and a ESM is that the input and output are separate actions in a LTS. This implies that a LTS allows for instance two consecutive inputs without an (probably empty) output of each of these inputs. Exactly one input and the associated output are combined to a single transition in an ESM. Moreover, an ESM has rich states where the "state" of an LTS is given by the current location in the LTS and the value of a set of global variables. For the abstraction level of web applications used here, the ESM-based view is more appropriate than a LTS-based view: we always want to consider the output associated to a given input.

2.2   Testing Conformance

The conformance relation states that for all inputs allowed after all traces of the specification, the input-output pair obtained from the iut should also occur in the specification. Since the number of different traces is unbounded for a general ESM, it is impossible to determine conformance by exhaustive testing. For a general ESM the real conformance can only be determined by model checking the specification and a model of the web application. That is a completely different technique from model-based testing. Here we want to treat the web application as a black box. We can apply an input to the web application and observe the generated output. No detailed model of its behavior is known. Hence, model checking is not an option.

Testing can however give a fair approximation of conformance. Moreover, a large number of correct transitions increases the confidence in the correctness of the iut. Experience shows that nonconformance is very often found rather quickly. Errors are found most often within thousands or even hundreds of transitions, rather than millions of transitions. Nevertheless, it is easy to design an iut with an error that can only be found with an enormous testing effort, but these kind of errors appear to be rare in practice.

Since checking the conformance by testing all possible traces is generally impossible, we test conformance by verifying a fixed number of traces. For each trace we check a finite number of transitions with the following algorithm:

$$\mathsf{testConf} : \mathbb{N} \times \mathbb{P}\, S_{spec} \times S_{iut} \to \mathsf{Verdict}$$
$$\mathsf{testConf}\,(n, s, u) = \mathbf{if}\ s = \emptyset$$

> **then** Fail
> **else if** $n = 0 \lor \text{init}(s) = \emptyset$
> **then** Pass
> **else** testConf $(n-1, t, v)$
> **where** $i \in \text{init}(s)$; $(o, v) = \text{iut}(u, i)$; $s \xrightarrow{i/o} t$

In this algorithm $n \in \mathbb{N}$ is the number of steps still to be tested in the current trace, $s \in \mathbb{P}\, S_{spec}$ is the set of possible states in the specification, $u \in S_{iut}$ is the abstract state of the iut, and Verdict is the result type that contains the elements Fail and Pass. Since the iut is a black box, the state u cannot be observed. We assume that the iut is available as a function of type $(S_{iut} \times I) \rightarrow (O^* \times S_{iut})$. The consistency predicate $P(o, t)$ is incorporated in the transition $s \xrightarrow{i/o} t$. Since the transition function yields a function, the new set of possible states is actually computed as $t = \{x \mid \forall s_i \in s, \forall f \in \delta_f(s_i, i), \forall x \in f(o), P(o, x)\}$. Due to the overloading of the transition notation we can write it concisely as $s \xrightarrow{i/o} t$.

Testing of a single trace is initiated by testConf $(N, \{s_0\}, S_{iut}^0)$, where N is the maximum length of this trace, s_0 the initial state of the specification, and S_{iut}^0 the initial abstract state of the iut. The input i used in each step is chosen arbitrarily from the set init(s). In the actual implementation it is possible to control this choice. The default algorithm generates input elements in pseudo random order and uses the first input element that is in init(s), i.e. $\exists x \in s.\delta_f(x, i) \neq \emptyset$.

2.3   Implementation

Apart from the representation of the specification the conformance relation used here is identical to the conformance relation implemented previously in G∀ST. The type of specifications handled by G∀ST are functions of type `Spec s i o`. Given a state `s` and an input `i`, the specifications yields a list of functions. Each of these functions yields a list of allowed targets states `[s]` after it receives the output obtained from the iut.

```
:: Spec s i o :== s → i → [[o]→[s]]
```

Since `s`, `i`, and `o` are type variables, one can choose any type for states inputs and outputs. In order to test web applications the test system has to behave as a browser for the web application. The web application expects an input and yields a new HTML-page as response. G∀STis extended by a module that selects the indicated input element from the current page and sends an input to the web application as if it were generated by a real browser. The page received as answer from the iut is used in the test of conformance. The additional predicate to check the consistency of the page and the states of the specification can be given as an option to the main test function:

```
testHtml :: [TestSMOption s i Html] → (Spec s i Html) → s →
            (*HSt → (Html,*HSt)) → *World → *World
```

The first argument is the list of test options. The options can control the number of traces used in the test and their length, the amount of detail written in log-files, the input selection algorithm etcetera. It is also possible to add a predicate checking the consistency of the current HTML-page and the state of the specification. G∀ST has reasonable defaults for all these parameters. Hence, it is often possible to leave this list of options empty. The second argument is the specification as shown above. The next argument is the initial state of the specification. The final arguments are the web application and Clean's world.

In order to facilitate testing of the received page, there are functions to query the data structure representing the HTML-page. For instance it is possible to obtain the list of all texts from the page, and to retrieve all text labeled with some name. These names are the anchors that are used in the page. Requiring anchors with specific names appears to be very convenient, but not necessary, in the testing of web-pages. For example `htmlTxts "Answer"`, applied to the current page yields the list of all strings labeled `"Answer"`.

3   Browser Navigation

In order to use our model-based test tool G∀ST to test web applications with browser navigation, we need a model of the desired behavior. First we determine the requirements for such a specification. An unattractive option is to add inputs `Back` and `Forward` to each specification and let the test engineer completely specify the semantics of these actions. *Requirement 1*: it should be easy to transform a specification ignoring browser navigation to a specification prescribing default behavior for browser navigation.

Even if the web application itself is a simple finite state machine with one or more loops the specification needs an unbounded amount of memory to record the potentially infinite number of browser navigation actions. *Requirement 2*: there is no artificial limit on the number of browser navigation actions.

Next we argue that using the back-button is not an undo of the previous transition in the specification. Consider the left state machine in figure 1. Suppose we know that the specification is in state S_0. When we apply the input i_1 to the iut and observe the output O_1 the set of possible states is $\{S_1, S_2\}$. After observing a transition i_2/O_3 the state is S_4. Hence the previous state was S_2. The back button brings the specification in this state S_2 via the transition $S_2 \xleftarrow{Back/O_1} S_4$ and not in $\{S_1, S_2\}$. This implies that if we apply the input i_2 again the only allowed output is O_3. *Requirement 3*: the back-button is a normal transition for the specification, not an undo action for the specification.

If the transition labeled i_2/O_2 should be allowed after the trace i_1/O_1; i_2/O_3; $Back/O_1$, we need a specification as depicted on the right in figure 1.

3.1   Persistent States

In the discussion above we have assumed that the web application stores its state in the web-page. This state can either be stored in visible parts like edit boxes and radio buttons, or in so-called *hidden fields* in the web-page. This content is invisible for the user in a normal browser window, but readable and writable for the web application. If the entire state of the web application is stored in the web-page, the web application goes to its previous state if the user goes a page back with the back-button of the browser.

Consider what would happen if the base converter (introduced in section 4.1) stores the number to be converted, the latest contents of the edit-box, in a persistent memory location, like in a cookie or some storage location on the web-server. If the user uses the back-button the browser displays the previous page, but the number to be converted is not changed even if it is different on the previous page which becomes actual. When the user chooses now a different base on this page not the displayed number is converted, but the number from the persistent memory.

For the number to be converted this is considered as undesirable behavior, but for a counter that keeps track of the total number of conversions done in this session this is exactly what is needed. This implies that the designer of the web application should determine the desired behavior for each variable in the web application.

In order to perform a model-based test of such a web application the model should reflect the persistent or volatile behavior of the modeled components of the state. Instead of splitting the state of each web application explicitly in a persistent and a volatile part, we ask the user to define a function that composes the new state of the specification from the last state and the previous state on a transition corresponding to a back-button. The default function yields the previous state. This corresponds to a complete volatile memory without any persistent component.

4 A Model Transformer to Model Browser Navigation

In this section we present a specification transformer that converts a specification without browser navigation to a specification that covers browser navigation. The transformed specification states that a Back just returns to the previous

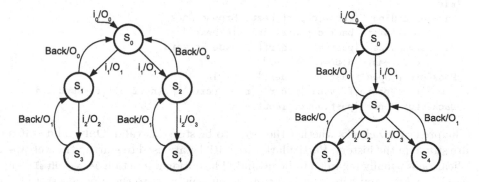

Fig. 1. Two nondeterministic state machines with back transitions

state in the specification without any state change corresponding to persistent state components. The `Forward` in the specification is always the undo of the corresponding `Back`-action, independent of the existence of persistent components in the state of the web application. The user can easily specify exceptions to this rule.

Web applications are specified most concisely using tailor made types for their input and state. Instances of the class `transInput` transform a tailor made type for inputs to the type `HtmlInput` required by the test system. It is undesirable to extend all types for inputs with their own back and forward buttons, and all types for state with their own history. This problem is solved by using a polymorphic type `BFInput i`. This type states that the input is either an element of the input type of the specification, a backward button from the browser, or a forward button from the browser.

```
:: BFInput i = SpecIn i | BrowserBack | BrowserForward
```

In a similar way we lift the type of a single state of the specification to a state with a history, `past`, and a future, `next`.

```
:: BFState s = {past :: [s], next :: [s]}
```

By convention the current state is the first state in the past:

```
toBFState :: s → BFState s
toBFState s = {past = [s], next = []}
```

Lifting a specification from an ordinary state `s` to a state `BFState s` that is also able to handle browser navigation is done by the function `toBackForwardSpec`. This function transforms both the state and the input to the types given above.

```
toBackForwardSpec ::    (Spec s i Html) (s→Bool) (Maybe (s→s→[Html]→s))
                    → (Spec (BFState s) (BFInput i) Html)
toBackForwardSpec s v Nothing = toBackForwardSpec s v (Just (λc p o→p))
toBackForwardSpec spec v (Just back) = BackForwardSpec
where
  BackForwardSpec {past=[c,p:r],next} BrowserBack
    = [λo→[{past=[back c p o:r],next=[c:next]}]]
  BackForwardSpec {past,next=[n:r]} BrowserForward
    = [λo→[{past=[n:past],next=r}]]
  BackForwardSpec {past=[c:r],next} (SpecIn i)
    = [λo→[{past=if (v c) [n,c:r] [n:r],next=[]}\\n←f o]\\f←spec c i]
  BackForwardSpec {past,next} input = []
```

The predicate `v` checks whether the state to be stored is valid. Only valid states are stored in the history. Particularly the initial state used to startup the web application is usually regarded to be invalid. The optional function `s→s→[Html]→s` can is used to copy persistent parts of the current state to the previous state for a `BrowserBack` input. Note the rather complex behavior specified for an ordinary input: each new state receives its own copy of the history.

4.1 Example: Base Converter

The first example is a web application that converts a decimal number to some other base. The bases supported are 2 (binary), 8 (octal), 12 (duodecimal), and 16 (hexadecimal). The base to be used is selected by the corresponding button. The number to convert is given in an integer edit box. In figure 2 a screen shot and the transition diagram of the Extended State Machine are given.

This example is clearly not a classic HTML-page, it contains buttons and performs computations rather than simple text and links. The state of the specification of this web application contains just the number to be transformed and the base to be used for this transformation. The state is represented by a record of type State containing the number and the base as an element of the enumeration type Base.

```
:: State = {n :: Int, b :: Base}
:: Base = Bin | Oct | Duo | Hex
```

The behavior of this web application is specified by the function BaseConvSpec:

```
BaseConvSpec :: State In → [[Html] → [State]]
BaseConvSpec s (BaseButton b) = [checkN2 {s&b=b} b s.n]
BaseConvSpec s (IntTextBox i) = [checkN2 {s&n=i} s.b i]

checkN2 :: State Base Int [Html] → [State]
checkN2 state b n html
    | findHtmlTexts "n2" html == [convert (toInt b) n] = [state]
    | otherwise                                        = []

convert :: Int Int → String
convert b i
    | i<0       = "-" + convert b (~i)
    | i<b       = baseDigits b !! i
    | otherwise = convert b (i/b) + baseDigits b !! (i rem b)
```

After each transition the specification checks whether the string labeled "n2" in the HTML-code received from the web application is equal to the string obtained

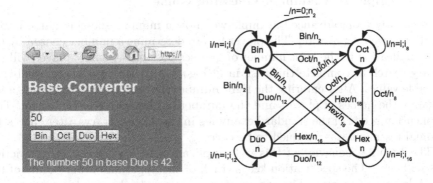

Fig. 2. Screen shot of the base converter and its Extended State Machine

by transforming the current number to a string in the current base. This example shows how we can use information from the parameterized state of the model and the actual HTML-code of the web application in the construction of the target state of the model. The initial state of the specification is:

```
initState = {n = 0, b = Bin}
```

After these preparations we can test an iData-based implementation of the base converter, called converter, by executing:

```
Start :: *World → *World
Start world = testHtml [] BaseConvSpec initState converter world
```

The web application is run by executing:

```
Start :: *World → *World
Start world = doHtmlServer converter world
```

Testing the web application converter with the specification BaseConvSpec does not reveal any issues. All observed traces are allowed by the specification.

The Base Converter with Browser Navigation. For the base converter we are happy with an implementation that treats the back-button of the browser as an undo of the last change. This implies that the implementation can store its entire state in the current page. That is the default choice of the iData, so converter can ignore browser navigation completely.

Using the specification transformer introduced here it is very easy to test whether the web application converter shows indeed the desired behavior. The specification transformer toBackForwardSpec imposes exactly the desired behavior. In order to execute the model-based tests one executes:

```
Start :: *World → *World
Start world = testHtml [] (toBackForwardSpec BaseConvSpec Nothing)
                          (toBFState initState) converter world
```

The results of this test show that the converter has the behavior prescribed by the specification lifted to the domain of browser navigation.

4.2   Example 2: A Number Guessing Game

As a slightly more advanced example we show a number guessing game implemented as web application. The player has to determine a number chosen by the web application in the least number of guesses possible. A smart player will use binary search to complete this task in $O(\log n)$ steps where n is the number of possible values. After entering the right number the web application shows a list of fame: the names of players and the number of guesses needed by them. This application is one of the standard examples in the iData-library. After successful manual testing it was assumed to be correct.

The required behavior of this web application is described by the function ngSpec below. The specification keeps track of the upper and lower bound of the possible correct answer. The specification also counts the number of tries and checks if this is correctly reported by the web application for a correct answer.

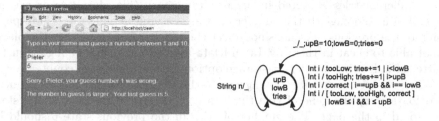

Fig. 3. The number guessing web application and a sketch of its state machine

```
:: NGState = {upB :: Int, lowB :: Int, tries :: Int}

newNGState = {upB = up, lowB = low, tries = 0}
initState  = {newNGState & tries = −1}

ngSpec :: NGState In → [[Html]→[NGState]]
ngSpec s  input  | s.tries<0 = [λ html = [newNGState]]  // used at startup
ngSpec s (StringTextBox n)  = [λ html = [s]]
ngSpec s (IntTextBox i)
  | i < s.lowB = [tooLow t]
  | i > s.upB  = [tooHigh t]
  | i == s.upB && i == s.lowB = [correct]
  | otherwise  = [tooLow {t & lowB = i+1},tooHigh {t & upB = i−1},correct]
where t = {s & tries = s.tries+1}

tooLow t html  |    htmlTxts "Hint" html == ["larger"]
                  && htmlTxts "Answer" html == ["Sorry"] = [t]
               | otherwise                               = []
tooHigh t html |    htmlTxts "Hint" html == ["smaller"]
                  && htmlTxts "Answer" html == ["Sorry"] = [t]
               | otherwise                               = []
correct   html | htmlTxts "Answer" html==["Congratulations"] = [newNGState]
               | otherwise                                   = []
```

Using this specification we tested the iData-implementation of this game. Testing shows an error: in contrast to the specification the web application chooses a new number to be guessed if the user enters a new name. Both choices for the behavior after a name change can be defended, but the choice in the specification and implementation has to be consistent. This shows that model-based testing of web applications is able to find data-related inconsistencies.

The Number Guessing Game with Browser Navigation. Using browser navigation, it seems attractive to cheat in this game in order to enter one's name high in the list of fame. A player guesses numbers until she knows the correct value. Then the user presses the back button until she is back to the HTML-page showing this task for the first time. Now she can enter the correct number immediately. In order to prevent this kind of cheating we require that the number of tries is stored in persistent memory (file, database or cookie) instead of in the page. If the number of tries is stored outside the HTML-page, going to the previous page does not affect the number of tries. Hence the player is not able to cheat in this way. In an iData-application such a change is just a matter of indicating a different storage option for the associated counter.

When we lift the specification ngSpec to the level of browser actions we need to deviate from the general rule that states that all components of the state are stored in the page. The number of tries in the previous state p should be identical to the number of tries in the current page c. Using our specification transformer this is expressed as:

```
liftedSpec          = toBackForwardSpec ngSpec valid (Just backNumGuess)
valid s             = s.tries ≥ 0
backNumGuess c p o  = {p & tries = c.tries}
```

Several other issues were found using model-based testing with this specification. **1)** The first issue is found by the predicate that the number of tries as text in the page should always be identical to number of tries in the specification. The first use of the back-button spoils this property. **2)** If one does not play the game to the end and starts a new one later, the web application continues with the old number of tries in persistent memory. **3)** Entering the same input twice in a row is counted as one try in the web application, but as two tries in the specification. **4)** The number to be guessed is stored in persistent memory by the web application, but the bounds are part of an ordinary state in the specification. This leads to inconsistencies in answers if one browses with the back-button over a correct guess and then continues with guessing. The specification prescribes consistency with the old bounds, while the answers of the web application are based on a new target. During the correction of these problems several small errors were introduced accidently and found by G∀ST.

Even testing a simple application that was assumed to be correct raised a number of serious issues. This shows that this framework is able to spot issues in real web applications. Testing with browser navigation often reveals issues related to the kind of storage used for parts of the state of the web application.

To demonstrate the possibilities of introducing additional changes in the lifted specification, we show how we can prevent going back to a previous game in the tests (corresponding to additional issue 4 above).

```
liftedSpec2 ls=:{past=[s,t:r]} | s.tries==0 = liftedSpec2 {ls & past=[s]}
liftedSpec2 s = toBackForwardSpec ngSpec valid (Just backNumGuess) s
```

If the number of tries in the current state is zero this implies that a new game is started. Going back to previous states is prevented by removing these states from the lifted specification. Note that only this additional requirement is defined, the general specification transformation keeps track of everything else.

By this additional requirement we only omit this behavior in the model. A real user might still provide this trace. When the model does not specify any behavior for such a trace, anything is allowed as behavior of the web application. So, if we have an opinion an the behavior of the iut in such a situation, we should specify it rather than remove it from the model.

5 More Browser Navigation

Most browsers provide more ways of browser navigation than just going a single page back or forward. A fairly standard option is to select one of the pages from the history or future to go n pages back or forward. It is straightforward to model such an transition and hence to test it using our model-based testing approach.

Most browsers allow also the possibility to clone a page. At any moment a user can decide to switch from the current page to such a clone or back and starts giving inputs from that page. This is slightly different from just going n pages back since a new input removes all forward pages (if they exist). A cloned page is not effected by a new input in some other page. In order to test this behavior we have to model it. This implies that we have to maintain a set of BFStates instead a single BFState. At the input Clone we copy the current state from the current BFState to a new BFState. At the input Switch the model makes another BFState the current state. Testing proceeds as before using this new state in the specification.

6 Related Work

Many other test tools for web applications exist, see www.softwareqatest.com for an overview. They often execute user-defined test scripts (like HttpUnit [2] see also httpunit.sourceforge.net). Browser navigation is only tested if it is explicitly included manually in the scripts. Our tool generates traces on-the-fly from the specification instead of executing predefined scripts. Other tools verify the HTML-code generated by the application, or the existence of the links in a generated page.

The paper by Andrews et al. [1] also specifies web applications by state machines in order to test the web applications. They argue that a huge number of errors is introduced by browser navigation. Hence, it is very worthwhile to test this. An important restriction of their approach is that they do not solve the *oracle problem*: their specification only specifies the inputs that should be accepted by the web application. The result of applying an input is not specified and cannot be tested. The reason the oracle problem is not solved is that an input to a web application can have many effects: e.g. an order can be printed or stored in an database. Hence, it is next to impossible to determine all effects of applying an input to a web application. Moreover, even the effect of input to the new HTML-page can be large. Usually we do not want to pinpoint every detail of the HTML-code that should be produced by the web application.

In our approach we cannot specify all effects of an input to a web application. Instead, we write a predicate over the resulting HTML-page. With a predicate we can specify the amount of detail needed, ranging from nothing at all to every detail of the HTML-code. Moreover, we use parameterized state machines rather than finite state machine like Andrews. This implies that we can store much data-related information (like counters, values and names) compactly in a parameterized state. This paper shows that we can specify elements of the page using this information and test these data by the model-based test tool G∀ST. As future research we will investigate how other effects of the web application on the world can be specified and tested.

Another popular approach to specifying transition systems is based on labeled transition systems, most notably the ioco approach and its variants as introduced by Tretmans [9]. In such a system the input and associated output have to be modeled by two separated actions. In our model of web applications the input and output are directly coupled: each input produces a new page as result. This is very convenient for the level of abstraction we want to consider here. In [3] Frantzen et al. describe the basis of an approach to test web services (instead of the web applications handled here). They use a Java like language as carrier for their specification which makes it less suited for function transformations that are the key of our approach. The state of the specification in their current implementation is mapped to a single integer. This implies that both examples used in this paper cannot be handled by their tooling.

We plan to extend G∀ST with asynchronous transitions in order to specify and test systems where the input and output are not necessarily tightly coupled. This would allow the handling of timeouts and web applications based on AJAX-technology.

7   Conclusions

It is a trend that new applications start using a browser as their universal graphical user interface. By design or not, these applications receive an interface with browser navigation. It is important to specify and test this behavior. We introduce a specification transformer that makes it easy to lift a specification that ignores browser navigation to a version that includes browser navigation. Only exceptions to the general behavior have to be specified explicitly. In this paper we demonstrate that this technique is capable of spotting errors in real web applications. We have shown that it really matters where the state of an application is stored. If the entire state is stored in the page the back-button corresponds to an undo-action. A state stored at the server is not influenced at all by using the back-button. The desired behavior of such a web application needs to be prescribed in a specification.

Specifying web applications by extended state machines has been shown to be a good basis for model-based testing. Representing the extended state machines by functions in a functional programming language yields very compact and elegant specifications. Due to the use of parameterized types and computations with these parameters, the specifications are clearer and more compact than corresponding graphical representations of the specification. Moreover, the representation of specifications by a function is much better suited for transformations, like lifting to the domain of browser navigation.

We show that this technique is able to spot issues in real web applications. In this paper we used web applications constructed with Clean's iData library, but that is not an inherent limitation of the technique described. For an arbitrary web application the test system will receive a textual version of the page in HTML rather than the data structure used here. The iData system contains a parser that is able to transform the textual representation to the data structure used here. If the test engineer would prefer, she can also use the textual representation of HTML (or any other representation preferred) in the specification and hence in the tests.

The formal treatment of conformance is improved in this paper. In our previous work [6], the predicate that checks the consistency of the output and the target state was added rather ad-hoc to the test algorithm. In this paper this predicate is part of the transition relation, and in that way smoothly integrated in the conformance relation and the test algorithm.

References

1. Andrews, A., Offutt, J., Alexander, R.: Testing Web Applications by Modelling with FSMs. Software Systems and Modeling 4(3) (August 2005)
2. Burke, E., Coyner, B.: Java Extreme Programming Cookbook. O'Reilly (2003)
3. Frantzen, L., Tretmans, J., Vries, R.d.: Towards model-based testing of web services. In: Polini, A. (ed.) WS-MaTe2006. International Workshop on Web Services - Modeling and Testing, Palermo, Italy, pp. 67–82 (June 9th, 2006)
4. Graunke, P., Findler, R., Krishnamurthi, S., Felleisen, M.: Modeling Web Interactions. In: Degano, P. (ed.) ESOP 2003 and ETAPS 2003. LNCS, vol. 2618, pp. 238–252. Springer, Heidelberg (2003)
5. Koopman, P., Plasmeijer, R.: Testing reactive systems with GAST. In: Gilmore, S. (ed.) Trends in Functional Programming, vol. 4, pp. 111–129 (2004)
6. Koopman, P., Plasmeijer, R., Achten, P.: Model-based testing of thin-client web applications. In: Havelund, K., Núñez, M., Roşu, G., Wolff, B. (eds.) FATES 2006 and RV 2006. LNCS, vol. 4262, Springer, Heidelberg (2006)
7. Plasmeijer, R., Achten, P.: iData For The World Wide Web - Programming Interconnected Web Forms. In: Hagiya, M., Wadler, P. (eds.) FLOPS 2006. LNCS, vol. 3945, Springer, Heidelberg (2006)
8. Plasmeijer, R., van Eekelen, M.: Concurrent CLEAN Language Report (version 2.0) (December 2001), http://www.cs.ru.nl/~clean/
9. Tretmans, J.: Testing Concurrent Systems: A Formal Approach. In: Baeten, J.C.M., Mauw, S. (eds.) CONCUR 1999. LNCS, vol. 1664, pp. 46–65. Springer, Heidelberg (1999)

High-Level Database Programming in Curry*

Bernd Braßel, Michael Hanus, and Marion Müller

Institut für Informatik, CAU Kiel, Germany
{bbr,mh,mam}@informatik.uni-kiel.de

Abstract. This paper presents an environment to support high-level database programming in the multi-paradigm declarative programming language Curry. We define an application programming interface (API) that abstracts from the concrete database access methods. The API supports transactions and exploits Curry's type system to ensure a strict separation between queries and updates. In order to ensure database updates that are safe w.r.t. an intended data model (e.g., containing specific relations between entities), we assume a description of the data dependencies in the entity-relationship (ER) model from which all access and update operations related to the database are generated. We propose a representation of ER diagrams in the declarative language Curry so that they can be constructed by various tools and then translated into this representation. Furthermore, we have implemented a compiler from this representation into a Curry program that provides safe access and update operations based on the API for database programming.

1 Motivation

Many applications in the real world need databases to store the data they process. Thus, programming languages for such applications must also support some mechanism to organize the access to databases. This can be done in a way that is largely independent on the underlying programming language, e.g., by passing SQL statements as strings to some database connection. However, it is well known that such a loose coupling is a source of security leaks, in particular, in web applications [15]. Thus, a tight connection or amalgamation of the database access into the programming language should be preferred.

In principle, logic programming provides a natural framework for connecting databases (e.g., see [4,6]) since relations stored in a relational database can be considered as facts defining a predicate of a logic program. Unfortunately, the well-developed theory in this area is not accompanied by practical implementations. For instance, distributions of Prolog implementations rarely come with a standard interface to relational databases. An exception is Ciao Prolog which has a persistence module [3] that allows the declaration of predicates where facts are persistently stored, e.g., in a relational database. This module supports a simple method to query the relational database, but updates are handled by predicates

---

* This work was partially supported by the German Research Council (DFG) under grant Ha 2457/5-2.

P. Hudak and D.S. Warren (Eds.): PADL 2008, LNCS 4902, pp. 316–332, 2008.

with side effects and transactions are not explicitly supported. A similar concept but with a clear separation between queries and updates has been proposed in [10] for the multi-paradigm declarative language Curry [7,14]. This will be the basis for the current framework that provides an environment for high-level programming with databases. The objectives of this work are:

- The methods to access and update the database should be expressed by language features rather than passing SQL strings around.
- Queries to the database should be clearly separated from updates that might change the outcome of queries.
- Safe transactions, i.e., sequence of updates that keep some integrity constraints, should be supported.
- The necessary code for these operations should be derived from specifications whenever possible in order to obtain more reliable applications.

In a first step, described in Section 2, we define an application programming interface (API) for database programming in Curry that abstracts from the concrete methods to access a given database by providing abstract operations for this purpose. This API exploits the type system in order to ensure a strict separation between queries and updates. To specify the logical structure of the data to be stored in a database, we use the entity-relationship (ER) model [2]. In order to be largely independent of concrete specification tools, we define in Section 3 a representation of ER diagrams in Curry so that concrete ER specification tools can be connected by defining a translator from the format used in these tools into this Curry representation. Finally, we develop a compiler that translates an ER diagram into a Curry module that contains access and update operations and operations to check integrity constraints according to the ER diagram. The generated code is based on the database API. The compilation method is sketched in Section 4. Finally, Section 5 contains our conclusions.

2   Database Programming in Curry

We assume familiarity with functional logic programming (see [12] for a recent survey) and Curry [7,14] so that we give in the following only a short sketch of the basic concepts relevant for this paper.

Functional logic languages integrate the most important features of functional and logic languages to provide a variety of programming concepts to the programmer. For instance, the concepts of demand-driven evaluation, higher-order functions, and polymorphic typing from functional programming are combined with logic programming features like computing with partial information (logic variables), constraint solving, and nondeterministic search. This combination leads to better abstractions in application programs such as implementing graphical user interfaces [8], programming dynamic web pages [9,11], or access and manipulation of persistent data possibly stored in databases [5,10].

As a concrete functional logic language, we use Curry in our framework but it should be possible to apply the same ideas also to other functional logic languages, e.g., TOY [16]. From a syntactic point of view, a Curry program is a functional program extended by the possible inclusion of free (logic) variables in conditions and right-hand sides of defining rules. Curry has a Haskell-like syntax [17], i.e., a Curry *program* consists of the definition of functions and data types on which the functions operate. Functions are first-class citizens and evaluated lazily. To provide the full power of logic programming, functions can be called with partially instantiated arguments and defined by conditional equations with constraints in the conditions. Function calls with free variables are evaluated by a possibly nondeterministic instantiation of demanded arguments (i.e., arguments whose values are necessary to decide the applicability of a rule) to the required values in order to apply a rule. Curry also offers other standard features of functional languages, like higher-order functions, modules, or monadic I/O [18].

The following Curry program defines functions for computing the concatenation of lists and the last element of a list:

```
conc :: [a] -> [a] -> [a]
conc []     ys = ys
conc (x:xs) ys = x : conc xs ys

last :: [a] -> a
last xs | conc ys [x] =:= xs   = x   where x,ys free
```

Thus, logic programming is supported by admitting function calls with free variables (see "conc ys [x]" above) and constraints in the condition of a defining rule. Conditional rules have the form $l \mid c = r$ specifying that l is reducible to r if the condition c is satisfied (see the rule defining `last` above). A *constraint* is any expression of the built-in type Success. For instance, the trivial constraint success is an expression of type Success that denotes the always satisfiable constraint. "$c_1 \& c_2$" denotes the *concurrent conjunction* of the constraints c_1 and c_2, i.e., this expression is evaluated by proving both argument constraints concurrently. An *equational constraint* $e_1 =:= e_2$ is satisfiable if both sides e_1 and e_2 are reducible to unifiable constructor terms. Specific Curry systems also support more powerful constraint structures, like arithmetic constraints on real numbers or finite domain constraints (e.g., PAKCS [13]).

Using functions instead of predicates has the advantage that the information provided by functional dependencies can be used to reduce the search space and evaluate goals in an optimal way [1]. However, there are also situations where a relational style is preferable, e.g., for database applications as considered in this paper. This style is supported by considering predicates as functions with result type Success. For instance, a predicate isPrime that is satisfied if the argument (an integer number) is a prime can be modeled as a function with type

```
isPrime :: Int -> Success
```

The following rules define a few facts for this predicate:

```
isPrime 2 = success
isPrime 3 = success
isPrime 5 = success
isPrime 7 = success
```

Apart from syntactic differences, any pure logic program has a direct correspondence to a Curry program. For instance, a predicate `isPrimePair` that is satisfied if the arguments are primes that differ by 2 can be defined as follows:

```
isPrimePair :: Int -> Int -> Success
isPrimePair x y = isPrime x & isPrime y & x+2 =:= y
```

In order to deal with information that is persistently stored outside the program (e.g., in databases), dynamic predicates are proposed in [10]. A *dynamic predicate* is a predicate where the defining facts (see `isPrime`) are not part of the program but stored outside. Moreover, the defining facts can be modified (similarly to dynamic predicates in Prolog). In order to distinguish between definitions in a program (that do not change over time) and dynamic entities, there is a distinguished type `Dynamic` for the latter.[1] For instance, in order to define a dynamic predicate `prime` to store prime numbers whenever we compute them, we provide the following definition in our program:

```
prime :: Int -> Dynamic
prime dynamic
```

If the prime numbers should be persistently stored, we replace the second line by

```
prime persistent "store"
```

where *store* specifies the storage mechanism, e.g., a directory for a lightweight file-based implementation [10] or a database specification [5].

There are various primitives that deal with dynamic predicates. First, there are combinators to construct complex queries from basic dynamic predicates. For instance, the combinator

```
(<>) :: Dynamic -> Dynamic -> Dynamic
```

joins two dynamic predicates, and the combinators

```
(|>)  :: Dynamic -> Bool    -> Dynamic
(|&>) :: Dynamic -> Success -> Dynamic
```

restrict a dynamic predicate with a Boolean condition or constraint, respectively. Since the operator "`<>`" binds stronger then "`|>`", the expression

```
prime x <> prime y |> x+2 == y
```

specifies numbers x and y that are prime pairs.[2] On the one hand, such expressions can be translated into corresponding SQL statements [5] so that the programmer is freed of dealing with details of SQL. On the other hand, one can use all elements and libraries of a universal programming language for database programming due to its conceptual embedding in the programming language.

---

[1] In contrast to Prolog, where dynamic declarations are often used for efficiency purposes, this separation is also necessary here due to the lazy evaluation strategy which makes it difficult to estimate *when* a particular evaluation is performed. Thus, performing updates by implicit side effects is not a good choice.

[2] Since the right argument of "`|>`" demands a Boolean value rather than a constraint, we use the Boolean equality operator "`==`" rather than the equational constraint "`=:=`" to compare the primes x and y.

Since the contents of dynamic predicates can change over time, one needs a careful concept of evaluating dynamic predicates in order to keep the declarative style of programming. For this purpose, we introduce the notion of "queries" that are evaluated in the I/O monad, i.e., at particular points of time in a computation.[3] Conceptually, a *query* is a method to compute solutions w.r.t. dynamic predicates. Depending on the number of requested solutions, there are different operations to construct queries, e.g.,

```
queryAll :: (a -> Dynamic) -> Query [a]
queryOne :: (a -> Dynamic) -> Query (Maybe a)
```

`queryAll` and `queryOne` construct queries to compute all and one (if possible) solution to an abstraction over dynamic predicates, respectively. For instance,

```
qPrimePairs :: Query [(Int,Int)]
qPrimePairs = queryAll (\(x,y) -> prime x <> prime y |> x+2==y)
```

is a query to compute all prime pairs. In order to access the currently stored data, there is an operation `runQ` to execute a query as an I/O action:

```
runQ :: Query a -> IO a
```

For instance, executing the main expression "`runQ qPrimePairs`" returns prime pairs w.r.t. the prime numbers currently stored in the dynamic predicate `prime`.

In order to change the data stored in dynamic predicates, there are operations to add and delete knowledge about dynamic predicates:

```
addDB    :: Dynamic -> Transaction ()
deleteDB :: Dynamic -> Transaction ()
```

Typically, these operations are applied to single ground facts (since facts with free variables cannot be persistently stored), like "`addDB (prime 13)`" or "`deleteDB (prime 4)`". In order to embed these update operations into safe transactions, the result type is "`Transaction ()`" (in contrast to the proposal in [10] where these updates are I/O actions). A *transaction* is basically a sequence of updates that is completely executed or ignored (following the ACID principle in databases). Similarly to the monadic approach to I/O [18], transactions also have a monadic structure so that transactions can be sequentially composed by a monadic bind operator:

```
(|>>=) :: Transaction a -> (a -> Transaction b) -> Transaction b
```

Thus, "`t1 |>>= \x -> t2`" is a transaction that first executes transaction `t1`, which returns some result value that is bound to the parameter `x` before executing transaction `t2`. If the result of the first transaction is not relevant, one can also use the specialized sequential composition "`|>>`":

```
(|>>) :: Transaction a -> Transaction b -> Transaction b
t1 |>> t2 = t1 |>>= \_ -> t2
```

A value can be mapped into a trivial transaction returning this value by the usual return operator:

```
returnT :: a -> Transaction a
```

---

[3] Note that we only use the basic concept of dynamic predicates from [10]. The following interface to deal with queries and transactions is new and more abstract than the concepts described in [10].

In order to define a transaction that depends on some data stored in a database, one can also embed a query into a transaction:

```
getDB :: Query a -> Transaction a
```

For instance, the following expression exploits the standard higher-order functions `map`, `foldr`, and "`.`" (function composition) to define a transaction that deletes all known primes that are smaller than 100:

```
getDB (queryAll (\i -> prime i |> i<100)) |>>=
foldr (|>>) (returnT ()) . map (deleteDB . prime)
```

Since such a sequential combination of transactions that are the result of mapping a list of values into a list of transactions frequently occurs, there is also a single function for this combination:

```
mapT_ :: (a -> Transaction _) -> [a] -> Transaction ()
mapT_ f = foldr (|>>) (returnT ()) . map f
```

To apply a transaction to the current database, there is an operation `runT` that executes a given transaction as an I/O action:

```
runT :: Transaction a -> IO (Either a TError)
```

`runT` returns either the value computed by the successful execution of the transaction or an error in case of a transaction failure. The type `TError` of possible transaction errors contains constructors for various kinds of errors, i.e., it is currently defined as

```
data TError = TError TErrorKind String

data TErrorKind = KeyNotExistsError | DuplicateKeyError
  | KeyRequiredError | UniqueError | NoRelationshipError
  | MinError | MaxError | UserDefinedError
```

but this type might be extended according to future requirements (the string argument is intended to provide some details about the reason of the error). `UserDefinedError` is a general error that could be raised by the application program whereas the other alternatives are typical errors due to unsatisfied integrity constraints according to ER diagrams. An error is raised inside a transaction by the operation

```
errorT :: TError -> Transaction a
```

where the specialization

```
failT :: String -> Transaction a
failT s = errorT (TError UserDefinedError s)
```

is useful to raise user-defined transaction errors. If an error is raised in a transaction, the transaction is aborted, i.e., the transaction monad satisfies the laws

$$\text{errorT } e \text{ |>>= } t = \text{errorT } e$$
$$t \text{ |>>= } \backslash x \text{ -> errorT } e = \text{errorT } e$$
$$\text{runT (errorT } e) = \text{return (Right } e)$$

Thus, the changes to the database performed in a transaction that raises an error are not visible.

There are a few further useful operations on transactions which are omitted here since they are not relevant for this paper. We summarize the important features of this abstract programming model for databases:

- Persistent data is represented in the application program as language entities (i.e., dynamic predicates) so that one can use all features of the underlying programming language (e.g., recursion, higher-order functions, deduction) for programming with this data.
- There is a clear separation between the data access (i.e., queries) and updates that can influence the results of accessing data. Thus, queries are purely declarative and are applied to the actual state of the database when their results are required.
- Transactions, i.e., database updates, can be constructed from a few primitive elements by specific combinators. Transactions are conceptually executed as an atomic action on the database. Transactions can be sequentially composed but nested transactions are excluded due to the type system (this feature is intended since nested transactions are usually not supported in databases).

This API for database programming is defined in a specific `Database` library[4] so that it can be simply used in the application program by importing it. This will be the basis to generate higher-level code from entity-relationship diagrams that are described next.

3   Entity-Relationship Diagrams

The entity-relationship model [2] is a framework to specify the structure and specific constraints of data stored in a database. It uses a graphical notation, called entity-relationship diagrams (ERDs) to visualize the conceptual model. In this framework, the part of the world that is interesting for the application is modeled by entities that have attributes and relationships between the entities. The relationships have cardinality constraints that must be satisfied in each valid state of the database, e.g., after each transaction.

There are various tools to support the data modeling process with ERDs. In our framework we want to use some tool to develop specific ERDs from which the necessary program code based on the `Database` library described in the previous section can be automatically generated. In order to become largely independent of a concrete tool, we define a representation of ERDs in Curry so that a concrete ERD tool can be applied in this framework by implementing a translator from the tool format into our representation. In our concrete implementation, we have used the free software tool Umbrello UML Modeller[5], a UML tool part of KDE that also supports ERDs. Figure 1 shows an example ERD constructed with this tool. The developed ERDs are stored in XML files in XMI (XML Metadata Interchange) format, a format for the exchange of UML models. Thus, it is a

---

[4] http://www.informatik.uni-kiel.de/~pakcs/lib/CDOC/Database.html
[5] http://uml.sourceforge.net

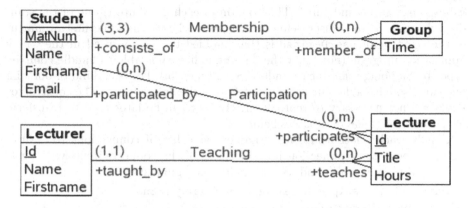

Fig. 1. A simple entity-relationship diagram for university lectures

standard XML transformation task to translate the Umbrello format into our
ERD format.

Unfortunately, there is no standard definition of ERDs so that different tools
support ERDs with different features. In the following, we provide a representation of ERDs that is sufficient for the Umbrello UML Modeller but it should
not be difficult to extend this representation to other kinds of ERDs (e.g., with
attributes for relations). The representation of ERDs as data types in Curry
is straightforward. In our case, a complete ERD consists of a name (that is
later used as the module name for the generated code) and lists of entities and
relationships:

```
data ERD = ERD String [Entity] [Relationship]
```

An entity has a name and a list of attributes, where each attribute has a name,
a domain, and specifications about its key and null value property:

```
data Entity = Entity String [Attribute]

data Attribute = Attribute String Domain Key Null

data Key = NoKey | PKey | Unique

type Null = Bool

data Domain = IntDom            (Maybe Int)
            | FloatDom          (Maybe Float)
            | CharDom           (Maybe Char)
            | StringDom         (Maybe String)
            | BoolDom           (Maybe Bool)
            | DateDom           (Maybe ClockTime)
            | UserDefined String (Maybe String)
            | KeyDom String    -- later used for foreign keys
```

Thus, each attribute is part of a primary key (PKey), unique (Unique), or not
a key (NoKey). Furthermore, it is allowed that specific attributes can have null

values, i.e., can be undefined. The domain of each attribute is one of the standard domains or some user-defined type. In the latter case, the first argument of the constructor `UserDefined` is the qualified type name used in the Curry application program (note that the `Database` library is able to handle complex types by mapping them into standard SQL types [5]). For each kind of domain, one can also have a default value (modeled by the `Maybe` type). The constructor `KeyDom` is not necessary to represent ERDs but will be later used to transform ERDs into relational database schemas.

Finally, each relationship has a name and a list of connections to entities (`REnd`), where each connection has the name of the connected entity, the role name of this connection, and its cardinality as arguments:

```
data Relationship = Relationship String [REnd]
data REnd = REnd String String Cardinality
data Cardinality = Exactly Int | Range Int (Maybe Int)
```

The cardinality is either a fixed integer or a range between two integers (where `Nothing` as the upper bound represents an arbitrary cardinality). For instance, the simple-complex (1:n) relationship `Teaching` in Figure 1 can be represented by the term

```
Relationship "Teaching"
            [REnd "Lecturer" "taught_by" (Exactly 1),
             REnd "Lecture"  "teaches"   (Range 0 Nothing)]
```

4   Compiling ER Diagrams into Curry Programs

This section describes the transformation of ERDs into executable Curry code. The generated code should contain dynamic predicates corresponding to the entities and relationships of an ERD as well as insertion, update, and delete operations for entities and relationships. The important issue of this work is the automatic checking of the integrity constraints of the conceptual data model: each operation that modifies entities or relationships should only be executable if the uniqueness and cardinality constraints specified in the corresponding ERD are satisfied in the modified database. For this purpose, we exploit transactions and the possibility to abort transactions by raising errors. For instance, if one tries to delete a student who participates in some lecture, the transaction error `KeyRequiredError` is raised, i.e., a student entity can be deleted only if it is not involved in any `Membership` or `Participation` relationship.

The transformation from ERDs into Curry code is done in the following order:

1. Translate an ERD into an `ERD` term.
2. Represent the relationships occurring in an `ERD` term as entities.
3. Map all entities into corresponding Curry code based on the `Database` library.

The first step depends on the format used in the ERD tool. As mentioned above, we have implemented a translator from the XMI format used by the Umbrello

UML Modeller into ERD terms. This part is relatively easy thanks to the presence of XML processing tools.

4.1 Transforming ERDs

The second step is necessary since the relational model supports only relations (i.e., database tables). Thus, entities as well as relationships must be mapped into relations. The mapping of entities into relations is straightforward by using the entity name as the name of the relation and the attribute names as column names. The mapping of relationships is more subtle. In principle, each relationship can be mapped into a corresponding relation. However, this simple approach might cause the creation of many relations or database tables. In order to reduce them, it is sometimes better to represent specific relations as foreign keys, i.e., to store the key of entity e_1 referred by a relationship between e_1 and e_2 in entity e_2. Whether or not this is possible depends on the kind of the relation. The different cases will be discussed next. Note that the representation of relationships as relations causes also various integrity constraints to be satisfied. For instance, if an entity has an attribute which contains a foreign key, the value of this attribute must be either null or an existing key in the corresponding relation. Furthermore, the various cardinalities of each relationship must be satisfied. Ideally, each transaction should modify the database only if all integrity constraints hold in the new state of the database.

Now we discuss the representation of the various kinds of relationships in the ER model. For the sake of simplicity, we assume that each relationship contains two ends, i.e., two roles with cardinality ranges (min, max) so that we can characterize each relationship by their related cardinalities $(min_A, max_A) : (min_B, max_B)$ between entities A and B (where max_i is either a natural number greater than min_i or ∞, $i \in \{A, B\}$).

Simple-simple (1:1) relations: This case covers all situations where each cardinality is at most one. In the case $(0, 1) : (1, 1)$, the key of entity B is added as an attribute to entity A containing a foreign key since there must be exactly one B entity for each A entity. Furthermore, this attribute is `Unique` to ensure the uniqueness of the inverse relation. The case $(0, 1) : (0, 1)$ can be similarly treated except that null values are allowed for the foreign key.

Simple-complex (1:n) relations: In the case $(0, 1) : (min_B, max_B)$, the key of entity A is added as a foreign key (possibly null) to each B entity. If $min_B > 0$ or $max_B \neq \infty$, the integrity constraints for the right number of occurrences must be checked by each database update. The case $(1, 1) : (0, max_B)$ is similarly implemented except that null values for the foreign key are not allowed.

Complex-complex (n:m) relations: In this case a new relation representing this relationship is introduced. The new relation is connected to entities A and B by two new relationships of the previous kinds.

Note that we have not considered relationships where both minimal cardinalities are greater than zero. This case is excluded by our framework (and rarely occurs in practical data models) since it causes difficulties when creating new entities of type A or B. Since each entity requires a relation to an existing entity of the other type and vice versa, it is not possible to create the new entities independently. Thus, both entities must be created and connected in one transaction which requires specific complex transactions. Therefore, we do not support this in our code generation. If such relations are required in an application (e.g., cyclic relationships), then the necessary code must be directly written with the operations of the Database library.

Based on this case distinction, the second step of our compiler maps an ERD term into a new ERD term where foreign keys are added to entities and new entities are introduced to represent complex-complex relations. Furthermore, each original entity is extended with an internal primary key to simplify the access to each entity by a unique scheme.

4.2   Code Generation for ERDs

After the mapping of entities and relationships into relations as described above, we can generate the concrete program code to organize the database access and update. As already mentioned, we base the generated code on the functionality provided by the library Database described in Section 2. The schemas for the generated code are sketched in this section. We use the notation En for the name of an entity (which starts by convention with an uppercase letter) and en for the same name where the first letter is lowercase (in order to satisfy the convention in Curry that data constructors and functions start with uppercase and lowercase letters, respectively).

The first elements of the generated code are data types to represent relations. For each entity En with attributes of types $at_1, \ldots, at_n$, we generate the following two type definitions:

```
data En = En Key at₁...atₙ
data EnKey = EnKey Key
```

Key is the type of all internal keys for entities. Currently, it is identical to Int. Thus, each entity structure contains an internal key for its unique identification. The specific type EnKey is later used to distinguish the keys for different entities by their types, i.e., to exploit the type system of Curry to avoid confusion between the various keys. For each relation that has been introduced for a complex-complex relationship (see above), a similar type definition is introduced except that it does not have an internal key but only the keys of the connected entities as arguments. Note that only the names of the types are exported but not their internal structure (i.e., they are *abstract* data types for the application program). This ensures that the application program cannot manipulate the internal keys. The manipulation of attributes is possible by explicit getter and setter functions that are described next.

In order to access or modify the attributes of an entity, we generate corresponding functions where we use the attribute names of the ERD for the names of the functions. If entity En has an attribute A_i of type at_i $(i = 1, \ldots, n)$, we generate the following getter and setter functions and a function to access the key of the entity:

$$enA_i \;::\; En \;\text{->}\; at_i$$
$$enA_i \;(En \; \_ \; \ldots \; x_i \; \ldots \; \_) = x_i$$

$$\mathrm{set}EnA_i \;::\; En \;\text{->}\; at_i \;\text{->}\; En$$
$$\mathrm{set}EnA_i \;(En \; x_1 \; \ldots \; \_ \; \ldots \; x_n) \; x_i = En \; x_1 \; \ldots \; x_i \; \ldots \; x_n$$

$$en\mathrm{Key} \;::\; En \;\text{->}\; En\mathrm{Key}$$
$$en\mathrm{Key} \;(En \; \mathrm{k} \; \_ \; \ldots \; \_) = En\mathrm{Key} \; \mathrm{k}$$

As described in Section 2, data can be persistently stored by putting them into a dynamic predicate. Thus, we define for each entity En a dynamic predicate

$$en\mathrm{Entry} \;::\; En \;\text{->}\; \mathtt{Dynamic}$$
```
enEntry persistent "..."
```

Since the manipulation of all persistent data should be done by safe operations, this dynamic predicate is not exported. Instead, a dynamic predicate en is exported that associates a key with the data so that an access is only possible to data with an existing key:

$$en \;::\; En\mathrm{Key} \;\text{->}\; En \;\text{->}\; \mathtt{Dynamic}$$
$$en \; \mathrm{key} \; \mathrm{obj} \; | \; \mathrm{key} =:= en\mathrm{Key} \; \mathrm{obj} = en\mathrm{Entry} \; \mathrm{obj}$$

Although these operations seem to be standard functions, the use of a functional logic language is important here. For instance, the access to an entity with a given key k can be done by solving the goal "en k o" where o is a free variable that will be bound to the concrete instance of the entity.

For each role with name rn specified in an ERD, we generate a dynamic predicate of type

$$rn \;::\; En_1\mathrm{Key} \;\text{->}\; En_2\mathrm{Key} \;\text{->}\; \mathtt{Dynamic}$$

where En_1 and En_2 are the entities related by this role. The implementation of these predicates depend on the kind of relationship according to their implementation as discussed in Section 4.1. Since complex-complex relationships are implemented as relations, i.e., persistent predicates (that are only internal and not exported), the corresponding roles can be directly mapped to these. Simple-simple and simple-complex relationships are implemented by foreign keys in the corresponding entities. Thus, their roles are implemented by accessing these keys. We omit the code details that depend on the different cases already discussed in Section 4.1.

Based on these basic implementations of entities and relationships, we generate code for transactions to manipulate the data and check the integrity constraints specified by the relationships of an ERD. In order to access an entity with a specific key, there is a generic function that delivers this entity in a transaction or raises a transaction error if there is no entry with this key:

```
getEntry :: k -> (k -> en -> Dynamic) -> Transaction en
getEntry key pred =
   getDB (queryOne (\info -> pred key info)) |>>=
   maybe (errorT (KeyNotExistsError "no entry for...")) returnT
```

This internal function is specialized to an exported function for each entity:

```
getEn :: EnKey -> Transaction En
getEn key = getEntry key en
```

In order to insert new entities, there is a "new" transaction for each entity. If the ERD specifies no relationship for this entity with a minimum greater than zero, there is no need to provide related entities so that the transaction has the following structure (if En has attributes of types $at_1, \ldots, at_n$):

```
newEn :: at₁ -> ⋯ -> atₙ -> Transaction En
newEn a₁ ... aₙ = check₁ |>> ... |>> checkₖ |>> newEntry ...
```

Here, $check_i$ are the various integrity checks (e.g., uniqueness checks for attributes specified as Unique) and newEntry is a generic operation to insert a new entity. If attribute A_i has a default value or null values are allowed for it, the type at_i is replaced by Maybe at_i in newEn.

For instance, consider the entity Student of Figure 1. It has an integer attribute MatNum which is unique, two string attributes Name and Firstname, and an attribute Email of the user-defined type Email where null values are allowed. Thus, the generated transaction to insert a new Student entity is as follows:

```
newStudent :: Int -> String -> String -> Maybe Email
              -> Transaction Student
newStudent matNum name firstname email =
  unique studentMatNum studentEntry matNum |>>
  newEntry (studentKeyToKey . studentKey)
           setStudentKey
           studentEntry
           (Student 0 matNum name firstname email)
```

The operation setStudentKey is an internal setter function generated similarly to the setter functions setEnA_i, and the internal function studentKeyToKey (of type StudentKey -> Key) strips off the StudentKey constructor.

The generic transaction unique implements a uniqueness check for arbitrary entities and attributes. It raises a UniqueError if an instance with a given attribute value already exists. The parameters are the attribute selector, the dynamic predicate representing this entity, and the new value of the attribute:

```
unique :: (en -> a) -> (en -> Dynamic) -> a -> Transaction ()
unique selector pred attr =
  getDB (queryOne (\x -> pred x |> attr == selector x)) |>>=
  maybe doneT
        (\_ -> errorT (TError UniqueError "error message"))
```

The generic transaction newEntry adds the new entity. Similarly to getEntry, it must be provided with parameters related to the specific entity, i.e., functions to access and modify the key of an entity, the dynamic predicate of the entity, and the initial value of the entity:

```
newEntry :: (en -> Key) -> (en -> Key -> en) -> (en -> Dynamic)
            -> en -> Transaction en
newEntry keyf keyset pred entry =
```

```
newDBKey keyf pred |>>= \k ->
let entrywithkey = keyset entry k in
addDB (pred entrywithkey) |>> returnT entrywithkey

-- get new key for an entity:
newDBKey :: (en -> Key) -> (en -> Dynamic) -> Transaction Key
newDBKey keyf pred =
  getDB (queryAll pred) |>>= \es ->
  returnT (if null es then 1 else foldr1 max (map keyf es) + 1)
```

If there are relationships for an entity with a minimum greater than zero, than the keys (in general, a list of keys) must be also provided as parameters to the operation new*En*. In this case, the name of the new operation is extended with a suffix explaining the meaning of the additional argument keys (an alternative to such long names would be a generated documentation explaining the meaning of these argument keys). For instance, the new operation for lectures according to the ERD in Figure 1 has the following type signature (since a Lecture entity contains a foreign Lecturer key representing the Teaching relationship):

```
newLectureWithLecturerTeachingKey :: Int -> String -> Maybe Int
                                  -> LecturerKey -> Transaction Lecture
```

The first three arguments are the values of the Id, Title and Hours attributes (where the attribute Hours has a default value so that the argument is optional). The last argument is the key of the lecturer required by the relationship Teaching. In a similar way, we generate "new" operations for each complex-complex relationship where the arguments are the keys of the associated entities.

Similarly to new*En*, we provide also operations to update existing entities. These operations have the following structure:

```
updateEn :: En -> Transaction ()
updateEn e = check₁ |>> ... |>> checkₖ |>> updateEntry ...
```

updateEn :: *En* -> Transaction ()
updateEn e = *check*₁ |>> ... |>> *check*ₖ |>> updateEntry ...

Again, the various integrity constraints must be checked before an update is finally performed. In order to get an impression of the kind of integrity constraints, we discuss a few checks in the following.

We have already seen the integrity constraint unique that checks the uniqueness property of attributes before inserting a new entity. If an entity contains a foreign key, each update must check the existence of this foreign key. This is the purpose of the generic transaction existsDBKey where the arguments are the getter function (*en*Key) for the key in the foreign entity, the dynamic predicate of the foreign entity, and the foreign key. If the key does not exist, a KeyNotExistsError is raised:

```
existsDBKey :: (en -> k) -> (en -> Dynamic) -> k -> Transaction ()
existsDBKey keyf pred key =
  getDB (queryOne (\x -> pred x |> key == keyf x)) |>>=
  maybe (errorT (TError KeyNotExistsError "error message"))
        (\_ -> doneT)
```

For instance, the operation `newLectureWithLecturerTeachingKey` to insert a new lecture as mentioned above is generated with the following code (the `Id` and `Title` attributes are unique and the attribute `Hours` has 4 as a default value):

```
newLectureWithLecturerTeachingKey iD title hours ltKey =
  unique lectureId lectureEntry iD |>>
  unique lectureTitle lectureEntry title |>>
  existsDBKey lecturerKey lecturerEntry ltKey |>>
  newEntry (lectureKeyToKey . lectureKey)
           setLectureKey
           lectureEntry
           (Lecture 0 iD title (maybe 4 id hours)
           (lecturerKeyToKey ltKey))
```

Furthermore, there are generic transactions to check minimum and maximum cardinalities for relationships and lists of foreign keys that can raise the transaction errors `MinError`, `MaxError`, or `DuplicateKeyError`. For each operation generated by our compiler, the necessary integrity checks are inserted based on the specification expressed by the `ERD` term.

Operations to delete entities or relationships are generated similarly to update operations but with different integrity tests (e.g., a lecturer can be deleted only if he does not teach any lecture, otherwise a `KeyRequiredError` is raised). An interesting topic for future work is the generation of complex delete operations for an entity that implicitly and recursively updates all other entities where this entity occurs as a key. However, complex delete operations must be used with care (e.g., the deletion of a lecturer requires the deletion of all his lectures and the participations by students). But if the programmer is aware of the consequences, he will appreciate the automatic generation of such operations as the correct order for deletion is not always obvious.

Even if our generated transactions ensure the integrity of the affected relations, it is sometimes useful to provide a global consistency check that is regularly applied to all data. This could be necessary if the database is modified by programs that do not use the safe interface but directly accesses the data. For this purpose, we also generate a global consistency test that checks all persistent data w.r.t. the ER model. If $E_1, \ldots, E_n$ are all entities (including the implicit entities for complex-complex relations) derived from the given ERD, the global consistency test is defined by

```
checkAllData :: Transaction ()
checkAllData = checkE₁ |>> ... |>> checkEₙ
```

The consistency test for each entity En is defined by

```
checkEn :: Transaction ()
checkEn = getDB (queryAll enEntry) |>>= mapT_ checkEnEntry

checkEnEntry :: En -> Transaction ()
checkEnEntry e = check₁ |>> ... |>> checkₖ
```

where the tests $check_i$ are similar to the ones used in new and update operations that raise transaction errors in case of unsatisfied integrity constraints.

5   Conclusions

We have presented an API as an abstract interface for database programming and a framework to compile conceptual data models specified as entity-relationship diagrams into executable code for database programming in Curry. This compilation is done in three phases: translate the specific ERD format into a tool-independent representation, transform the relationships into relations according to their complexity, and generate code for the safe access and update of the data.

Due to the importance of ERDs to design conceptual data models, there are also other tools with similar objectives. Most existing tools support only the generation of SQL code, like the free software tools DB-Main[6] or DBDesigner4[7]. The main motivation for our work was the seamless embedding of database programming in a declarative language and the use of existing specification methods like ERDs as the basis to generate most of the necessary code required by the application programs. The advantages of our framework are:

- The application programmer must only specify the data model in a high-level format (ERDs) and all necessary code to deal with this data is generated.
- The interface used by the application programs is type safe, i.e., the types specified in the ERD are mapped into types of the programming language so that ill-typed data cannot be constructed.
- Updates to the database are supported as transactions that automatically checks all integrity constraints specified in the ERD.
- Checks for all integrity constraints are derived from the ERD for individual tables and the complete database so that they can be periodically applied to verify the integrity of the current state of the database.
- The generated code is based on a high-level interface for database programming so that it is readable and well structured. Thus, it can be easily modified and adapted to new requirements. For instance, integrity constraints not expressible in ERDs can be easily added to individual update operations, or complex delete operations can be inserted in the generated module.

The database API and the ERD compiler described in this paper are freely available with the latest distribution of PAKCS [13]. For future work we intend to increase the functionality of our framework, e.g., to extend ERDs by allowing the specification of more complex integrity constraints or attributes for relations, which is supported by some ER tools, or to provide also complex delete operations for particular entities. Finally, it could be also interesting to generate access and update operations for existing databases by analyzing their data model. Although this is an issue different from our framework, one can reuse the API described in Section 2 and some other techniques of this paper for such a purpose.

---

[6] http://www.db-main.be
[7] http://www.fabforce.net/dbdesigner4

References

1. Antoy, S., Echahed, R., Hanus, M.: A Needed Narrowing Strategy. Journal of the ACM 47(4), 776–822 (2000)
2. Chen, P.P.-S.: The Entity-Relationship Model—Toward a Unified View of Data. ACM Transactions on Database Systems 1(1), 9–36 (1976)
3. Correas, J., Gómez, J.M., Carro, M., Cabeza, D., Hermenegildo, M.: A Generic Persistence Model for (C)LP Systems (and Two Useful Implementations). In: Jayaraman, B. (ed.) PADL 2004. LNCS, vol. 3057, pp. 104–119. Springer, Heidelberg (2004)
4. Das, S.K.: Deductive Databases and Logic Programming. Addison-Wesley, Reading (1992)
5. Fischer, S.: A Functional Logic Database Library. In: WCFLP 2005. Proc. of the ACM SIGPLAN 2005 Workshop on Curry and Functional Logic Programming, pp. 54–59. ACM Press, New York (2005)
6. Gallaire, H., Minker, J. (eds.): Logic and Databases. Plenum Press, New York (1978)
7. Hanus, M.: A Unified Computation Model for Functional and Logic Programming. In: Proc. of the 24th ACM Symposium on Principles of Programming Languages, Paris, pp. 80–93 (1997)
8. Hanus, M.: A Functional Logic Programming Approach to Graphical User Interfaces. In: Pontelli, E., Santos Costa, V. (eds.) PADL 2000. LNCS, vol. 1753, pp. 47–62. Springer, Heidelberg (2000)
9. Hanus, M.: High-Level Server Side Web Scripting in Curry. In: Ramakrishnan, I.V. (ed.) PADL 2001. LNCS, vol. 1990, pp. 76–92. Springer, Heidelberg (2001)
10. Hanus, M.: Dynamic Predicates in Functional Logic Programs. Journal of Functional and Logic Programming 2004(5) (2004)
11. Hanus, M.: Type-Oriented Construction of Web User Interfaces. In: PPDP 2006. Proceedings of the 8th ACM SIGPLAN International Conference on Principles and Practice of Declarative Programming, pp. 27–38. ACM Press, New York (2006)
12. Hanus, M.: Multi-paradigm Declarative Languages. In: Dahl, V., Niemelä, I. (eds.) ICLP 2007. LNCS, vol. 4670, pp. 45–75. Springer, Heidelberg (2007)
13. Hanus, M., Antoy, S., Braßel, B., Engelke, M., Höppner, K., Koj, J., Niederau, P., Sadre, R., Steiner, F.: PAKCS: The Portland Aachen Kiel Curry System (2007), http://www.informatik.uni-kiel.de/~pakcs/
14. Hanus, M. (ed.): Curry: An Integrated Functional Logic Language (Vers. 0.8.2) (2006), http://www.informatik.uni-kiel.de/~curry
15. Huseby, S.H.: Innocent Code: A Security Wake-Up Call for Web Programmers. Wiley, Chichester (2003)
16. López-Fraguas, F., Sánchez-Hernández, J.: TOY: A Multiparadigm Declarative System. In: Narendran, P., Rusinowitch, M. (eds.) RTA 1999. LNCS, vol. 1631, pp. 244–247. Springer, Heidelberg (1999)
17. Peyton Jones, S. (ed.): Haskell 98 Language and Libraries—The Revised Report. Cambridge University Press, Cambridge (2003)
18. Wadler, P.: How to Declare an Imperative. ACM Computing Surveys 29(3), 240–263 (1997)

Author Index

Lecture Notes in Computer Science

Sublibrary 2: Programming and Software Engineering

For information about Vols. 1– 4227
please contact your bookseller or Springer

Vol. 4554: C. Stephanidis (Ed.), Universal Acess in Human Computer Interaction, Part I. XXII, 1054 pages. 2007.

Vol. 4553: J.A. Jacko (Ed.), Human-Computer Interaction, Part IV. XXIV, 1225 pages. 2007.

Vol. 4552: J.A. Jacko (Ed.), Human-Computer Interaction, Part III. XXI, 1038 pages. 2007.

Vol. 4551: J.A. Jacko (Ed.), Human-Computer Interaction, Part II. XXIII, 1253 pages. 2007.

Vol. 4550: J.A. Jacko (Ed.), Human-Computer Interaction, Part I. XXIII, 1240 pages. 2007.

Vol. 4542: P. Sawyer, B. Paech, P. Heymans (Eds.), Requirements Engineering: Foundation for Software Quality. IX, 384 pages. 2007.

Vol. 4536: G. Concas, E. Damiani, M. Scotto, G. Succi (Eds.), Agile Processes in Software Engineering and Extreme Programming. XV, 276 pages. 2007.

Vol. 4530: D.H. Akehurst, R. Vogel, R.F. Paige (Eds.), Model Driven Architecture - Foundations and Applications. X, 219 pages. 2007.

Vol. 4523: Y.-H. Lee, H.-N. Kim, J. Kim, Y.W. Park, L.T. Yang, S.W. Kim (Eds.), Embedded Software and Systems. XIX, 829 pages. 2007.

Vol. 4498: N. Abdennahder, F. Kordon (Eds.), Reliable Software Technologies - Ada-Europe 2007. XII, 247 pages. 2007.

Vol. 4486: M. Bernardo, J. Hillston (Eds.), Formal Methods for Performance Evaluation. VII, 469 pages. 2007.

Vol. 4470: Q. Wang, D. Pfahl, D.M. Raffo (Eds.), Software Process Dynamics and Agility. XI, 346 pages. 2007.

Vol. 4468: M.M. Bonsangue, E.B. Johnsen (Eds.), Formal Methods for Open Object-Based Distributed Systems. X, 317 pages. 2007.

Vol. 4467: A.L. Murphy, J. Vitek (Eds.), Coordination Models and Languages. X, 325 pages. 2007.

Vol. 4454: Y. Gurevich, B. Meyer (Eds.), Tests and Proofs. IX, 217 pages. 2007.

Vol. 4444: T. Reps, M. Sagiv, J. Bauer (Eds.), Program Analysis and Compilation, Theory and Practice. X, 361 pages. 2007.

Vol. 4440: B. Liblit, Cooperative Bug Isolation. XV, 101 pages. 2007.

Vol. 4408: R. Choren, A. Garcia, H. Giese, H.-f. Leung, C. Lucena, A. Romanovsky (Eds.), Software Engineering for Multi-Agent Systems V. XII, 233 pages. 2007.

Vol. 4406: W. De Meuter (Ed.), Advances in Smalltalk. VII, 157 pages. 2007.

Vol. 4405: L. Padgham, F. Zambonelli (Eds.), Agent-Oriented Software Engineering VII. XII, 225 pages. 2007.

Vol. 4401: N. Guelfi, D. Buchs (Eds.), Rapid Integration of Software Engineering Techniques. IX, 177 pages. 2007.

Vol. 4385: K. Coninx, K. Luyten, K.A. Schneider (Eds.), Task Models and Diagrams for Users Interface Design. XI, 355 pages. 2007.

Vol. 4383: E. Bin, A. Ziv, S. Ur (Eds.), Hardware and Software, Verification and Testing. XII, 235 pages. 2007.

Vol. 4379: M. Südholt, C. Consel (Eds.), Object-Oriented Technology. VIII, 157 pages. 2007.

Vol. 4364: T. Kühne (Ed.), Models in Software Engineering. XI, 332 pages. 2007.

Vol. 4355: J. Julliand, O. Kouchnarenko (Eds.), B 2007: Formal Specification and Development in B. XIII, 293 pages. 2006.

Vol. 4354: M. Hanus (Ed.), Practical Aspects of Declarative Languages. X, 335 pages. 2006.

Vol. 4350: M. Clavel, F. Durán, S. Eker, P. Lincoln, N. Martí-Oliet, J. Meseguer, C. Talcott, All About Maude - A High-Performance Logical Framework. XXII, 797 pages. 2007.

Vol. 4348: S. Tucker Taft, R.A. Duff, R.L. Brukardt, E. Plödereder, P. Leroy, Ada 2005 Reference Manual. XXII, 765 pages. 2006.

Vol. 4346: L. Brim, B.R. Haverkort, M. Leucker, J. van de Pol (Eds.), Formal Methods: Applications and Technology. X, 363 pages. 2007.

Vol. 4344: V. Gruhn, F. Oquendo (Eds.), Software Architecture. X, 245 pages. 2006.

Vol. 4340: R. Prodan, T. Fahringer, Grid Computing. XXIII, 317 pages. 2007.

Vol. 4336: V.R. Basili, H.D. Rombach, K. Schneider, B. Kitchenham, D. Pfahl, R.W. Selby (Eds.), Empirical Software Engineering Issues. XVII, 193 pages. 2007.

Vol. 4326: S. Göbel, R. Malkewitz, I. Iurgel (Eds.), Technologies for Interactive Digital Storytelling and Entertainment. X, 384 pages. 2006.

Vol. 4323: G. Doherty, A. Blandford (Eds.), Interactive Systems. XI, 269 pages. 2007.

Vol. 4322: F. Kordon, J. Sztipanovits (Eds.), Reliable Systems on Unreliable Networked Platforms. XIV, 317 pages. 2007.

Vol. 4309: P. Inverardi, M. Jazayeri (Eds.), Software Engineering Education in the Modern Age. VIII, 207 pages. 2006.

Vol. 4294: A. Dan, W. Lamersdorf (Eds.), Service-Oriented Computing – ICSOC 2006. XIX, 653 pages. 2006.

Vol. 4290: M. van Steen, M. Henning (Eds.), Middleware 2006. XIII, 425 pages. 2006.

Vol. 4279: N. Kobayashi (Ed.), Programming Languages and Systems. XI, 423 pages. 2006.

Vol. 4262: K. Havelund, M. Núñez, G. Roşu, B. Wolff (Eds.), Formal Approaches to Software Testing and Runtime Verification. VIII, 255 pages. 2006.

Vol. 4260: Z. Liu, J. He (Eds.), Formal Methods and Software Engineering. XII, 778 pages. 2006.

Vol. 4257: I. Richardson, P. Runeson, R. Messnarz (Eds.), Software Process Improvement. XI, 219 pages. 2006.

Vol. 4242: A. Rashid, M. Aksit (Eds.), Transactions on Aspect-Oriented Software Development II. IX, 289 pages. 2006.

Vol. 4229: E. Najm, J.-F. Pradat-Peyre, V.V. Donzeau-Gouge (Eds.), Formal Techniques for Networked and Distributed Systems - FORTE 2006. X, 486 pages. 2006.